National Geographic Picture Atlas of

OurWorld

National Geographic Picture Atlas of

OurWorld

National Geographic Picture Atlas of

Our World

Published by
The National Geographic Society

Gilbert M. Grosvenor
President and
Chairman of the Board

Owen R. Anderson
Executive Vice President

Robert L. Breeden
Senior Vice President,
Publications and
Educational Media

Prepared by
National Geographic
Book Service

Charles O. Hyman
Director

Ross S. Bennett
Associate Director

Margaret Sedeen
Managing Editor

Susan C. Eckert
Director of Research

Staff for this book

Mary B. Dickinson
Editor

Jean Kaplan Teichroew
Assistant Editor and
Map Coordinator

Linda B. Meyerriecks
Illustrations Editor

David M. Seager
Art Director

Marguerite Suarez Dunn
Chief Researcher

Jennifer Gorham Ackerman
Catherine Herbert Howell
Edward Lanouette
David F. Robinson
Writer-Editors

Joseph Alper
Elisabeth B. Booz
Margo Browning
Carol Dana
Elizabeth L. Newhouse
Catherine O'Neill
Melanie Patt-Corner
Suzanne K. Poole
Margaret Sedeen
John Thompson
Anne E. Withers
Contributing Writers

Ratri Banerjee
Cathryn P. Buchanan
Paulette L. Claus
Anne Elizabeth Ely
James B. Enzinna
Joyce B. Marshall
Lise Swinson Sajewski
Penelope A. Timbers
Editorial Researchers

James B. Enzinna
Art Coordinator

Charlotte Golin
Design Assistant and
Color Specialist

Greta Arnold
Assistant Illustrations
Editor

Laurie A. Smith
Jean C. Stringer
Illustrations Assistants

Karen F. Edwards
Traffic Manager

Richard S. Wain
Production Manager

Andrea Crosman
Assistant Production Manager

Emily F. Gwynn
Production Assistant

Manufacturing and
Quality Management
John T. Dunn
Director
David V. Evans
Manager

R. Gary Colbert
Executive Assistant

Teresita Cóquia Sison
Editorial Assistant

George I. Burneston, III
Indexer

Maps by Publications Art
John D. Garst, Jr.
Virginia L. Baza
Isaac Ortiz
Peter J. Balch
Gary M. Johnson
Sven M. Dolling
Daniel J. Ortiz
Andrew J. Karl
Timothy E. Burdick
Darrah Long
Elizabeth G. Jevons

World Map
Mapping Specialists, Ltd.

Globe maps by
Tibor G. Toth

Artwork by
Shusei Nagaoka

Flags by
Cartographic Division
Kevin P. Allen
Neal J. Edwards

Janet Crane
Staff Geographer

Contributions by
Aileen Buckley
Alexander M. Tait

Jonathan B. Tourtellot
Planning Consultant

Sue Appleby Purcell
Educational Consultant

John P. Augelli,
   The University of Kansas,
   Latin America
Stephen S. Birdsall,
   The University of North Carolina
   at Chapel Hill, *North America*
Michael E. Bonine,
   The University of Arizona,
   North Africa and Middle East
John D. Eyre,
   The University of North Carolina
   at Chapel Hill, *Oceania*
Jack D. Ives,
   University of California
   at Davis, *The Poles*
C. Gregory Knight,
   The Pennsylvania State
   University, *Sub-Saharan Africa*
Thomas R. Leinbach,
   University of Kentucky,
   Southeast Asia
Clifton W. Pannell,
   The University of Georgia,
   Far East
Joseph E. Schwartzberg,
   University of Minnesota,
   Twin Cities, *South Asia*
Craig ZumBrunnen,
   University of Washington,
   Europe
Regional Consultants

Cover photography: Michel
Tcherevkoff.

Copyright© 1990, 1991. National
Geographic Society, Washington,
D. C. All rights reserved. Repro-
duction of the whole or any part of
the contents without written permission is prohibited. Library of
Congress CIP data, page 256.

First edition: 300,000 copies
Second printing: 35,000 copies
256 pages, 261 illustrations,
120 maps, 27 paintings.

Contents

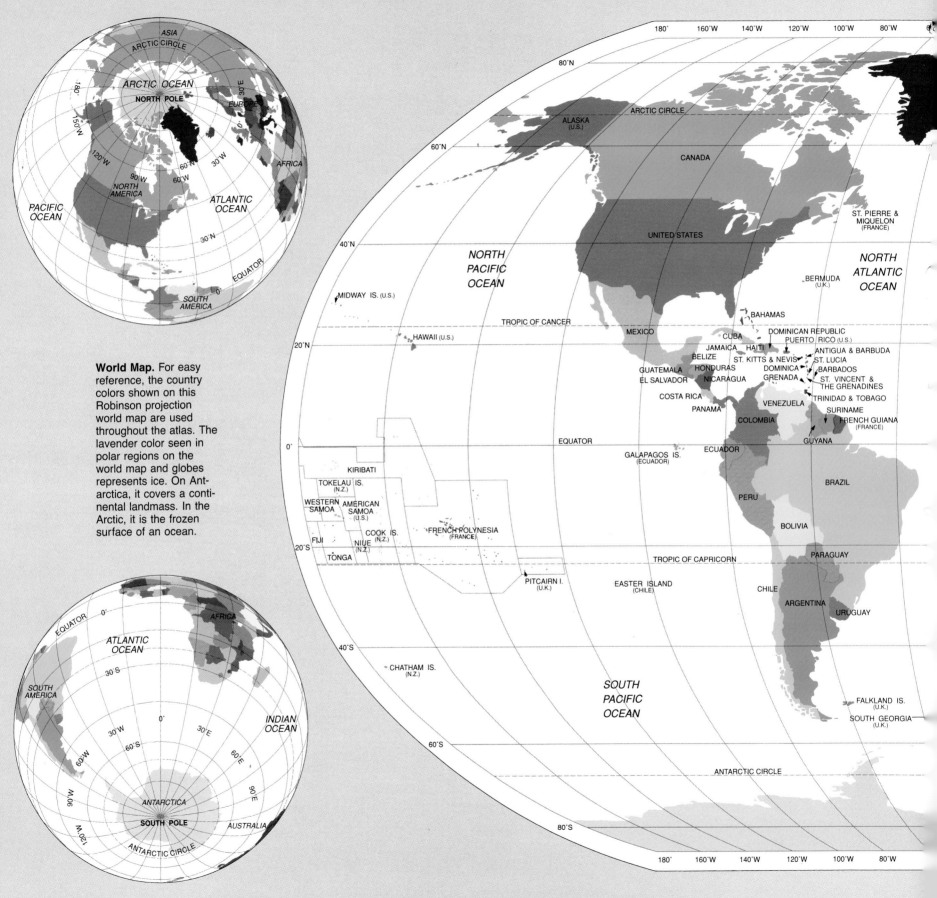

World Map. For easy reference, the country colors shown on this Robinson projection world map are used throughout the atlas. The lavender color seen in polar regions on the world map and globes represents ice. On Antarctica, it covers a continental landmass. In the Arctic, it is the frozen surface of an ocean.

ASIA
ARCTIC CIRCLE
ARCTIC OCEAN
NORTH POLE
EUROPE
30°E
30°W
30°N
AFRICA
PACIFIC OCEAN
NORTH AMERICA
90°W
60°W
ATLANTIC OCEAN
30°N
EQUATOR
SOUTH AMERICA
180°
150°W
120°W
0°

EQUATOR
0°
AFRICA
ATLANTIC OCEAN
30°S
30°W
0°
30°E
INDIAN OCEAN
SOUTH AMERICA
60°S
60°E
60°W
90°W
90°E
ANTARCTICA
SOUTH POLE
AUSTRALIA
120°W
ANTARCTIC CIRCLE

180° 160°W 140°W 120°W 100°W 80°W

80°N
ARCTIC CIRCLE
ALASKA (U.S.)
60°N
CANADA
NORTH PACIFIC OCEAN
40°N
UNITED STATES
ST. PIERRE & MIQUELON (FRANCE)
NORTH ATLANTIC OCEAN
BERMUDA (U.K.)
TROPIC OF CANCER
20°N
MEXICO
BAHAMAS
CUBA
DOMINICAN REPUBLIC
PUERTO RICO (U.S.)
JAMAICA HAITI
ANTIGUA & BARBUDA
BELIZE
ST. KITTS & NEVIS
ST. LUCIA
GUATEMALA HONDURAS
DOMINICA
BARBADOS
EL SALVADOR NICARAGUA
GRENADA
ST. VINCENT & THE GRENADINES
COSTA RICA
VENEZUELA
TRINIDAD & TOBAGO
PANAMA
SURINAME
COLOMBIA
FRENCH GUIANA (FRANCE)
GUYANA
MIDWAY IS. (U.S.)
HAWAII (U.S.)
GALAPAGOS IS. (ECUADOR)
EQUATOR
ECUADOR
0°
KIRIBATI
PERU
BRAZIL
TOKELAU IS. (N.Z.)
WESTERN SAMOA
AMERICAN SAMOA (U.S.)
BOLIVIA
FIJI
COOK IS. (N.Z.)
FRENCH POLYNESIA (FRANCE)
NIUE (N.Z.)
20°S
TONGA
PARAGUAY
TROPIC OF CAPRICORN
PITCAIRN I. (U.K.)
EASTER ISLAND (CHILE)
CHILE
ARGENTINA
URUGUAY
40°S
CHATHAM IS. (N.Z.)
SOUTH PACIFIC OCEAN
FALKLAND IS. (U.K.)
SOUTH GEORGIA (U.K.)
60°S
ANTARCTIC CIRCLE
80°S
180° 160°W 140°W 120°W 100°W 80°W

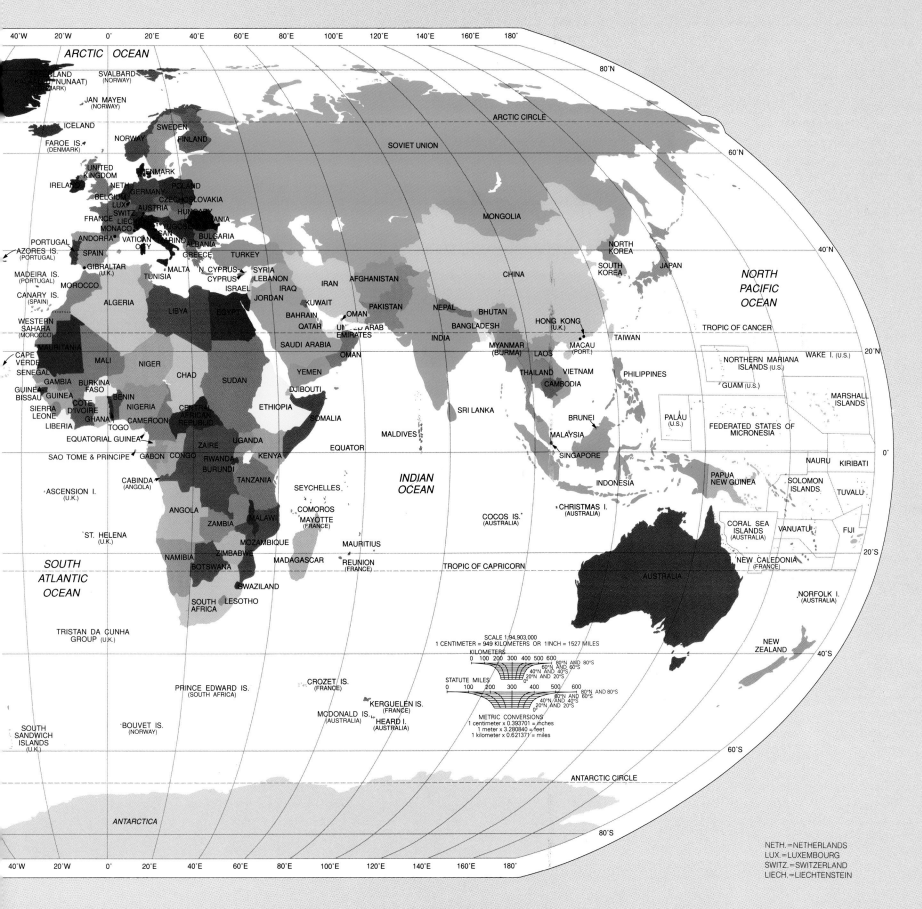

ARCTIC OCEAN

SVALBARD (NORWAY)

JAN MAYEN (NORWAY)

ARCTIC CIRCLE

80°N

ICELAND

FAROE IS. (DENMARK)

NORWAY SWEDEN FINLAND

SOVIET UNION

60°N

UNITED KINGDOM

IRELAND NETH. DENMARK

BELGIUM GERMANY POLAND
LUX. CZECHOSLOVAKIA
FRANCE SWITZ. AUSTRIA HUNGARY
LIECH. ROMANIA
MONACO
ANDORRA SAN MARINO YUGOSLAVIA BULGARIA
VATICAN CITY ALBANIA

MONGOLIA

NORTH KOREA
40°N

PORTUGAL
AZORES IS. (PORTUGAL)
SPAIN GREECE TURKEY
GIBRALTAR (U.K.) MALTA N. CYPRUS SYRIA
CYPRUS LEBANON
MADEIRA IS. (PORTUGAL) TUNISIA ISRAEL IRAQ IRAN AFGHANISTAN
CANARY IS. (SPAIN) MOROCCO JORDAN
ALGERIA KUWAIT
LIBYA EGYPT BAHRAIN
QATAR PAKISTAN NEPAL BHUTAN

CHINA

SOUTH KOREA JAPAN

NORTH PACIFIC OCEAN

TROPIC OF CANCER
HONG KONG (U.K.)
MACAU (PORT.) TAIWAN
20°N

WESTERN SAHARA (MOROCCO)
MAURITANIA
CAPE VERDE
SENEGAL
GUINEA BISSAU GUINEA
SIERRA LEONE
LIBERIA

MALI NIGER
CHAD SUDAN
BURKINA FASO
GAMBIA
COTE D'IVOIRE BENIN NIGERIA
GHANA
TOGO CAMEROON
CENTRAL AFRICAN REPUBLIC

SAUDI ARABIA
OMAN
YEMEN
DJIBOUTI
ETHIOPIA
SOMALIA

UNITED ARAB EMIRATES
INDIA
MYANMAR (BURMA) LAOS
THAILAND VIETNAM
CAMBODIA

SRI LANKA

PHILIPPINES

NORTHERN MARIANA ISLANDS (U.S.) WAKE I. (U.S.)

GUAM (U.S.)

MARSHALL ISLANDS

BRUNEI PALAU (U.S.) FEDERATED STATES OF MICRONESIA

EQUATORIAL GUINEA
SAO TOME & PRINCIPE GABON CONGO
ZAIRE UGANDA
RWANDA
CABINDA (ANGOLA) BURUNDI KENYA
TANZANIA

MALDIVES

EQUATOR

MALAYSIA

SINGAPORE

INDONESIA

NAURU KIRIBATI

PAPUA NEW GUINEA
SOLOMON ISLANDS TUVALU

0°

ASCENSION I. (U.K.)

ANGOLA
ZAMBIA MALAWI
NAMIBIA
BOTSWANA ZIMBABWE
MOZAMBIQUE

SEYCHELLES

COMOROS
MAYOTTE (FRANCE)

INDIAN OCEAN

COCOS IS. (AUSTRALIA)

CHRISTMAS I. (AUSTRALIA)

CORAL SEA ISLANDS (AUSTRALIA)

VANUATU FIJI

NEW CALEDONIA (FRANCE)

20°S

ST. HELENA (U.K.)

MADAGASCAR MAURITIUS
REUNION (FRANCE)

TROPIC OF CAPRICORN

AUSTRALIA

NORFOLK I. (AUSTRALIA)

SOUTH ATLANTIC OCEAN

SWAZILAND
SOUTH AFRICA LESOTHO

SCALE 1/94,903,000
1 CENTIMETER = 949 KILOMETERS OR 1INCH = 1527 MILES
KILOMETERS
0 100 200 300 400 500 600
80°N AND 80°S
60°N AND 60°S
40°N AND 40°S
20°N AND 20°S
0°

NEW ZEALAND
40°S

TRISTAN DA CUNHA GROUP (U.K.)

CROZET IS. (FRANCE)

STATUTE MILES
0 100 200 300 400 500 600
80°N AND 80°S
60°N AND 60°S
40°N AND 40°S
20°N AND 20°S
0°

PRINCE EDWARD IS. (SOUTH AFRICA)

KERGUELEN IS. (FRANCE)

METRIC CONVERSIONS
1 centimeter x 0.393701 = inches
1 meter x 3.280840 = feet
1 kilometer x 0.621371 = miles

SOUTH SANDWICH ISLANDS (U.K.)

BOUVET IS. (NORWAY)

MCDONALD IS. (AUSTRALIA) HEARD I. (AUSTRALIA)

60°S

ANTARCTIC CIRCLE

ANTARCTICA

80°S

NETH.=NETHERLANDS
LUX.=LUXEMBOURG
SWITZ.=SWITZERLAND
LIECH.=LIECHTENSTEIN

Mapping Our World

The word "geography" was on everyone's lips when our staff began planning this Picture Atlas. Americans, it seemed, were not particularly good at it. In 1988, the National Geographic Society's centennial year, the Society commissioned an international Gallup survey to test geographic literacy. The countries tested besides the United States were Sweden, West Germany, Japan, France, Canada, the United Kingdom, Italy, and Mexico.

Americans ranked in the bottom third. One in seven people could not identify the United States on a world map and one in four could not find the Pacific Ocean. Fewer than half could pick out countries often mentioned in the news such as the United Kingdom, France, South Africa, and Japan. The results were worst among young Americans between the ages of 18 and 24.

Announcing the survey results, National Geographic President Gilbert M. Grosvenor stressed "the urgency of National Geographic's long-term commitment to improve geography teaching in our classrooms." To understand global economics, population and hunger problems, arms control, and the need for international care of the environment, it was essential that children come to know the world. The Society had already established its Geography Education Program in 1985 to restore geography to the country's classrooms. The next year it launched an annual Summer Geography Institute for elementary and secondary school teachers.

Since 1988, the Society has embarked on a series of programs to interest children in geography. They range from a telecommunications-based science and geography curriculum for schools called National Geographic Kids Network to an interactive computer and videodisc system called GTV and the National Geography Bee. The response has been rewarding. Interest in geography is clearly on the rise.

As 1988 advanced into 1989, plans for the Picture Atlas focused on bringing the world into the family living room—on capturing within the pages of a book the blue marble that astronauts see floating in space. The first need was to relate each country to its continental and global setting. Geography is very much like a detective story, with clues piling up in the form of population, location, natural resources, physical terrain, politics, and relations with neighboring countries, until the pattern of life for a whole region emerges. No country exists in a vacuum. It's that interweaving of relationships that makes geography such an exciting subject. Each map supports our theme of mapping the whole world. Locator maps place each country in its continental context, and the world map in the front of the atlas provides a global setting.

Children needed to *see* that world too, in photographs. Picture choices were aimed at a lively mix of human and physical geography. It was a real challenge to find recent photography for countries where civil wars rage, or for those where foreign photographers are not welcome.

In the fall of 1989, the world map suddenly became necessary just to interpret the daily newspaper headlines. Countries whose locations would not have been familiar to those taking our Gallup poll followed one another into the news in the wake of the Soviet Union's accelerating move to *glasnost*—openness: Hungary, Poland, Czechoslovakia, Bulgaria, Romania. Often known collectively as Eastern Europe, they suddenly assumed individual identities and became household words, their demands for democratic reform matters of daily speculation.

East Germans, too, were demonstrating, and the Berlin Wall opened up so that East Berliners might walk freely into the rest of their city for the first time in 28 years. A glance at the map showed the large silhouette that was historic Germany, soon to be united once more. Even Albania, the most steadfast of communist countries, made cautious overtures toward glasnost.

As we approach press time on the atlas, it is hard to stay abreast of the world. In March 1990 Namibia won independence from South Africa. In May the two Yemens united as one country. In July Benin changed its flag. Lithuania, Latvia, and other regions of the Soviet Union are demanding independence. Croatia and Slovenia threaten to secede from Yugoslavia. It is an exhilarating time to study the domino effect of self-determination. This atlas reflects the most up-to-date developments in the ever-evolving task of mapping our changing world.

Mary B. Dickinson

Where in the World?

Finding your way around the globe is like using a street map. Suppose you want to meet a friend on the corner of Third Avenue and Main Street. To find the intersection on a map, you might follow Third Avenue until it meets Main Street. On a globe, there are no streets or avenues to guide you to a particular spot. Instead, you can use the grid formed by lines of latitude and lines of longitude. By following these lines, you can find any place on Earth.

Lines of latitude run east and west around the globe and are evenly spaced from the Equator to the North and South Poles. They are also called parallels, because they are parallel to each other. Parallels become shorter toward the Poles.

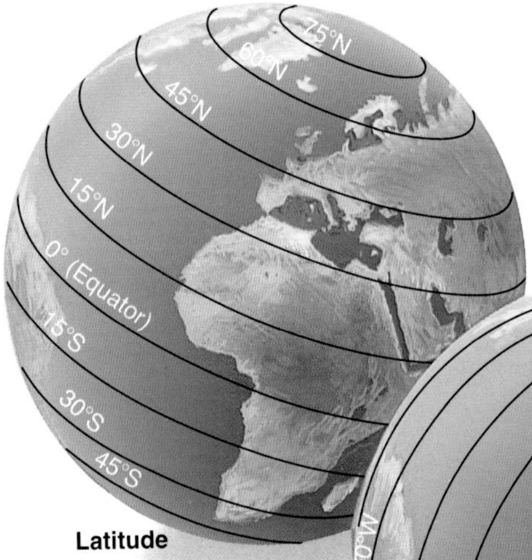

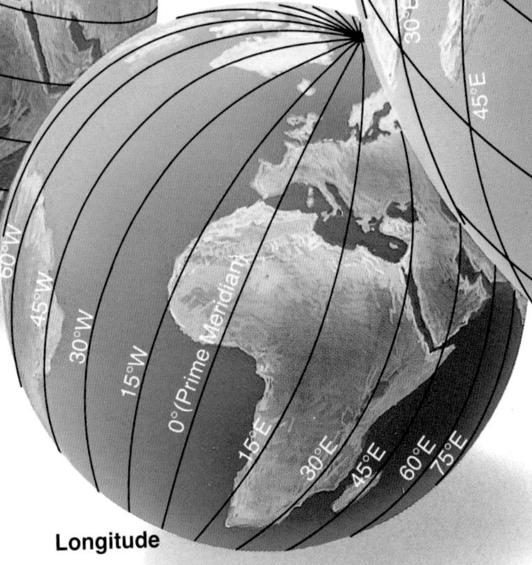

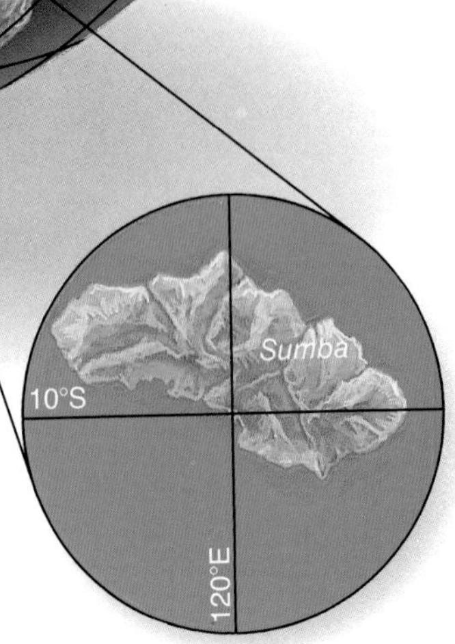

Latitude

Longitude

90°N (North Pole)

Finding Sumba. *Globes do not show every line of latitude or longitude, but just a few at regular intervals. The two small globes above show lines of* latitude *(left) and* longitude *(right) spaced 15 degrees apart. The Equator is at 0° latitude, and the Prime Meridian is at 0° longitude. Combining the two sets of lines*

forms a grid, shown on the large globe. You can use this grid to find any spot on Earth. For example, Sumba, one of the Lesser Sunda Islands of Indonesia, is located at about latitude 10° S, longitude 120° E. To find it, follow the Equator east to 120° E, then go south. Just before 15° S, you will find Sumba.

Lines of longitude run north and south. They are also called meridians. All meridians are the same length, and they come together at the North and South Poles. By international agreement, the meridian that runs through Greenwich, England, is called the Prime Meridian.

Together, meridians and parallels form an imaginary grid that defines positions on Earth in terms of their distance from the Equator and Prime Meridian. Latitude measures distance north or south of the Equator, and longitude is the distance east or west of the Prime Meridian. Both latitude and longitude are measured in degrees (°). Latitude goes from 0° to 90° north and south of the Equator, and longitude from 0° to 180° east and west of the Prime Meridian. Each degree is further divided into 60 minutes ('), and each minute is divided into 60 seconds ("). Geographers use all these measurements to pinpoint the locations of places in the world.

Parallels never meet, so the distance between two lines of latitude does not change. One degree of latitude is about 69 miles (111 km), one minute of latitude is about 1.15 miles (1.85 km), and one second of latitude is approximately 101 feet (31 m). Because meridians do meet, one degree of longitude is shorter at the Poles than at the Equator. However, no matter where, 15 degrees of longitude equals the amount of the Earth that passes the sun in one hour.

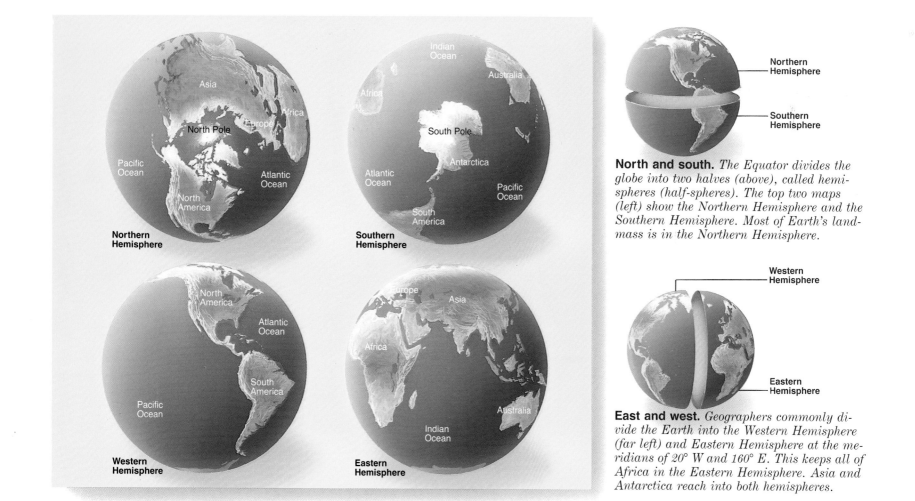

North and south. *The Equator divides the globe into two halves (above), called hemispheres (half-spheres). The top two maps (left) show the Northern Hemisphere and the Southern Hemisphere. Most of Earth's landmass is in the Northern Hemisphere.*

East and west. *Geographers commonly divide the Earth into the Western Hemisphere (far left) and Eastern Hemisphere at the meridians of 20° W and 160° E. This keeps all of Africa in the Eastern Hemisphere. Asia and Antarctica reach into both hemispheres.*

The Round Earth on Flat Paper

Maps teach us about the world by showing the sizes and shapes of countries, displaying Earth's mountains, rivers, lakes, and other features, and showing the distance between places. Maps can also show us the worldwide distribution of such things as deserts, cities, people, or resources like oil fields. Maps, though, are not the best way to show the round Earth. A globe is.

A globe is a scale model of the Earth showing its shape, lands, distances, and directions in their true proportions. But a globe is too bulky and awkward to carry around, and pictures of a globe do not make good maps in an atlas. For one thing, they show only half of the world at a time. So mapmakers make flat maps instead.

Changing the globe into a map is not simple, however. Imagine cutting a globe in half and trying to flatten the two hemispheres. They would wrinkle, and their shapes would distort. In fact, every map has some distortion. A map can show either the correct *size* of countries or the correct *shapes* of small areas, but not both.

There are many ways to project a round globe onto flat paper. Each produces a certain type of map. Imagine a glass globe with lines etched on it. Lines running parallel to the Equator are called parallels of latitude; those connecting the Poles are called meridians of longitude. Shining a light through the globe onto paper projects shadows of the lines and landmasses onto the paper (see below). These can be copied on paper to make a map, but the method is limited. Computers are needed to make most map projections.

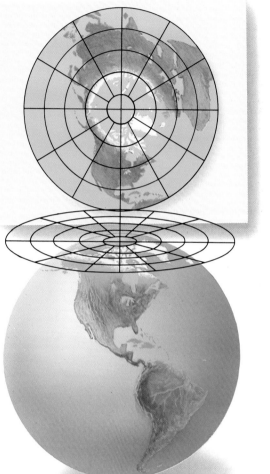

Plane projection. *Each type of map is suited for displaying a particular view of the world. The map above is useful for displaying an entire hemisphere. It also represents areas in their proper proportions: If you put a dime over two different places on the map, the areas represented under each coin will be the same size. This map is called a Lambert Azimuthal Equal-Area map, and it is made by projecting half of the Earth onto a plane that touches the globe at one point. That point becomes the central projection point of the map. Directions from the map's center to another point on the map are correct, but all other directions are distorted. This projection also distorts the shapes of countries.*

Conic Projection. *A Lambert Conformal Conic map is made by projecting the globe onto a cone. The latitude lines where the cone and globe touch, shown darker than the others, are called the standard parallels. The word "conformal" means that this map represents the shape of limited areas accurately. Conic maps are used to show parts of the globe that run primarily east and west in the middle latitudes. The United States would be one example. Unlike the map at left, this one distorts size from one area to another.*

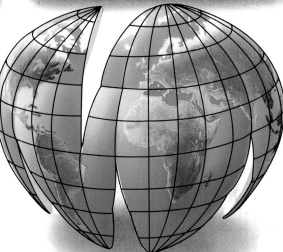

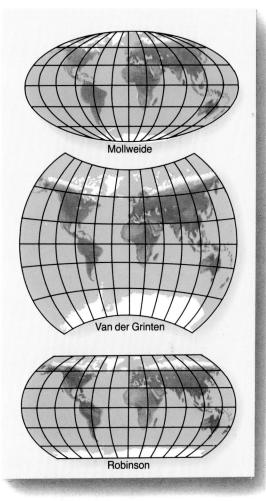

Mollweide

Van der Grinten

Robinson

Cylindrical projection. *The Mercator projection map is very commonly used. It is best for navigating at sea because a line connecting any two points gives the best possible compass direction between them. For areas close to the Equator, this type of map accurately represents the* shape, *but it badly distorts the relative sizes of landmasses the nearer they are to the North and South Poles. Alaska, for example, looks about half the size of South America on such a map, while in fact, South America is more than 11 times bigger.*

Interrupted projection. *If you peeled an orange and flattened it out, you might have something that looked like Goode's Interrupted Homolosine map. Such a map shows the continents or oceans with very little distortion in shape or size. To achieve this, each continent or ocean is centered on its own central meridian. Interrupted projections can be made to feature ocean areas by cutting apart the continents instead.*

Map evolution. *Cartographers are always looking for a more accurate way to project the round Earth onto flat paper. The Mollweide projection (top), developed in 1805, is good for accurately representing the relative* size *of the world's landmasses, but it distorts their* shapes. *The Van der Grinten projection (middle) became the National Geographic Society's standard map in 1922. It does a better job of representing* shapes, *but it distorts the relative* sizes *of many countries, particularly Canada, Greenland, and the Soviet Union. In 1988 the Society adopted a map based on the Robinson projection as its official standard, believing that it provides the best compromise in representing both* shape *and* size.

Spinning Through Day and Night

While people on North America's west coast stir in early morning slumber at 4 a.m., those on the east coast are eating breakfast, and the residents of central Africa have finished their midday meal. Because it is 8 to 10 p.m. in Australia, people there are probably thinking about bed. The reason for these time differences is that the Earth rotates from west to east, spinning through 15 degrees of longitude every hour.

In the days when communication among different areas was slow, each town set its clocks by observing the sun's position—it was 12 noon local time when the sun was directly overhead. Thus in the United States, at noon in Washington, D. C., it was 12:12 p.m. farther east in New York City. But as transportation and communication technology advanced, it became important to have a standard system of time.

In 1883, U. S. railroad officials created four time zones, each 15 degrees wide, to span the country. These zones were centered on the meridians at 75°, 90°, 105°, and 120° west of the Prime Meridian running through Greenwich, England. Soon other countries began adopting this system, creating a series of standard time zones centered on meridians spaced 15 degrees apart. Today, all but a few countries set their local time according to these time zones. As a result, we can determine accurately what time it is anywhere in the world.

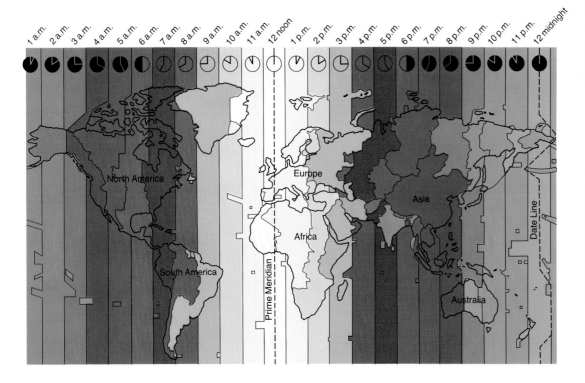

World time zones. *The map above shows the 24 standard time zones. The colors correspond to the meridians on which they are centered, which encircle the globe at right. Notice that the borders of each time zone are not straight lines. That is so that entire countries or neighboring communities can have the same time zone. For example, the international date line, at 180° longitude, zigs and zags to avoid splitting up island groups in the Pacific Ocean. China, by decree of its government, has only one time zone even though it spans some 60 degrees of longitude. It shows up as a single zone under the Asia label.*

Earth's rotation. *A day—approximately the time it takes the Earth to complete one rotation on its axis—is divided into 24 hours. Because the planet is divided into 360 degrees, it travels 15 degrees each hour. The globe below shows the meridians, spaced at intervals of 15 degrees longitude. Each hour a different meridian is opposite the sun. The white line is the Prime Meridian at 0° longitude, and the time zone centered on it is called Universal Time (UT), formerly Greenwich Mean Time (GMT). The zigzagging green line on the opposite side of the Earth is the date line, the place where each day on Earth begins.*

Revolving with the Seasons

Every 365¼ days, the Earth completes its orbit of the sun. During that trip, the weather over much of the world changes in a regular pattern known as seasons. Year after year, spring, summer, fall, and winter follow one another. Spring always begins around March 21 in the Northern Hemisphere, while fall starts on that same date in the Southern Hemisphere.

The Earth has seasons because its axis is tilted. You can see by looking at a mounted globe that the North and South Poles are tipped at an angle of about 23½ degrees. The Earth always leans in the same direction as it revolves around the sun, so the amount of sunlight hitting the Northern and Southern Hemispheres changes seasonally as the planet orbits the sun.

On about June 22, when the Northern Hemisphere is tilted toward the sun, countries such as the United States enjoy the first day of summer. This is the longest day of the year, and the sun's rays are never more direct. Meanwhile, it is the shortest day in the Southern Hemisphere, as the South Pole points away from the sun.

Six months later, the Southern Hemisphere leans toward the sun. Winter grips northern latitudes, while Australia heads into summer. Between the extremes of summer and winter come spring and fall. During these seasons, Earth's axis is perpendicular to the sun's rays, and neither hemisphere has much sunlight advantage.

Cockeyed world. *As Earth orbits the sun, most areas pass through four seasonal phases (below). On about June 22, the Tropic of Cancer receives the sun's most direct rays. This is the summer solstice in the Northern Hemisphere, when summer begins. As Earth moves on around the sun, the rays strike the globe most directly farther south, crossing the Equator about September 23, the fall equinox. By about December 22, the winter solstice in the Northern Hemisphere, the Tropic of Capricorn is exposed to the sun's most direct rays. They move north across the Equator again on the spring equinox, about March 21. On the two equinoxes, most places on Earth have nearly equal hours of daylight and dark.*

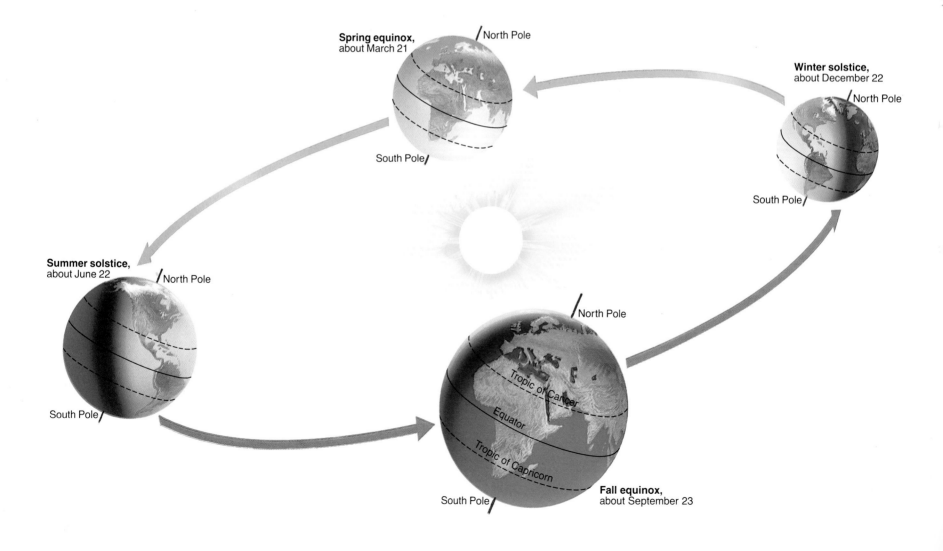

Spring equinox, about March 21 / North Pole
South Pole /

Winter solstice, about December 22 / North Pole
South Pole /

Summer solstice, about June 22 / North Pole
South Pole /

North Pole /
Tropic of Cancer
Equator
Tropic of Capricorn
South Pole /

Fall equinox, about September 23

Arctic zone

Temperate zone

Tropical zone

Heat and light. *Temperatures may change with the seasons, but it is always warmer at the Equator than it is near the North and South Poles. The reason for this is that the Earth is round. In the world's tropical areas, symbolized by the tropical hut, the sun's rays hit the Earth nearly vertically, and the ground and air above it become warm. But because the Earth is curved, the angle of the sun's rays becomes lower as you move away from the Equator. A house in the United States (middle, above) receives less direct sunlight. In the Arctic, still less reaches the igloo, because the sun's rays are nearly parallel to the ground. The sun's energy is dissipated and the Arctic stays generally colder.*

Nature's Power Shapes the Land

Earth's changing surface is formed of thick slabs of rock called plates. They divide the planet's rigid crust into a patchwork of seven vast pieces and several small ones. The huge plates carry the continents and form the ocean floor.

Propelled by forces from within the planet, the plates move slowly around the globe. Most of the time, plate movement is so gradual that it can't be felt. The slabs of rock usually advance only a few inches each year. As they move, the plates interact. They may plow into each other, pull apart, or slide past each other. Geologists call this activity plate tectonics.

Plate tectonics is the force that creates many of Earth's physical features. In fact, "tectonic" comes from a Greek word that means "builder."

Where plates collide, great mountain chains rise, such as the Himalaya in Asia. Where the edge of one plate slides beneath another, creating deep valleys called trenches, the interaction triggers volcanic activity. Around three sides of the Pacific Plate, hundreds of active volcanoes form the zone known as the Ring of Fire.

As plates sliding alongside each other catch,

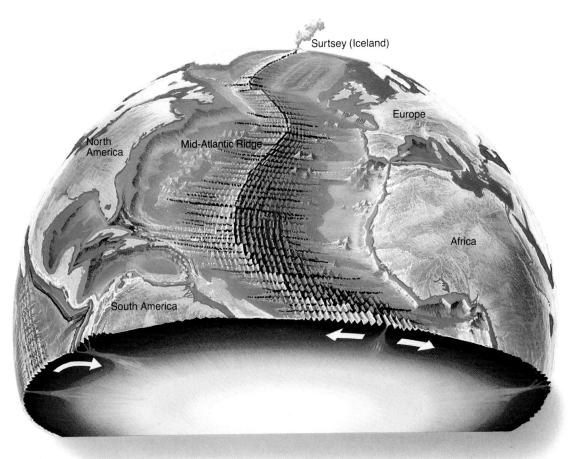

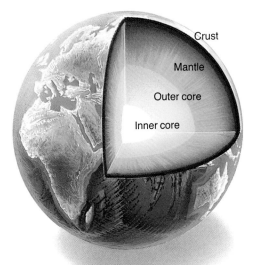

Layered Planet. *A superhot, solid inner core lies at the center of the planet. It is surrounded by the liquid outer core. The mantle, a thick layer of hot, dense rock, lies above the iron core. The crust, Earth's rocky shell, forms the surface. As little as 5 miles (8 km) thick in places, it is Earth's thinnest layer.*

Mid-Atlantic Ridge. *The diagram above shows a section of the Mid-Ocean Ridge. A rift, or deep crack, splits the ridge. From the rift, molten rock called magma wells up between the plates. The magma hardens into rock, creating ocean floor and volcanic landforms such as the distant island of Surtsey.*

Patchwork of Plates. *Seven large plates and several small ones form Earth's crust. Red lines on the map below represent plate boundaries. Yellow dots stand for the many active volcanoes found along them. Volcanic zones develop where molten material from inside Earth spills through weak points in the crust.*

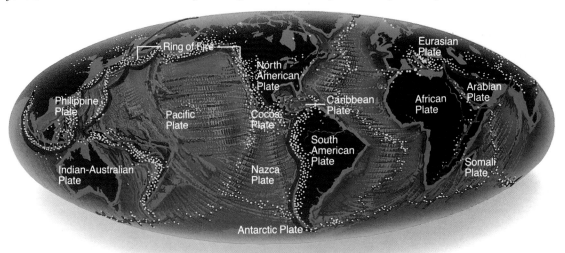

Along a fault. *Earthquakes happen along faults, or cracks, in the Earth's rigid outer crust. The dark vertical line on the diagram below shows the location of a fault. As two plates of crust grind past each other along a fault, strain builds up in the rocks. Eventually the strain becomes so great that the rocks* snap and move. *This movement releases pent-up energy along the fault, causing an earthquake. The ground trembles as shock waves move through it away from the place where the rocks snapped apart. Earthquakes can topple houses and power lines and tear apart sections of roads and railroad tracks.*

they build up tension. When the tension releases, it causes earthquakes such as those that have repeatedly shaken California. Where plates pull apart, usually on the floor of the oceans, molten rock from within the Earth wells up. This material creates new seafloor and builds an undersea mountain chain that rings the Earth, the Mid-Ocean Ridge.

Earth scientists have not pinpointed exactly what fuels plate tectonics. But they think that heat rising from the Earth's core may set off currents of slow movement in the mantle, the thick layer of rock just below the crust. Over millions of years, these slowly churning currents may have shifted the plates around.

Scientists estimate that plate tectonics has been shaping the Earth's surface for from 2.5 to 4 billion years. The activity continues today. The peaks of the Himalaya are getting higher as the Indian landmass pushes against them; Hawaii is inching toward Japan; Europe and North America are drifting apart. Millions of years from now, plate tectonics will have sculpted a whole new face for our dynamic planet.

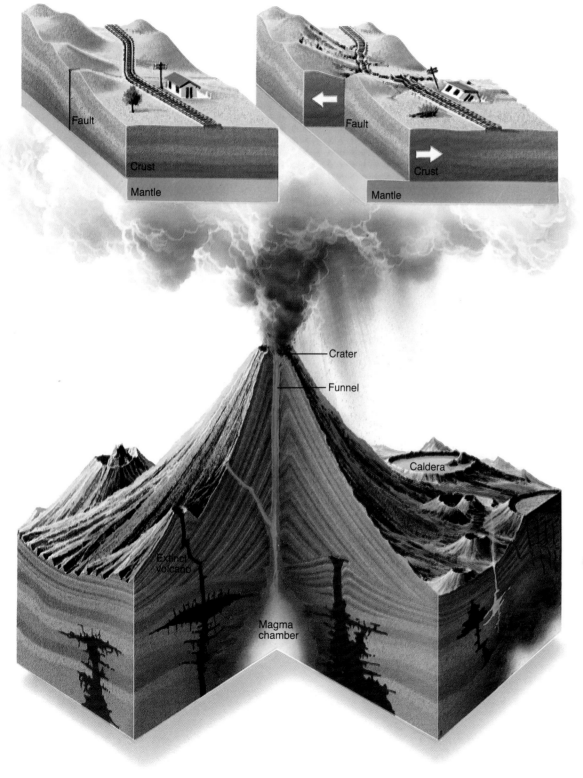

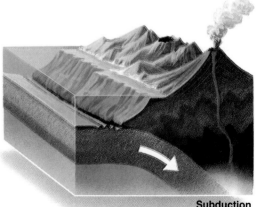

Volcanic eruption. *A cloud of ash and gas spews from a volcano's vent as red-hot magma rises to the surface (left). Volcanoes form along boundaries where one plate plunges beneath another (above). The rocky slab melts as it dives down into the hot mantle, and the molten material rises to forge volcanoes.*

The Language of Maps

archipelago—a group or chain of islands.

bay—a body of water partially surrounded by land; bays are usually smaller and less deeply indented than **gulfs.**

canyon—a deep, narrow valley with steep sides; it is wider and longer than a gorge.

cape—a piece of land that extends into a river, a lake, or an ocean.

delta—a lowland composed of silt, sand, and gravel deposited by a river at its mouth.

divide—the high boundary between areas drained by different river systems; water flows in a different direction on either side.

dormant volcano—a temporarily inactive volcano; a totally inactive one is called extinct.

escarpment—a cliff separating two nearly flat land surfaces that lie at different levels.

glacier—a large, slowly moving mass of ice.

harbor—a body of water sheltered by natural or artificial barriers and deep enough to moor ships.

iceberg—a large floating chunk of ice broken away from a glacier or an ice shelf (see map, page 236).

isthmus—a narrow strip of land that connects two larger landmasses and has water on two sides.

lagoon—a shallow body of water that opens on the sea, but is protected by a sandbar or coral reef.

mesa—a broad, flat-topped landform with steep sides found in arid or semiarid regions.

oasis—a green area in a desert, with a spring or waterhole, often fed by an underground aquifer.

peninsula—a long piece of land almost surrounded by water, but connected to a larger landmass.

plateau—a large, flat area that rises higher than the land around it; larger than a mesa.

reef—an offshore ridge of rocks, coral, or sand.

sound—a long, broad ocean inlet usually parallel to the coast, or a long stretch of water separating an island from the mainland.

strait—a narrow passage of water that connects two larger bodies of water.

tributary—a stream that flows into a larger river.

How to Read Our Maps

Each map in this book is full of information. To find the locations of towns, rivers, and other features, you can read the place-name labels. If you understand the symbols, you can discover even more. When looking at the maps, refer to the key below. On this map, you'll see that Argentina's capital is Buenos Aires. The label size also tells you that, like Montevideo, it has a population of more than a million. The towns of Viedma and Rawson have the smallest size dot and label, meaning they have fewer than 50,000 people.

The other symbols represent man-made and physical features. Look at the painting of a geographical landscape on the opposite page. Keep that picture in mind when you see a canal, waterfall, glacier, or reef symbol on a map.

In this Picture Atlas each country appears on a map like the one at right and on a locator map to place it on its continent. Each has a story and a fact box, and flags are shown for all independent countries. Foreign words and place-names in the stories often have accent marks called diacriticals that help in pronunciation. Diacriticals appear on the wall map that comes with this book, but they are not on the book's own maps.

⊛ *Country Capital*

⊙ *Dependency Capital*

● **Montevideo** *1 million people and over*

● **Cordoba** *100,000 to under 1 million people*

● Copiapo *50,000 to under 100,000 people*

• Viedma *under 50,000 people*

Lake, Reservoir		*Swamp*	
Intermittent Lake		*Internal Boundary*	
Dry Salt Lake		*Disputed Area*	
River		*Road*	
Intermittent River		*Railroad*	
Disappearing River		*Pass, Tunnel*	)(
Canal		*Waterfall*	//
Reef		*Dam*	I
Mountains		*Mountain Peak*	+
Glaciers		*Site*	□

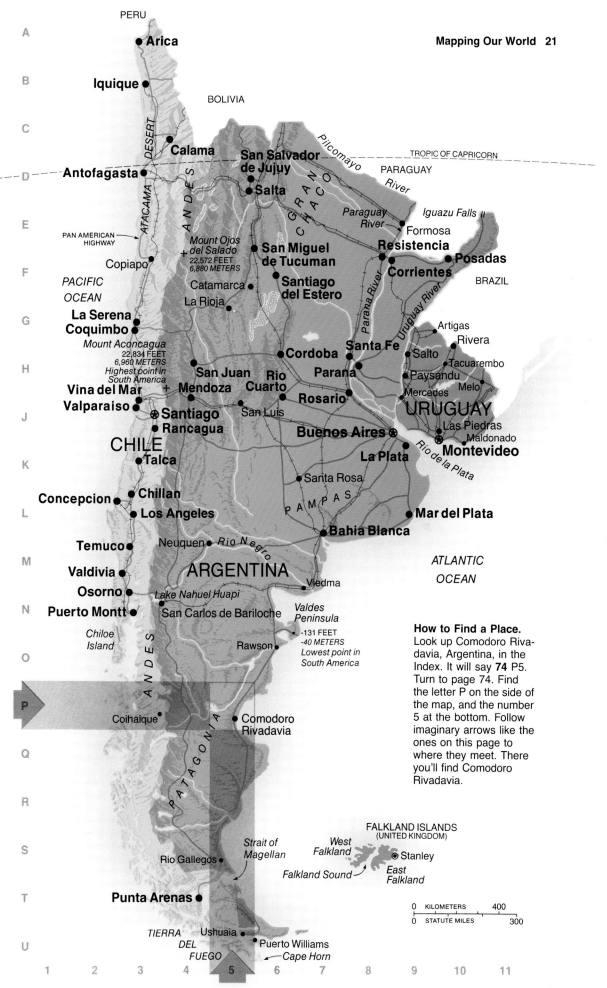

How to Find a Place.
Look up Comodoro Rivadavia, Argentina, in the Index. It will say **74** P5. Turn to page 74. Find the letter P on the side of the map, and the number 5 at the bottom. Follow imaginary arrows like the ones on this page to where they meet. There you'll find Comodoro Rivadavia.

North America

The first humans set foot on North America in what is now Alaska about 30,000 years ago. These early migrants crossed from Asia on a strip of land long since submerged under the Bering Strait. Their descendants survive today as the Indians of the Americas. As they spread southward, they peopled a continent that ranks third out of seven in size, after Asia and Africa.

North America measures some 4,000 miles (6,437 km) between the coasts of Alaska and Newfoundland, but it pinches to 31 miles (50 km) at its southernmost reach in Central America. There, North America is about 500 miles (805 km) from the Equator. Its northernmost point, a tip of the world's largest island, Greenland, comes about that close to the North Pole.

North America's great geographical diversity has led to great diversity in the way people live. Along the continent's Atlantic coast and the Gulf of Mexico runs a low coastal plain. Much of this land abounds in fertile soil that has grown cotton, corn, tobacco, and other important crops since the days when European colonists settled there. Rich oil deposits lie in the southern part of the plain and in the Gulf of Mexico. Their development often threatens the region's ecology.

The forested ridges of the Appalachian Mountains stretch from Newfoundland to the southern United States. The Appalachians are among Earth's oldest mountains; 300 million years ago they stood perhaps as high as today's Rocky Mountains. As erosion wore down the mountains, layers of mud, silt, and sand buried dead plants. Millions of years of heat and pressure underground turned them into coal. This resource has brought wealth to Kentucky, West Virginia, and other states, but at a cost: Mines scar Appalachian hillsides. Miners risk accidents and lung disease, and shutdowns have brought poverty.

Rapids and waterfalls mark places where rivers rush from the Appalachian foothills to meet the coastal plain. In the early days of the United States, ships could sail no farther upriver, and cities grew where there was waterpower for industry. They now form a string of densely populated metropolitan areas along the East Coast.

In Canada, the lowlands of the St. Lawrence River lie west of the Appalachians. This river highway to the Great Lakes and its fertile valley helped cities to thrive. Once the development of steam power freed industry from its dependence on rushing water, cities grew up near raw materials such as iron and coal. Just as eastern cities drew immigrants, first from Europe, later from Asia and Latin America, these inland cities became home to many different cultural groups.

In the center of the continent, plains and lowlands sweep west from the Appalachians to the foot of the Rocky Mountains. Some 14,000 years ago, glaciers covered parts of the northern plains. These ice sheets sculptured a rolling landscape with thousands of lakes, the biggest of which are the five Great Lakes. Great river systems formed from the runoff of melting glaciers. Among others, the Missouri, Mississippi, and Ohio became highways traveled by Indians and pioneers and by today's barges and ships.

The western plains lie in the rain shadow of the Rocky Mountains. Too dry for forests, the plains were grasslands until settlers' plows broke the sod. Now farmers grow wheat and ranchers graze cattle. In Canada's southern prairies, agriculture and mineral resources have brought wealth, and cities have flourished.

In Canada's north, the prairies give way to the conifer forests of the taiga and, farther north, to tundra. People in isolated lumber camps, mining towns, and fishing villages face a frigid climate and harsh terrain. To the east, shaped like an enormous broken doughnut, the Canadian Shield arcs around Hudson Bay and dips into parts of the United States. The Shield is named for the rock that lies under its thin soil, rock that formed about three billion years ago, when the first forms of life appeared on Earth.

To the west, the plains slope upward to the Rocky Mountains, a jagged range of lofty peaks stretching from northern Alaska through western Canada almost to Mexico. These are young mountains. At the southern end, volcanic explosions that ended ten million years ago created peaks and basins, and the rich mineral deposits that drew prospectors and miners. The spine of the Rockies forms part of the Continental Divide. East of the divide, rivers flow to the Gulf of Mexico and the Atlantic or to the Arctic Ocean. West of it they flow to the Pacific.

Between the Rockies and the Pacific coast ranges of the United States lies a series of plateaus and basins, the latter flooded thousands of

A Missouri tallgrass prairie

The Continental Divide in Montana

A Lake Superior shoreline in Wisconsin

ASIA

ARCTIC OCEAN

BERING SEA

GREENLAND

Aleutian Islands

Yukon River

Ellesmere Island

BAFFIN BAY

+Mt. McKinley
20,320 FEET
6,194 METERS
Highest point in
North America

Mackenzie River

Baffin Island

GULF OF ALASKA

Canadian

ARCTIC CIRCLE

PACIFIC OCEAN

Vancouver Island

HUDSON BAY

Great

Shield

NORTH

Hawaiian Islands

Coast Range

Great Basin

Great Plains

AMERICA

Great Lakes

St. Lawrence River

Newfoundland

Colorado River

ROCKY MOUNTAINS

Central Lowlands

Niagara Falls

APPALACHIAN MTS.

Death Valley
−282 FEET
−86 METERS
Lowest point in
North America

Grand Canyon

ATLANTIC OCEAN

TROPIC OF CANCER

Gulf of California

Sierra Madre Occidental

Rio Grande

Mississippi River

Coastal

Bermuda Islands

Plain

GULF OF MEXICO

WEST INDIES

CENTRAL AMERICA

CARIBBEAN SEA

EQUATOR

Isthmus of Panama

SOUTH AMERICA

TROPIC OF CAPRICORN

ASIA

ARCTIC OCEAN

Bering Sea

GREENLAND
(KALAALLIT NUNAAT)
(DENMARK)

ARCTIC CIRCLE

Yukon River

ALASKA
(UNITED STATES)

Nuuk
(Godthab)

Mackenzie River

Great Bear
Lake

Great Slave
Lake

CANADA

Hudson
Bay

Island of
Newfoundland

Nelson River

Edmonton

Vancouver
Island

Columbia
River

Calgary

Lake
Winnipeg

St. Lawrence River

ST. PIERRE AND MIQUELON
(FRANCE)

Seattle

Winnipeg

Missouri River

Lake
Superior

Lake
Huron

Montreal

PACIFIC
OCEAN

Snake River

Mississippi River

Lake
Michigan

Ottawa

Toronto

Detroit

Lake
Ontario

Lake
Erie

New York

ATLANTIC
OCEAN

San Francisco

UNITED STATES

Denver

Chicago

Philadelphia

Washington, D. C.

Colorado River

Arkansas River

Ohio River

Los Angeles

San Diego

Rio Grande

Dallas

Tennessee River

Atlanta

BERMUDA
(UNITED KINGDOM)

TROPIC OF CANCER

Houston

Monterrey

Gulf of
Mexico

Miami

BAHAMAS

Nassau

PUERTO RICO
(UNITED STATES)

MEXICO

Guadalajara

Havana

CUBA

DOMINICAN
REPUBLIC

Mexico

HAITI

Santo Domingo

Port-au-Prince

JAMAICA

Kingston

CARIBBEAN SEA

LESSER ANTILLES

BELIZE

Belmopan

HONDURAS

GUATEMALA

Tegucigalpa

Guatemala

San Salvador

NICARAGUA

Port of Spain

EL SALVADOR

Managua

TRINIDAD AND
TOBAGO

COSTA RICA

Panama
Canal

Panama

San Jose

PANAMA

SOUTH AMERICA

years ago with huge lakes. Now the dry lake beds are hard and flat as pavement. On one of them, shuttles land after their sojourns in space. Across one plateau the Colorado River slices the mile-deep Grand Canyon, the biggest gorge on Earth. Irrigation allows some farming, but much of this region is rangeland and desert.

Along the Pacific coast grew the greatest conifer forest on Earth before loggers came to it. Today's remnants are a reminder of what western North America was like before Europeans appeared. Redwoods here are the world's tallest trees, giant sequoias are the largest, and bristlecone pines are more than 4,000 years old, among the oldest living things on Earth.

To the south, a high, rugged plateau forms the heart of Mexico, rimmed on east and west by mountains that converge in volcanic peaks. In sight of these peaks stands one of the world's fastest growing urban areas, Mexico City. Seeking work, impoverished peasants flood into the city. Millions of Mexicans and other Latin Americans have found their way legally or illegally into the United States.

The smaller nations of North America range through Central America and arc across the Caribbean Sea. Many of the Caribbean islands are the peaks of submerged volcanoes. Coastal plains and sandy beaches edge the islands. Some are among the world's most densely populated places. Much of the good land is on plantations owned by wealthy people, and businesses are often owned by outsiders. A major source of income in Mexico and the islands is remittances, money sent home by those who leave to work in Canada or the United States. Still, the Caribbean nations have made great strides in building up their tourist industry, which became their prime foreign-currency earner in the mid-1980s.

Most of North America's poorer people aspire to the affluence of the American lifestyle. With some of the world's greatest resources at their disposal, the United States and Canada have developed standards of living largely unmatched in the rest of the world. In recent years, though, a greater understanding has grown of the vulnerability of those natural assets and of the need to protect the environment, to check consumption, to lessen air pollution—to preserve the quality as well as the abundance of life.

Mexico City, like many cities, faces overcrowding and pollution.

Facts About North America

Area: 9,357,293 sq mi (24,235,280 sq km)
Population: 416,664,500
Highest Point: Mt. McKinley, Alaska, 20,320 ft (6,194 m) above sea level
Lowest Point: Death Valley, California, 282 ft (86 m) below sea level
Largest Country: (by area) Canada 3,849,674 sq mi (9,970,610 sq km)
Largest Country: (by population) United States 243,400,000
Largest Island: *Greenland, 840,004 sq mi (2,175,600 sq km)
Largest Metropolitan Areas: (by population)

Mexico City, Mexico	19,370,000
New York, U. S.	18,120,000
Los Angeles, U. S.	13,770,000

Longest Rivers: (mi and km)

Mackenzie-Peace	2,635	4,241
Missouri	2,540	4,088
Mississippi	2,340	3,766

Largest Lakes: (sq mi and sq km)

Superior, U. S.-Canada	31,699	82,100
Huron, U. S.-Canada	23,012	59,600

*World record

Glossary

campesino—a resident of a Latin American rural area.

contras—an organized group of rebels who fought the Sandinista government in Nicaragua.

Creole—a mixture of several languages, which serves as an indigenous form of speech.

ejido—in Mexico, redistribution of farmland by the government to individuals or collectives after the 1910 Mexican Revolution.

guerrilla—a person who carries on warfare behind enemy lines through ambushes, raids, and sabotage of transport and communications.

hacienda—a large estate or plantation in Latin America, or its main house.

Maya—an Indian civilization of Central America, which built cities and temple-pyramids and devised a calendar and a writing system.

patois—a regional dialect.

plantation—a large estate that grows a cash crop; usually worked by unskilled or semiskilled labor.

taiga—subarctic coniferous forest largely consisting of firs and spruces.

tundra—a treeless plain found mostly in Arctic regions, that has permanently frozen subsoil and low-growing plants.

Seattle
Columbia
River
WASH.
Portland
OREGON
IDAHO
Boise
Snake River
CASCADE RANGE
SIERRA NEVADA
NEVADA
Great
Salt
Lake
Salt Lake City
San Francisco
UTAH
Mt. Whitney
14,494 FEET
4,418 METERS
Highest point in 48
+ contiguous states
San Jose
CALIF.
Colorado River
Death Valley
−282 FEET
−86 METERS
Lowest point in
North America
Las Vegas
Los Angeles
ARIZONA
Albuquerque
San Diego
Phoenix
NEW
MEXICO
PACIFIC
OCEAN
MEXICO
El Paso

CANADA
MONTANA
NORTH
DAKOTA
MINNESOTA
Lake
Superior
GREAT PLAINS
SOUTH
DAKOTA
St. Paul
WIS.
Lake
Michigan
Lake
Huron
Minneapolis
Milwaukee
MICH.
WYOMING
Missouri River
Lake
Ontario
Buffalo
N.Y.
Lake
Erie
Detroit
Cleveland
PA.
Mississippi
River
Chicago
NEBRASKA
IOWA
Platte River
INDIANA
OHIO
Pittsburgh
ROCKY MOUNTAINS
Denver
COLO.
+
Pikes Peak
14,110 FEET
4,301 METERS
Omaha
Kansas
City
UNITED STATES
Indianapolis
Columbus
W. VA.
KANSAS
St. Louis
MISSOURI
Ohio River
KY.
VA.
OZARK
PLATEAU
Nashville
Oklahoma City
TENN.
APPALACHIAN MOUNTAINS
N.C.
Charlotte
OKLAHOMA
ARKANSAS
Memphis
S.C.
Red River
Atlanta
Mississippi
River
ALA.
GEORGIA
Fort Worth
Dallas
LA.
MISS.
TEXAS
Austin
New Orleans
Houston
San Antonio
Rio Grande
GULF OF
MEXICO
FLORIDA
Jacksonville
Cape Canaveral
Tampa
Miami

ME.
VT.
N.H.
Hudson
River
N.Y.
Boston
MASS.
CONN.
R.I.
New York
N.J.
Philadelphia
DEL.
Baltimore
MD.
Washington, D. C.
ATLANTIC
OCEAN
Outer
Banks

0 KILOMETERS 500
0 STATUTE MILES 250
For map legend see page 21.

Of the 50 United States, 48 are contiguous, which means they touch each other. That leaves two: Alaska, which borders on Canada, and Hawaii in the Pacific Ocean. To fit these states on the same pages as the contiguous states, the maps here show them far out of

their true geographical location. You can locate Alaska and Hawaii correctly on the top map on the facing page. Hawaii (opposite) has been enlarged. The round symbol on that map, a compass rose, indicates which way is north, south, east, or west.

Barrow
BROOKS RANGE
ARCTIC CIRCLE
Nome
Yukon River
CANADA
Fairbanks
ALASKA
Mount McKinley +
20,320 FEET
6,194 METERS
Highest point in
North America
BERING
SEA
Anchorage
Juneau
GULF OF
ALASKA
Kodiak
Island
Sitka
ALEUTIAN ISLANDS

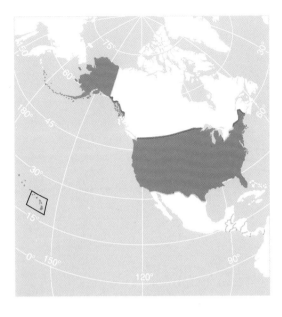

United States

Ocean waves slap the rocks of Oregon and wash the sands of Florida. Deserts cover the Southwest and forests the Pacific Northwest. In California's Death Valley it seldom rains; at the top of Hawaii's Mount Waialeale the rain seldom stops. Few other nations match the United States' variety of landscapes and climates.

The fourth largest country in both area and population was born on the East Coast while Spanish colonists settled the Southwest. It grew westward, from 13 colonies on the Atlantic coast to 50 states stretching as far as Alaska and Hawaii. In longitude it reaches a third of the way around the globe. In latitude it spans more than 50 degrees, from southernmost Hawaii where the ground never freezes to northernmost Alaska where the ground never thaws.

Three-fourths of the United States lies west of the Mississippi River. But more than half of the 30 largest metropolitan areas lie east of it. As you travel east to west, you see reasons why.

On the East Coast, colonists built towns and cleared farmland. Abundant resources such as lumber, fish, and iron, and crops such as tobacco and cotton funneled through seaports en route to other colonies and Europe. Cities with skyscrapers now stand where ports grew around harbors on the coast and up the rivers.

In the hilly Northeast, swift rivers gave power for factories run by waterwheels. So along with farming and lumbering, a host of industries such as textiles and firearms arose. With the coming of railroads, industrial hubs such as Detroit and Pittsburgh prospered, close to both transportation and sources of raw materials.

In the Southeast, land and climate were ideal for planting cotton and tobacco. Some of the millions of blacks brought over as slaves worked these fields. Descendants of slaves now make up about a tenth of the U. S. population.

Inland, you reach the low Appalachian Mountain ridges. Their mines help make the United States the world's top producer of coal. But for many years these forested ridges slowed westward travel. To the east the colonies threw off British rule and forged a nation of 13 states, while lands to the west and south remained largely Indian territory. But settlers soon crowded out the Native Americans whose land this had been for thousands of years.

The land smoothes out in the central farmlands and dairy pastures and the Great Plains beyond. Here farmers grow half the world's corn and more wheat for export than any other country. Here, too, lie sheep and cattle ranges.

Cities sprinkle the nation's midsection and the rugged Rocky Mountain area. Many started as mining towns, others as rail hubs where cattle and crops were shipped, still others as port cities along rivers like the Mississippi that served as vital highways of commerce and expansion.

Farther west you cross deserts in the rain shadow of the Sierra Nevada mountains. Over that range lie California croplands and the Coast Range, then the Pacific Ocean.

Head northwest past the dense forests of the Pacific Northwest and you find Alaska, where some fishing towns are linked by air and sea without a road across the rugged land. Far out to sea you come to the Hawaiian Islands, the summits of undersea volcanoes, where pineapples and sugarcane ripen and tourists frolic.

The United States is the world's leading industrial power. Machines now do much of the work of farms and factories, driving millions of people to desert the fields and mills of small-town America and turn to service jobs in the cities: banking, finance, government, entertainment, and medical care. Less than two Americans in a hundred work on a farm. But as cities have swelled, so have their problems, and those of smaller towns, too: economic worries, overcrowding, pollution, crime, drugs.

Americans trace their roots to immigrants. Some were refugees from hard times or political upheavals in Europe. Some were brought against their will from Africa. Many now pour in from Southeast Asia and Latin America. The American people are as varied as their land, a mix more diverse than in any other nation.

Official name: *United States of America*
Area: *3,618,770 sq mi (9,372,614 sq km)*
Population: *243,400,000*
Capital: *Washington, D. C. (pop. 622,000)*
Ethnic groups: *white, black, Hispanic, Asian, Native American*
Language: *English*
Religious groups: *Christian, Jewish, other*
Economy: *Agr: grains, cotton, tobacco, oilseeds, livestock, sugar, vegetables, fruit. Ind: machinery, metals, food processing, chemicals, motor vehicles, aerospace, telecommunications, oil, electronics, consumer goods, fishing, lumber, paper, mining*
Currency: *U. S. dollar*

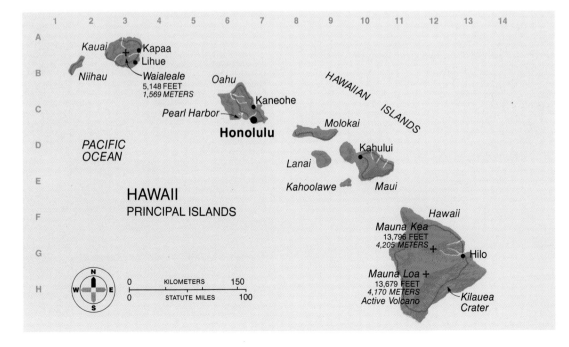

HAWAII
PRINCIPAL ISLANDS

United States

1 *Autumn paints the hills of Burke Hollow in Vermont, a New England state famed for fall colors and winter skiing.*

2 *Space shuttle* Columbia *roars off the pad at Cape Canaveral, Florida, home base for U. S. space vehicles since the 1950s.*

3 *New York City lights up the night. Lights and cars help make the United States the world's biggest consumer of energy.*

4 *A high school band joins a presidential inaugural parade in Washington, D. C., the nation's capital since 1800.*

5 *Fishermen explore a Louisiana bayou. Such slow-moving streams crisscross the Mississippi Delta, where the river fans out near its mouth.*

1 *Vermont, U. S.*

2 *Florida, U.S.*

3 *New York, U.S.*

4 *Washington, D.C., U.S.*

5 *Louisiana, U.S.*

1 *Washington, U. S.*

United States

1 *A self-leveling combine harvests wheat on a slope in Washington. This state ranked fifth in U. S. wheat production in 1989.*

2 *Freeways tie a knot in Los Angeles. Such high-speed roads link the city's downtown core to its sprawling suburbs.*

3 *Mount McKinley, North America's highest peak, soars over campers in Alaska. Indians call the mountain Denali, "high one."*

4 *Logs for export, cut from vast forests of the Pacific Northwest, crowd both the ships and the water at Longview, Washington.*

5 *Indian cowboys rope a calf on an Apache ranch, one of several cooperatives that raise cattle on grasslands of the Fort Apache Reservation in Arizona.*

2 *California, U. S.*

3 *Alaska, U. S.*

4 *Washington, U. S.*

5 *Arizona, U. S.*

A B C D E F G H J K L M N O P Q R S T U

GREENLAND SEA

ARCTIC OCEAN

Alert

Ellesmere Island

GREENLAND
(KALAALLIT NUNAAT)
(DENMARK)

Qaanaaq (Thule)
Thule Air Base

North Magnetic Pole

Parry Islands

Baffin Bay

ARCTIC CIRCLE

Tasiilaq

BEAUFORT SEA

Banks Island

Resolute

Ilulissat

Aasiaat

Davis Strait

Sisimiut

ALASKA
(UNITED STATES)

Tuktoyaktuk

Inuvik

Victoria Island

Baffin Island

Maniitsoq

Nuuk (Godthab)

Cape Farewell

Paamiut

Qaqortoq

YUKON TERRITORY

Mount Logan
19,850 FEET
6,050 METERS

Mackenzie River

Cambridge Bay

Great Bear Lake

LABRADOR SEA

Yukon River

Whitehorse

Great Slave Lake

NORTHWEST TERRITORIES

Iqaluit

Hudson Strait

Yellowknife

Rankin Inlet

Ivujivik

Ungava Peninsula

ATLANTIC OCEAN

BRITISH COLUMBIA

Hay River

CANADA

Kuujjuaq

NEWFOUNDLAND

Fort Smith

Lake Athabasca

HUDSON BAY

LABRADOR

Churchill Falls

Prince Rupert

Churchill River

Churchill

St. John's

Dawson Creek

ALBERTA

Nelson River

Fort Severn

QUEBEC

TRANS-CANADA HIGHWAY

Island of Newfoundland

Prince George

Fraser River

Fort George

Sept-Iles

PACIFIC OCEAN

Edmonton

SASKATCHEWAN

MANITOBA

James Bay

Gulf of St. Lawrence

ST. PIERRE AND MIQUELON (FRANCE)

Vancouver Island

Prince Albert

Lake Winnipeg

Fort Albany

PRINCE EDWARD ISLAND

Saskatoon

Calgary

ONTARIO

St. Lawrence River

NEW BRUNSWICK

Charlottetown

Victoria

Vancouver

Lethbridge

Regina

Winnipeg

Fredericton

Halifax

TRANS-CANADA HIGHWAY

TRANS-CANADA HIGHWAY

Quebec

NOVA SCOTIA

Thunder Bay

Lake Superior

Sudbury

Montreal

Bay of Fundy

UNITED STATES

Lake Huron

Ottawa

Oshawa

Toronto

Lake Ontario

Lake Michigan

London

Hamilton

Lake Erie

Windsor

Most of Greenland, the world's largest island, lies above the Arctic Circle. Most of Canada sprawls below it. In these two lands, people live farther north than anywhere else in the Western Hemisphere. Far more Canadians

live in the south, though, near the border with the contiguous United States, the world's longest open border. Some 88 million people cross it every year.

0 KILOMETERS 600
0 STATUTE MILES 400

For map legend see page 21.

1 2 3 4 5 6 7 8 9 10 11 12 13 14 15 16 17 18 19

Canada

Look at a Canadian ten-dollar bill and you'll see the words "Ten Dollars Dix." *Dix* is the French word for ten. It's there because Canada's history has given the country two official languages.

In 1497 John Cabot sailed to Newfoundland and staked a claim for England. Nearly 40 years later, Jacques Cartier sailed to the mouth of the St. Lawrence River and laid claim for France. While English settlements sprouted along the seaboard and Hudson Bay, the French headed inland. Their settlements in the present-day province of Quebec became part of New France, the French colonial empire in North America that lasted for more than a century until the British seized control in 1763.

Canada is now a democracy, modeled in part after British law and government. The country recognizes the British Queen as its sovereign, a largely ceremonial echo of British rule. But in Quebec, French is the main language, and the legal system is much like that of France. Montreal, Quebec's largest city, is the largest French-speaking city in the world except Paris.

Canada and the United States share an unfortified border more than 5,000 miles (8,045 km) long. Eight out of ten Canadians live within 100 miles (160 km) of it. That leaves almost 80 percent of this huge land nearly uninhabited. Yet this wilderness is Canada's treasure chest. Forty percent of the world's newsprint, the paper in your newspaper, comes from forests that cover half the country. Hundreds of mines make Canada the world's leading exporter of minerals.

Canada is the largest country in area after the Soviet Union. Five regions make up this immense landmass. At the northern end of the Appalachian Mountains is a region of hills and rolling plains stretching from New Brunswick to Newfoundland. A neighboring region of fertile flatlands rims the Great Lakes and the St. Lawrence River. Half of Canada's people live in these two regions. Half of its vegetables and nearly all of its corn come from farms there.

In the last 50 years steel mills, refineries, car factories, and other plants have been built along the shores of the Great Lakes in Ontario. Ontario's abundant hydroelectricity and, lately, nuclear power have contributed greatly to industrial development. The St. Lawrence River waterway links industrial centers such as Toronto and Montreal with seaports of the world.

Most of eastern Canada rests on an ancient sheet of bedrock called the Canadian Shield that extends into the United States. Thick evergreen forests cover its southern reaches. Farther north, taiga forests overlap the permafrost region. In the latter, the subsoil is permanently frozen, and most plants are tundra species such as low shrubs and lichens. Few plants survive in the ice and snow of the Shield's Arctic extremes.

West of the Shield lies a belt of plains, wooded in the north, rippling with wheat in the south. Besides bumper crops that rank Canada second only to the United States as a wheat exporting country, the region yields lumber and minerals.

West of these forests and wheatfields rise the majestic Canadian Rockies, the beginning of a mountainous region that stretches to the Pacific coast. Rough terrain and a cold climate help keep this region sparsely settled, though Vancouver and other coastal centers thrive on fishing, shipping, and other activities.

A land of striking contrasts, Canada embraces the extremes of wilderness and urban development, of agriculture and industry, of European and indigenous cultures. Its vast natural resources and far-flung population supply an urbanized, industrial heartland with the raw materials that keep the economy going.

Official name: *Canada*
Area: *3,849,670 sq mi (9,970,610 sq km)*
Population: *25,354,000*
Capital: *Ottawa (pop. 300,800)*
Ethnic groups: *British, French, and other European origin, indigenous Indian and Inuit*
Language: *English, French*
Religious groups: *Roman Catholic, Protestant*
Economy: *Agr: wheat, livestock, feed crops, oilseeds, tobacco, fruit, vegetables. Ind: transportation equipment, food processing, petroleum products, wood and paper products, chemicals, metals, minerals, fishing*
Currency: *Canadian dollar*

Greenland

Greenland is like an elongated bowl filled with ice. A huge ice sheet, two miles thick in places, covers nearly all the island. Its heavy weight helps push the land down below sea level, leaving a surrounding rim of mountains.

Greenland is the world's biggest island. Here, in the tenth century, Viking explorer Erik the Red found patches of green in fjords and coastal meadows. To lure settlers from Iceland, he named the island Greenland. Other people already lived there. Inuit hunters had crossed the ice from Ellesmere Island generations before.

From their day to ours, most people have found the ice-choked northern coasts unfit to live on, and have settled on Greenland's southwestern coastal fringe. There, commercial fishermen can put out to sea and herders can grow hay and tend sheep or reindeer. Many residents of Greenland fish for salmon, halibut, and cod, or work in plants that process the catch. Few roads link towns along the rugged coast; boats, snowmobiles, and aircraft take people to visit, attend school, or find a job.

Nearly all Greenlanders are of Inuit or Inuit-European descent. They govern themselves, but their island, known officially by its Greenlandic name, Kalaallit Nunaat, remains part of Denmark, home of Vikings centuries ago. There is a movement toward full independence.

Official name: *Greenland (Kalaallit Nunaat)*
Area: *840,004 sq mi (2,175,600 sq km)*
Population: *55,000*
Capital: *Nuuk (Godthåb) (pop. 10,972)*
Ethnic groups: *Greenlander, Danish*
Language: *Danish, Greenlandic*
Religious groups: *Lutheran*
Economy: *Agr: hay, sheep, vegetables. Ind: fishing, lead and zinc mining, sealing, handicrafts*
Currency: *Danish krone*

St. Pierre and Miquelon

Of its once-great Canadian lands, France holds only these eight rocky islets. With little soil for gardens, the islanders—French citizens, but self-governing—raise vegetables and livestock for home use and work in a fishing fleet and a fish processing plant. Tourism helps the economy.

Official name: *Territorial Collectivity of St. Pierre and Miquelon*
Area: *93 sq mi (242 sq km)*
Population: *6,000*
Capital: *St.-Pierre (pop. 5,415)*

1 *British Columbia, Canada*

Canada

1 *Lions Gate Bridge leads toward Vancouver, Canada's most important Pacific port, where tall forests grow down to the sea.*

2 *Grain elevators store wheat in Saskatchewan, one of the Prairie Provinces and a leading grower of wheat.*

3 *Canadian Rockies peaks frame a camper in Banff National Park in Alberta, a province famed for high-country scenery.*

2 *Saskatchewan, Canada*

4 *Quebec, Canada*

5 *Newfoundland, Canada*

3 *Alberta, Canada*

6 *Greenland*

Canada

4 *Château Frontenac hotel towers over Quebec, Canada's oldest city and capital of the French-speaking province of Quebec.*

5 *Atlantic codfish are netted inshore in Newfoundland. Inshore and offshore fishing have yielded a rich catch for centuries.*

Greenland

6 *Inuit hunters make sealskin leather. Inuits, or Eskimos, range North America's Arctic and subarctic regions.*

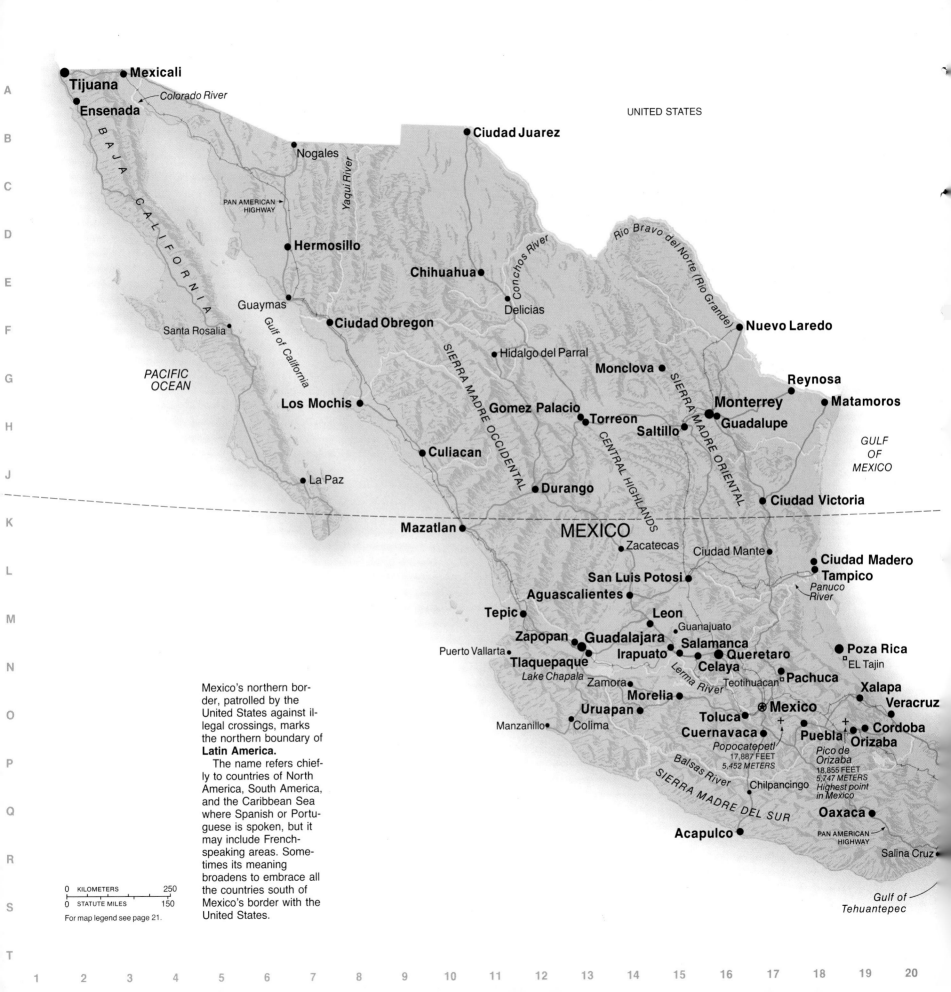

A

B

C

D

E

F

G

H

J

K

L

M

N

O

P

Q

R

S

T

Tijuana ● Mexicali

Ensenada

Colorado River

UNITED STATES

BAJA CALIFORNIA

● Ciudad Juarez

Nogales

Yaqui River

PAN AMERICAN
HIGHWAY

● Hermosillo

Conchos River

Rio Bravo del Norte (Rio Grande)

Chihuahua ●

Guaymas

Delicias

● Ciudad Obregon

● Nuevo Laredo

Santa Rosalia ●

Gulf of California

Hidalgo del Parral ●

Monclova ●

Reynosa

PACIFIC
OCEAN

Los Mochis ●

SIERRA MADRE OCCIDENTAL

Gomez Palacio ●
● Torreon

Monterrey ●●
Saltillo ● Guadalupe

Matamoros

SIERRA MADRE ORIENTAL

GULF
OF
MEXICO

Culiacan ●

CENTRAL HIGHLANDS

La Paz ●

Durango ●

● Ciudad Victoria

Mazatlan ●

MEXICO

Zacatecas ●

Ciudad Mante ●

● Ciudad Madero
Tampico

Panuco River

San Luis Potosi ●

Aguascalientes ●

Tepic ●

Leon ●
Guanajuato

● Poza Rica
□ EL Tajin

Zapopan ● ● Guadalajara

Puerto Vallarta ●

Tlaquepaque

Irapuato ●
Salamanca ●
● Queretaro
Celaya

Lerma River

Lake Chapala

Zamora ●

Teotihuacan □
● Pachuca

Xalapa ●

Veracruz

Morelia ●

Uruapan ●

Toluca ●
Manzanillo ● ● Colima

⊕ Mexico

Cordoba ●

Cuernavaca ●

Puebla ●
Orizaba

Popocatepetl
17,887 FEET
5,452 METERS

*Pico de
Orizaba*
18,855 FEET
5,747 METERS
*Highest point
in Mexico*

Balsas River

Chilpancingo ●

SIERRA MADRE DEL SUR

Oaxaca ●

Acapulco ●

PAN AMERICAN
HIGHWAY

Salina Cruz ●

*Gulf of
Tehuantepec*

Mexico's northern bor-
der, patrolled by the
United States against il-
legal crossings, marks
the northern boundary of
Latin America.
The name refers chief-
ly to countries of North
America, South America,
and the Caribbean Sea
where Spanish or Portu-
guese is spoken, but it
may include French-
speaking areas. Some-
times its meaning
broadens to embrace all
the countries south of
Mexico's border with the
United States.

0 KILOMETERS 250
0 STATUTE MILES 150

For map legend see page 21.

1 2 3 4 5 6 7 8 9 10 11 12 13 14 15 16 17 18 19 20

Mexico

Like a great stone wall, a range of mountains winds through western Central America and deep into Mexico. There it splits into two ranges, the Sierra Madre Oriental (East) and Occidental (West). Between them spreads a cool, high plateau, 500 miles (805 km) wide and 1,500 miles (2,415 km) long that is home to half of Mexico's people. Where the ranges divide stands Mexico City with one of the highest city populations in the world. Latest estimates run to about 20 million residents in the metropolitan area.

Frequent earthquakes jolt the city. Pollution fouls its air, partly because the surrounding mountains often keep winds from blowing away factory smoke and the exhaust of cars, buses, and trucks. Yet thousands more people arrive in Mexico City each week, looking for jobs and a place to live. Many end up jobless in the shantytowns at the city's fringes.

For thousands of years this central plateau has been a magnet for settlers. Indians found a pleasant climate, fertile soil, and enough rainfall for their staple crops of corn, beans, and squash. Six centuries ago the Aztec Indians built their capital here, on an island in a lake. Now the lake is gone, drained and filled in by Spanish conquerors for a capital that developed into modern Mexico City. But Indians remain. About a third of Mexico's people descend from the Indian peoples who farmed and traded in Mexico before the Spaniards came. The rest are mostly mestizos of mixed Indian and Spanish blood.

The Spaniards divided the plateau, and much of the rest of Mexico, into haciendas, sprawling estates where landowners prospered on cattle ranching and farming. Today a government program called *ejido* has redistributed nearly half of the farmland to individuals or to community groups. Despite this effort, reminders of the old hacienda system linger today in large landholdings worked by campesinos, farm workers who often have no farmland of their own.

Little more than a tenth of Mexico's land is good for farming. Only a small fraction of that is permanently cultivated, often by using irrigation. In the deserts of the north and west there is not enough rain for crops; in the mountains the terrain is too steep and the climate too cold; the southeast lacks dependable water sources. Yet farming is still the mainstay of Mexico's economy. Large farms yield coffee, cotton, fruit, and vegetables and export much of the crop.

In rural areas, campesinos tend plots to feed their families or work for pay on the commercial farms. When crop prices fall, landholders cannot make a profit on crops they grow to sell, and thus cannot pay the campesinos. Out of jobs, the workers move to urban centers. Mexico's population boom forces still more people into the already crowded cities.

Some do find jobs in Mexico's well-developed industries. Workers help produce chemicals, textiles, and steel, and assemble everything from audiocassettes to automobiles. Many factories are in the central plateau, but an increasing number are in the arid north and west near the U. S. border. Here more than a thousand factories called *maquiladoras* receive parts from American firms and ship back assembled goods to the United States.

Mexico is a world leader in silver production. Miners also extract gold, sulfur, lead and zinc ores, and about 40 other minerals. In the 1970s a big oil discovery in the hot, humid lowlands along the Gulf of Mexico gave the nation's economy a much-needed boost. Then oil prices fell, leaving Mexico with massive foreign debt.

Tourists, most of them from the United States, help ease the nation's money problems. They come to seaside resorts such as Puerto Vallarta and Acapulco on the Pacific shore, and island getaways such as Cancún and Cozumel in the Caribbean Sea. Many travelers visit the impressive Maya Indian ruins that dot the Yucatán Peninsula, a riverless flatland so dependent on rainfall that the Maya worshiped a rain god.

Mexicans come to the United States too, but most aren't on vacation. Millions live legally in the United States. No one knows how many more have crossed the border illegally. These people are refugees from Mexico's population boom and lack of jobs.

Officially, Latin America ends at the U. S. border. But Mexico once stretched much farther north, and the border states still have strong Spanish ties. Today Mexico has the highest population of any Spanish-speaking country in the world. Its roots are in Spain, and in the former grandeur of civilizations such as those of the Aztec and Maya Indians.

Official name: *United Mexican States*
Area: *756,066 sq mi (1,958,201 sq km)*
Population: *86,740,000*
Capital: *Mexico (City) (pop. 8,831,079, met. pop. 19,370,000)*
Ethnic groups: *mestizo, Indian, white*
Language: *Spanish, Indian languages*
Religious groups: *Roman Catholic*
Economy: *Agr: corn, wheat, coffee, cotton, sugarcane, fruit, vegetables, sorghum, oilseeds, livestock, tobacco. Ind: oil, food processing, chemicals, steel, minerals, textiles, motor vehicles, tourism, fishing*
Currency: *peso*

TROPIC OF CANCER

Cancun Island

Progreso

Merida

Cozumel Island

Chichen Itza

Uxmal

Bay of Campeche

Campeche

YUCATAN PENINSULA

Chetumal

Usumacinta River

BELIZE

Villahermosa

Palenque

Tuxtla Gutierrez

Salinas River

Grijalva River

GUATEMALA

Tapachula

1 *Mexico*

Mexico

1 *Popocatépetl, sacred volcano of Aztec Indians, towers over a church built by Spanish conquerors atop an Aztec temple-pyramid.*

2 *Near pyramids built between A.D. 300 and 1100 at El Tajín, Totonac Indians tend corn much as their ancestors did.*

3 *Imitating the gaudy quetzal, a bird prized by Aztec and Maya Indians, dancers honor old beliefs at a fair near Mexico City.*

4 *Mexicans wade the Rio Grande at Ciudad Juárez. Some make money carrying others across this border with the United States.*

5 *Sparks fly as factory workers make car exhaust pipes in Querétaro. The U. S.-owned factory helps boost Mexico's economy.*

6 *Once a fishing village, Cancún was chosen in 1970 to be a big tourist center. Now hotels fill this islet in the Caribbean Sea.*

7 *Cacao pods ripen in southeastern Mexico. The beans inside are used to make cocoa.*

2 *Mexico*

3 *Mexico*

4 *Mexico*

5 *Mexico*

6 *Mexico*

7 *Mexico*

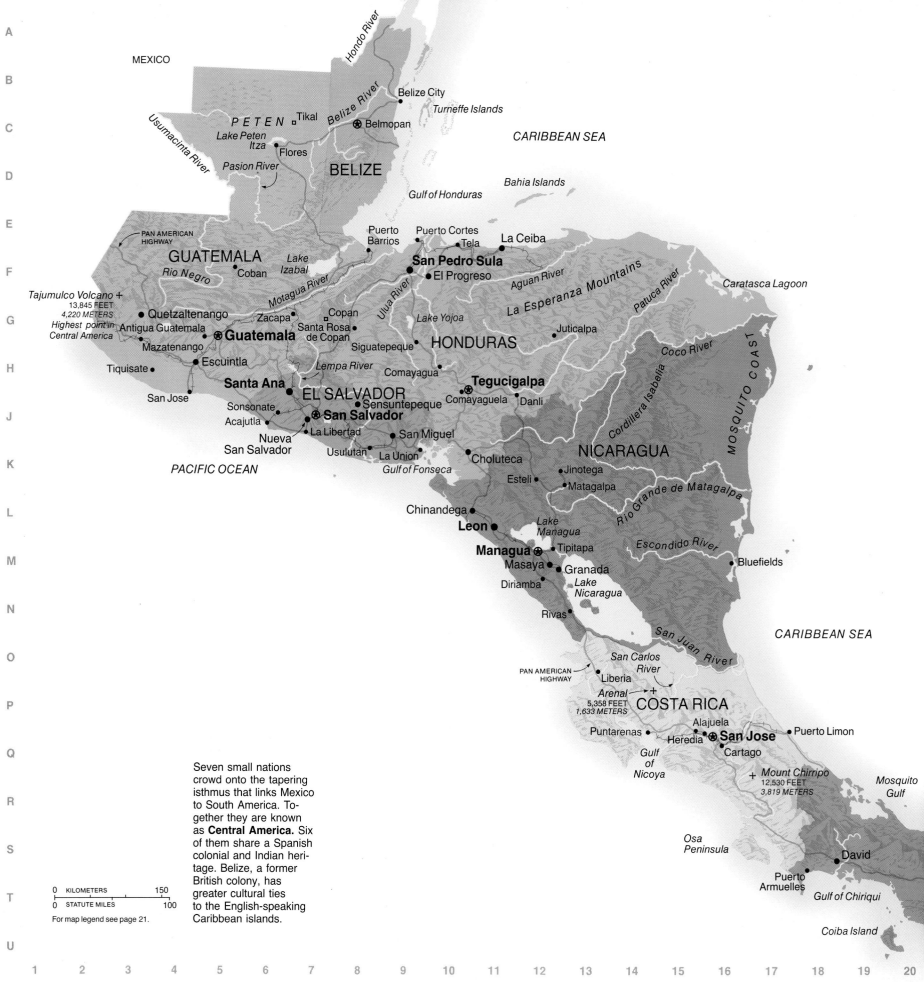

A B C D E F G H J K L M N O P Q R S T U

MEXICO

Hondo River

Belize City
Turneffe Islands

☐ Tikal
P E T E N

⊗ Belmopan

CARIBBEAN SEA

Usumacinta River
Lake Peten Itza
• Flores

Belize River

BELIZE

Pasion River

Gulf of Honduras

Bahia Islands

PAN AMERICAN
HIGHWAY

GUATEMALA

Puerto
Barrios
Puerto Cortes
• Tela
La Ceiba

*Lake
Izabal*

San Pedro Sula
• El Progreso

Aguan River

La Esperanza Mountains

Caratasca Lagoon

Rio Negro
• Coban

Motagua River

Patuca River

+ *Tajumulco Volcano*
13,845 FEET
4,220 METERS
*Highest point in
Central America*

• Quetzaltenango
Zacapa •
☐ Copan
Santa Rosa
de Copan •
Siguatepeque

Ulua River

Lake Yojoa

Juticalpa •

Antigua Guatemala •
⊗ **Guatemala**

Mazatenango •
Comayagua

HONDURAS

Coco River

Cordillera Isabelia

Tiquisate •
• Escuintla

Lempa River

Santa Ana

EL SALVADOR

Comayagua

⊗ **Tegucigalpa**

M O S Q U I T O   C O A S T

San Jose •

Sonsonate •
⊗ **San Salvador**

• Sensuntepeque

Comayaguela
• Danli

Acajutla •
Nueva
San Salvador
• La Libertad
Usulutan •

San Miguel •

NICARAGUA

PACIFIC OCEAN

La Union •

Gulf of Fonseca

• Choluteca

Rio Grande de Matagalpa

Jinotega •
Esteli •
• Matagalpa

Chinandega •

*Lake
Managua*

Escondido River

Leon •

Managua ⊗
• Tipitapa
Masaya •
Diriamba •
• Granada

*Lake
Nicaragua*

• Bluefields

CARIBBEAN SEA

Rivas •

San Juan River

PAN AMERICAN
HIGHWAY

*San Carlos
River*
• Liberia

+ *Arenal*
5,358 FEET
1,633 METERS

COSTA RICA

Puntarenas •

Alajuela •
Heredia •
⊗ **San Jose**
Cartago •

• Puerto Limon

*Gulf
of
Nicoya*

+ *Mount Chirripo*
12,530 FEET
3,819 METERS

*Mosquito
Gulf*

*Osa
Peninsula*

• David

Puerto
Armuelles •

Gulf of Chiriqui

Coiba Island

Seven small nations
crowd onto the tapering
isthmus that links Mexico
to South America. To-
gether they are known
as **Central America.** Six
of them share a Spanish
colonial and Indian heri-
tage. Belize, a former
British colony, has
greater cultural ties
to the English-speaking
Caribbean islands.

0   KILOMETERS   150
0   STATUTE MILES   100

For map legend see page 21.

1 2 3 4 5 6 7 8 9 10 11 12 13 14 15 16 17 18 19 20

Guatemala

Cool southern highlands hold most of Guatemala's people and industries. There stands the biggest city in Central America—Guatemala City, the nation's capital. The metropolitan area's population has grown fourfold in three decades. Farmers come in from the countryside to seek jobs because they own little or no land to farm. Half the farmland is owned by less than 5 percent of the population, who prosper on coffee, bananas, cotton, and other export crops.

Other people flee to the city from rural homelands wracked by decades of war between government troops and rebel guerrillas. Thousands more flocked in when their villages crumbled in a mighty earthquake in 1976.

Among the highlands volcanoes rise—a few still active, but most of them dormant like Tajumulco, Central America's highest peak. In the sparsely settled northern third of the country, the Petén, stand Maya ruins such as Tikal, a maze of stone palaces and temple-pyramids.

About half of Guatemala's people are Indians. Nowhere on the North American continent is there an Indian culture so little changed by the coming of Europeans. Most Indians speak Maya languages and tend plots of corn, beans, and squash as their forebears did.

Official name: *Republic of Guatemala*
Area: *42,042 sq mi (108,889 sq km)*
Population: *8,935,000*
Capital: *Guatemala (City) (pop. 754,243)*
Ethnic groups: *Indian, ladino*
Language: *Spanish, Maya languages*
Religious groups: *Roman Catholic, Protestant*
Economy: *Agr: coffee, cotton, sugarcane, bananas, corn, beans, livestock, rubber, cardamom. Ind: food processing, textiles, chemicals, oil, tourism*
Currency: *quetzal*

Belize

Legend says English sailors shipwrecked in 1638 founded the first British settlement in what is now Belize. Established as a crown colony named British Honduras in 1862, Belize won independence in 1981. English is the official language, and most Belizeans also speak an English Creole somewhat like those of the Caribbean islands. The British influence gives Belize a distinctive flavor in Central America.

From coastal swamps and forests the terrain slopes upward to low mountains. Two natural treasures bring in much needed tourist income: a spectacular coral reef second in size to Australia's Great Barrier Reef, and a rain forest full of tropical birds and animals. Sugarcane, fruit, and fish are the other mainstays of an economy with very little manufacturing.

Belize has the smallest population in Central America. Half its people trace roots to black Africa. Most Belizeans live in Belize City and other coastal communities, where steady sea breezes relieve the hot, humid climate.

Official name: *Belize*
Area: *8,867 sq mi (22,965 sq km)*
Population: *176,000*
Capital: *Belmopan (pop. 4,500)*
Ethnic groups: *black, mestizo, Indian*
Language: *English, English Creole, Spanish*
Religious groups: *Roman Catholic, Protestant*
Economy: *Agr: sugarcane, citrus fruit, bananas, corn, rice, beans, livestock. Ind: food processing, clothing, fertilizer, lumber, rum, fishing, tourism*
Currency: *Belize dollar*

El Salvador

El Salvador lies along a double row of volcanoes, and some of them are very much alive. Yet Salvadoran peasants farm even the steep sides of the cones. Land is precious in the smallest and most densely populated country in Central America, and much of the farmland is owned by an elite few.

On the slopes the farmers tend small plots of corn and other staples, tilling with hoes and planting with pointed sticks. Many live in squarish thatched-roof houses with dirt floors. After the fall harvest, thousands trek to commercial plantations in the highlands to pick the coffee beans that sustain El Salvador's economy.

Although 40 percent of Salvadoran workers are employed in agriculture, the country is highly industrialized. Factories are located around the larger cities and towns. The economy is in trouble, though, slowed by drought and a devastating 1986 earthquake, and sabotaged by a civil war that has dragged on for a decade. Tens of thousands of civilians have died in the war's cross fire, and perhaps a million have fled their homeland. The tourist industry has suffered too; far fewer visitors come to enjoy the lakes and mountains of the cool interior or the beaches along the Pacific Ocean fringe.

Official name: *Republic of El Salvador*
Area: *8,124 sq mi (21,041 sq km)*
Population: *5,125,000*
Capital: *San Salvador (pop. 452,614)*
Ethnic groups: *mestizo, Indian*
Language: *Spanish*
Religious groups: *Roman Catholic*
Economy: *Agr: coffee, cotton, corn, sugarcane, beans, rice, sorghum, wheat. Ind: food processing, textiles, clothing, chemicals, oil, cement, fishing*
Currency: *Salvadoran colón*

Honduras

In the late 16th century, Spanish prospectors found silver in the mountainous interior of Honduras. Mule paths that linked scattered dwellings later became the winding streets of Tegucigalpa, once a mining town, today the capital. Some say its name comes from an ancient Indian language: *taguzgalpa*, meaning "silver hill."

Honduran miners still dig for silver and other minerals, mainly in the western mountains. And the manufacturing of textiles, cement, and wood products has begun to develop, especially in San

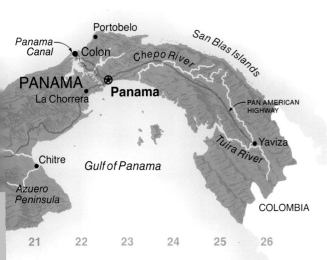

Portobelo
Panama Canal
Colon
PANAMA
La Chorrera
Panama
San Blas Islands
Chepo River
PAN AMERICAN HIGHWAY
Chitre
Gulf of Panama
Tuira River
Yaviza
Azuero Peninsula
COLOMBIA

Pedro Sula. Shrimp, lobsters, coffee, and meat bring in export income, but bananas rule the economy. They grow mostly in lowlands along the Caribbean Sea, where American firms own large plantations.

Honduras is the least developed and poorest country in Central America. Sparsely populated, it is a haven for refugees from strife-torn neighboring nations. Primary education is free, but there are few teachers. Nearly half the people cannot read or write. To fight illiteracy, Hondurans with six years of school are required to teach reading and writing to two adults.

Official name: *Republic of Honduras*
Area: *43,277 sq mi (112,088 sq km)*
Population: *4,982,000*
Capital: *Tegucigalpa (pop. 597,512)*
Ethnic groups: *mestizo, Indian, black*
Language: *Spanish, Black Carib*
Religious groups: *Roman Catholic*
Economy: *Agr: bananas, coffee, sugarcane, corn, beans, rice, tobacco, livestock. Ind: food processing, textiles, clothing, wood products, mining, fishing*
Currency: *lempira*

Nicaragua

Two big lakes called Lake Managua and Lake Nicaragua nestle between the mountain ranges of western Nicaragua. Most Nicaraguans make their home in the plains along the Pacific coast and the highlands around the lakes. There campesinos herd cattle and grow cotton, coffee, and bananas in the fertile volcanic soil. There too stand most of Nicaragua's urban areas, including the biggest, the capital city of Managua.

Earthquakes wrecked Managua in 1931 and again in 1972. Ghostly ruins dot the old downtown area, while businessmen and government workers come and go in the rebuilt city. Textile and food-processing plants cluster nearby.

Sandinista rebels seized power in 1979 after overthrowing the 43-year dictatorship of the Somoza family. Then the Sandinistas fought for nearly a decade against U. S.-backed guerrillas known as contras. Now, with the election as president of opposition leader Violeta Barrios de Chamorro, a new government struggles to revive an economy crippled by years of strife.

The country looks like a big triangle set askew. From the mountainous western region, the hills slope down eastward to broad, swampy plains, thick with tropical forests but only thinly populated. Indians such as the Miskito dwell along the Caribbean shore, known as the Mosquito Coast. Thousands of Miskitos jammed refugee camps in Honduras when the Sandinistas leveled their villages and tried to resettle them in new ones out of the path of war.

Official name: *Republic of Nicaragua*
Area: *50,193 sq mi (130,000 sq km)*
Population: *3,503,000*
Capital: *Managua (pop. 819,679)*
Ethnic groups: *mestizo, white, black, Indian*
Language: *Spanish*
Religious groups: *Roman Catholic*
Economy: *Agr: coffee, cotton, sugarcane, rice, corn, beans, sorghum, cattle, bananas. Ind: food processing, chemicals, metal products, textiles, oil refining*
Currency: *new córdoba*

Costa Rica

Costa Rica lies across the Central American isthmus like a saddle, its sides dropping to seacoasts, its middle rising to mountains. The capital city, San José, sits squarely in the seat on a central highland in the ridge that runs the country's length.

Politically, Costa Rica is like the calm eye of one of the hurricanes that on rare occasions roar in from the Caribbean Sea. In 1949 the Costa Ricans, who call themselves Ticos, abolished their armed forces. Since then their country has become known as a haven of peace in a region of strife. In 1987 President Oscar Arias Sánchez received a Nobel Peace Prize for his plan to restore peace to Central America.

Ticos take pride in the highest literacy rate in Central America. Nine out of ten adults can read and write, and nearly all children of school age attend school. To guard a natural heritage of rain forests, volcanoes, and sandy beaches, a park system protects a tenth of the nation's lands, a model for other countries worldwide. The economy balances agriculture—mainly coffee, bananas, and beef—with food processing, chemical, and textile industries.

Official name: *Republic of Costa Rica*
Area: *19,730 sq mi (51,100 sq km)*
Population: *2,954,000*
Capital: *San José (pop. 274,832)*
Ethnic groups: *white, mestizo, black*
Language: *Spanish*
Religious groups: *Roman Catholic*
Economy: *Agr: coffee, bananas, sugarcane, rice, corn, cattle. Ind: food processing, textiles, chemicals*
Currency: *Costa Rican colón*

Panama

Panama is like two bridges: a land link between continents and a sea link between oceans. Panama's mountainous S-curve connects the North and South American continents by land. Since 1914 the Panama Canal has sliced across Central America to link the Pacific Ocean with the Atlantic via the Caribbean Sea. Built by the United States, the canal is jointly administered by the U. S. and Panama.

Panama City, the capital, located on the canal's Pacific end, and Colón, about 50 miles (80 km) away on the Caribbean end, have prospered from trade that funnels through the strategic Big Ditch. Panama normally receives millions of dollars a month for use of the canal and an oil pipeline that crosses the isthmus.

By treaty, Panama will take over the canal in the year 2000. With the announced aim of protecting American lives and the canal treaties, the U. S. sent troops to Panama in 1989 to remove dictator Manuel Antonio Noriega, who had seized control of the government. Power was restored to the government elected earlier in 1989, which Noriega had blocked from taking office. And for the first time, a Panamanian became head of the Panama Canal Commission.

Panama has about 100 banks that serve customers worldwide. Merchant ships of many nations sail under Panamanian registry, making it a world leader in the licensing of cargo ships. Perhaps a quarter of Panama's workers are farmers who tend family plots or grow cash crops. But the country's economy relies on the Canal Zone and its service industries.

Official name: *Republic of Panama*
Area: *29,762 sq mi (77,082 sq km)*
Population: *2,370,000*
Capital: *Panama (City) (met. pop. 424,204)*
Ethnic groups: *mestizo, black, white, Indian*
Language: *Spanish, English*
Religious groups: *Roman Catholic*
Economy: *Agr: bananas, sugarcane, coffee, rice, corn, beans. Ind: finance, transport, food processing*
Currency: *balboa*

Costa Rica

1 *Arenal Volcano fumes and rumbles in the northern mountains of Costa Rica. Volcanoes that sprinkle the ridges of the Central American isthmus mark the seams where great shifting slabs of Earth's crust, called tectonic plates, slowly collide and grind against each other.*

1 *Costa Rica*

Panama

1 *Skyscrapers sprout in Panama's capital, Panama City, the Pacific Ocean gateway to the canal that cuts across the isthmus.*

El Salvador

2 *A Salvadoran harvests red, ripe coffee berries, each containing two coffee beans, from shrubs in the highlands.*

Nicaragua

3 *Wreckage of guerrilla warfare scars the life of a girl in northern Nicaragua.*

Guatemala

4 *Steep pyramids crowned with temples jut from the Guatemalan jungle at Tikal, a sprawling Maya ruin.*

Honduras

5 *Streets and sidewalks pulse with life in Comayagüela. Workers tote the wares of stores and open-air market stalls.*

Belize

6 *Rainbows of fish in coral gardens lure divers to Lighthouse Reef and other undersea wonders just off the shore of Belize.*

1 *Panama*

2 *El Salvador*

3 *Nicaragua*

4 *Guatemala*

5 *Honduras*

6 *Belize*

UNITED STATES

Grand Bahama Island

Freeport

Abaco Island

BERMUDA
(UNITED KINGDOM)

St. George's Island

Somerset Island

St. David's Island

Hamilton ◉

Bermuda Island

0 KILOMETERS 15
0 STATUTE MILES 10

Eleuthera Island

Nassau ✪

New Providence Island

Andros Island

Cat Island

San Salvador

Straits of Florida

TROPIC OF CANCER

BAHAMAS

Havana ✪ **Guanabacoa**
● Cardenas

Great Exuma

Long Island

Matanzas

Pinar del Rio ●

Santa Clara ●

Cienfuegos ●

CUBA

Bay of Pigs

Isle of Youth

Sancti Spiritus ●

● **Ciego de Avila**

Acklins Island

Mayaguana Island

Camaguey ●

Turks and Caicos Islands
(UNITED KINGDOM)

Victoria de las Tunas ● ● **Holguin**

Great Inagua Island

◉ Grand Turk

Manzanillo ● **Bayamo**

Santiago de Cuba ● ● **Guantanamo**

Cap-Haitien

ATLANTIC OCEAN

Port-de-Paix

Puerto Plata

Cayman Islands
(UNITED KINGDOM)

George Town ◉

Gonaives ●

Santiago ●

San Francisco de Macoris ●

G R E A T E R

HAITI

DOMINICAN REPUBLIC

San Juan —
Bayamon

Montego Bay ●

JAMAICA

Port-au-Prince ✪

● San Juan

Santo Domingo ✪

La Romana

Mandeville ●

May Pen ●

Kingston ✪

HISPANIOLA

Bani ●

San Pedro de Macoris

PUERTO RICO
(UNITED STATES)

Ponce

Spanish Town

Les Cayes ●

CARIBBEAN SEA

A N T I L L E S

When Columbus sighted these islands in 1492, he thought he had reached islands near India in Asia, and so he named them the Indies. Now they are known as the **West Indies,** because of their location in the Western Hemisphere. The two main island groups in the West Indies are the Greater Antilles and Lesser Antilles. The Antilles separate the Caribbean Sea from the Atlantic Ocean. A third group, the Bahamas, lies in the Atlantic.

0 KILOMETERS 250
0 STATUTE MILES 150

For map legend see page 21.

ARUBA
(NETHERLANDS)

NETHERLANDS ANTILLES
(NETHERLANDS)

Oranjestad ◉

Curacao

Bonaire

Willemstad ◉

L E S S E R

COLOMBIA

VENEZUELA

A B C D E F G H J K L M N O P Q R S T U

1 2 3 4 5 6 7 8 9 10 11 12 13 14 15 16 17 18 19 20

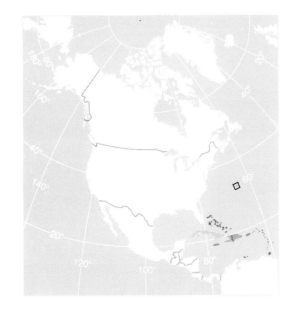

U.S. Virgin Islands
British Virgin Islands
Anguilla (UNITED KINGDOM)
St. Martin (St. Maarten) (FRANCE & NETHERLANDS)
harlotte
malie
Saba (NETH.) St. Barthelemy (FRANCE)
Croix St. Eustatius Basseterre Barbuda
S.) (NETH.) St. John's ANTIGUA AND
ST. KITTS-NEVIS Antigua BARBUDA
Redonda Montserrat (UNITED KINGDOM)
Guadeloupe Abymes
(FRANCE) Pointe-a-Pitre
Basse-Terre
DOMINICA
Roseau
A
N
T
I
L
L
E
S
St.-Pierre Martinique
Fort-de-France (FRANCE)
Castries ST. LUCIA
St. Vincent BARBADOS
Kingstown Bridgetown
ST. VINCENT AND
THE GRENADINES
GRENADA
St. George's
Tobago
TRINIDAD AND TOBAGO
Port of Spain Arima
Trinidad
San Fernando

Bermuda

The British colony of Bermuda is made up of hundreds of coral islands lying 650 miles (1,046 km) east of North Carolina. Only 20 are inhabited. Many are too small to show up on our map.

Nowhere else in the world do you find coral islands this far north. Bermuda's famed beaches owe their pink tint to grains of coral. The warm Gulf Stream ensures balmy breezes, flowers—and tourists, the core of Bermuda's prosperity. Exports of flowers and bananas, plus a little manufacturing, round out a healthy economy.

Spanish explorer Juan de Bermudez spotted the hilly islands in 1503. The first occupants were British seafarers shipwrecked in 1609. Later, African slaves were brought in; today three-fifths of Bermudians descend from them.

Official name: *Bermuda*
Area: *20 sq mi (53 sq km)*
Population: *58,000*
Capital: *Hamilton (pop. 1,617)*
Ethnic groups: *black, white*
Language: *English*
Religious groups: *Protestant, Roman Catholic*
Economy: *Agr: bananas, vegetables, Easter lilies, citrus fruit. Ind: tourism, finance, manufacturing*
Currency: *Bermuda dollar*

Bahamas

On one of the 700 Bahama Islands, Columbus first landed in the New World five centuries ago. Later a British colony, the Bahamas won independence in 1973. Today more than three million visitors come to this beach-fringed nation each year, making tourism its leading industry. Finance ranks second, with more than 300 banks serving customers around the world. Shipping adds to an economy that includes little agriculture.

Nowhere in the world can you find clearer seas than here, because these low, sandy islands have no rivers to cloud the water with silt. Though 29 islands are inhabited, six out of ten Bahamians live on only one: New Providence, site of the major port and capital city, Nassau.

Official name: *The Commonwealth of The Bahamas*
Area: *5,382 sq mi (13,939 sq km)*
Population: *247,000*
Capital: *Nassau (pop. 110,000)*
Ethnic groups: *black, white*
Language: *English, English Creole*
Religious groups: *Protestant, Roman Catholic*
Economy: *Agr: vegetables, fruit, livestock. Ind: tourism, banking, shipping, cement, rum, fishing*
Currency: *Bahamian dollar*

British Dependencies

Once the British West Indies embraced many islands, but now only a sprinkling remain under British rule. These include the **British Virgin Islands**, a double arc of some 15 inhabited islands and about 20 islets. More than three-fourths of the people of this volcanic archipelago live on Tortola. Most are black; about 10 percent are of white or other origin. Poor soils and hilly terrain make large-scale farming or herding difficult, and there are few industries. The economy relies on tourists, many of whom sail the clear waters to coves where 18th-century pirates like Blackbeard and Captain Kidd lurked between raids on passing ships.

Abundant rain gives mountainous **Montserrat** a wealth of streams, waterfalls, and dense tropical forests. Its economy also depends on tourism, along with fruit, vegetable, and livestock farming. One 1989 visitor was most unwelcome: Hurricane Hugo left almost all of the island's 12,000 residents homeless.

In recent years the low-lying **Cayman Islands** have become an important financial center and tax haven. A turtle farm founded on the Caymans in 1968 breeds the endangered green sea turtle. Some are released into the wild and some eaten locally. The low, dry **Turks and Caicos Islands** are another financial center. On rocky **Anguilla** people make salt by drying seawater. Islanders also fish for clawless lobsters and for conch, the large marine snails eaten here.

Cuba

The world's top exporter of sugar, Cuba sold most of its output to the United States until a revolt led by Fidel Castro turned the island nation to communism in 1959. Since then the Soviet Union has supported Cuba's economy, providing cheap oil and cut-rate loans while buying sugar at up to triple the going price. Cuba is also a world leader in nickel exports, and the Soviets buy most of that too. But shortages persist, and food and clothing must be rationed. Many people have emigrated.

Sugarcane covers more than half of Cuba's farmland, most of which lies in the fertile central plains. Before Castro, three-fourths of the cropland was owned by foreigners. Tenant farmers worked the cane, chopping the thick stalks with heavy knives called machetes. Farmhands still do, but now the state owns most of the land.

The state owns the factories too. Cigars, the

best-known product, have been a Cuban export since Columbus's sailors saw Indians puffing on rolls of leaves they called *tobacos*. The Indians died out long ago. Today's Cubans are mostly blacks, whites, and mulattos, descendants of Spaniards and their black plantation slaves.

Cuba's fine climate, beaches, and mountain scenery attract a growing tourist trade. Visitors once flocked to Havana, largest city in the Caribbean, for its old Spanish buildings, showy nightclubs, and nonstop fun. Though the glamour has faded, Cuba's capital remains a busy port and commercial hub.

Official name: *Republic of Cuba*
Area: *42,804 sq mi (110,861 sq km)*
Population: *10,450,000*
Capital: *Havana (pop. 2,036,799)*
Ethnic groups: *mulatto, white, black*
Language: *Spanish*
Religious groups: *Roman Catholic*
Economy: *Agr: sugarcane, tobacco, rice, root crops, citrus fruit, coffee, livestock. Ind: oil refining, food processing, nickel, textiles, chemicals, fishing*
Currency: *Cuban peso*

Jamaica

"*Irie,*" say some Jamaicans of their island. In their dialect it means "wonderful." Tourists agree as they raft down a river or admire the scenery of this mountainous tropical island, third largest in the Caribbean. Many enjoy beach resorts, where they sip local rum and dance to reggae. Most tourists do not see Jamaica's other, grimmer face: the slums of urban areas like Kingston, the capital.

Three-fourths of Jamaicans descend from African slaves who worked plantations under British colonial rule. Many now tend small farms all over the island, raising corn, yams, coffee, or other crops—even marijuana. Some work modern sugarcane and banana plantations, or make clothing, tires, cement, and other manufactured goods in urban centers. Few countries surpass Jamaica's output of bauxite—the ore from which aluminum is made—a major export.

Official name: *Jamaica*
Area: *4,244 sq mi (10,991 sq km)*
Population: *2,485,000*
Capital: *Kingston (pop. 104,041)*
Ethnic groups: *black, mulatto*
Language: *English, English Creole*
Religious groups: *Protestant*
Economy: *Agr: sugarcane, citrus fruit, bananas, pimiento, coconuts, coffee, cacao, tobacco. Ind: bauxite, tourism, textiles, food processing, rum, cement*
Currency: *Jamaican dollar*

Haiti

In the 1700s Haiti was a rich French colony of sugarcane and coffee plantations, one of the best farming areas in the world. Today this western third of the island of Hispaniola is one of the world's poorest countries. Forests that covered its mountainous terrain are all but gone. As erosion strips away the exposed soil, Haitians continue to cut trees to make charcoal for fuel. Coffee is still an important export, but most farmers tend only small plots of corn, rice, and beans to feed their families. Factories assemble toys, electronic equipment, and sporting goods, including baseballs.

Most Haitians descend from African slaves who revolted and formed the world's first black republic in 1804. Many practice voodoo, a blend of African and Christian beliefs. After decades of rule by dictators, chiefly the Duvalier family, Haitians plan once more to hold free elections.

Official name: *Republic of Haiti*
Area: *10,714 sq mi (27,750 sq km)*
Population: *6,382,000*
Capital: *Port-au-Prince (pop. 461,464)*
Ethnic groups: *black, mulatto*
Language: *French, Haitian Creole*
Religious groups: *Roman Catholic, voodoo*
Economy: *Agr: coffee, sugarcane, corn, rice, beans, cacao. Ind: food processing, textiles, manufacturing*
Currency: *gourde*

Dominican Republic

In 1492 some of Columbus's sailors settled on the island that he named Hispaniola. There, four years later, Spanish colonists founded Santo Domingo, the first permanent European settlement in the New World. Today it's the capital of the Dominican Republic, a nation that occupies the eastern two-thirds of the island.

The highest point in the Caribbean is in the middle of this mountainous country: 10,417-foot (3,175 m) Pico Duarte in the Cordillera Central, one of four ranges that corrugate the landscape. To its north lies the Cibao Valley, a major farming area. Another is the wide plain in the southeast, where sugarcane plantations and sugar refineries produce the nation's leading export. Small farms yield much of the coffee crop, another important export. Farming employs almost half the country's workers.

Miners dig silver, nickel, and other minerals. The nation has the biggest active gold mine in the Caribbean. Yet most Dominicans are poor, their economy crippled by dictatorship, unrest, and falling sugar prices. New resorts help, as tourists discover Dominican beaches, sportfishing grounds, and old Spanish-style architecture.

Official name: *Dominican Republic*
Area: *18,816 sq mi (48,734 sq km)*
Population: *7,018,000*
Capital: *Santo Domingo (pop. 1,313,172)*
Ethnic groups: *mulatto, white, black*
Language: *Spanish*
Religious groups: *Roman Catholic*
Economy: *Agr: sugarcane, coffee, rice, cacao, tobacco. Ind: food processing, mining, textiles, cement*
Currency: *Dominican Republic peso*

Puerto Rico

Commonwealth, state, or independent nation? For many years Puerto Ricans have argued over what their island should be. Since 1952 it has been a self-governing commonwealth, part of the United States but without a vote in Congress. Puerto Ricans can't vote for president, but they don't pay federal income tax either.

During four centuries of Spanish control, the fortunes of this mountainous island depended on sugarcane, coffee, and tobacco. By the 1950s, the markets for these crops had declined, fields had become unproductive, and there was not enough food or work for the booming population. Being U. S. citizens, Puerto Ricans could emigrate freely to the mainland. More than half a million people left the island in search of jobs. Most crowded into neighborhoods called barrios in cities like New York and Chicago.

Federal aid and investment by U. S. companies helped the Puerto Rican government create jobs in industries such as clothing, electrical equipment, and food processing. Thousands who had left came home. Many settled around San Juan, the capital. Now manufacturing and tourism help to make Puerto Rico one of the wealthiest Caribbean islands, though still poorer than the poorest U. S. state.

Official name: *Commonwealth of Puerto Rico*
Area: *3,435 sq mi (8,897 sq km)*
Population: *3,301,000*
Capital: *San Juan (pop. 424,600)*
Ethnic groups: *Hispanic*
Language: *Spanish, English*
Religious groups: *Roman Catholic*
Economy: *Agr: livestock, sugarcane, coffee, bananas, yams, pineapples. Ind: medicines, petrochemicals, food processing, electronics, textiles*
Currency: *U. S. dollar*

United States Virgin Islands

There is not much level land in the 3 hilly islands and about 50 islets of the U. S. Virgin Islands. Rainfall is erratic; when it comes, most of it runs off the hard clay soil, sometimes in floods. Yet for 250 years, Dutch, British, French, then Danish planters raised sugarcane and other crops on plantations sprawling up the hillsides.

After slaves were set free in the mid-1800s, the plantations fell idle. Today visitors roam ruins of sugar mills and homes on islands that now belong to the U. S., bought from Denmark in 1917. More than a million tourists come here each year. Many arrive on big cruise ships that dock, sometimes a dozen a day, at Charlotte Amalie, the capital and seaport on **St. Thomas.** There they find resorts and duty-free shops.

Some take a ferry to **St. John,** where a national park covers half the island and more than 5,000 acres (2,025 ha) of coral gardens offshore. The largest island is **St. Croix,** site of rum distilleries and of one of the world's largest oil refineries.

These islands depend on tourists. But there aren't enough islanders to staff the hotels and cafés, drive the cabs, and sell the souvenirs. Thousands of people from poorer islands have come here for jobs.

Official name: *Virgin Islands of the United States*
Area: *136 sq mi (352 sq km)*
Population: *109,000*
Capital: *Charlotte Amalie (pop. 11,842)*
Ethnic groups: *black, white*
Language: *English, Spanish, French*
Religious groups: *Protestant, Roman Catholic*
Economy: *Agr: vegetables, fruit, sorghum, cattle. Ind: tourism, oil refining, watches, rum, textiles*
Currency: *U. S. dollar*

St. Kitts and Nevis

St. Kitts and Nevis are one country, but they are almost like two. On St. Kitts, the larger island, workers raise sugarcane on government plantations that cover the lower slopes of its volcanic peaks. Factories turn out electronic goods, textiles, and shoes. Resorts cater to upscale tourists, who pour into shops and casinos in the fast-paced capital, Basseterre.

Two miles (3 km) away on Nevis, cotton and vegetables ripen on the slopes of a single peak, its summit hidden in clouds nearly every day. Gone are the sugarcane plantations of British colonial times; renovated sugar mills and houses now welcome tourists as quaint, quiet inns.

In 1623 St. Kitts became the first British settlement in the Caribbean. Together St. Kitts and Nevis won independence in 1983, but Nevisians kept the right to secede from the union.

Official name: *Federation of St. Kitts and Nevis*
Area: *101 sq mi (261 sq km)*
Population: *40,000*
Capital: *Basseterre (pop. 14,161)*
Ethnic groups: *black*
Language: *English*
Religious groups: *Protestant*
Economy: *Agr: sugarcane, cotton, coconuts. Ind: sugar, tourism, clothing, beverages, electronics*
Currency: *East Caribbean dollar*

Antigua and Barbuda

Antiguans say that if you visit a beach a day, it will take you a year to see all the beaches on their hilly island of many coves and bays. In a bay called English Harbour, a British fleet set up a base in the 1700s to protect its Caribbean colonies. For 185 years a family named Codrington leased nearby Barbuda from Britain's monarchs for "one fat pig" a year, and used the island for fishing and raising livestock to feed slaves on Antigua's sugarcane plantations.

In 1981 a nation was formed of Antigua, low, forested Barbuda, and uninhabited Redonda. The country is striving to ease its dependence on tourism with fishing, farming, and the manufacture of appliances, clothing, and rum.

Official name: *Antigua and Barbuda*
Area: *170 sq mi (440 sq km)*
Population: *64,000*
Capital: *St. John's (pop. 36,000)*
Ethnic groups: *black*
Language: *English, local dialects*
Religious groups: *Protestant*
Economy: *Agr: cotton, livestock, fruit, vegetables. Ind: tourism, clothing, appliances, rum, fishing*
Currency: *East Caribbean dollar*

French Overseas Departments

Now and then, disaster hits mountainous **Martinique**—a hurricane, an earthquake, a volcanic eruption. One of the worst struck in 1902, when Mount Pelée erupted and wiped out the old capital, St.-Pierre. In minutes, more than 30,000 people died. Today St.-Pierre is a quiet village rich in history, and a new capital flourishes at sophisticated, French-flavored Fort-de-France.

The eruption crippled the sugar industry, the main source of export income during 350 years of French rule. Much cropland is still owned by *békés*, descendants of white settlers, but now most sugar goes to the island's rum distilleries. Bananas and pineapples add to an economy that includes oil refining, cement making, tourism, and subsidies from the French government.

Guadeloupe, some 70 miles (113 km) north, is an archipelago of islands and islets. The main landmass is not one island but two. A salt-water channel named Rivière Salée separates the volcanic western island from the low, rolling eastern island. Sugar is important here too, and so is coffee, but bananas bring in half of Guadeloupe's export income.

Administered as part of Guadeloupe are France's other Caribbean possessions: small, quiet St. Barthélemy, whose name is often shortened to St. Barts, and St. Martin, the northern two-thirds of an island whose southern third is Dutch. Both have deposits of salt.

Dominica

Forests cover much of this rugged, rainy island nation, a British possession until 1978. Bananas, coconuts, and limes ripen in its rich soil, and factories process foodstuffs and make soap and cigars.

Dominica has few white sand beaches and no casinos or nightlife to lure tourists as other Caribbean islands do. Instead, nature lovers hike to gauzy waterfalls, lush rain forests, hot springs, and a boiling lake in a volcanic basin.

With high peaks to wring out clouds, parts of Dominica get up to 20 feet (6 m) of rain a year, so much that it exports water to other islands. It has the only reservation for Caribs, once-fierce Indians who gave the Caribbean Sea its name. Some Dominicans speak both English and a French patois, an echo of British-French wrangling over the island in the 1700s. On the reservation you can hear the ancient Carib language.

Official name: *Commonwealth of Dominica*
Area: *290 sq mi (751 sq km)*
Population: *83,000*
Capital: *Roseau (pop. 8,346)*
Ethnic groups: *black, Carib Indian*
Language: *English, French patois*
Religious groups: *Roman Catholic, Protestant*
Economy: *bananas, citrus fruit, coconuts, soap*
Currency: *East Caribbean dollar*

St. Lucia

Before becoming a British colony in 1814, St. Lucia changed hands 14 times as France and Britain vied for control. The British profited for the next 165 years from sugarcane plantations in the island's broad valleys. Most St. Lucians descend from the African plantation slaves. English is the official language, but many people speak instead a French patois left over from the years of conflict. The nation gained independence in 1979.

Bananas and coconuts in sprawling groves ripen in the rich volcanic soil. But hurricanes often ruin the crops. The economy has been broadened to include manufacturing and food processing. Tourists come in growing numbers, drawn by beaches, mountain scenery, and bubbling sulfur springs left from the island's volcanic origin. Oil tankers come too, for near the capital of Castries stands a modern tanker port.

Official name: *St. Lucia*
Area: *238 sq mi (617 sq km)*
Population: *150,000*
Capital: *Castries (pop. 50,700)*
Ethnic groups: *black, mixed, East Indian*
Language: *English, French patois*
Religious groups: *Roman Catholic*
Economy: *Agr: bananas, coconuts, cacao. Ind: clothing, beverages, cardboard boxes, tourism*
Currency: *East Caribbean dollar*

St. Vincent and the Grenadines

This small nation of islands was a British colony until 1979. It is the world's leading grower of arrowroot, a source of starch used in medicines and flour. The plant is also now used in paper that makes copies without carbons and in computer paper, giving growers and the economy a boost. Bananas, rum, and flour are the mainstays. Still, the main island of St. Vincent remains one of the eastern Caribbean's poorest.

Vincentians are a little better off on the Grenadines, a kite-tail of six main islands and nearly a hundred islets strung out to the south. Many tourists visiting this country go to the swanky resorts in the Grenadines or explore their bays and beaches by private yacht. The southernmost Grenadines belong to Grenada.

Mountainous St. Vincent faces constant peril. Soufrière, one of the region's two most active volcanoes (the other is Pelée on Martinique), erupted in 1979 and could again any day. Hurricanes can also ravage the islands.

Official name: *St. Vincent and the Grenadines*
Area: *150 sq mi (388 sq km)*
Population: *105,000*
Capital: *Kingstown (pop. 24,764)*
Ethnic groups: *black, mulatto, white*
Language: *English, French patois*
Religious groups: *Protestant, Roman Catholic*
Economy: *Agr: bananas, arrowroot, coconuts. Ind: food processing, cement, furniture, rum*
Currency: *East Caribbean dollar*

Barbados

"Not British but English," says one Barbadian of this nation's heritage. Settled by Englishmen in 1627, Barbados never changed hands until independence in 1966. Generations of English landlords ran sugarcane plantations and molasses and rum operations on the coastal lowlands and slopes of the central ridge. These families still own much of the land, but descendants of slaves make up most of the population, one of the world's densest at more than 1,500 people per square mile. Barbadians call their island Bimshire and themselves Bajans.

Tourism and small factories now surpass sugar on this easternmost Caribbean island. Unlike its volcanic neighbors, it is a low coral outcrop.

Official name: *Barbados*
Area: *166 sq mi (430 sq km)*
Population: *259,000*
Capital: *Bridgetown (pop. 7,466)*
Ethnic groups: *black, mulatto, white*
Language: *English*
Religious groups: *Protestant*
Economy: *Agr: sugarcane. Ind: tourism, food processing, electronic components assembly, clothing*
Currency: *Barbados dollar*

Grenada

The oval on the left of Grenada's flag is a nutmeg. Grind the seed inside, and you have the spice that flavors cookies and eggnog. Grind the lacy husk around the seed, and you have mace, another spice. For 200 years the nutmeg has ripened on the fertile slopes of this volcanic outcrop, often called the Isle of Spice. Sugar ruled before that. Now descendants of the sugarcane plantation slaves grow nutmeg, fruit, and vegetables on small plots sprinkled over the wooded island.

Once a British colony, Grenada became a nation in 1974. When radicals staged a coup and began executing rivals, the United States and several Caribbean countries invaded in 1983 to restore democracy. Though it includes Carriacou and islets to the north, Grenada is one of the Western Hemisphere's tiniest nations.

Official name: *Grenada*
Area: *133 sq mi (344 sq km)*
Population: *85,000*
Capital: *St. George's (pop. 7,500)*
Ethnic groups: *black, mulatto*
Language: *English, French patois*
Religious groups: *Roman Catholic, Protestant*
Economy: *nutmeg, mace, cacao, bananas, tourism*
Currency: *East Caribbean dollar*

Trinidad and Tobago

Imagine a lake of black, oozy tar. On the island of Trinidad there really is one: Pitch Lake, the world's leading source of natural asphalt. Petroleum has oozed up through porous rock to create this 100-acre (40 ha) wonder. One of the first nations in the world to drill for oil, Trinidad now produces its own and refines oil from the Middle East.

Lying off the east coast of Venezuela, Trinidad and Tobago together were a British colony before they became a nation in 1962. But while Tobago is a quiet, mountainous tourist haven, Trinidad has steel mills, chemical plants, factories, and livestock farms. Big estates, mostly on the western side, grow sugarcane. Small farms produce cacao and other crops.

Trinidad has resorts too. They fill up during Carnival, two days of merrymaking before the 40 fasting days of Lent. Costumed bands hammer on steel drums made from oil barrels, adding witty lyrics to a catchy beat in music called calypso. Nearly half of the people descend from black slaves, most of the rest from Indian workers brought in when slavery ended.

Official name: *Republic of Trinidad and Tobago*
Area: *1,981 sq mi (5,130 sq km)*
Population: *1,244,000*
Capital: *Port of Spain (pop. 59,649)*
Ethnic groups: *black, East Indian, mixed*
Language: *English, English Creole, other*
Religious groups: *Christian, Hindu*
Economy: *Agr: sugarcane, cacao, coffee, rice, citrus fruits. Ind: oil, chemicals, tourism, food processing*
Currency: *Trinidad and Tobago dollar*

Netherlands Dependencies

Remembering three of these six islands is as easy as ABC: Aruba, Bonaire, and Curaçao. The ABCs lie close to Venezuela. The others are some 500 miles (805 km) northeast: St. Eustatius, Saba, and St. Maarten, part of an island that also holds French St. Martin. The Netherlands has ruled these islands known as the **Netherlands Antilles** for most of their history. In 1986 **Aruba** split off from the others to become a separate dependency with its own capital, Oranjestad. Aruba is set for independence in 1996.

The hallmark of these islands is diversity. The ABCs are mainly coral, the others mostly volcanic. Schools teach in Dutch on the ABCs and in English on the other islands. In the ABCs people also speak Papiamento, a mix of Spanish, Portuguese, Dutch, English, and African dialects that mirrors the history of the Caribbean.

Tourism is a major industry on all the islands. Four have fine beaches, but rugged Saba and St. Eustatius jut from the sea without the wide, sandy beaches that many tourists seek. They offer serenity and scenery instead. Saba has lush vegetation, but arid Aruba is nearly barren.

Dutch merchants have made Willemstad, the Netherlands Antilles capital on Curaçao, a commercial and financial center. It is also a visual delight with its colorful, ornamented wooden shops and houses. Curaçao has one of the Western Hemisphere's biggest ship-repair drydocks. Workers on this island mine phosphates. On Bonaire and St. Maarten they produce salt. Bonaire is also a major grower of aloes—plants used in medicines and ointments—and a magnet for scuba divers lured to its fish-filled coral reefs. Oil from Venezuela once fed refineries on the ABCs, but the oil industry has recently declined, causing serious economic hardship.

French Overseas Departments

1 *Mount Pelée looms over St.-Pierre on volcanic Martinique. An eruption in 1902 wiped out the capital city that stood here.*

Trinidad and Tobago

2 *Swirls of scarlet frame a masquerader at Trinidad's Carnival, a pre-Lenten funfest held also in Tobago.*

Grenada

3 *Just picked on Grenada, nutmegs show red husks that yield a spice called mace. Seeds inside yield another spice, nutmeg.*

1 *Martinique, French Overseas Departments*

2 *Trinidad, Trinidad and Tobago*

3 *Grenada*

1 *Haiti*

2 *New Providence Island, Bahamas*

3 *United States Virgin Islands*

4 *Barbados*

5   *Cuba*

6   *Dominican Republic*

Haiti

1   *Haitians at a sacred waterfall join a voodoo festival that commemorates a vision of the Virgin of Miracles, Vyèj Mirak.*

Bahamas

2   *Nassau schoolchildren decorated this Bahamian street with colors and images of island life: fishing, marketing, churchgoing.*

United States Virgin Islands

3   *A diver swims among fragile corals in the Buck Island Reef National Monument.*

Barbados

4   *Sugarcane burdens a Barbadian field hand. Leaves are used for tying bundles; sap in the stalk yields sugar.*

Cuba

5   *Havana cigar makers sample their world-famous product. They can puff all the cigars they want by day and take one home.*

Dominican Republic

6   *Villagers take a break in the western hill country near the border with Haiti.*

South America

Among the seven continents of the world, South America is middle size—fourth after Asia, Africa, and North America. But unlike some other continents, South America is largely wilderness—a land of high mountains, sweeping forests, and sprawling plains. The continent extends about 4,700 miles (7,560 km) between the sunny beaches of the Caribbean Sea and the cold, storm-lashed islands of Tierra del Fuego near Antarctica. Most people find much of the land inhospitable—too hot or too cold or too dry or too wet.

South America is a continent of extravagances. The Andes form the longest mountain range on any continent. They are second in height only to Asia's Himalaya. More than 45 Andean peaks rise above 20,000 feet (6,100 m), half of them higher than any summit in North America. Angel Falls in Venezuela is the world's highest waterfall, and the falls of Iguazú, shared by Argentina and Brazil, are among the most spectacular.

Want to find one of the world's stormiest places? Then try the coast of Chile, around 40 or 50 degrees south latitude—the roaring forties and furious fifties that have made Cape Horn a notorious graveyard of ships and sailors.

Between the Andes and the Pacific Ocean lies a narrow strip of coastal plain. Here you find the Atacama Desert, the world's driest place. Before 1971 some parts of the Atacama hadn't felt a drop of rain in centuries. Ocean currents flowing from Antarctica cool the air along the coast, preventing the buildup of rain clouds.

Many Andean mountains are volcanoes formed by molten rock bubbling up through the Earth's crust as the continent slowly grinds up over the floor of the Pacific Ocean. Ecuador alone has some 50 volcanoes, about 30 of them active. From time to time earthquakes rumble through the mountains. Or volcanoes spew ash and lava onto surrounding slopes. Over the last half century or so about 100,000 Andean people have been killed in landslides and avalanches touched off by earthquakes.

Though destructive, volcanic eruptions add minerals to the soil, creating fertile fields in which farmers can grow their crops.

In the northern half of the Andes, broad, high plateaus or valleys called altiplanos lie between parallel mountain ranges. Many of the people who live on these altiplanos are Indians, descendants of the Inca and other groups that flourished here before the arrival of Spanish explorers in the 16th century. They live in small communities isolated from one another and the outside world by rugged terrain and lack of good roads. Most villagers are farmers who grow barely enough food to feed themselves, and herd sheep or llamas and alpacas. In recent years, many farmers have taken to growing coca as a cash crop. It's easy to see why: An acre of coca, the raw ingredient of cocaine, brings in $5,000 to $10,000; an acre of corn, $150 or so.

Because of altitude, life in the highlands can be uncomfortably cold, even in the summer. People who have lived there for generations have enlarged hearts and lungs that enable them to live and work in the rarefied air. Visitors unaccustomed to such heights find it impossible to get about without gasping for breath.

South America has other highlands, too, but much lower ones than the Andes. In the north, the Guiana Highlands border the Amazon Basin and are covered with tropical forests. South of the Amazon rise the Brazilian Highlands, mostly rolling hills and plateaus.

Farther south, the Brazilian Highlands give way to the grassy plains, or Pampas, of Uruguay and Argentina—a region known for cattle ranches and farms that grow huge crops of wheat, rice, oats, and corn. Beyond the Pampas, where the continent narrows, stretch the rolling tablelands of Patagonia, a cold, windy, almost treeless place where sheep are raised.

Between the Guiana and Brazilian Highlands lies the Amazon Basin, a hot, humid region nearly as big as the contiguous United States. Through the lowlands flows the 4,000-mile-long (6,437 km) Amazon River and more than a thousand of its tributary streams. Seven tributaries are more than 1,000 miles (1,600 km) long. One of them, the Madeira River, winds 2,013 miles (3,240 km) through the forest. All in all, the mighty Amazon carries more water than the combined flow of the world's next ten largest rivers—and it carries the water through the world's largest rain forest.

The mouth of the Amazon measures 200 miles (320 km) across, wide enough to hold Marajó, an

Salt lakes amid volcanic peaks in the high Andes

Angel Falls in Venezuela

NORTH AMERICA

CARIBBEAN SEA

CENTRAL AMERICA

AFRICA

TROPIC OF CANCER

Llanos

Orinoco River

Angel Falls

GUIANA
HIGHLANDS

Marajo Island

Amazon

Amazon River

EQUATOR

Galapagos Islands

River

Basin

SOUTH AMERICA

BRAZILIAN

Madeira

Mato
Grosso
Plateau

HIGHLANDS

Sao Francisco River

Lake Titicaca

Altiplano

Atacama Desert

PACIFIC
OCEAN

Paraguay River

Gran

Chaco

TROPIC OF CAPRICORN

Iguazu Falls

Parana River

Uruguay River

ATLANTIC
OCEAN

Easter Island

A
N
D
E
S

Pampas

Rio de la Plata

Mt. Aconcagua
22,834 FEET
6,960 METERS
Highest point in
South America

Patagonia

Valdes Peninsula
−131 FEET
−40 METERS
Lowest point in
South America

Falkland Islands

South Georgia

Tierra del Fuego

Strait of Magellan

Cape Horn

South Sandwich Islands

ANTARCTIC CIRCLE

ANTARCTICA

NORTH AMERICA

CARIBBEAN SEA

Lake Maracaibo

⊗ Caracas

VENEZUELA

Georgetown ⊗
Paramaribo
Cayenne ⊙

GUYANA

FRENCH GUIANA
(FRANCE)

SURINAME

• Medellin
⊗ Bogota

COLOMBIA

Orinoco River

EQUATOR

⊗ Quito

ECUADOR

Rio Negro

Amazon River

Fortaleza •

Galapagos Islands
(ECUADOR)

Iquitos •

Ucayali R.

Purus River

Madeira River

Xingu River

BRAZIL

Recife •

PERU

Sao Francisco River

Lima ⊗

Mamore River

Salvador •

Lake Titicaca

La Paz ⊗

Brasilia ⊗

BOLIVIA

⊗ Sucre

Belo
Horizonte •

PACIFIC
OCEAN

PARAGUAY

Parana River

Sao Paulo •

Rio de Janeiro •

TROPIC OF CAPRICORN

Asuncion ⊗

ATLANTIC
OCEAN

Porto
Alegre •

Uruguay River

Cordoba •

Mirim Lake

CHILE ⊗
Santiago

URUGUAY ⊗

Buenos
Aires ⊗

Montevideo •

ARGENTINA

FALKLAND ISLANDS
(UNITED KINGDOM)

Strait of Magellan →

⊗ Stanley

SOUTH GEORGIA
(UNITED KINGDOM)

*TIERRA DEL
FUEGO*

Cape Horn

island nearly the size of Denmark. Large ocean-going vessels travel 1,000 miles (1,600 km) upstream to the city of Manaus. Smaller ships can navigate all the way to Iquitos in Peru, 2,300 miles (3,700 km) from the Atlantic Ocean.

Tropical rain forest covers much of the Amazon Basin. Nearly 300 tree species can be found in a single square mile, among them hardwoods such as mahogany and cedar; edible palms; rubber trees; the Brazil nut tree; and the cumaru, from which come perfumes and medicines. By contrast, temperate forests have only about 30 tree species per square mile.

Much of the forest is deeply shadowed and parklike, covered by a dense, leafy canopy that blocks out sunlight. Near clearings or along riverbanks where light reaches the ground, the forest becomes a jungle, a tangle of vegetation impenetrable to anyone on foot without a machete to hack through the undergrowth.

But now the rain forest is in trouble. To encourage settlement and develop the interior, Brazilians have been bulldozing roads through the wilderness and cutting or burning vast tracts of forest to open up new lands for crops and cattle.

Today about 90 percent of all South Americans live within 200 miles (320 km) of the coast in large, modern cities such as São Paulo, Rio de Janeiro, Buenos Aires, Santiago, and Lima. About half of them speak Spanish. The other half—in Brazil—speak Portuguese because Portugal colonized Brazil about 500 years ago.

Today, the more temperate parts of South America, a broad band running from southern Brazil and Uruguay to central Chile and Argentina, are among the world's most rapidly industrializing areas. Only about a quarter of all South Americans still work on farms and ranches. Since 1950 people have moved to cities in droves, hoping to escape rural poverty and the turmoil caused by roving terrorist bands. This migration of millions of people has placed Buenos Aires, Rio de Janeiro, and São Paulo among the world's ten largest and fastest growing metropolitan areas. But on the outskirts of these gleaming, skyscrapered cities, huddle vast slums—sprawling shantytowns largely filled with country folk seeking jobs and a better life for themselves and their children.

Development imperils the Amazon rain forest in Brazil.

Facts About South America

Area: 6,880,637 sq mi (17,820,770 sq km)
Population: 290,015,000
Highest Point: Mount Aconcagua, Argentina, 22,834 ft (6,960 m) above sea level
Lowest Point: Valdes Peninsula, Argentina, 131 ft (40 m) below sea level
Largest Country: *(by area)* Brazil 3,286,488 sq mi (8,511,965 sq km)
Largest Country: *(by population)* Brazil 147,393,000
Largest Metropolitan Areas: *(by population)*

São Paulo, Brazil	18,420,000
Buenos Aires, Argentina	11,580,000
Rio de Janeiro, Brazil	11,120,000
Lima, Peru	6,500,000

Longest Rivers: *(mi and km)*

Amazon	4,000	6,437
Paraná	2,485	3,999
Purus	2,100	3,380

Largest Lakes: *(sq mi and sq km)*

Maracaibo, Venezuela	5,217	13,512
Titicaca, Peru-Bolivia	3,200	8,288

Highest Waterfall:
* Angel Falls, Venezuela, 3,212 ft (979 m)

*World record

Glossary

alpaca—a domesticated mammal with long, woolly hair; related to the llama.

altiplano—a high plateau or valley between higher mountains.

coca—a shrub whose leaves are made into a drug called cocaine.

conquistador—a soldier in the Spanish conquest of the Americas.

coup, coup d'état—a sudden, usually successful act to overthrow a government from within.

guanaco—a mammal with a soft, thick coat; probably the original ancestor of both the alpaca and the llama.

Inca—an empire in the Andes that ruled an area from Colombia to Chile before the Spanish conquest.

landlocked country—a country surrounded by land, without access to the sea.

llama—a mammal used as a pack animal and a source of wool; related to the camel.

llano—an open, grassy plain.

mestizo—a Latin American of mixed European and American Indian ancestry.

pampa—an extensive grassland.

rain forest—dense forest composed mainly of broad-leaved evergreens found in wet tropical regions.

CARIBBEAN SEA

Guajira Peninsula

Paraguana Peninsula

Margarita Island

Paria Peninsula

Santa Marta
Riohacha

Coro

Barranquilla

Cristobal Colon Peak
+ 18,947 FEET
5,775 METERS

Maracaibo

Caracas
Petare
⊗

Cumana

TRINIDAD AND TOBAGO

Cartagena

Valledupar

Cabimas

San Felipe

Barcelona

Magdalena River

Barquisimeto

Valencia

Baruta
Maracay

Sincelejo

Lake Maracaibo

Valera

Acarigua

Maturin

ATLANTIC OCEAN

Monteria

Guanare

LLANOS

PANAMA

Merida

Barinas

Orinoco River

Ciudad Guayana

PAN AMERICAN HIGHWAY

+ Bolivar Peak
16,427 FEET
5,007 METERS

Apure River

San Fernando de Apure

Ciudad Bolivar

Atrato River

Cucuta

San Cristobal

VENEZUELA

Bucaramanga

Caura River

GUYANA

Barrancabermeja

Arauca

Puerto Paez

≈ Angel Falls

Medellin
Bello

Puerto Carreno

GUIANA

HIGHLANDS Mt. Roraima
9,094 FEET
2,772 METERS +

Quibdo

Tunja

ANDES

LLANOS

Meta River

PACIFIC OCEAN

Manizales

LA GRAN SABANA

Armenia
Pereira

⊗ **Bogota**

Ibague

Villavicencio

Buenaventura

Palmira

Guaviare River

Obando

Cali

Orinoco River

Neiva

COLOMBIA

Casiquiare River

Popayan

San Jose del Guaviare

Guainia River

Florencia

ANDES

San Felipe

Tumaco

Rio Negro

Pasto

Vaupes River

ECUADOR

Caqueta River

BRAZIL

EQUATOR

Puerto Leguizamo

AMAZON BASIN

Putumayo River

PERU

La Pedrera

Arica

Amazon River

Leticia

0 KILOMETERS 250
0 STATUTE MILES 150

For map legend see page 21.

Follow the broad band of the Andes as they curve along the coasts of Colombia and Venezuela before disappearing into the Caribbean Sea. Notice that the mountains are parallel ranges, folded like a rug shoved against the wall as South America's western edge slowly collides with an underlying oceanic plate. (See pages 18-19 for a discussion of plate tectonics.)

Lake Maracaibo, the site of vast oil deposits in Venezuela, is regarded as South America's largest lake, even though it is actually an inlet of the sea. In 1960 Venezuela became the only non-Middle Eastern founding member of OPEC, the Organization of Petroleum Exporting Countries, which sets oil prices worldwide.

Colombia

Colombia is the only South American nation with coastlines washed by both the Caribbean Sea and the Pacific Ocean. Its land is rugged and varied. It includes snowcapped mountains nearly 19,000 feet (5,800 m) high, rolling hills and upland plateaus, coastal deserts, and low-lying tropical rain forests.

Most of Colombia's people live in the mountainous western third of the country. There, in broad, high valleys, rich volcanic soil provides fertile farmland, and the weather is usually cool and comfortable. East of the mountains, cattle graze the grasslands. To the south spreads the Amazon Basin, a hot, humid region cut by streams that flow into the Amazon River.

Gold brought Spanish settlers to Colombia in the early 1500s. Soon after, they began to hear stories of a golden man—El Dorado, they called him. He was an Indian chief, it was said, whose subjects dusted him with gold on ceremonial occasions. Spanish treasure hunters soon took up the search for the chieftain. They never found him or his treasure, but they did find gold and forced Indian slaves to mine it for them.

To this day Colombia is one of South America's leading gold producers. It is rich in emeralds, too, mining about 90 percent of the world's supply of the lustrous green gems. Colombia has many other minerals as well, chiefly salt, coal, and metal ores such as copper and iron.

The nation's capital, Bogotá, is also its largest city. Situated on a plateau about 8,600 feet (2,620 m) high, it is home to nearly four million

people. Cartagena, a port on the Caribbean Sea, ranks as one of Colombia's oldest cities. Founded in 1533, its massive fortress guarded against pirate attacks on treasure fleets that gathered there to sail back to Spain. In both cities modern, high-rise buildings stand amid carefully preserved tile-and-stucco homes and churches of those bygone colonial days.

Medellín, the second largest city, is an industrial center noted for its textile mills and steel plants. Surrounded by mountains, it lies in a rich coffee-growing region. Most Colombian coffee is grown on small family farms. Prized for its flavor, it is an important source of export income.

In recent years, Medellín has also become a major center for illegal drugs such as marijuana and cocaine. The cocaine is processed in jungle hideouts and shipped to the United States. So far, the city's drug lords have defied government attempts to halt the trade. Another important drug center is Cali, to the south.

Colombia's position at the meeting place of two continents, and its variety of terrain and climate, give it many different kinds of plants and animals, including about 1,500 bird species—a world record. The birds range from moth-size hummingbirds to the large harpy eagle that can swoop off with a monkey or a sloth. Pumas, jaguars, and ocelots roam the wilds, and Colombia counts more species of bats, including the bloodthirsty vampire, than any other country.

Official name: *Republic of Colombia*
Area: *439,737 sq mi (1,138,914 sq km)*
Population: *31,192,000*
Capital: *Bogotá (met. pop. 3,982,941)*
Ethnic groups: *mestizo, white, mulatto, black*
Language: *Spanish*
Religious groups: *Roman Catholic*
Economy: *Agr: coffee, grains, potatoes, sugarcane, bananas, cotton, livestock, flowers. Ind: textiles, food processing, oil, chemicals, metals, cement, mining*
Currency: *Colombian peso*

Venezuela

Venezuela jumped into the modern world in the 1920s when it began to produce oil, lots of it. The oil was found in vast deposits beneath the waters of Lake Maracaibo on the Caribbean coast. Soon Venezuela was the richest country in South America. By 1926 oil had replaced coffee as the nation's most important export. Cities boomed, burgeoning with glass-and-steel buildings. Highways called *autopistas* linked major urban centers.

But then trouble struck. Over the years Venezuela had borrowed heavily from international banks to expand and modernize its farms and develop its industries. When the price of oil suddenly dropped in 1986, the deeply indebted nation could not pay off its loans. Today the government has much less money to spend on factories and schools and hospitals and jobs.

Venezuela has 2,000 miles (3,220 km) of coast along the northern reaches of the continent. Two-thirds of its people—and most of its major cities, including the capital, Caracas—are found in the highlands that stretch along the Caribbean Sea. The highlands are spurs of the Andes. Their altitude gives them a mild climate, and some of the higher mountains in the west are snow covered year-round.

A thin strip of land between the sea and the mountains, known as the Maracaibo lowlands, extends from the delta of the Orinoco River to Lake Maracaibo. The large, shallow lake is dotted with thousands of oil-drilling derricks.

Sixteenth-century explorers sailing along the coast found Indians living on the lake in houses built on stilts. Houses and canoes reminded the explorers of Venice, Italy, so they named the place Venezuela, Spanish for Little Venice.

Maracaibo, a large modern city near the lake, is a commercial and industrial center, and home to nearly a million Venezuelans.

In the interior, beyond the mountains and north of the Orinoco River, stretch the Llanos, or plains. This is cattle ranching country, populated by cowboys called *llaneros* and great herds of humpbacked zebu cattle. The government has begun to develop industries in the Llanos, because of their rich iron and aluminum ore deposits and immense new oil reserves.

South of the river lie the Guiana Highlands, a barely explored forest from which rise high, flat-topped mountains known as *tepuis*. From one of them, Auyan Tepui, the Devil's Mountain, spills the world's highest waterfall, 3,212-foot (979 m) Angel Falls. It was discovered in 1935 by an American aviator, Jimmy Angel, while searching for gold and diamonds—deposits modern prospectors still hope to find.

Official name: *Republic of Venezuela*
Area: *352,144 sq mi (912,050 sq km)*
Population: *19,149,000*
Capital: *Caracas (pop. 1,232,254)*
Ethnic groups: *mestizo, white, black, Indian*
Language: *Spanish*
Religious groups: *Roman Catholic*
Economy: *Agr: corn, fruit, sugarcane, coffee, rice. Ind: oil, iron ore, building materials, food processing, textiles, steel, aluminum, motor vehicles*
Currency: *bolívar*

1 *Colombia*

2 *Colombia*

3 *Colombia*

4 *Venezuela*

5 *Venezuela*

Colombia

1 *Stone walls of a 17th-century fortification surround the high-rise heart of Cartagena. The walls, 60 feet (18 m) thick in places, were built to protect the city from pirates.*

2 *Emeralds from a mine near Bogotá are prized worldwide for their color and brilliance. Found only in small clusters, the stones must be dug out with hand tools.*

3 *A Colombian farmer harvests coca leaves, used to make cocaine. Demand for the illegal drug makes coca an irresistible cash crop for poor farmers of the Andes.*

Venezuela

4 *Oil-drilling rigs rise from the waters of Lake Maracaibo. These wells tap petroleum deposits lying beneath the lake bed.*

5 *Flat-topped Mount Roraima rises 9,094 feet (2,772 m) through the mist. Rare birds and plants live in isolation on this mesa called a* tepui, *Indian for "mountain."*

6 *A Makiritare Indian girl from the rain forest of the Orinoco region rests in a hammock with her pet toucan.*

6 *Venezuela*

A B C D E F G H J K L M N O P Q R S T U

Esmeraldas

Ibarra

EQUATOR

Quito ⊗

COLOMBIA

Ecuador got its name because the Equator—*el ecuador* in Spanish—runs right through it.

For many years before Mount Everest's height was measured in the 1850s, Ecuador's tallest volcano, Chimborazo, was believed to be the highest mountain on Earth. Surveys revealed that other peaks besides Everest topped it, including the two shown here in Peru.

The Galápagos Islands, part of Ecuador since 1832, get their name from the giant tortoises—*galápagos* in Spanish—that live there.

Latacunga

+ *Cotopaxi*
19,347 FEET
5,897 METERS

Napo River

Manta

Portoviejo

Quevedo

Ambato

Chimborazo +
20,702 FEET
6,310 METERS

Riobamba

ECUADOR

Putumayo River

Guayaquil

Gulf of Guayaquil

Cuenca

Tumbes

Machala

Iquitos

Amazon River

Loja

Talara

A N D E S

Sullana

Piura

SECHURA DESERT

Maranon River

AMAZON BASIN

Yurimaguas

Moyobamba

Chachapoyas

Ucayali River

Huallaga River

Chiclayo

Cajamarca

BRAZIL

PACIFIC OCEAN

PERU

Trujillo

Pucallpa

Yungay + *Mount Huascaran*
22,205 FEET
6,768 METERS

Chimbote

Huaraz

Huanuco

Urubamba River

0 KILOMETERS 250
0 STATUTE MILES 150

For map legend see page 21.

← PAN AMERICAN HIGHWAY

Cerro de Pasco

La Oroya

Callao

Lima ⊗

Huancayo

Puerto Maldonado

A L T I P L A N O

Huancavelica

Ayacucho

Machu Picchu

A N D E S

Pisco

Abancay

Cuzco

Apurimac River

Ica

A N D E S

BOLIVIA

Nazca

Mount Coropuna +
21,079 FEET
6,425 METERS

Lake Titicaca

Puno

Arequipa

Mollendo

Moquegua

Tacna

CHILE

GALAPAGOS ISLANDS
(ECUADOR)

0 KILOMETERS 100
0 STATUTE MILES 75

PACIFIC OCEAN

Pinta Island

Marchena Island

EQUATOR

San Salvador Island

Fernandina Island

Santa Cruz Island

Isabela Island

Baqueriza Moreno

San Cristobal Island

Santa Maria Island

Espanola Island

1 2 3 4 5 6 7 8 9 10 11 12 13 14 15 16 17 18 19

Ecuador

There are two kinds of eruptions you can almost always count on in Ecuador, volcanoes and politics. This Equator-straddling country has about 30 active volcanoes. From time to time they rumble and belch ashes onto surrounding villages.

Almost as restless as the volcanoes are the politicians. Until recently, few presidents managed to serve out a full, four-year term. Coups and countercoups were a way of life as government after government was overthrown. At one stage in its modern history, Ecuador had 22 presidents or heads of state within 23 years.

Geography and the state of the economy play a big part in Ecuador's political instability. About half of its people live in the fertile, coastal lowlands, where bananas, coffee, cacao, and other export crops flourish. The major city here is Guayaquil, a busy modern port that has grown rapidly since the late 1960s when oil was discovered in the eastern provinces. Most lowlanders are of European or mixed Indian-European extraction. Living near the coast encourages them to be outward-looking in matters of trade and commerce, and exposes them to new ideas.

The other half of Ecuador's people—many of them Indians—live in isolated highland towns and villages nestled in the Andes. Most highlanders lead traditional, slow-paced lives as farmers who raise dairy cattle or wheat, corn, barley, and potatoes. Their isolation makes them less receptive to change.

Quito, the capital, lies in the highlands at an altitude of 9,300 feet (2,830 m). Its churches, plazas, and public buildings preserve some of South America's finest examples of Spanish colonial architecture. Change comes slowly to Quito—and to most highlanders. Getting them to agree with lowlanders on politics can be tricky.

East of the mountains stretches Ecuador's oil region, a sparsely populated area covered by dense tropical forests. Oil discovered here in 1967 helped to fuel Ecuadorian prosperity until oil prices fell in the mid-1980s. Today Ecuador, like other South American oil producers, faces slow economic growth and heavy debt from borrowing when oil prices were high.

Ecuador's offshore waters swarm with tuna, shrimp, and other fish. Farther offshore, some 600 miles (965 km) to the west, lie the Galápagos Islands. This cluster of volcanic islands belonging to Ecuador is home to giant tortoises, marine lizards, and other animals found nowhere else. They have fascinated scientists ever since naturalist Charles Darwin visited the islands in 1835. In 1959 Ecuador declared most of the archipelago a national park.

Official name: *Republic of Ecuador*
Area: *109,484 sq mi (283,561 sq km)*
Population: *10,450,000*
Capital: *Quito (pop. 1,093,278)*
Ethnic groups: *Indian, mestizo, white, black*
Language: *Spanish, Quechua*
Religious groups: *Roman Catholic*
Economy: *Agr: bananas, coffee, cacao, sugarcane, corn, potatoes, rice, livestock. Ind: food processing, textiles, chemicals, fishing, lumber, oil, shrimp*
Currency: *sucre*

Peru

Peru, stronghold of the once proud Inca Empire, is a land high, wild, beautiful—and cruel. Many of South America's highest mountains rise here, snowcapped peaks thrusting 20,000 feet (6,100 m) or more above the sea. Although these Andean mountains are beautiful, they are also deadly. In 1962 Peru's highest mountain, 22,205-foot (6,768 m) Huascarán, let loose a cascade of mud and ice that killed 4,000 people. And in 1970 an earthquake touched off a series of avalanches that killed 60,000 people.

Streams and rivers have carved awesome canyons in the highlands and plateaus where half of Peru's people live. Some of these gorges plunge two miles (3 km)—twice as deep as the Grand Canyon. After the conquest of Peru by Spain in 1532, Inca survivors may have hidden out in the mountains north of the old Inca capital of Cuzco. Here, on a ridge between two mountain peaks rising from the forest, stands Machu Picchu, now thought to be a royal estate built by Pachacuti, founder of the Inca Empire.

Most of the people who live in the central highlands and valleys are Indians, Quechua-speaking descendants of the Incas whose fabulously rich empire reached from Chile to Colombia. Many of them farm small plots of corn, potatoes, and coca (much of which is shipped to Colombia to be made into cocaine). Their children herd sheep and llamas, valued for meat and wool. Still others work in copper, lead, and silver mines.

The high plateau, or Altiplano, of southern Peru is also the site of Lake Titicaca, shared by Peru and Bolivia. Indians here live in reed huts and sail the lake in boats made of reed bundles.

Living for generations at elevations of 12,000 to 14,000 feet (3,660 to 4,270 m), highland Indians have developed extra-large lungs and hearts. Most of them are desperately poor. They have few roads, schools, or hospitals. One out of ten babies dies before its first birthday. These problems have led to social unrest and the formation of armed rebel bands who try to overthrow the government with terrorist tactics.

Narrow coastal lowlands fringe the western flanks of the mountains. They are mainly desert, created by a cold ocean current, the Peru Current, which cools the air flowing across it so that rain clouds don't form. The current also supports shoals of anchovies that are ground into pig and chicken feed, and sold all over the world.

Peru's capital, Lima, founded on this coastal strip by conquistadors in 1535, is a center of commerce, art, and industry, along with its port city, Callao. Most lowlanders descend from Spanish or Spanish and Indian ancestors.

East of the mountains lies the great basin through which flow the headwaters of the Amazon River. The thick, largely unexplored forests of this region cover about 60 percent of Peru, but are home to only 5 percent of its people. The discovery of oil and gas here in 1976 and the development of roads and farms may someday bring people flocking to Peru's "wild East."

Official name: *Republic of Peru*
Area: *496,225 sq mi (1,285,220 sq km)*
Population: *21,449,000*
Capital: *Lima (met. pop. 6,500,000)*
Ethnic groups: *Indian, mestizo, white*
Language: *Spanish, Quechua, Aymara*
Religious groups: *Roman Catholic*
Economy: *Agr: sugarcane, potatoes, rice, corn, coffee, cotton, livestock. Ind: minerals, oil, fishing, textiles, food processing, cement, motor vehicles, steel*
Currency: *inti*

1 *Peru*

2 *Peru*

3 *Peru*

Peru

1 *Spinning wool into yarn, an Indian woman near Cuzco uses a spindle to twist the fibers together. Mother and napping child wear traditional dyed-wool clothing.*

2 *Farmers in the Andean highlands harvest potatoes, a crop that can grow successfully at altitudes of up to 14,000 feet (4,270 m).*

3 *Machu Picchu, built by the Inca Indians in the 15th century, crowns a ridge in the Andes. Scientists now believe the ruins were once part of a royal estate.*

Ecuador

4 *Shoppers stroll amid an open-air market in Quito. South America's oldest capital, Quito was established in 1534 and preserves much of its colonial heritage.*

5 *A giant tortoise in the Galápagos Islands displays its armor. These endangered animals can weigh up to 600 pounds (270 kg) and may live 150 years.*

4 *Ecuador*

5 *Ecuador*

A B C D E F G H J K L M N O P Q R S T U

VENEZUELA

GUYANA

SURINAME

FRENCH GUIANA
(FRANCE)

COLOMBIA

Georgetown
Linden
Nieuw Nickerie
Paramaribo
Devil's Island
Lake Van Blommestein
Kourou
Cayenne

GUIANA HIGHLANDS

ATLANTIC OCEAN

Neblina Peak
9,888 FEET
+ 3,014 METERS

EQUATOR

Rio Negro

Amazon River

Marajo Island

Belem

Amazon River

Manaus

AMAZON BASIN

Madeira River

Tapajos River

TRANS-AMAZON HIGHWAY

Tocantins River

Sao Luis

Fortaleza

Teresina
Crateus

BRAZIL

Purus River

Parnaiba River

Natal

Joao Pessoa

Recife

Rio Branco

PERU

Porto Velho

Xingu River

Sao Francisco River

Juazeiro

Maceio

Aracaju

Feira de Santana

Salvador

MATO GROSSO

BRAZILIAN HIGHLANDS

BOLIVIA

PLATEAU

⊕**Brasilia**

Goiania

Brazil, the giant of South America, covers nearly half the continent. It extends some 2,700 miles (4,345 km) from north to south and east to west. It holds more than half the continent's population, too. The Portuguese colonized coastal areas in the 1500s, and because of the rugged interior, most cities remain near the coast.

Guyana, Suriname, and French Guiana to Brazil's north, are the only countries in South America without a Portuguese or Spanish heritage. The first two are former British and Dutch colonies, while the third still is French.

Campos

Campo Grande

Belo Horizonte

Vitoria

Parana River

Ribeirao Preto

Juiz de Fora

Campinas

Sorocaba

PARAGUAY

Rio de Janeiro

Sao Paulo
Santos

Sao Jose dos Campos

TROPIC OF CAPRICORN

Iguazu Falls

Curitiba

ARGENTINA

Uruguay River

Porto Alegre

Patos Lagoon

URUGUAY

0 KILOMETERS 500
0 STATUTE MILES 300

For map legend see page 21.

1 2 3 4 5 6 7 8 9 10 11 12 13 14 15 16 17 18

Guyana

In Guyana they speak English. It's the country's official language, which makes Guyana the only English-speaking nation in South America. That's because, for 150 years—until it won independence in 1966—Guyana was a colony ruled by the United Kingdom. It was known as British Guiana.

Guiana is an Indian word. It means "land of waters" and refers to the coastal swamps, marshes, and lagoons formed by four major rivers as they flow into the Atlantic Ocean from the interior highlands. Spanish explorers sailing along the coast here in 1498 took one look at all the mud, silt, jungles, and alligators—and sailed on to Venezuela. It was the Dutch, in the early 1600s, who realized that so much mud and water was worth a king's ransom in rich farmland, but only if the water could be drained.

Dutch settlers dredged and built and brought in slaves from Africa to work on their sugarcane plantations. The British eventually took over, and brought in thousands of indentured workers from India, Portugal, and China.

Today, Guyanese call their country "the land of six peoples." Most of them live in the humid coastal lowlands. They grow rice and sugarcane. Only a few native Indians, descendants of the Caribs and Arawaks, live inland. Georgetown, the capital, is a city of wooden buildings, many of them raised on stilts to escape flooding.

Gold and diamonds have been found in Guyana's interior, but the nation's real mineral wealth lies in its immense deposits of bauxite.

During World War II Guyana supplied the United States with nearly all the bauxite needed for aluminum to build fighter planes and bombers.

Official name: *Co-operative Republic of Guyana*
Area: *83,000 sq mi (214,969 sq km)*
Population: *766,000*
Capital: *Georgetown (pop. 72,049)*
Ethnic groups: *East Indian, black, mixed, Indian*
Language: *English*
Religious groups: *Christian, Hindu, Muslim*
Economy: *Agr: sugarcane, rice, fruit, vegetables. Ind: bauxite, lumber, fishing, textiles, gold, rum*
Currency: *Guyana dollar*

Suriname

The British and the Dutch arranged a land swap in 1667. In exchange for a colony named Nieuw Amsterdam in North America, the Dutch got part of a British colony in South America. Nieuw Amsterdam would become New York City and Dutch Guiana became Suriname, which won its independence in 1975.

Suriname rises gradually from a low, swampy coastal belt to heavily forested interior highlands. About 90 percent of the land is covered by thousands of different kinds of trees. One of them, the rot-resistant greenheart, has wood so dense and hard that it will not float.

Suriname's biggest export is the bauxite dug from its mines and processed into aluminum. Power to run the factories comes from a hydroelectric plant that taps one of the world's largest man-made lakes, 600-square-mile (1,555 sq km) Lake Van Blommestein.

Most of Suriname's people live along the coast on farms and plantations that export rice and bananas. Here, too, stands the capital, Paramaribo, a city of about 180,000 people. Suriname's citizens, like those in neighboring Guyana, came originally from many lands. Most Surinamers speak a polyglot tongue commonly called Taki Taki, which is made up of English, Dutch, French, African, and Asian words.

Official name: *Republic of Suriname*
Area: *63,037 sq mi (163,265 sq km)*
Population: *397,000*
Capital: *Paramaribo (met. pop. 180,000)*
Ethnic groups: *East Indian, Creole, Javanese, black, Indian*
Language: *Dutch, Sranan Tongo (Taki Taki)*
Religious groups: *Christian, Hindu, Muslim*
Economy: *Agr: rice, bananas, sugarcane. Ind: bauxite, wood products, food processing, shrimp*
Currency: *Suriname guilder*

French Guiana

French Guiana is noted mainly for two things: the spicy red pepper named after its capital, Cayenne, and Devil's Island, the dreaded prison colony surrounded by sharks and swirling currents. Between 1852 and 1946, some 70,000 prisoners languished in several prisons here, now shut. Most never lived to see France again.

Long a colony, French Guiana became an overseas *département* in 1946, with an elected representative in Paris. Its people, chiefly of African descent, are French citizens. Most live in and around Cayenne. The heavily forested countryside has few roads and, away from the coast, rises to low hills. Shrimp processing and rum distilling are among French Guiana's industries, along with a commercial rocket-launching station at Kourou, which takes advantage of Earth's greater rotational speed near the Equator to loft rockets into orbit.

Official name: *Department of French Guiana*
Area: *34,749 sq mi (90,000 sq km)*
Population: *95,000*
Capital: *Cayenne (pop. 38,091)*
Ethnic groups: *black, mulatto, white, East Indian, Chinese, Indian*
Language: *French, French Creole*
Religious groups: *Roman Catholic*
Economy: *Agr: rice, cassava, bananas, vegetables, sugarcane. Ind: construction, shrimp, lumber, rum*
Currency: *French franc*

Brazil

Almost everything about Brazil is big: big land, big forests, big rivers, big cities—big debt. Brazil is far and away the largest nation in South America. It covers nearly half the continent and shares a common border with all other South American countries except Chile and Ecuador. Brazil is also the only Portuguese-speaking nation in South America, thanks to its discovery by Portuguese mariners in 1500.

The country's Atlantic coast extends more than 4,600 miles (7,400 km). About 90 percent of the Brazilian people—a mixture of Europeans, Africans, Indians, and Asians—live along a coastal strip between the ocean and a wall-like escarpment that averages 2,600 feet (790 m) high. Behind the escarpment spread large plateaus and the Amazon Basin.

Part of the plateaus and basin are covered with grass and shrubs—excellent for cattle ranching. But most of the basin is covered by a rain forest so immense it could blanket much of the United States. Many giants live in this shadowy world—trees more than 200 feet (60 m) high, lily pads big enough for small children to float on, toads and spiders as big as dinner plates, snakes big enough to swallow a deer.

Here, too, flows the 4,000-mile-long (6,437 km) Amazon River, second in length only to Egypt's 4,145-mile (6,671 km) Nile. But the Amazon carries 60 times more water than the Nile.

Millions of plant and animal species live in the Amazon forest, many of them barely known to science. One tree, *pau-brasil*—brazilwood—gave the country its name, and provided 16th-century Europe with a valuable red dye.

But now the forest is in danger. Over the years great swaths have been cut down, burned, or flooded so that farmers, ranchers, and miners could move into the interior. In one recent year a forest area bigger than Belgium went up in smoke. In the 1950s, to encourage settlement, a new national capital, Brasília, was built 600 miles (965 km) inland from the old coastal capital, Rio de Janeiro. Roads were built to link the new capital with the *sertão*, the backcountry.

Scientists and conservationists warn that if such destruction continues, global weather might be seriously affected, and thousands of useful plants and animals might disappear before we can learn about them. The livelihood of forest-dwelling Indians is also threatened.

Brazil is a rich country. Its forests yield lumber, nuts, wax, and latex from rubber trees. Its farms grow a third of the world's coffee and much of its cacao, soybeans, sugarcane, and oranges. Mills and factories in large, modern industrial cities such as São Paulo and Rio turn out cars, textiles, and television sets. Brazil's mines have some of the world's richest deposits of iron ore, bauxite, gold, manganese, and gemstones.

Brazil also has the biggest debts of any developing nation. Over the years it borrowed heavily to develop farms and factories; to build roads, dams, and cities. Today its foreign debt is so staggering that many Brazilians say: "This is a land of the future—and always will be!"

Official name: *Federative Republic of Brazil*
Area: *3,286,488 sq mi (8,511,965 sq km)*
Population: *147,393,000*
Capital: *Brasília (pop. 1,576,657)*
Ethnic groups: *white, mulatto, black, Indian*
Language: *Portuguese*
Religious groups: *Roman Catholic*
Economy: *Agr: coffee, rice, corn, sugarcane, cacao, soybeans, cotton, cassava, oranges, livestock, wheat. Ind: textiles, chemicals, cement, lumber, iron ore, steel, motor vehicles, metals, manufacturing, fishing*
Currency: *cruzado*

1 *Brazil*

2 *Brazil*

3 *Brazil*

4 *French Guiana*

Brazil

1 *Hacked from the heart of the Amazon forest, the Carajás iron mine in the northern Brazilian Highlands holds the world's largest deposit of high-quality iron ore.*

2 *A woolly spider monkey uses its tail as an extra "hand." Fewer than 400 of these monkeys survive as development destroys their coastal forest habitat.*

3 *Steep-sided mountains called* morros *give Rio de Janeiro its distinctive cityscape.*

French Guiana

4 *Wayana Indian children examine a new toy—a Rubik's Cube. Despite the remoteness of the Wayanas' rain-forest home, modern products are changing their lives.*

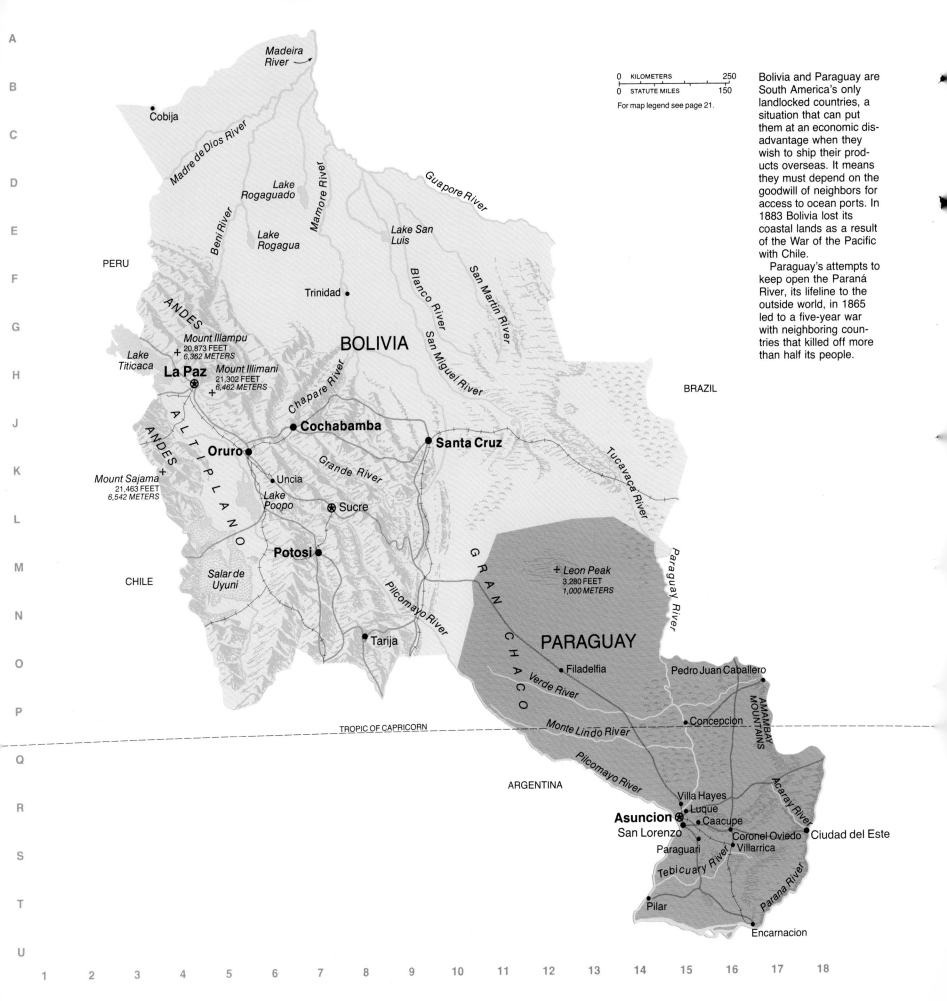

Bolivia and Paraguay are South America's only landlocked countries, a situation that can put them at an economic disadvantage when they wish to ship their products overseas. It means they must depend on the goodwill of neighbors for access to ocean ports. In 1883 Bolivia lost its coastal lands as a result of the War of the Pacific with Chile.

Paraguay's attempts to keep open the Paraná River, its lifeline to the outside world, in 1865 led to a five-year war with neighboring countries that killed off more than half its people.

0 KILOMETERS 250
0 STATUTE MILES 150

For map legend see page 21.

Bolivia

The capital of Bolivia, La Paz, lies at such a high altitude—12,000 feet (3,660 m) above sea level—that visitors from the lowlands find themselves huffing and puffing if they try to walk fast. At that height it takes six minutes to boil a three-minute egg, airplanes need extra-long runways to take off, and the people who live there have enlarged lungs that help them breathe the rarefied air more efficiently.

The world's highest city, La Paz is located on the Altiplano, the high, windswept plateau that lies between parallel ranges of the Andes. Here, amid snow-covered mountain peaks, condors with 10-foot (3 m) wingspans ride the updrafts, and llamas and alpacas graze the grasses. A few miles away from La Paz sparkles Lake Titicaca, the world's highest navigable lake.

With about a million inhabitants, La Paz is Bolivia's largest city and a center of business. It is also one of two Bolivian capitals. The presidential palace and most of the nation's government offices are found there. The other capital, Sucre, is the judicial capital. It houses Bolivia's judges and courts of law.

About half of Bolivia's citizens live on the Altiplano. Most are Aymara and Quechua Indians or mestizos, people of mixed Spanish and Indian ancestry. The Indian women are noted for their colorful clothes—bright shawls and skirts worn over a dozen or so petticoats. Men wear *chullos*, colorful knitted caps with earflaps.

Most of the Indians are desperately poor.

They earn about $500 a year as laborers, miners, herders, and small farmers. Many cannot read or write, and some speak no Spanish.

In the foothills east of the Andes lie the *yungas*—deep, fertile valleys from which come major crops such as coca, coffee, grains, and fruit. By some estimates, three-quarters of Bolivia's cultivated land is used to grow coca, despite all government attempts to stamp out the practice. The Indians themselves chew dried coca leaves to dull the pain of hunger and cold.

The nation has long been known as a storehouse of mineral wealth. Its silver, tin, and copper mines have been among the world's richest. From 1544 to about 1600, Bolivian mines produced half the world's silver. Even today its minerals are an important source of foreign earnings. And the development of oil and gas deposits in the Gran Chaco and near Santa Cruz may someday bring prosperity to its people.

But for now, prosperity eludes Bolivia. Since it won independence from Spain in 1825, Bolivia has lost about two-thirds of its territory in wars with more powerful neighbors. This has left it a landlocked nation, without ports to ship its goods overseas. Political squabbling has done even more damage. In its 165-year history, the republic has suffered 195 coups d'état. From 1978 to 1980, it underwent three general elections, four revolutions, five temporary governments, and more than a thousand strikes by unhappy workers. Such instability helps keep Bolivia in a chronic state of poverty.

Official name: *Republic of Bolivia*
Area: *424,164 sq mi (1,098,581 sq km)*
Population: *7,086,000*
Capital: *La Paz, administrative (pop. 1,033,288)*
    Sucre, legal and judicial (pop. 88,774)
Ethnic groups: *Indian, mestizo, white*
Language: *Spanish, Quechua, Aymara*
Religious groups: *Roman Catholic*
Economy: *Agr: sugarcane, potatoes, grains, fruit, coffee, cotton. Ind: minerals, oil, lumber, textiles*
Currency: *boliviano*

Paraguay

He could be brutal and he sometimes was. He was Alfredo Stroessner, the red-headed son of a Bavarian father and a Paraguayan mother. For nearly 35 years he ruled his country, Paraguay, with an iron fist as a *caudillo*, a military dictator. On friends he lavished power and wealth. Political enemies, on the other hand, were beaten or jailed or thrown out of Paraguay . . . or killed.

But General Stroessner also built roads, bridges, schools, dams—even a new city. More important, he brought a measure of peace and stability to a land that had long been torn by wars, uprisings, and grinding poverty. Many of his countrymen supported him. Others remained silent or fled the country.

And the general himself fled to Brazil—after a coup in 1989 toppled him from power.

A landlocked nation in the middle of South America, Paraguay has long been off the beaten track of commerce and industry. For much of its history, the Paraguay River, which divides the country in half, provided the only access, via the Paraná River, to the outside world. Sometimes the nation's isolation was deliberate, decreed by dictators who governed Paraguay from the time it won independence from Spain in 1811.

The first dictator, a despot known as *El Supremo*, The Supreme One, held office for 30 years. He cut off all foreign trade and contact. A later ruler involved Paraguay in a war that cost the nation about a third of its land and the lives of more than half its people.

Most Paraguayans are part Guaraní Indian and part Spanish. They speak both languages. About 95 percent of them live in the eastern half of the country, a wooded, rolling plateau with fertile soil. Here they cultivate soybeans, coffee, and rice, as well as tropical fruit. Paraguay has few minerals and not much industry besides selling lumber, making cement, and smuggling everything from cars to cocaine.

The western part of the country, the Gran Chaco, is a grassland area parched in the dry season and swampy when it rains. Here cattle roam on large ranches, and Mennonite farmers near Filadelfia produce fruit, vegetables, and dairy products for sale in the capital, Asunción. The Mennonites, a religious group, migrated to the Chaco from Canada and Europe in the 1920s.

Today, as Paraguay shakes off decades of dictatorship, more than half of its earnings come from the sale of electricity to Brazil. The power is generated by hydroelectric projects on the Paraná River. Initiated by General Stroessner, they were part of his modernization program.

Official name: *Republic of Paraguay*
Area: *157,048 sq mi (406,752 sq km)*
Population: *4,157,000*
Capital: *Asunción (pop. 457,210)*
Ethnic groups: *mestizo, Indian*
Language: *Spanish, Guaraní*
Religious groups: *Roman Catholic*
Economy: *Agr: oilseeds, soybeans, cotton, cassava, sweet potatoes, tobacco, corn, rice, sugarcane, coffee. Ind: meat packing, brewing, textiles, cement, lumber*
Currency: *guaraní*

1 *Paraguay*

2 *Paraguay*

3 *Bolivia*

Paraguay

1 Soccer players become airborne during a match in Asunción. Futbol is Paraguay's most popular sport.

2 Vaqueros, Paraguayan cowboys, round up calves, crossbreeds of zebu and Brahmans, before driving them to fresh pastures.

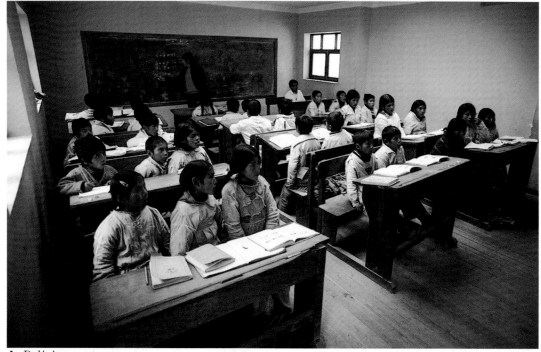

4 *Bolivia*

5 *Bolivia*

6 *Bolivia*

Bolivia

3 *Lake Titicaca's clear waters lie 12,500 feet (3,810 m) above sea level. Indians fish the lake in boats made of bundled totora reeds.*

4 *Sharing a one-room village schoolhouse, two teachers instruct Indian children in two languages, Spanish and Aymara. Separate classes sit back-to-back.*

5 *Tin miners extract ore deep inside a mountain at Potosí. Working in harsh conditions of extreme heat and thin air, they earn about a dollar a day.*

6 *An Aymara Indian plays a* sampoña, *a reed panpipe, on the streets of Potosí. The music has a breathy, haunting quality.*

PERU

A · Arica

B · Iquique

BOLIVIA

0 KILOMETERS 400
0 STATUTE MILES 300
For map legend see page 21.

C

Calama · San Salvador de Jujuy

Pilcomayo

TROPIC OF CAPRICORN

D · Antofagasta · Salta · PARAGUAY

Paraguay River

Paraguay River · Iguazu Falls

E · Mount Ojos del Salado 22,572 FEET 6,880 METERS · San Miguel de Tucuman · Formosa · Resistencia · Posadas

PAN AMERICAN HIGHWAY

Copiapo · Catamarca · Santiago del Estero · Corrientes · BRAZIL

F · PACIFIC OCEAN · La Rioja

G · La Serena · Coquimbo · Artigas · Rivera

Mount Aconcagua 22,834 FEET 6,960 METERS Highest point in South America · Cordoba · Santa Fe · Salto · Tacuarembo

H · San Juan · Rio Cuarto · Parana · Paysandu · Melo · Mercedes

Vina del Mar · Mendoza · Rosario · URUGUAY

J · Valparaiso · Santiago · San Luis · Buenos Aires · Las Piedras · Maldonado · Montevideo

Rancagua

CHILE · La Plata · Rio de la Plata

K · Talca · Santa Rosa

Chillan

L · Concepcion · Los Angeles · P A M P A S · Mar del Plata

Bahia Blanca

M · Temuco · Neuquen · Rio Negro

ARGENTINA · ATLANTIC OCEAN

Valdivia · Viedma

N · Osorno · Lake Nahuel Huapi · Valdes Peninsula

Puerto Montt · San Carlos de Bariloche

Chiloe Island · -131 FEET -40 METERS Lowest point in South America

O · Rawson

ANDES

P · Coihaique · Comodoro Rivadavia

PATAGONIA

Q

South America's highest and lowest points, Mount Aconcagua and Valdes Peninsula, are both in Argentina. Cape Horn, at the continent's southern tip, lies only about 600 miles (965 km) from Antarctica. Until the opening of the Panama Canal in 1914, sailors voyaging from New York to San Francisco had to face the cape's ferocious storms as well as an extra journey of 9,000 miles (14,485 km).

R · FALKLAND ISLANDS (UNITED KINGDOM)

S · Rio Gallegos · Strait of Magellan · West Falkland · Stanley · East Falkland

Falkland Sound

A piece of Chile lies 2,300 miles (3,700 km) to its west: Easter Island (see pages 227 and 231).

T · Punta Arenas

U · TIERRA DEL FUEGO · Ushuaia · Puerto Williams · Cape Horn

1 2 3 4 5 6 7 8 9 10 11

Chile

Chilli, "where the land ends." That's what the Indians called the world's longest and skinniest country, the Republic of Chile. Pinched between the Pacific Ocean and the high ridges of the southern Andes, Chile extends some 2,650 miles (4,260 km), about the distance between New York and San Francisco. Nowhere is it more than 250 miles (400 km) wide.

Chile is a country of great beauty and stark contrasts. In some places, snowcapped peaks rise straight out of the water. The northern third of the country includes the Atacama Desert, a region so dry that parts of it go centuries without rain. The desert is also a mother lode of mineral wealth—copper, silver, gold, and immense deposits of sodium nitrate.

By contrast, Chile's southern part, a wooded maze of fjords and islands, is one of the world's wettest and stormiest places. Some 200 inches (500 cm) of rain a year drench thick forests. Near the continent's tip, winds of up to 200 miles (320 km) an hour lash ice fields and granite peaks. Around the Strait of Magellan, sheep outnumber people fifty to one, and hardy sheepherders mingle with oil and gas drillers. Here, too, live most of Chile's Indians, Mapuche descendants of the warlike Araucanians who successfully resisted armed conquest by Inca and Spaniard.

Most Chileans live in the central section of their country, a region of mild climate and fertile soil. Here farms and ranches produce abundant fruit, vegetables, grains, meats, and dairy products. Here, too, stands Chile's capital,

Santiago, and most of its other major cities. The lake district south of Concepción is widely regarded as one of the world's most beautiful resort areas, a land of shimmering lakes and waterfalls set amid sometimes active volcanoes.

Chile's dependence on world copper prices and recent political turmoil cloud its future. In 1970 a communist president was elected to office. Unable to stabilize the nation's economy, he died during a coup three years later and was succeeded by a dictator. Now the country labors to get its economy rolling again under a new, democratically elected president.

Official name: *Republic of Chile*
Area: *292,135 sq mi (756,626 sq km)*
Population: *12,960,000*
Capital: *Santiago (met. pop. 4,318,305)*
Ethnic groups: *mestizo, white, Indian*
Language: *Spanish*
Religious groups: *Roman Catholic*
Economy: *Agr: grains, vegetables, sugar beets, fruit, cattle. Ind: copper, minerals, fishing, wood products*
Currency: *Chilean peso*

Argentina

In Argentina they have a saying: "Mexicans descended from the Aztecs. Peruvians descended from the Incas. But we descended from boats." They say this because the ancestors of about 95 percent of the nation's 32 million people came by boat from Europe. Unlike most Latin American countries, Argentina has a very small population of mixed Spanish and Indian blood, and there are few blacks. Most Argentine ancestors came from Italy and Spain. Many also came from France, Germany, Austria, Russia, Great Britain, Switzerland, and Poland.

Perhaps this explains why the capital, Buenos Aires, looks and feels more like a busy European metropolis than most other Latin American cities. Offices and public buildings stand amid chic shops and restaurants along tree-lined boulevards. The area is also home to about a third of Argentina's people. Its factories turn out everything from cars and chemicals to television sets and washing machines.

Argentina is a land of many lands. In the west, along the border with Chile, soar the peaks of the Andes. One of them, 22,834-foot (6,960 m) Mount Aconcagua, is the highest mountain in all the Americas. Amid the mountains farther south lies San Carlos de Bariloche, resembling a town in Switzerland. Settled by Swiss,

Germans, and northern Italians, the town has become a resort noted for its chalet-style houses, chocolate shops, and challenging ski runs.

Sweeping eastward across the continent from the foot of the mountains are Argentina's plains—the dry scrublands of the Gran Chaco in the north, the fertile grasslands called Pampas in the middle, and the windswept Patagonian plateau in the south.

Large parts of the Pampas are cattle country, home of the hard-riding gaucho, or cowboy. Here, too, live the wild guanaco, related to the llama, and the ostrich-like rhea. Beef cattle and wheat grown on large *estancias*, ranches, have long provided major Argentine exports. And in Patagonia's desolate reaches roam large flocks of sheep, many of them on ranches established by Scots and Welsh settlers in the 1800s.

At the tip of the continent lies Tierra del Fuego, the Land of Fire, named for the Indian campfires seen by explorer Ferdinand Magellan in 1520 as he sailed through the strait that bears his name. And in the northeast, near Brazil and Paraguay, spread subtropical forests and a tongue of land that reaches to spectacular Iguazú Falls shared by Brazil and Argentina.

But for all its beauty and productive land, Argentina is a country that has gone from riches to rags. In the early 1900s, to be "rich like an Argentine" was to be superwealthy. But years of misrule has left the nation's economy in shambles. Enormous foreign debts and skyrocketing inflation now threaten the fragile democracy established with the election of a popular civilian president in 1983.

Official name: *Argentine Republic*
Area: *1,068,302 sq mi (2,766,889 sq km)*
Population: *31,930,000*
Capital: *Buenos Aires (met. pop. 11,580,000)*
Ethnic groups: *white, mestizo, Indian*
Language: *Spanish*
Religious groups: *Roman Catholic*
Economy: *Agr: grains, sugarcane, oilseeds, livestock. Ind: food processing, motor vehicles, textiles, hides, chemicals, petrochemicals, metals, fishing*
Currency: *austral*

Uruguay

For much of this century Uruguay has seemed blessed. It is a land of gently rolling hills and pasturelands that supports millions of sheep and cattle. Meat, hides, and wool sold abroad have brought widespread prosperity unknown to most other Latin American countries.

The government has been generous, providing free schools, hospitals, and other social services.

Nearly half of all Uruguayans live in or around the capital, Montevideo, a modern city at the mouth of the Río de la Plata. Beautiful beaches line the coast. Uruguay's climate is mild, and enough rain falls to grow bountiful crops of sugar, rice, and wheat. In the spring, wildflowers called verbena color the hills, giving Uruguay its nickname, "the purple land."

But in the 1970s, with agricultural production slumping, oil prices and the cost of social services soared. Inflation grew, making the peso worth less and less. Terrorist bands and economic hard times nearly destroyed the nation. The military took control in 1973 and waged a ruthless campaign against the guerrilla bands and leftist political opposition. Today, under a civilian president, Uruguay struggles to repay its debts to foreign lenders, rebuild its shattered economy, and regain its place as one of South America's leading democracies.

Official name: *Oriental Republic of Uruguay*
Area: *68,037 sq mi (176,215 sq km)*
Population: *2,989,000*
Capital: *Montevideo (pop. 1,247,920)*
Ethnic groups: *white, mestizo, black*
Language: *Spanish*
Religious groups: *Roman Catholic*
Economy: *Agr: livestock, wheat, rice, corn. Ind: food processing, leather, textiles, rubber, cement, fishing*
Currency: *Uruguayan new peso*

Falkland Islands

Islands at the end of the world, the Falklands made headlines in 1982 during a brief but bloody war between Argentina and the United Kingdom, which has ruled the Falklands as a colony since 1833. Though defeated, Argentina still claims this Connecticut-size archipelago of some 200 islands that it calls Islas Malvinas. About 2,000 people, mostly sheep ranchers of British extraction, live on these windswept islands near Antarctica. Seals, seabirds, and penguins inhabit their crags and coves; offshore waters teem with squid. The sale of wool provides a major source of island income.

Official name: *Colony of the Falkland Islands*
Area: *4,700 sq mi (12,173 sq km)*
Population: *2,000*
Capital: *Stanley (pop. 1,239)*
Ethnic groups: *British*
Language: *English*
Religious groups: *Protestant*
Economy: *Agr: sheep. Ind: wool, hides, skins*
Currency: *pound sterling*

1 *Argentina*

2 *Argentina*

3 *Falkland Islands*

4 *Chile*

Argentina

1 *Gauchos lead a cattle drive in Argentina, where rich grasslands called Pampas nourish beef raised for export.*

2 *Crowds jam the movie district in Buenos Aires, the capital of Argentina. Its metropolitan area has the second largest population in South America.*

Falkland Islands

3 *Black-browed albatrosses perch on cliffs overlooking the South Atlantic Ocean. Their island home lies 300 miles (480 km) off Argentina's coast.*

Chile

4 *Near the southern reaches of the Andes, the glaciated peaks of Torres del Paine National Park harbor rare animal species.*

5 *Nearly four miles (6 km) above sea level, miners break up chunks of sulfur. The mine is on Aucanquilcha, a volcano that rises 20,262 feet (6,175 m) in the Andes.*

5 *Chile*

Europe

Europe is more a reflection of human culture than of the Earth's geography. Physically, it is little more than a large, irregular peninsula hanging off the enormous Eurasian landmass that stretches from the Atlantic to the Pacific Ocean. It is less than one-fourth the size of Asia, and only slightly larger than the United States. Of all the continents, only Australia is smaller. Still, Europe's role in world history has been great. At one time or another, Europeans have controlled the vast majority of land on Earth. As a result, some traces of European culture—languages, customs, or systems of government—are visible nearly everywhere in the world.

Europe's most important geographical distinction is that no point is very far from an arm of the ocean. This has been a key to its development, for it has given Europeans easy access to the rest of the world. The Arctic Ocean borders it in the north, the Atlantic in the west, and the Mediterranean Sea in the south. Its 50,000-mile (80,470 km) coastline is more fragmented than that of any other continent, being indented with thousands of fjords and other types of inlets.

Many seas with narrow openings are created by Europe's numerous peninsulas and islands. Water is never far away. Of the more than 30 European countries, only 9 are landlocked and lack direct access to the sea. Even along the continent's eastern border, formed by the Ural Mountains that cross the Soviet Union, the Kara Sea and the Black Sea are reachable. It is not surprising that Europeans have been known for centuries as good sailors.

The Atlantic Ocean has a great effect on Europe's weather too. Its currents keep winters mild and summers moderate on much of the continent. Westerly winds from the ocean provide ample rainfall. Because the climate in the western regions is similar to that of the eastern United States, Americans might think that England is straight across the Atlantic Ocean from New York. It's actually opposite icy Labrador.

Europe is also blessed with a large number of navigable rivers, scoured out of the landscape when the glaciers retreated at the end of the Ice Age. Most of Europe's major cities, as well as its factories, are on rivers, some of which are fed by the remnants of these glaciers.

Four land features dominate the European continent. Rugged highlands cover large parts of the British Isles, Brittany, Scandinavia, and the Iberian Peninsula. Here, glaciers scraped away most of the earth, leaving behind thin soil and barren rock. As a result, many of the people became herders and fishermen. These regions are some of the most sparsely settled in Europe.

The alpine mountain system lies across much of southern Europe, though not as a continuous range. The Pyrenees, Alps, Apennines, Balkans, Dinaric Alps, and Carpathians are the major mountain chains. Many peaks rise more than 10,000 feet (3,050 m) above sea level, and some reach 15,000 feet (4,570 m) or more. Breaks within these ranges are few, but those passes that do exist provide important routes through which settlers, traders, and armies have passed between southern and northern Europe. The alpine system is still geologically active, so that earthquakes and volcanic eruptions periodically shake southern Europe.

North of the Alps lies an upland zone of hilly, rugged plateaus that crosses central Europe. Great rivers, such as the Danube and the Rhine, have carved deep valleys. The rivers that flow here have long served as important routes for commerce. This region usually has cool temperatures and abundant rainfall—weather in which grasses and fodder crops thrive. Dairy and livestock farming are important enterprises. Because of rich mineral resources, this area is also a center of mining and industry.

The Northern European Plain stretches across the continent from the Pyrenees to the Ural Mountains. Many of the world's great cities and industrial areas have flourished here amid the gently rolling lowlands. Moderate temperatures and year-round light rains, together with rich soils, have allowed farmers in this part of Europe to be among the most productive in the world. They need to be, in order to help support one of the most densely populated regions on Earth. Though Europe covers only 7 percent of the world's land, it is home to more people than North and South America combined.

Dozens of ethnic groups speaking some 40 languages live in Europe, though not always in harmony. Open plains, mountain passes, and navigable rivers have allowed them to move freely across the continent. European

The headwaters of the Rhône River

The Cliffs of Moher on Ireland's west coast

civilization started with the ancient Greek and Roman cultures. Much of its history is the story of migrations, conquests, and retreats, as different cultures rose to power and then fell before the advance of a stronger group. As the Roman Empire waned, the spread of Christianity provided a common thread for the continent.

Over the centuries, strong military leaders have waged war in attempts to unify Europe under one banner, but without lasting success. Today, Europeans are taking a different route toward unity, letting politicians instead of generals lead the way. Twelve countries formed the European Community (EC): Belgium, Denmark, France, Greece, Ireland, Italy, Luxembourg, the Netherlands, Portugal, Spain, the United Kingdom, and West Germany. In 1990 the latter united with East Germany. By 1993 EC countries expect to have free trade and open borders between them.

Austria, Finland, Iceland, Norway, Sweden, and Switzerland are members of another group, the European Free Trade Association. They are negotiating trade agreements with the European Community, which would create a still larger economic body. With the rise of democracy in Eastern Europe, it is possible that former communist countries will eventually join such an alliance to form a loose but powerful federation.

Even before Europeans started forging new economic ties, they began facing up to their continent's rapidly deteriorating environment. Because winds and rivers carry pollutants across national boundaries, it is difficult to enforce environmental protection laws. Toxic chemicals dumped into rivers and streams contaminate drinking water. Automobiles and factories produce life-threatening smog. Scientists blame acid rain, produced by burning large amounts of coal as fuel in factories, for the widespread destruction of Europe's forests. In central Europe, barren plateaus stretch for more than 350 miles (565 km) where thick forests once stood. Germany's fabled Black Forest is dying, and the suspected cause is acid rain.

With the advances in economic cooperation have come discussions of how to meet these environmental challenges. Europe's countries have launched the decade of the 1990s by declaring a "green" war on pollution.

Austrian factories belch chemical-laden smoke.

Black Forest trees may be victims of acid rain.

Facts About Europe

Area: 4,065,945 sq mi (10,530,750 sq km)
Population: 715,233,800
Highest Point: Mount Elbrus, U.S.S.R., 18,510 ft (5,642 m) above sea level
Lowest Point: Caspian Sea, Europe-Asia, 92 ft (28 m) below sea level
Largest Countries: *(by area)*
   European U.S.S.R. 2,150,975 sq mi (5,571,000 sq km). France 210,026 sq mi (543,965 sq km)
Largest Countries: *(by population)*

European U.S.S.R.	216,556,000
Germany	78,048,000

Smallest Country: *(by area and population)*
  * Vatican City 0.2 sq mi (0.4 sq km); pop. 830
Largest Metropolitan Areas: *(by population)*

London, England	10,570,000
Moscow, U.S.S.R.	9,390,000
Paris, France	8,510,000

Longest Rivers: *(mi and km)*

Volga	2,194	3,531
Danube	1,776	2,858

Largest Lake: *(sq mi and sq km)*

Ladoga, U.S.S.R.	6,835	17,703

*World record

Glossary

autonomy—the right of self-government or freedom from external control.

city-state—an independent country made up of a city and sometimes the surrounding area.

dialect—a regional variety of a language.

duchy—the territory ruled by a duke or duchess.

fjord—a narrow, steep-sided ocean inlet that reaches far into a coastline.

geothermal power—energy provided by heat from inside the Earth.

hydroelectric power—electricity produced by capturing the energy of moving water.

maritime—bordering the sea; concerning navigation or commerce on the sea.

medieval—referring to a period of European history known as the Middle Ages, roughly from A.D. 500 to 1500.

monarchy—a government having undivided rule by a single person, such as a king or queen.

moor—an open expanse of rolling land covered with grass or other low vegetation.

parliament—a group of representatives who meet to discuss national affairs and make laws.

tartan—a plaid textile design usually associated with a distinctive Scottish clan.

ARCTIC CIRCLE

Akureyri

ICELAND

Egilsstadir

Thjorsa River

Vatnajokull

⊗ Reykjavik

Selfoss

ATLANTIC
OCEAN

Heimaey
Surtsey

Vik

FAROE ISLANDS
(DENMARK)

Streymoy

Torshavn   Sandoy

Suduroy

KILOMETERS   200

STATUTE MILES   150

For map legend see page 21.

North Cape

Hammerfest

Tromso

LAPLAND

Lofoten
Islands

Narvik

Kebnekaise
6,926 FEET
2,111 METERS

Kiruna

Tornio River

Kemi River

Vestfjorden

Bodo

Lule River

ARCTIC CIRCLE

Rovaniemi

SOVIET
UNION

NORWEGIAN
SEA

Kemi

Lulea

Oulu

Oulu
River

Angerman River

Ume River

Skelleftea

Namsen
River

Trondheimsfjorden

NORRLAND

Umea

FINLAND

Trondheim

Ornskoldsvik

Ostersund

Vaasa

Kuopio

Joensuu

Alesund

NORWAY

SWEDEN

Sundsvall

LAKE

Jyvaskyla

REGION

Savonlinna

Galdhopiggen
2,489 FEET
8,166 METERS

Lagen River

Glama River

Klar River

GULF
OF BOTHNIA

Tampere

Mikkeli

Lake
Saimaa

Lappeenranta

Sognefjorden

Dal River

Pori

Lahti

Bergen

Aland
Islands

Turku

⊗ Helsinki

Kotka

ATLANTIC

Haugesund

Drammen

⊗ Oslo

SVEALAND

Uppsala

GULF OF FINLAND

OCEAN

Stavanger

Karlstad

Vasteras

Lake
Malaren

⊗ Stockholm

Sklen

Lake
Vanern

Orebro

Kristiansand

SKAGERRAK

Norrkoping

Linkoping

NORTH
SEA

Goteborg

Lake
Vattern

Frederikshavn

Boras

Jonkoping

Visby

KATTEGAT

GOTALAND

Gotland

Alborg

DENMARK

Oland

BALTIC
SEA

JUTLAND

Arhus

Helsingborg

Karlskrona

Esbjerg

Copenhagen

Odense

Fyn

Malmo

ZEALAND

Bornholm

Lolland   Falster

GERMANY

Norway, Sweden, and
Denmark are referred to
jointly as **Scandinavia.**
Sometimes geographers
include Iceland and Fin-
land because of cultural
similarities. The entire
region is known as
Nordic Europe.
   The homeland of the
Saami people above the
Arctic Circle, called

Lapland, crosses political
boundaries. North, in the
Arctic Ocean, lie Jan Ma-
yen and Svalbard, island
territories that belong
to Norway (see map,
page 80).

Norway

Fifteen thousand years ago, Ice Age glaciers slowly ground across what is today Norway. On the seacoast they carved narrow, steep-sided valleys. When the ice eventually melted, the sea level rose and water flooded the valleys, creating fjords and a long, jagged coastline.

Most of Norway is mountainous, and about a quarter of it is covered by forest. Only 3 percent of the land is suitable for farming, much of it in the southeast. Farmers here raise livestock or grow potatoes and barley. A warm ocean current makes the climate temperate along the coast and especially in the south where most Norwegians live, mainly in urban areas. Chief among these is Norway's capital and largest city, Oslo, which is the country's leading industrial, financial, and transportation center.

About a third of Norway lies above the Arctic Circle. Here in the Land of the Midnight Sun, the sun is above the horizon 24 hours a day all summer. In winter it is never seen. The long, dark winters and rugged landscape may have sparked the imagination of storytellers long ago. Norse mythology from the ninth century tells of a family of gods battling hostile giants to protect humans. Rich folklore was succeeded by a literary tradition that produced writers such as the 19th-century playwright Henrik Ibsen.

The sea has always brought wealth to Norway. Its large merchant marine fleet carries cargo around the world. The warm ocean current keeps most harbors ice-free all year. Bergen was a major port and fish market when the Vikings lived there a thousand years ago. The ocean's latest gifts to Norway are oil and natural gas deposits under the North Sea. Since the mid-1970s they have accounted for about half of Norway's export income.

Today Norwegians live in one of the world's richest countries. The government provides free education and health care, and unemployment remains low. Every year more than 2,000 immigrants become Norwegian citizens.

Official name: *Kingdom of Norway*
Area: *125,182 sq mi (324,220 sq km)*
Population: *4,225,000*
Capital: *Oslo (pop. 445,357)*
Ethnic groups: *Norwegian, Saami (Lapp)*
Language: *Norwegian, Lappish*
Religious groups: *Lutheran*
Economy: *Agr: livestock, feed crops, potatoes, fruit, vegetables. Ind: oil, natural gas, food processing, paper products, machinery, metals, chemicals, fishing*
Currency: *Norwegian krone*

Denmark

Denmark is made up of the Jutland Peninsula and almost 500 islands, connected by a number of ferries and bridges. Throughout history, the country's geographic location has made it a crossroads for people and goods, its islands acting like stepping-stones between Europe and Scandinavia.

Low, rolling grasslands and a moist, mild climate allow the Danes to farm more than 70 percent of their country. Farmland is considered an important national asset. Before young farmers can purchase land, they must earn a farming license. Danish farmers have long specialized in exports, especially butter and other dairy products. They feed their pigs skim milk, a butter-making leftover. Another well-known Danish export is ham.

Despite their agricultural tradition, nearly a quarter of all Danes are employed in industry. A highly skilled work force manufactures a wide range of goods, but most raw materials must be imported. In recent years, products such as ships and diesel engines, furniture and silverware, delicate porcelain figures, and plastic Lego building blocks have accounted for more than 60 percent of the country's export income.

Most factories are near the capital, Copenhagen. More than one-fourth of the population lives in or around this eastern port. Here cargo is collected from vessels too large to enter the shallow Baltic Sea and transferred to smaller freighters. Overlooking Copenhagen's harbor is a statue of the Little Mermaid, a character from the works of the 19th-century Danish author, Hans Christian Andersen. "The Ugly Duckling" and his many other tales are told the world over.

Denmark ruled Nordic Europe 600 years ago. Today it only has two self-governing possessions in the North Atlantic—Greenland and the **Faroe Islands,** where fishing provides most of the export income. Only about 6 percent of the rocky archipelago is cultivated, chiefly for potatoes. Grass is another main crop, and a vital one since sheep greatly outnumber people.

Official name: *Kingdom of Denmark*
Area: *16,638 sq mi (43,092 sq km)*
Population: *5,133,000*
Capital: *Copenhagen (pop. 478,615)*
Ethnic groups: *Danish*
Language: *Danish*
Religious groups: *Lutheran*
Economy: *Agr: livestock, dairy products, grains, root crops. Ind: food processing, machinery, textiles, furs, chemicals, electronics, furniture, fishing*
Currency: *Danish krone*

Iceland

Even in winter's chill, Icelanders swim outdoors—in natural hot springs. The springs are heated by volcanoes of an undersea mountain chain called the Mid-Atlantic Ridge. Iceland, part of this chain, rises above the sea and is at the mercy of Earth's continual volcanic activity. Every five years, at least one of the country's 200 volcanoes erupts.

Icelanders make the most of life in an unstable environment. They tap geothermal energy to heat most of their homes, buildings, and swimming pools. Greenhouses give them vegetables, tropical fruit, and flowers year-round, defying the short subarctic growing season. Swift rivers supply 96 percent of their electric power.

About half the population lives in Reykjavik, the capital city. The rest graze sheep and cattle on farms in scattered coastal valleys or live in fishing villages. Because less than 2 percent of the island can be farmed, Icelanders have always turned to the sea to make a living. Iceland's economy depends on fishing, which earns about 70 percent of its export income.

Official name: *Republic of Iceland*
Area: *39,769 sq mi (103,000 sq km)*
Population: *251,000*
Capital: *Reykjavik (pop. 91,497)*
Ethnic groups: *Icelander*
Language: *Icelandic*
Religious groups: *Lutheran*
Economy: *Agr: livestock, hay, potatoes, turnips. Ind: fishing, aluminum, ferrosilicon, wool*
Currency: *Icelandic krona*

Sweden

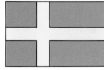

Alfred Nobel, the Swede who invented dynamite in 1866, established the Nobel Peace Prize to help make amends for his destructive creation. His explosives empire marked Sweden's beginning as an industrial nation. By 1890, when industry finally brought prosperity, one million Swedes had emigrated to Wisconsin, Minnesota, and Illinois.

Since then Sweden has exploited its natural resources of iron ore, timber, and waterpower. Today the country is a leader in industry, helped by its powerful northern rivers that generate inexpensive hydroelectricity. The heart of Swedish economy is steel production. Near the Arctic town of Kiruna, huge iron ore deposits supply the factories that manufacture automobiles, machinery, and ships. Timber from the country's extensive forests provides lumber for furniture and wood pulp for newsprint. Forest products account for over a fourth of Sweden's exports.

Much of the northern work force is composed of Saami, or Lapps, an ethnic group that lives north of the Arctic Circle. Traditionally the Saami moved across Lapland herding their reindeer. Now many work in mining and forestry.

Although less than 8 percent of Sweden is suitable for agriculture, its farms furnish nearly all its food. Much of the fertile land is in the south where the climate is mildest. Here farmers raise livestock for dairy products and meat, and grow sugar beets, potatoes, wheat, and barley.

Most major cities and industrial centers are in the south, too. Stockholm, the capital and largest city, is built on a group of islands and is a leading port on the Baltic Sea. Here 90 percent of the residents live in apartments. Even though there is ample land for single homes, large buildings that house many people are more economical to heat during the frigid winters.

In the midst of winter, when the sun shines no more than six hours, one day is devoted to St. Lucia, the patron saint of light. On December 13, girls wear crowns of lighted candles and everyone celebrates the coming of longer days.

Official name: *Kingdom of Sweden*
Area: *173,732 sq mi (449,964 sq km)*
Population: *8,462,000*
Capital: *Stockholm (pop. 666,810)*
Ethnic groups: *Swedish, Finnish, Saami (Lapp)*
Language: *Swedish, Finnish, Lappish*
Religious groups: *Lutheran*
Economy: *Agr: livestock, grains, sugar beets, potatoes. Ind: iron, steel, machinery, electronics, wood products, paper, food processing, chemicals, fishing*
Currency: *Swedish krona*

Finland

Finland's location between Sweden and the Soviet Union makes it a border country between Western and Eastern Europe. Dominated by Sweden for almost 700 years, Finland became part of Russia in 1809, then declared independence in 1917. Many Swedish customs remain and, along with Finnish, Swedish is an official language.

Unlike most other European peoples, the Finns came from what is now west-central Siberia in the Soviet Union. Probably around 2,000 years ago they settled the town of Turku. Most Finns still live in this region on the southwestern coastal plain, primarily in cities. Helsinki, the capital, is Finland's busiest port.

The southwest is also where Finland's best farmland lies. Farmers raise livestock for dairy products and meat, providing all the country's needs. They also grow potatoes and the hardy grains of rye, barley, and oats for domestic use. Finland has a short growing season, so most fruit and vegetables must be imported.

Forests of spruce, pine, and birch that cover about two-thirds of Finland are its greatest resource. Paper, wood, and pulp earn more than a third of its export income. Timber is also an important source of energy. Peat bogs provide some fuel, and rivers furnish hydroelectric power. Most of the country's rivers flow from the 55,000 or more lakes that glaciers have carved throughout Finland.

Lacking natural gas and oil, Finland relies heavily on the Soviet Union for these sources of energy. In turn, the Soviets import entire Finnish factories. One-fifth of Finland's foreign trade is with its eastern neighbor.

With snow on the ground for almost six months, Finns begin skiing at a young age. Schoolchildren get a February ski holiday, and they can attend the national winter sports festival held in the city of Lahti. Traditionally Finns relax after rigorous activity in a sauna, a small wooden room heated by water sizzling on hot stones. One sauna exists for every five Finns.

Official name: *Republic of Finland*
Area: *130,558 sq mi (338,145 sq km)*
Population: *4,953,000*
Capital: *Helsinki (pop. 487,521)*
Ethnic groups: *Finnish, Swedish, Saami (Lapp)*
Language: *Finnish, Swedish*
Religious groups: *Lutheran*
Economy: *Agr: livestock, grains, sugar beets, potatoes. Ind: wood and paper products, metals, electronics, food processing, textiles, chemicals, machinery*
Currency: *markka*

1 *Iceland*

2 *Iceland*

Iceland

1 *Bathers take advantage of naturally heated waters at a geothermal electric plant near Reykjavik, the country's capital.*

2 *A couple shares the task of turning Icelandic wool into distinctively patterned sweaters. This profitable cottage industry helps pass the time during long winter evenings.*

1 *Denmark*

Denmark

1 *Amid the warm glow of Christmas candles, an artist paints a dish with a Royal Copenhagen pattern dating back to 1775.*

Norway

2 *A 12th-century stave church stands on the coast of the Sognefjorden in western Norway. Staves, or wooden posts, form the interior framework of the building.*

Finland

3 *Helsinki's Western Harbor is one of five that make up Finland's biggest seaport. Its shipyards specialize in building icebreakers that keep sea-lanes open in winter.*

Sweden

4 *Actors perform in the public square of Stockholm's Old Town, Gamla Stan, where buildings are centuries old.*

5 *A Saami reindeer race draws a crowd in northern Sweden. Reindeer herding was the traditional livelihood of the Saami, but few of them still follow this occupation.*

2 *Norway*

3 *Finland*

4 *Sweden*

5 *Sweden*

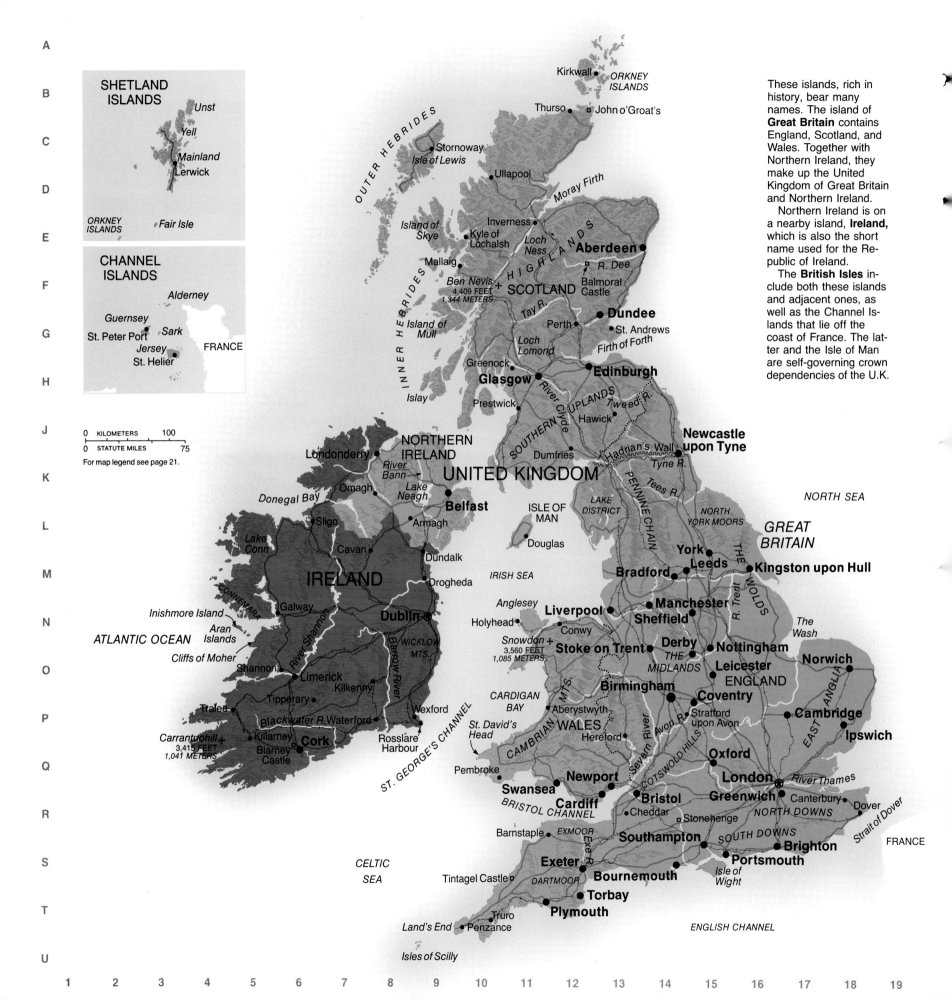

SHETLAND ISLANDS

Unst
Yell
Mainland
Lerwick

ORKNEY ISLANDS
Fair Isle

CHANNEL ISLANDS

Alderney
Guernsey
St. Peter Port   Sark
Jersey
St. Helier   FRANCE

0   KILOMETERS   100
0   STATUTE MILES   75

For map legend see page 21.

These islands, rich in history, bear many names. The island of **Great Britain** contains England, Scotland, and Wales. Together with Northern Ireland, they make up the United Kingdom of Great Britain and Northern Ireland.

Northern Ireland is on a nearby island, **Ireland,** which is also the short name used for the Republic of Ireland.

The **British Isles** include both these islands and adjacent ones, as well as the Channel Islands that lie off the coast of France. The latter and the Isle of Man are self-governing crown dependencies of the U.K.

ORKNEY ISLANDS
Kirkwall
Thurso   John o'Groat's

OUTER HEBRIDES
Stornoway
Isle of Lewis
Ullapool
Moray Firth
Island of Skye
Inverness
Kyle of Lochalsh
Loch Ness
Aberdeen
Mallaig
Ben Nevis
4,409 FEET
1,344 METERS
HIGHLANDS
R. Dee
Balmoral Castle
Island of Mull
SCOTLAND
Tay R.
Dundee
Perth
St. Andrews
INNER HEBRIDES
Loch Lomond
Firth of Forth
Greenock
Edinburgh
Glasgow
Islay
Prestwick
River Clyde
SOUTHERN UPLANDS
Tweed R.
Hawick

NORTHERN IRELAND
Londonderry
River Bann
UNITED KINGDOM
Dumfries
Hadrian's Wall
Newcastle upon Tyne
Tyne R.
Omagh
Lake Neagh
PENNINE CHAIN
Tees R.
Belfast
Armagh
ISLE OF MAN
LAKE DISTRICT
NORTH YORK MOORS
Sligo
Lake Conn
Cavan
Dundalk
Douglas
GREAT BRITAIN
IRELAND
Drogheda
IRISH SEA
York
THE WOLDS
CONNEMARA
Bradford
Leeds
Kingston upon Hull
Galway
River Shannon
Dublin
Anglesey
Liverpool
Manchester
R. Trent
Inishmore Island
Holyhead
Sheffield
The Wash
Aran Islands
WICKLOW MTS.
Conwy
ATLANTIC OCEAN
Cliffs of Moher
Snowdon
3,560 FEET
1,085 METERS
Stoke on Trent
Derby
Nottingham
Norwich
Shannon
Barrow River
THE MIDLANDS
Leicester
Limerick
Kilkenny
ENGLAND
Tipperary
Birmingham
Coventry
EAST ANGLIA
CARDIGAN BAY
Aberystwyth
Cambridge
Tralee
Wexford
Stratford upon Avon
Carrantuohill
3,415 FEET
1,041 METERS
Blackwater R.
Waterford
CAMBRIAN MTS.
Avon R.
Ipswich
Killarney
Rosslare Harbour
WALES
Severn River
Oxford
Blarney Castle
Cork
St. David's Head
Hereford
COTSWOLD HILLS
London
Pembroke
Newport
Greenwich
River Thames
ST. GEORGE'S CHANNEL
Swansea
Canterbury
Cardiff
Bristol
NORTH DOWNS
Dover
BRISTOL CHANNEL
Cheddar
Stonehenge
Strait of Dover
Barnstaple
EXMOOR
SOUTH DOWNS
FRANCE
CELTIC SEA
EXETER
Exe R.
Southampton
Brighton
Exeter
DARTMOOR
Bournemouth
Portsmouth
Tintagel Castle
Isle of Wight
Torbay
NORTH SEA
Land's End
Truro
Plymouth
Penzance
ENGLISH CHANNEL

Isles of Scilly

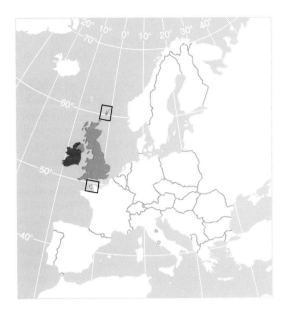

includes James Joyce and George Bernard Shaw. Efforts have long been under way to preserve the Irish language, which is spoken today only in parts of the far west and south of Ireland.

Official name: *Republic of Ireland*
Area: *27,137 sq mi (70,284 sq km)*
Population: *3,547,000*
Capital: *Dublin (pop. 525,360; met. pop. 915,115)*
Ethnic groups: *Irish, English*
Language: *English, Irish*
Religious groups: *Roman Catholic*
Economy: *Agr: livestock, barley, potatoes, sugar beets, wheat. Ind: food processing, electronics, chemicals, textiles, machinery, tourism, glass, fishing*
Currency: *Irish pound*

Ireland

Shaped like a saucer with a wide rim of hills, the Emerald Isle looks lush and inviting from the air. The landscape is nourished by limestone that lies just under the soil and by constant rain and mist.

The Republic of Ireland, formerly ruled by the United Kingdom, won independence in 1922. Predominantly Roman Catholic, the republic occupies five-sixths of the island that also holds Northern Ireland. The latter, mostly Protestant, chose to remain with the U.K.

Ireland's eastern half contains most of the country's people, cities, and industry. Some 890 foreign companies have invested in factories here. Dublin, the capital, is the manufacturing, publishing, and communications center, and home to a quarter of the people. Waterford in the south is famous for its fine crystal.

In the midlands farmers chiefly raise cattle. Dry periods are too short here for grain to ripen, but it grows in the drier east. The country's damp climate was partly responsible for the Great Potato Famine of the 1840s. Infected by a fungus, the staple crop rotted in the ground. Starving Irish left by the thousands, most of them emigrating to the United States.

In the west, sheep farms and peat bogs give way to a mountainous landscape that in places drops down sheer cliffs to the sea. One-seventh of Ireland is covered with peat, a spongy, partially decayed moss that is used as a fuel source.

The Irish are blessed with a gift for language. Their large share of world-renowned writers

United Kingdom

Famed for much of its history as an island fortress, Great Britain hasn't always been an island. In prehistoric times it was connected to continental Europe. Stone Age hunters could walk there. Eventually the sea rose and successive groups of Celts, Romans, Anglo-Saxons, Vikings, and Normans sailed across the English Channel or the North Sea to Great Britain and Ireland. Regional cultures evolved into the countries of England, Scotland, Wales, and Ireland, which merged as the United Kingdom in 1801. The Republic of Ireland won its independence in 1922.

London, near the mouth of the Thames, has been the country's economic center since Roman times and remains one of the largest financial and commercial centers in the world. It is the seat of a parliamentary democracy. While a king or queen reigns in the United Kingdom, the country is governed by a parliament of elected members (the House of Commons) and hereditary or lifetime peers (the House of Lords). Ceremony is a trademark of this great capital.

The Thames, Great Britain's longest river, wanders through lowlands that cover the southeast—a pleasant land of rolling hills and patchwork fields bordered by hedges, stone fences, and rows of trees. Resort towns line the south coast from Dover to the wild cliffs and countryside of Land's End. The country's best cropland lies in the southeast. Only about 2 percent of the work force is employed in farming, so the United Kingdom must import much of its food.

The most crowded region of this densely populated country besides Greater London and the southeast is the Midlands. Here the industrial revolution began in the 1700s. Iron and steel, textile, shipbuilding, and coal industries thrived

in northern England, Scotland, and Wales, aided by raw materials from the former British Empire. About a quarter of the work force remains in industry, but foreign competition has led to decline, creating serious unemployment.

North of the Pennines, the country's mountain backbone, beyond the Scottish Southern Uplands, lie Scotland's lowlands and two largest cities, Edinburgh and Glasgow. Most of Scotland's people, farmland, and industry are found here. Still farther north stretch the windswept Scottish Highlands, with their heather-covered moors, deep lakes, or lochs, and few trees. Inhabitants raise sheep or fish the seas. The North Sea oil boom near Aberdeen has brought prosperity, but also the threat of pollution to fishing grounds and coastal wildlife.

In mountainous Wales the few people who live in the north tend sheep or quarry for limestone and slate. Most of the Welsh live along the coast or in the green valleys of the south, center of a large but now struggling coal industry. Wales is renowned for its poets and singers, who kept the mythology of the Celts alive for centuries before a written language existed.

Across the Irish Sea is Northern Ireland, a countryside of gentle mountains, valleys, and fertile lowlands. Its livestock and dairy products are exported to Great Britain and Europe, while Irish tweed and linen produced in Londonderry are famous worldwide. Belfast is its major city and port. Northern Ireland's Protestant majority chose in 1922 to stay under British rule when the Republic of Ireland split away, but the Catholic minority feels strongly that all of Ireland should be united. The two groups have clashed repeatedly, with tragic loss of life.

The English Channel, nature's moat protecting the island fortress, has long given the British a sense of national identity. But since joining the European Community in 1973, the United Kingdom has looked more and more to Europe for trade. A man-made link, a Channel tunnel scheduled to open in 1993, will once more join the island of Great Britain to the rest of Europe.

Official name: *United Kingdom of Great Britain and Northern Ireland*
Area: *94,248 sq mi (244,100 sq km)*
Population: *57,265,000*
Capital: *London (met. pop. 10,570,000)*
Ethnic groups: *English, Scottish, Irish, Welsh*
Language: *English, Welsh, Gaelic*
Religious groups: *Protestant, Roman Catholic*
Economy: *Agr: wheat, barley, potatoes, sugar beets, livestock. Ind: metals, machinery, oil, coal, banking, textiles, chemicals, clothing, electronics, motor vehicles, aircraft, shipbuilding, food processing, fishing.*
Currency: *pound sterling*

1 *England, U.K.*

United Kingdom

1 *Senior judges in ceremonial dress gather at the Palace of Westminster in London for the State Opening of Parliament.*

2 *A familiar London landmark, the Tower Bridge has spanned the River Thames since completion in 1894.*

3 *Coal dust blackens the face of a miner in Rhondda Valley, heart of the Welsh mining industry, which lies outside Cardiff.*

4 *Surrounded by piles of Scottish tartans, a worker stacks up cloth in a cloth-finishing factory at Hawick, a thriving wool center.*

Ireland

5 *A glass cutter touches up a sample of the fine glassware for which Waterford has been famous since the 18th century.*

6 *Stone walls on Inishmore Island protect man-made soil of sand and seaweed, which transforms barren rock to fertile fields.*

2 *England, U.K.*

3 *Wales, U.K.*

4 *Scotland, U.K.*

5 *Ireland*

6 *Ireland*

A B C D E F G H J K L M N O P Q R S T U

1 2 3 4 5 6 7 8 9 10 11 12 13 14 15 16 17 18

DENMARK

Sylt

North Frisian Islands

BALTIC SEA

● Flensburg

Kiel Bay *Fehmarn* *Rugen*

Helgoland

● **Kiel** Stralsund ●

Usedom

Rostock ●

NORTH SEA

Lubeck ● Wismar Neubrandenburg ●

MECKLENBURG

P O M E R A N I A

East Frisian Islands

Bremerhaven ● Schwerin ●

West Frisian Islands Emden ●

Wilhelmshaven ●

Hamburg

Lake Muritz

Groningen ●

F R I E S L A N D

Oldenburg ●

Bremen ●

E U R O P E A N P L A N

Elbe River

Oder River

POLAND

NETHERLANDS

● Edam *Elevoland Polder*

Ems River

Weser River

Wolfsburg ● Brandenburg ●

Berlin ●

BRANDENBURG

Frankfurt an der Oder

IJsselmeer

Mittelland Canal

Haarlem ●

Amsterdam ● **Enschede**

Hannover ●

Braunschweig ●

Magdeburg ●

Potsdam

Leiden ●

Osnabruck ●

The Hague ● Delft ● **Utrecht** ●

Arnhem ●

Munster ●

Bielefeld ●

HARZ MOUNTAINS

Dessau ●

Cottbus ●

Rotterdam ●

WESTPHALIA

Barrier dam →

Dordrecht ● **Nijmegen** ●

Rhine

Hamm ●

Gottingen ● Stolberg ●

Halle ●

Neisse R.

Oosterschelde →

Maas River

Essen ● **Dortmund** ●

Ruhr River

Saale R.

Leipzig ●

Eindhoven ●

Duisburg ●

Wuppertal ●

Kassel ●

S A X O N Y

Ostend ● **Brugge** ● **Antwerp** ● **Dusseldorf** ●

Gent ●

Fulda

Erfurt ●

Gera ● **Chemnitz** ●

Dresden ●

Gorlitz

FLANDERS

Schelde River

BELGIUM

Monchen-Gladbach ●

Koln ●

GERMANY

Gotha ● **Jena** ●

ORE MOUNTAINS

Brussels ●

Bonn ●

Zwickau ●

Waterloo ●

Aachen ●

Werra River

Plauen ●

Charleroi ●

Liege ●

EIFEL

Namur ●

ARDENNES

Koblenz ●

River

CZECHOSLOVAKIA

LUXEMBOURG

Mosel River

Wiesbaden ● **Frankfurt am Main** ●

Main River

Bamberg ●

B O H E M I A N F O R E S T

Mainz ● **Darmstadt** ● **Wurzburg** ●

Esch ● Luxembourg ●

Mannheim ●

FRANCE

Saarbrucken ● **Heidelberg** ●

Nurnberg ●

Heilbronn ●

Regensburg ●

Karlsruhe ●

BAVARIA

JURA

Danube River

Stuttgart ●

BLACK FOREST

Neckar River

SWABIAN

Ulm ●

Augsburg ●

Inn River

Rhine River

Munich ●

Freiburg ●

Neuschwanstein Castle ▫

BAVARIAN ALPS

Lake Constance

Garmisch-Partenkirchen ●

SWITZERLAND

+ *Zugspitze* 9,719 FEET 2,962 METERS

AUSTRIA

This map shows the boundaries of the recent-ly reunited country of **Germany.** Soon after World War II ended, the victorious Allied powers split Germany into East Germany and West Ger-many. The two agreed to reunification in 1990.

On July 1 the Germa-nys merged their econo-mies. A treaty signed with the former Allies completed the prelimi-naries, and full political union was achieved on October 3.

0   KILOMETERS   100

0   STATUTE MILES   75

For map legend see page 21.

Dutch are able to export cheese, vegetables, and flowers. Their most beloved export, though, may be the tradition of a December visit from St. Nicholas—Sinterklaas. In the United States, this saint's nickname is Santa Claus.

Official name: *Kingdom of the Netherlands*
Area: *16,023 sq mi (41,499 sq km)*
Population: *14,850,000*
Capital: *Amsterdam (pop. 677,360)*
The Hague, seat of government (pop. 444,313)
Ethnic groups: *Dutch*
Language: *Dutch*
Religious groups: *Roman Catholic, Protestant*
Economy: *Agr: livestock, flowers, grains, potatoes, sugar beets. Ind: food processing, chemicals, oil, metal products, natural gas, machinery, electronics*
Currency: *Netherlands guilder*

Netherlands

Netherlands means "the lowlands," and true to its name nearly half of this small, flat country lies below sea level. Over the centuries the Dutch have learned how to protect their land and how to reclaim more from the sea.

They stabilized the natural sand dunes along the coasts and built dikes to keep the sea out. Then they cut ditches and canals for drainage and pumped the wetlands dry. Once run by windmills, pumps are now driven by steam and electricity. Polders, drained lands claimed from the sea, have rich soil for farming, but the Dutch must balance many needs. Factories, airports, and even towns are built on polders.

Without sea defenses, high tides would flood almost half the country twice a day. The latest engineering feat, the Delta Project completed in 1986, built four huge barriers to keep the North Sea from overflowing the estuary of the Rhine, Maas, and Schelde Rivers during storms.

In the 17th century the Netherlands was a leading sea power, and world trade brought riches. Historic cities such as Amsterdam, Leiden, Delft, and The Hague preserve the art and architecture of this golden age. Still an active trading country, the Netherlands has the world's busiest port at Rotterdam.

The Netherlands is one of the world's most densely populated countries. The Dutch use space cleverly. Houses one room wide rise four stories; apartments span highways. High technology makes small farms so productive that the

Belgium

Belgium's lowlands have been a battleground over the centuries. Most recently, British and American troops fought the Germans there in World War II. From a wide coastal plain the land rolls gently upward to the hilly Ardennes region.

Ruled at times by Spain, Austria, France, or the Netherlands, Belgium won independence from the Dutch in 1830. The country remains divided: In the south live French-speaking Walloons, and in the north dwell Dutch-speaking Flemings. Rivalry is so intense that each group insists on having its own regional government in addition to national rule. By law Brussels, the capital, is bilingual. Its street signs and official documents are printed in both languages.

Though split at home, Belgium promotes unity in Europe. After World War II, Belgium, the Netherlands, and Luxembourg formed Benelux, an economic alliance for tax-free trade. This was the forerunner of the European Community, a Western European trade organization with headquarters in Brussels.

Located near the industrial regions of France, Germany, and the Netherlands, Belgium has long been a trade center. One of the first European countries to industrialize in the 1800s, Belgium has since had a strong manufacturing economy, fed by large coal deposits. As aging factories and mines close in the south and the northern Flemish birthrate exceeds that of the southern Walloons, Belgium's economic power is shifting north, increasing regional tensions.

Most Belgians live in crowded urban areas. The old cities, such as Gent, Brugge, Liège,

and the port of Antwerp (an important diamond-cutting center), charm tourists with the architecture of their medieval buildings.

Official name: *Kingdom of Belgium*
Area: *11,783 sq mi (30,518 sq km)*
Population: *9,886,000*
Capital: *Brussels (pop. 139,678; met. pop. 973,500)*
Ethnic groups: *Fleming, Walloon, mixed*
Language: *Dutch, French, German*
Religious groups: *Roman Catholic*
Economy: *Agr: livestock, grains, sugar beets, potatoes, flax. Ind: metals, chemicals, food processing, textiles, glass, oil, coal, motor vehicles, diamonds*
Currency: *Belgian franc*

Luxembourg

The Grand Duchy of Luxembourg began as a castle built in 963 on a rocky cliff, once the site of a Roman fort. Walled towns grew up around the castle, turning the area into a strong fortress whose rulers won great power in the Middle Ages. Today Luxembourg survives as one of Europe's smallest countries. Bordered by Belgium, Germany, and France, the duchy is only 51 miles (82 km) long and 35 miles (56 km) wide.

Scenic forests and deep river valleys in the north give way to the Bon Pays, or "good land," a farming region where wheat, oats, potatoes, and livestock flourish. Along the Mosel River, wine grapes grow in terraced vineyards. Iron ore deposits in the south, which once supported Luxembourg's iron and steel industry, are nearly gone; today most raw materials must be imported from France. The capital city, also called Luxembourg, is an international financial center where more than 100 banks have branches.

Luxembourg has three official languages: French and German (used in schools, government, and the press), and Letzeburgish, a Germanic dialect used in conversation. In crowded cities that mix modern and medieval buildings, Luxembourgers enjoy a high standard of living. Not surprisingly, their national anthem proclaims, "We want to remain what we are."

Official name: *Grand Duchy of Luxembourg*
Area: *998 sq mi (2,586 sq km)*
Population: *376,000*
Capital: *Luxembourg (pop. 78,900)*
Ethnic groups: *Luxembourger, Portuguese, Italian*
Language: *Letzeburgish, French, German*
Religious groups: *Roman Catholic*
Economy: *Agr: grains, livestock, potatoes, grapes. Ind: banking, iron, steel, food processing, chemicals*
Currency: *Luxembourg franc*

Germany

A reunited Germany. The tremendous political changes that swept Eastern Europe in 1989 and 1990 brought in their wake the reunification of East and West Germany. Berlin became once more the official German capital.

In a dramatic move in 1989, the East German communist government opened the Berlin Wall. For the first time since 1961, East Germans could pass freely into West Berlin. East German demonstrators had already been demanding political freedom and an end to the harsh life of communist rule. Within weeks the Communist Party leaders resigned and free elections were held. Soon the newly elected East German government started making plans with West German leaders to reunite the Germanys. Unification took place on October 3, and all-German elections followed in December.

The German people have played a key role in history for many centuries, but Germany was previously united as a country for only 74 years. A group of diverse states joined together in 1871 to form Germany. It grew into a strong industrial and military power but was defeated in two world wars. After World War II, the four Allied countries divided Germany into four sectors.

In 1949 the area controlled by the United States, France, and the United Kingdom became the Federal Republic of Germany, or West Germany. A communist state known as the German Democratic Republic, or East Germany, was created out of the German lands occupied by Soviet forces. The border between the two Germanys ran south from Lübeck to just beyond the Werra River, then cut east toward Plauen.

The capital, Berlin, was divided, too. East Germany made East Berlin its capital. West Germany, while maintaining ties with West Berlin, set up a separate capital in Bonn. In 1961 East Germans built the Berlin Wall.

Berlin, Germany's largest city, stands on the Northern European Plain and has long been the focal point of the northeast. Urban centers of the northwest include Hamburg, the second largest city and an important port. Near the North and Baltic Seas, lakes and marshes punctuate a landscape scattered with large moraines. The soil here is better suited to pasture than cultivation. On the southern edge of the plain, windblown dust and silt called loess creates fertile soil for farms. Small but productive farms were typical of West Germany, while large collectives were the rule in East Germany.

West Germany had risen from the ruins of World War II to become one of the world's top economic powers. Its hardworking and well-educated citizens, helped by about two million "guest workers," mostly from Turkey, Italy, and Yugoslavia, made it one of the most important trading nations in the world. At its heart stood Frankfurt, an international banking center, where a cathedral and town hall dating back to the Middle Ages rise in a cityscape of modern skyscrapers. Frankfurt is located on the Main River, a tributary of the Rhine. The Rhine, flowing on through Germany's chief industrial belt, is Europe's major commercial waterway.

The Ruhr River Valley, in western Germany, is the most heavily industrialized region in Europe, producing coal, steel, and other goods such as chemicals and automobiles. In the east, swift streams in the central uplands provide hydroelectric power for one of Europe's most important textile industries based in Chemnitz, formerly known as Karl Marx Stadt. Germany's industrial regions are some of the continent's most polluted areas.

Pollution may well be affecting the fabled Black Forest in the southwest, home of German legends and fairy tales. Rugged mountains covered with dark fir trees give the area its name. In recent years large numbers of trees have died, the suspected cause being acid rain.

The Danube River flows east from the Black Forest toward Bavaria, the largest state in southern Germany. Bavaria's capital and industrial center, Munich, is famed for its beer gardens and Oktoberfest, a 16-day annual spree of feasting and beer-drinking. To the south, the Bavarian Alps rise above dairy farms, bogs, and sparkling glacial lakes. Here, perched high on a steep crag, sits ornate Neuschwanstein Castle, built in the 19th century by King Ludwig II, patron of the German composer Richard Wagner.

Germany's borders encompass a wealth of resources and Europe's largest population outside the Soviet Union. The Berlin Wall became the symbol of a divided Germany. Opening the Wall signaled the end to that division. Germany now has the potential to help bridge the former divisions between Eastern and Western Europe.

Official name: *Federal Republic of Germany*
Area: *137,857 sq mi (357,046 sq km)*
Population: *78,048,000*
Capital: *Berlin (pop. 3,102,500)*
Ethnic groups: *German*
Language: *German*
Religious groups: *Protestant, Roman Catholic*
Economy: *Agr: grains, potatoes, sugar beets, fruit, livestock. Ind: iron, steel, motor vehicles, machinery, chemicals, electronics, cement, shipbuilding, coal, machine tools, food processing, textiles, beer, wine*
Currency: *Deutsche mark*

1 *Germany*

2 *Belgium*

4 *Netherlands*

Germany

1 *A German gymnast performs on the high bar. Between 1968 and 1990 East and West Germany competed separately in the Olympics, but now they will be united.*

Belgium

2 *A Godiva worker applies drops of chocolate to fondant-covered cherries. The Brussels-based company is known worldwide.*

Germany

3 *Built in the 19th century for "Mad" King Ludwig II, Neuschwanstein Castle embodied his fantasy of the ideal castle. It inspired the one at Disneyland.*

Netherlands

4 *Street-straddling apartments solve Rotterdam's limited space problem. The city has been largely rebuilt since World War II.*

3 *Germany*

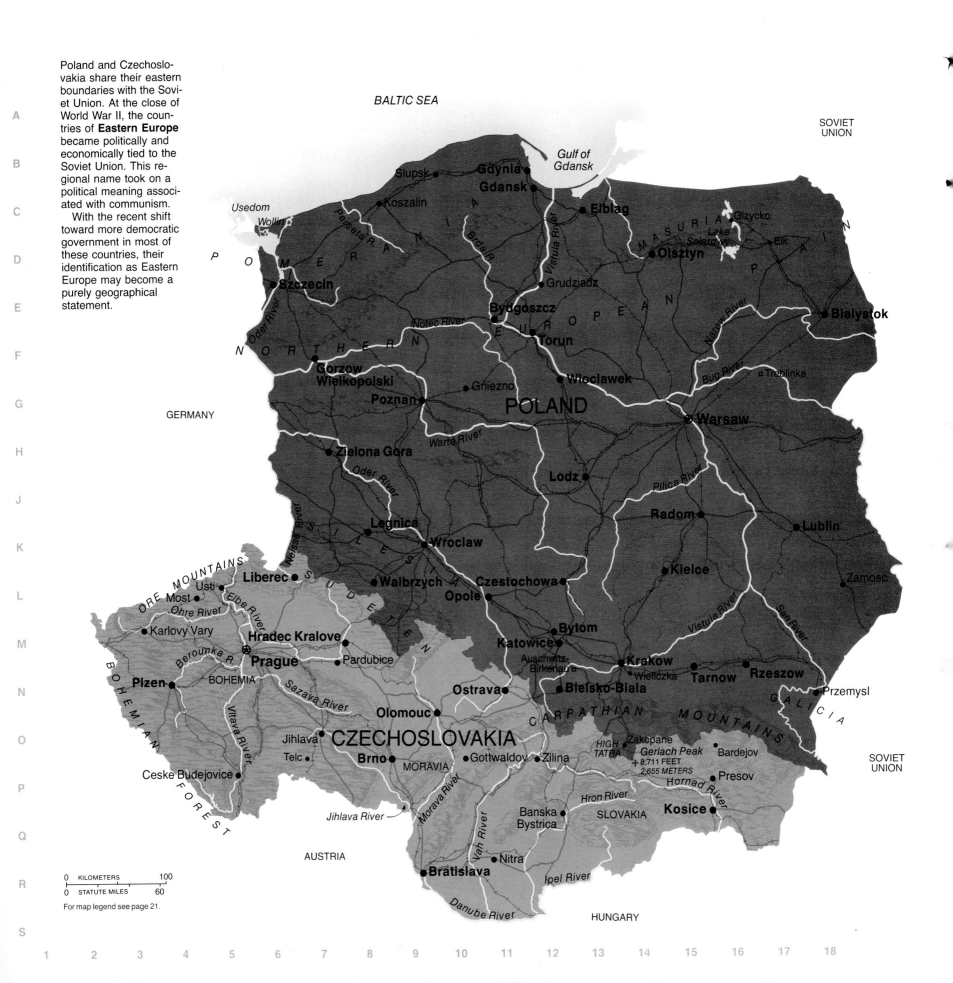

Poland and Czechoslovakia share their eastern boundaries with the Soviet Union. At the close of World War II, the countries of **Eastern Europe** became politically and economically tied to the Soviet Union. This regional name took on a political meaning associated with communism.

With the recent shift toward more democratic government in most of these countries, their identification as Eastern Europe may become a purely geographical statement.

BALTIC SEA

SOVIET UNION

Gulf of Gdansk

Gdynia
Gdansk
Slupsk
Koszalin
Elblag
Gizycko
Lake Sniardwy
Elk

Usedom
Wollin
Olsztyn

MASURIA

Szczecin

Grudziadz

Bialystok

Parseta R.
Brda R.
Vistula River

Bydgoszcz

Notec River
Torun

Narew River

Bug River
Treblinka

Gorzow Wielkopolski

Wloclawek

Gniezno

POLAND

Poznan

Warsaw

GERMANY

Warta River

Zielona Gora
Oder River

Lodz
Pilica River

Legnica
Wroclaw

Radom
Lublin

Ore Mountains
Liberec
Usti
Most
Ohre River
Karlovy Vary

SUDETEN

Walbrzych
Opole

Czestochowa

Kielce

Zamosc

Elbe River

Hradec Kralove
Pardubice

Bytom
Katowice
Krakow
Auschwitz-Birkenau
Wieliczka

Vistula River

San River

Prague
Berounka R.

BOHEMIA

Ostrava

Tarnow

Rzeszow

Bielsko-Biala

GALICIA

Przemysl

Plzen

Sazava River

Vltava River

Olomouc

CZECHOSLOVAKIA

CARPATHIAN MOUNTAINS

SOVIET UNION

Jihlava
Telc

Brno

MORAVIA

Gottwaldov
Zilina

Zakopane
HIGH TATRA
Gerlach Peak
+ 8,711 FEET
2,655 METERS

Bardejov
Presov

Ceske Budejovice

Jihlava River

Morava River

Vah River

Banska Bystrica

Hron River

SLOVAKIA

Kosice

Hornad River

BOHEMIAN FOREST

Nitra

Ipel River

Bratislava

Danube River

AUSTRIA

HUNGARY

Poland

Although Communists controlled Poland for more than 40 years after World War II, Poles never accepted communism. Ours is like a radish, they'd say: red on the outside only. The Poles' love of freedom and strong ties to the Roman Catholic Church and to Western Europe kept communism from profoundly changing their society. Peasant resistance to Soviet-style collective farms left most of their land in private hands.

Situated on the huge Northern European Plain, Poland is protected by the Baltic Sea in the north and the Carpathian Mountains in the south, but lies open to east and west. It has been an easy target for invading armies since its founding in the tenth century, when a Christian ruler united groups of Slavs living between the Vistula and Oder Rivers. In the late 1700s, Prussia, Austria, and Russia carved up Poland and wiped it off the map.

In 1918 Poland became a nation again, but not for long. Twenty-one years later, Hitler's German troops overran it in an invasion that started World War II. Poland suffered greatly during the war. At least six million Poles died, many in notorious concentration camps such as Treblinka and Auschwitz-Birkenau. Large areas of the country were destroyed. Warsaw, the capital since 1596, was reduced to ashes and rubble.

After peace came in 1945, the Poles rebuilt their historic capital, using old paintings and photographs for guidance. Modern Warsaw sprang up around it. Today factories sprawl on its outskirts, and farms beyond produce fruit and flowers. Crops of rye are raised in northern and central Poland and wheat in the south. Potatoes, the chief staple, grow all over.

Poland's troubles did not end in 1945. The Soviet Union annexed provinces in eastern Poland and gave the country western lands belonging to defeated Germany, thus sliding Poland westward like a piece in a board game. Millions of people were forced to migrate, and the population shrank to a postwar low of about 24 million.

Poland's population has risen a dramatic 58 percent since the war. The increase has chiefly been in towns and cities, reflecting the Communists' strong push for industrialization. The most valuable lands acquired in 1945 contain the Silesian coalfields. These and other rich mineral deposits in the south and southwest have fueled an enormous growth in shipbuilding, engineering, and automobile and chemical plants. But the heavy industries were developed at the cost of frequent shortages in food and consumer goods; and with industrialization has come some of the worst water and air pollution in Europe.

In 1980, with the value of wages dropping and food prices soaring, industrial workers led by Lech Walesa formed Solidarity, the first free postwar trade union in Eastern Europe. The government banned the union. Then, in the space of a stunning four months in 1989, it gave in to pressures for open elections, and a Solidarity leader became prime minister. The new government has taken on the immense challenge of transforming the rigid communist economic system into a more flexible capitalist one.

Official name: *Republic of Poland*
Area: *120,725 sq mi (312,677 sq km)*
Population: *38,170,000*
Capital: *Warsaw (pop. 1,659,400)*
Ethnic groups: *Polish*
Language: *Polish*
Religious groups: *Roman Catholic*
Economy: *Agr: grains, potatoes, sugar beets, oilseeds, livestock. Ind: machinery, iron, steel, mining, chemicals, shipbuilding, food processing, textiles*
Currency: *zloty*

Czechoslovakia

On New Year's Eve 1989, tens of thousands of Czechoslovaks flooded into Prague's central Wenceslas Square, singing and exploding firecrackers to celebrate the election of the first non-Communist president in more than 40 years. In the space of only a few weeks a mass democratic movement had peacefully pushed the Communists from power.

It was a sweet victory for a people who had seen an earlier attempt at liberal reform, the "Prague Spring" of 1968, crushed by a Soviet-led invasion. In the two decades that followed, the communist government had tried to suppress most forms of free expression.

Two distinct nationalities make up landlocked Czechoslovakia: the Czechs in the western regions of Bohemia and Moravia, and the Slovaks in the east. The Czech regions, and especially Bohemia, have traditionally been the most developed and prosperous parts of the country. Artistic and intellectual ties to Western Europe have been strong since the Middle Ages. The Elbe River, flowing through Bohemia's fertile wheat and sugar-beet fields, has long carried ideas and goods to and from the West. Palaces and churches fill the heart of the country's medieval capital, Prague, known as the "golden city." Prague today is a thriving commercial and industrial center.

The other Czech region, Moravia, contains Czechoslovakia's most important coalfields and steel plants. Brno, the regional capital in South Moravia, also dates back to medieval times.

Mountainous Slovakia, once a traditional peasant society, has increasingly turned to industry. Farming, now collectivized, employs only about 15 percent of the work force, who raise livestock and grow crops of grain and potatoes. Huge government investments in hydroelectric power, mining, and industries such as engineering, chemicals, and wood products have helped bring living standards up sharply.

Czechoslovakia had a democratic government before Nazi Germany occupied the country during World War II. At war's end Soviet troops liberated most of Czechoslovakia and thus influenced the move to a communist government.

As freedom rang again in Wenceslas Square, crowds cheered and jingled key chains to symbolize the opening of doors long closed. They sang a song made popular in 1968: "May peace be with this land. Let hate, envy, fear, and conflict pass. May they pass, may they pass."

Official name: *Czech and Slovak Federal Republic*
Area: *49,371 sq mi (127,870 sq km)*
Population: *15,632,000*
Capital: *Prague (pop. 1,190,576)*
Ethnic groups: *Czech, Slovak, Hungarian*
Language: *Czech, Slovak, Hungarian*
Religious groups: *Roman Catholic, Protestant*
Economy: *Agr: wheat, barley, potatoes, sugar beets, livestock. Ind: machinery, iron, steel, cement, glass, motor vehicles, chemicals, mining, textiles, shoes*
Currency: *koruna*

1 *Poland*

Poland

1 *A master craftsman tunes the back of a violin that he is making. Poles produce some of the world's finest string instruments.*

2 *The High Tatra Mountains form a backdrop to farmers pitching hay onto a wagon. A fifth of the Polish people live on farms, where horses still outnumber tractors.*

Czechoslovakia

3 *Evening falls on the town of Banská Bystrica. Founded in 1255, it is known as the "pearl on the Hron River."*

4 *A worker stitches leather in a shoe factory in Bardejov, near the Polish border. Czechoslovaks manufacture some 125 million pairs of shoes a year.*

2 *Poland*

3 *Czechoslovakia*

4 *Czechoslovakia*

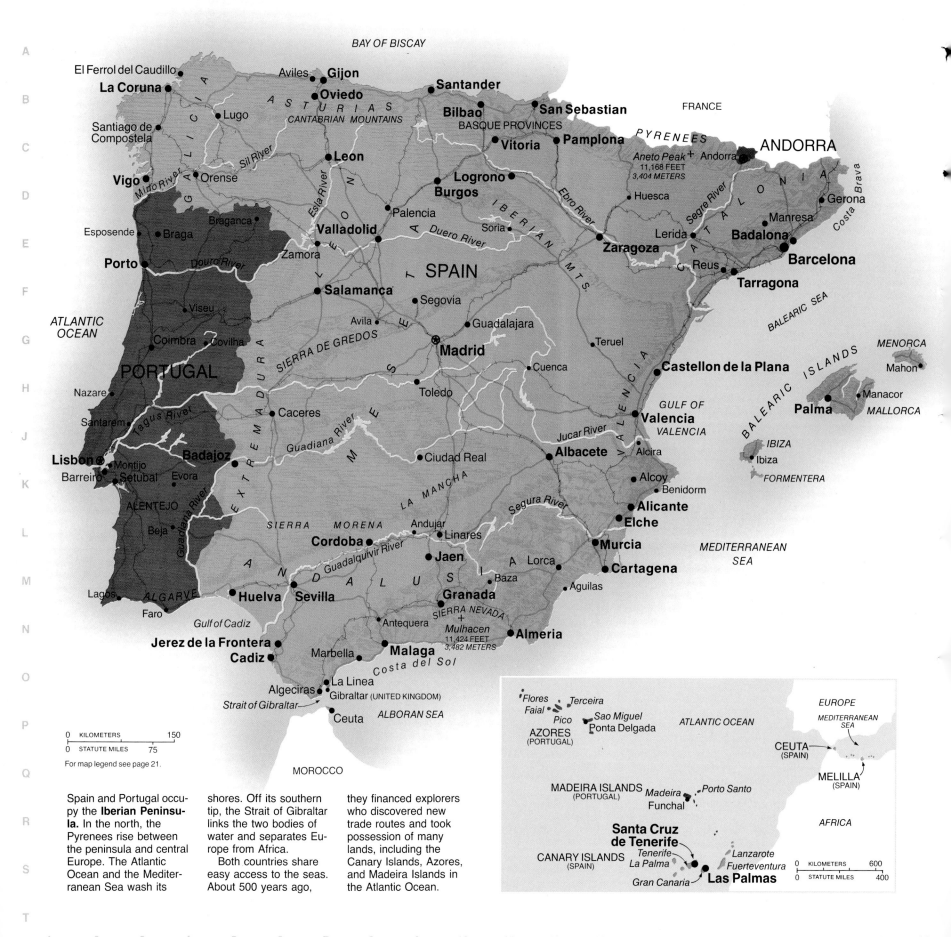

BAY OF BISCAY

FRANCE

ANDORRA

La Coruna
El Ferrol del Caudillo
Aviles
Gijon
Santander
San Sebastian
Lugo
GALICIA
ASTURIAS
CANTABRIAN MOUNTAINS
Oviedo
Bilbao
BASQUE PROVINCES
PYRENEES
Aneto Peak
11,168 FEET
3,404 METERS
Andorra
Santiago de Compostela
Sil River
Leon
Vitoria
Pamplona
Huesca
Gerona
Vigo
Mino River
Orense
Esla River
Logrono
Ebro River
Segre River
Manresa
Lerida
CATALONIA
Costa Brava
Burgos
Palencia
Soria
IBERIAN
Zaragoza
Badalona
Esposende
Braga
Braganca
Valladolid
Zamora
Duero River
Reus
Barcelona
Porto
Douro River
SPAIN
MTS.
Tarragona
Salamanca
Segovia
Guadalajara
BALEARIC SEA
Viseu
Avila
Teruel
MENORCA
ATLANTIC OCEAN
Coimbra
Covilha
SIERRA DE GREDOS
Madrid
Cuenca
Castellon de la Plana
Mahon
Nazare
PORTUGAL
Caceres
Toledo
BALEARIC ISLANDS
Manacor
Santarem
Tagus River
EXTREMADURA
Guadiana River
Jucar River
Valencia
VALENCIA
Palma
MALLORCA
Lisbon
Montijo
Badajoz
Ciudad Real
Alcira
IBIZA
Barreiro
Setubal
Evora
Ibiza
LA MANCHA
Alcoy
Albacete
FORMENTERA
ALENTEJO
Beja
Guadiana River
SIERRA MORENA
Andujar
Segura River
Benidorm
Alicante
Elche
Lagos
ALGARVE
Huelva
Sevilla
Cordoba
Guadalquivir River
Linares
Jaen
Lorca
Baza
Murcia
Cartagena
MEDITERRANEAN SEA
Faro
Gulf of Cadiz
Antequera
Granada
SIERRA NEVADA
Mulhacen
11,424 FEET
3,482 METERS
Aguilas
Almeria
Jerez de la Frontera
Marbella
Malaga
Cadiz
Costa del Sol
La Linea
Algeciras
Gibraltar (UNITED KINGDOM)
Strait of Gibraltar
ALBORAN SEA
Ceuta

MOROCCO

0 KILOMETERS 150
0 STATUTE MILES 75
For map legend see page 21.

Spain and Portugal occupy the **Iberian Peninsula.** In the north, the Pyrenees rise between the peninsula and central Europe. The Atlantic Ocean and the Mediterranean Sea wash its

shores. Off its southern tip, the Strait of Gibraltar links the two bodies of water and separates Europe from Africa.

Both countries share easy access to the seas. About 500 years ago,

they financed explorers who discovered new trade routes and took possession of many lands, including the Canary Islands, Azores, and Madeira Islands in the Atlantic Ocean.

Flores
Terceira
Faial
Pico
Sao Miguel
Ponta Delgada
AZORES (PORTUGAL)
ATLANTIC OCEAN
EUROPE
MEDITERRANEAN SEA
CEUTA (SPAIN)
MADEIRA ISLANDS (PORTUGAL)
Madeira
Porto Santo
Funchal
MELILLA (SPAIN)
AFRICA
Santa Cruz de Tenerife
Tenerife
La Palma
Lanzarote
Fuerteventura
CANARY ISLANDS (SPAIN)
Gran Canaria
Las Palmas
0 KILOMETERS 600
0 STATUTE MILES 400

The **Azores** and **Madeira,** two volcanic island groups hundreds of miles away from Portugal in the Atlantic Ocean, are autonomous regions of the Portuguese Republic. The Azores, covered with lush vegetation, are home to about 250,000 people. Their main products are pineapples, tea, and canned fish. On Madeira, the mineral-rich soil, abundant sunshine, and moist sea breezes result in a profusion of flowers. The 267,000 inhabitants support an economy based on sugar, wine, bananas, and hand embroidery, boosted by a growing tourist trade. Visitors arriving by sea or by air are greeted with vistas of plunging cliffs and terraced fields and gardens.

Official name: *Portuguese Republic*
Area: *35,672 sq mi (92,389 sq km)*
Population: *10,406,000*
Capital: *Lisbon (pop. 807,167)*
Ethnic groups: *Portuguese*
Language: *Portuguese*
Religious groups: *Roman Catholic*
Economy: *Agr: grains, potatoes, grapes, olives. Ind: textiles, shoes, chemicals, wood and cork products, paper, wine, appliances, ceramics, fishing, tourism*
Currency: *Portuguese escudo*

Portugal

The Portuguese are proud of their seagoing history. Builders of Europe's first great maritime empire, Portuguese explorers established colonies around the world in the 15th and 16th centuries. Their language is still spoken by 200 million people in Portugal's former possessions in Africa, Asia, and South America.

Today Western Europe's poorest nation, Portugal is struggling to expand its economy. To supplement the traditional pursuits of fishing and farming, the country manufactures such products as textiles, shoes, and chemicals. Lisbon and Porto are the main industrial centers and largest cities, but most Portuguese still live in rural areas, along the coast or in river valleys.

The Tagus River flows across the middle of Portugal, dividing it roughly in two. To the north, farmers plant mostly grain crops and potatoes in cool, wet highlands. In vineyards of the Douro River Valley grow the grapes for port wine, one of Portugal's most important exports. The gently rolling plains south of the Tagus River produce fruit, olives, and the cork oak trees that provide another important export, cork. Seventy percent of the world's supply comes from Portugal, chiefly from the Alentejo region.

The Portuguese pour heart and soul into cultural traditions such as the fado—a bittersweet folk song accompanied by two guitars—and popular sports such as soccer and bullfighting. In Portugal, skillful *cavaleiros* fight the bull on horseback, and the bull is not killed at the end.

Spain

In Europe, only Switzerland and Austria are more mountainous than Spain. The Cantabrian Mountains rise on Spain's northern coast, while the Sierra Nevada stretch across the south. The Meseta, a tableland slashed by deep river valleys, covers much of the interior, and the Pyrenees cut off Spain from central Europe. Other ranges ripple across the land, dividing it into distinct geographic regions that are further set apart by speech. Nearly 75 percent of all Spaniards speak Castilian Spanish, the dialect of Castile, Spain's central region. It is the country's official language. Other regional languages include Catalan, Galician, and Basque.

Provinces in the western Pyrenees have been home to the Basques for 5,000 years. Bilbao, one of Spain's biggest ports and a center of shipbuilding and steel manufacturing, is located there. Struggling to make their homeland independent, Basque separatists have clashed frequently with Spanish police.

Between its Atlantic coast and the Mediterranean shore, Spain encompasses three climates and agricultural zones. Farmers grow corn, apples, pears, beans, and potatoes in the cool, wet northwest. They raise beef and dairy cattle there, on the country's best pastureland. On the

Meseta, the hot summers, cold winters, and sparse rainfall are better suited for grazing sheep and goats, and for growing wheat and barley. The southern coast, with its dry summers and mild winters, abounds in citrus fruit, wine grapes, and olives—major export crops. Spain trades its fruit, vegetable, and grain crops with other countries in the European Community.

Madrid, Spain's capital and largest city, is located on the Meseta. It is a busy, rapidly growing financial center. Yet it follows a traditional Spanish rhythm of leisurely two-hour lunches and late-night suppers. Diners rarely sit down before nine o'clock.

Outside Madrid, most Spaniards live in cities on the Mediterranean coast. Spain's second largest city, Barcelona, is a major industrial port. In the 1950s Spain began to modernize its economy, stressing industry rather than agriculture. Automobile production grew rapidly; it now ranks fourth in Europe. Tourism, another important source of income, attracts more than 50 million visitors a year to sunny beaches, national festivals, and historic sites.

In 711 North Africans later called Moors conquered Spain. One of their castles, the Alhambra, overlooks the city of Granada. Carved with elaborate Islamic designs, its rooms open onto tiled courtyards with splashing fountains. Spain drove out the last of the Moors in 1492, the year it sponsored Christopher Columbus's voyage to North America. By the mid-1500s Spain controlled a rich empire in the Americas and was the most powerful country in Europe.

Over the next centuries, Spain suffered a series of wars and rebellions, and eventually lost its empire. In 1936 civil war broke out. Gen. Francisco Franco's forces won in 1939, and he ruled as dictator until his death in 1975. Today the king is chief of state and presides over a parliamentary monarchy. Spain's territories include two ocean communities: the hilly Balearic Islands in the Mediterranean Sea and the Canary Islands, a group of small volcanic islands in the Atlantic Ocean. Awaiting autonomy are the cities of **Ceuta** and **Melilla** on the North African coast, the last of Spain's overseas empire.

Official name: *Kingdom of Spain*
Area: *194,897 sq mi (504,782 sq km)*
Population: *39,193,000*
Capital: *Madrid (met. pop. 3,217,461)*
Ethnic groups: *Spanish, Catalan, Galician, Basque*
Language: *Spanish, Catalan, Galician, Basque*
Religious groups: *Roman Catholic*
Economy: *Agr: grains, fruit, vegetables, olives, livestock. Ind: motor vehicles, iron and steel, chemicals, food processing, textiles, machinery, shoes, electronics, shipbuilding, wine, fishing, tourism*
Currency: *Spanish peseta*

Andorra

Tucked into six glacier-carved valleys high in the Pyrenees mountains, Andorra covers an area only one-fifth the size of Rhode Island. The country is landlocked between France and Spain. The President of France governs this coprincipality jointly with a Spanish bishop under an arrangement made in 1278.

Some residents, particularly immigrants, are trying to establish a more democratic government. Many Andorrans still hold to tradition but are slowly giving up their age-old system that favors long-established families.

Because it is governed by France and Spain, Andorra has no constitution or political parties of its own. Its small army fires rifles only at official ceremonies. Although the country's language is Catalan, most children are taught in French or Spanish. Both francs and pesetas are accepted currency.

Until the 1950s, Andorra was a poor country of sheepherders, tobacco growers, and smugglers. Since then tourism has made it prosperous. Tax-free shopping and a six-month ski season attract 12 million visitors each year.

Official name: *Principality of Andorra*
Area: *175 sq mi (453 sq km)*
Population: *50,000*
Capital: *Andorra La Vella (pop. 16,200)*
Ethnic groups: *Catalan, Spanish, French*
Language: *Catalan, Spanish, French*
Religious groups: *Roman Catholic*
Economy: *tourism, banking, sheep, potatoes, tobacco*
Currency: *Spanish peseta, French franc*

Gibraltar

On a peninsula in southern Spain, the Rock of Gibraltar rises 1,394 feet (425 m) into the sky. It overlooks the Strait of Gibraltar, the narrow link between the Atlantic Ocean and the Mediterranean Sea. The British won Gibraltar from Spain 300 years ago, and administer it as a colony. Spain still claims Gibraltar, but the British are reluctant to give it up. Tourism, banking, construction, and a naval yard employ most Gibraltarians. On the Rock lives a group of monkeys called Barbary apes. Folklore says that as long as the apes live there, the British will stay.

Official name: *Gibraltar*
Area: *2.3 sq mi (6 sq km)*
Population: *30,000*
Capital: *Gibraltar (pop. 26,479)*

1 *Spain*

2 *Spain*

3 *Spain*

Spain

1 *Shoppers stroll along Toledo's Calle del Comercio. Building is strictly regulated in this city, a national monument since 1941.*

2 *Farmers stuff pork sausages beneath Torre de Riu castle in Catalonia. The region has its own folkways, language, and cuisine.*

3 *Andalusian dancers in traditional dress honor a saint at a romería, a festival that combines pilgrimage with celebration.*

Portugal

4 *Across the bay from an Algarve resort, fishermen prepare to launch their boat, its bow painted with protective symbols.*

4 *Portugal*

UNITED KINGDOM

BELGIUM

ENGLISH CHANNEL

LUXEMBOURG

GERMANY

Strait of Dover

Dunkerque
Calais
Lille

Dieppe • **Amiens**

Cherbourg
Le Havre • **Rouen**
Caen

GULF OF ST.-MALO

N O R M A N D Y

Seine River

Reims

Versailles
Paris

Chartres

Metz
Moselle River

Nancy

Strasbourg

Meuse River

Brest
St.-Brieuc
St.-Malo

B R I T T A N Y

Quimper

Lorient

Rennes

Le Mans

Orleans

Troyes

C H A M P A G N E

Marne River

Mulhouse

Basel

Lake Constance

Rhine River

LIECHTENSTEIN

Vaduz

AUSTRIA

Angers

St.-Nazaire

Nantes

Tours

Bourges

Loire River

B U R G U N D Y

Dijon

Besancon

JURA MOUNTAINS

Zurich

Luzern

Lake Lucerne

Davos
St. Moritz

ATLANTIC OCEAN

BAY OF BISCAY

La Rochelle

Poitiers

Vienne River

FRANCE

Montlucon

Vichy

Chalon-sur-Saone

Saone River

Roanne

Lausanne

Lake Neuchatel

Lake Geneva

Bern

SWITZERLAND

Lake Maggiore

Lake Lugano

Cognac

Limoges

Clermont-Ferrand

M A S S I F

Lyon

Geneva

Matterhorn 14,692 FEET 4,478 METERS

Dufourspitze 15,203 FEET 4,634 METERS

Mont Blanc 15,771 FEET 4,807 METERS

ITALY

Brive-la-Gaillarde

St.-Etienne

C E N T R A L

Grenoble

Bordeaux

Dordogne River

Lot River

Valence

Rhone River

Isère River

Garonne River

Montauban

L A N G U E D O C

Bayonne

Pau

G A S C O N Y

Ariege R.

Toulouse

Montpellier

Beziers

Nimes

Avignon

Durance River

P R O V E N C E

MONACO

Nice Monte-Carlo
Monaco
Cannes

Riviera

Aix-en-Provence

Marseille

Toulon

GULF OF LIONS

Perpignan

SPAIN

P Y R E N E E S

MEDITERRANEAN SEA

CORSICA

Bastia

Ajaccio

France is the nearest country in continental Europe to the United Kingdom. Already linked by air and English Channel ferries, the two are scheduled to be joined in 1993 by the submarine Eurotunnel, popularly known as the Chunnel.

The French language is spoken in the western part of Switzerland. In the south, next to Italy, the Swiss chiefly speak Italian and the local Romansch language. The native tongue of most Swiss people is German, but for everyday conversation they use a dialect called Schwyzerdütsch—Swiss German.

0 KILOMETERS 150
0 STATUTE MILES 100

For map legend see page 21.

A B C D E F G H J K L M N O P Q R S T

1 2 3 4 5 6 7 8 9 10 11 12 13 14 15 16 17 18 19 20

France

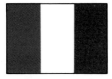

The biggest country in Western Europe, *la belle France* offers the greatest variety of landscapes. Beaches beckon on the English Channel, the Atlantic Ocean, and the Mediterranean Sea. Mountains draw tourists to the Pyrenees on Spain's border, to the Alps and Western Europe's highest peak, Mont Blanc, and to the forested Vosges near Germany. Fishing villages on Brittany's rocky coast attract sightseers. Tourists boost the economy, and the French themselves are enthusiastic travelers, piling into cars and trains each summer.

Most of France is blessed with rich farmland, making it Western Europe's leading agricultural country. Markets in many towns display fresh farm produce on outdoor stalls. There are nearly 300 kinds of French cheese. In sunny Provence, olives are grown for their oil and fields of lavender provide essence for perfume. Vineyards flourish everywhere, but the best known wines come from the regions of Bordeaux, Burgundy, and Champagne. France earns more export income from wine than any other country. People throughout France share a love of good food and make an art of cooking it. The French dishes of quiche lorraine, bouillabaisse, and boeuf bourguignon are familiar the world over.

Paris, the capital, on the Seine River in northern France, is by far the biggest city. Fifteen percent of the population lives there. Famous for its broad boulevards and sidewalk cafés, and for monuments such as the Eiffel Tower and the Arc de Triomphe, Paris is the center of French politics, government, and culture. Most major roads, railways, and a network of canals converge there. From Paris barges transport goods by river and canal all the way to Marseille, France's busiest Mediterranean port, and to neighboring countries.

French people take great pride in their culture, which has led the way in art, literature, music, and the sciences for centuries. French manners were copied in other countries and French was spoken by diplomats and educated people around the world until the 20th century, when English became the favored international language. Majestic Gothic cathedrals rose throughout France in the Middle Ages. Later, kings and nobles built elegant *châteaux* along the Loire River. King Louis XIV, the Sun King, erected a magnificent palace at Versailles in the 1600s, when France was at a peak of cultural splendor and world power.

The French Revolution of 1789 put an end to monarchy and France became a republic. Napoléon, an army general, seized control, named himself emperor, and set out to conquer all of Europe. He was defeated in 1815 at Waterloo in Belgium by British and Prussian forces. Although France later acquired colonies overseas, it never regained its former power. Two world wars fought on French soil weakened it further. Gen. Charles de Gaulle, who led the French resistance to the Nazis during World War II, became president of France in 1958 and helped restore French pride and confidence.

To complement its agricultural strength, France has become an industrial giant, ranked fifth in the world. It joined its neighbors in 1957 to form the Common Market that grew into the European Community. France has developed its own defense strategy and nuclear weapons.

French people today are caught in a conflict between old traditions and new technology, between national pride and international needs. They wonder how to cope with the growing American influence on French culture and how to maintain the purity of their language.

Official name: *French Republic*
Area: *210,026 sq mi (543,965 sq km)*
Population: *56,123,000*
Capital: *Paris (pop. 2,188,960; met. pop. 8,510,000)*
Ethnic groups: *French*
Language: *French*
Religious groups: *Roman Catholic*
Economy: *Agr: livestock, grains, sugar beets, vegetables, fruit. Ind: iron, steel, machinery, transportation equipment, electronics, chemicals, textiles, food processing, wine, tourism, mining, fishing*
Currency: *French franc*

Switzerland

Spectacular mountain scenery and powdery ski slopes have made Switzerland Europe's most famous winter vacation spot. Tourism is one of its biggest businesses. Villages of traditional wooden chalets, their window boxes overflowing with flowers, compete for visitors. Quiet electric trains carry people throughout the country with all the punctuality of Swiss-made watches and clocks.

Many of Europe's highest mountains lie in the Swiss Alps. Their glaciers feed the headwaters of two of the continent's major rivers, the Rhine and the Rhône. The Jura Mountains, lower than the Alps, form a long range on Switzerland's western border. In summertime, lush mountain pastures fatten cows whose rich milk makes cheese and milk chocolate. Villagers give dairy herds a festive send-off each spring.

Between the Alps and the Jura lies a hilly plateau where the main cities are found and where three-fourths of the Swiss people live. Big factories in this region turn out machinery, precision instruments, medicines, and chemicals.

This small country has four languages: German, French, Italian, and Romansch, a language of Latin origin. Most Swiss speak at least two, and often English as well. In Bern, the capital, and Zürich, the biggest city and chief banking center, German is the primary language. French-speaking Geneva is headquarters for some 150 international organizations.

Switzerland has remained neutral for more than 400 years, refusing to take sides in other countries' wars. However, its big, modern army can mobilize for defense in 48 hours. Swiss men between ages 20 and 50 have had army training and keep their uniforms and firearms at home.

Staunchly democratic since 1291, when three small cantons formed a union, Switzerland now has 26 cantons, or states, and a federal government somewhat like that of the United States. A seven-member federal council takes turns at being president by serving terms of one year each.

Official name: *Swiss Confederation*
Area: *15,941 sq mi (41,288 sq km)*
Population: *6,607,000*
Capital: *Bern (pop. 137,134)*
Ethnic groups: *German, French, Italian*
Language: *German, French, Italian, Romansch*
Religious groups: *Roman Catholic, Protestant*
Economy: *Agr: dairy products. Ind: banking, machinery, chemicals, watches, textiles, precision instruments, tourism, metal products, food processing*
Currency: *Swiss franc*

Liechtenstein

Tinkling cowbells, Alpine meadows, and terraced vineyards greet visitors to Liechtenstein, one of the smallest, richest countries in the world. Most of its people work in modern factories that produce precision instruments, false teeth, and other goods in an economic union with Switzerland. Low taxes have persuaded about 25,000 foreign companies to establish offices here. Liechtenstein has had no army, only local police, for more than a hundred years. A prince heads the conservative government, which first allowed women to vote in 1984. His castle overlooks the capital of Vaduz, situated in a valley between the Alps and the Rhine River.

Official name: *Principality of Liechtenstein*
Area: *62 sq mi (160 sq km)*
Population: *28,000*
Capital: *Vaduz (pop. 4,927)*
Ethnic groups: *Alemannic, Italian*
Language: *German, Alemannic dialect*
Religious groups: *Roman Catholic*
Economy: *Agr: livestock, grains, vegetables, grapes. Ind: banking, electronics, metal products, textiles, ceramics, chemicals, tourism, stamps*
Currency: *Swiss franc*

Monaco

Some of the world's most luxurious yachts anchor in Monaco's sunny harbor. The tiny principality on France's southeast coast draws wealthy visitors to its beaches and to the famous casino in Monte Carlo. Low taxes also attract many foreign businesses and residents, most of them French. Monégasques, the native people, are now a minority. The laws free them from taxes but forbid them to gamble in the casino. Princes of the Grimaldi family have ruled Monaco off and on for centuries. If a prince should die without a male heir, Monaco would become part of France.

Official name: *Principality of Monaco*
Area: *0.6 sq mi (1.9 sq km)*
Population: *28,000*
Capital: *Monaco*
Ethnic groups: *French, Monégasque, Italian*
Language: *French, Monégasque, Italian*
Religious groups: *Roman Catholic*
Economy: *Ind: tourism, medicines, plastics, precision instruments, banking, stamps*
Currency: *French franc*

1 *France*

2 *France*

3 *France*

4 *Switzerland*

5 *Switzerland*

France

1 *Built in honor of the French Revolution, the Eiffel Tower arcs above the École Militaire and heavy traffic in downtown Paris.*

2 *Sleek high-speed trains fill a rail yard. The Trains à Grande Vitesse hurtle from Paris to Lyon at 168 miles (270 km) per hour.*

3 *A cellar master drains Bordeaux wine into a fresh cask. Candlelight helps reveal the presence of unwanted sediment.*

Switzerland

4 *Crowned with flowers and evergreens, a cow returns to her valley home after a summer spent in high Alpine pastures.*

5 *Greenbacks join other foreign currencies in Swiss banks, known worldwide for their dependability and discretion.*

A B C D E F G H J K L M N O P Q R S T U

1 2 3 4 5 6 7 8 9 10 11 12 13 14 15 16 17 18 19

SWITZERLAND

AUSTRIA

Brenner Pass

+ *Mont Blanc*
15,771 FEET
4,807 METERS

*Lake
Maggiore*

*Lake
Como*

Bolzano

Udine

YUGOSLAVIA

FRANCE

*Lake
Lugano*

Novara

Milan

Bergamo

Lake Garda

Verona

Adige R.

Trieste

Playe River

Turin

Brescia

Padova

Venice

*GULF
OF VENICE*

Alessandria

Po River

Parma

Po River

Ferrara

Modena

LIGURIA

Genoa

Bologna

Ravenna

*GULF OF
GENOA*

La Spezia

Rimini

Prato

⊗ **SAN MARINO**
San Marino

Pisa

Florence

Ancona

*LIGURIAN
SEA*

Livorno

Arno River

TUSCANY

Tiber River

Siena

*Lake
Trasimeno*

Perugia

Elba

UMBRIA

*Lake
Bolsena*

Terni

ITALY

Pescara

*A D R I A T I C
S E A*

CORSICA
(FRANCE)

Civitavecchia

ABRUZZI

VATICAN CITY

Campobasso

Foggia

Rome

*Volturno
River*

Strait of Bonifacio

Bari

T Y R R H E N I A N   S E A

*Mount Vesuvius
4,203 FEET
1,281 METERS*

Naples +

Potenza

Brindisi

Sassari

Olbia

Herculaneum

Salerno

*Gulf of
Naples*

*Isle of
Capri*

Pompeii

Taranto

SARDINIA

Tirso River

+ *Punta La Marmora
6,017 FEET
1,834 METERS*

*GULF OF
TARANTO*

Cosenza

*IONIAN
SEA*

Cagliari

Catanzaro

Stromboli

Vulcano

KILOMETERS 15
STATUTE MILES 10

Gozo

Victoria

N
W E
S

Palermo

Messina

Reggio di Calabria

Comino

Marfa

SICILY

*Mount Etna
10,902 FEET
3,323 METERS*

*Strait of
Messina*

MALTA

Rabat

Sliema
Valletta ⊗

Salso

*Strait of
Sicily*

Catania

Malta

Gela

Syracuse

MEDITERRANEAN SEA

M E D I T E R R A N E A N   S E A

0 KILOMETERS 120
0 STATUTE MILES 80

For map legend see page 21.

Active volcanoes contin-
ually threaten the south-
ern part of Italy. One of
the most famous, Mount
Vesuvius near Naples,
erupted in A.D. 79 and
destroyed the towns of
Pompeii and Herculane-
um. Their ruins are pre-
served as tourist sites.
Mount Etna, on the is-
land of Sicily, erupts an
average of once every
ten years. In the Tyrrhe-
nian Sea, the volcanic islands of Stromboli and
Vulcano still smolder.

Italy

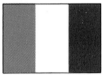

Shaped like a high-heeled boot, Italy has one of the most recognizable outlines on the globe. The toe of the boot seems about to touch the Italian island of Sicily, where fruit and olives grow. Another island, sheep-raising Sardinia, lies 140 miles (225 km) offshore, near the knee.

Two great mountain ranges influence Italy's economy. Snowmelt from the Alps on the northern border ensures natural irrigation and hydroelectric power for the Po River Valley, where two-fifths of the population lives. Here farmers grow wheat, corn, and vegetables, and the factories of Milan, Genoa, and Turin turn out goods such as shoes, textiles, computers, and automobiles. Italy's strength lies in manufacturing and fine design; it has to import most raw materials. In the north, employment is high and families live well, owning cars and often vacation homes.

Italy's southern half is less fortunate. The Apennine mountains that run 840 miles (1,350 km) down the peninsula form part of a rocky, dry landscape. Farmers herd sheep and goats or grow grapes for wine, one of Italy's major exports. In the warmest regions they grow oranges, lemons, and olives. Earning a living is hard. Families live in small villages and enjoy few luxuries. Naples, the south's only big city, suffers from overcrowding and unemployment.

Rome, Italy's capital, sits halfway down the peninsula. Before their empire fell, the ancient Romans controlled all the Mediterranean countries. Around the 12th century, the area north of Rome split into rival city-states.

Chief among these was Venice, built on a cluster of islands. Canals wind through the modern city, and people travel by boat. Among other important city-states, Florence sparked the Renaissance, a period from the 14th to the 17th century when the arts flourished in Europe. Rome, under the control of the Roman Catholic Church, became a center of culture and Christianity. Italy's art, architecture, and ancient history attract millions of tourists each year.

Unification of the peninsula did not occur until 1870. Thus modern Italy is a young country, and many Italians still put regional loyalties ahead of national feeling. Some say Italy was truly united in 1982, when its soccer team won the World Cup. Then, in towns all over the country, people danced in the streets in celebration.

Official name: *Italian Republic*
Area: *116,324 sq mi (301,277 sq km)*
Population: *57,558,000*
Capital: *Rome (pop. 2,815,457)*
Ethnic groups: *Italian*
Language: *Italian*
Religious groups: *Roman Catholic*
Economy: *Agr: fruit, vegetables, grains, olives. Ind: machinery, motor vehicles, iron, steel, chemicals, textiles, shoes, food processing, wine, tourism*
Currency: *Italian lira*

San Marino

Wholly surrounded by Italian territory, the tiny Republic of San Marino is a survivor of some 200 city-states that existed before Italy was united in 1870. Its walled capital stands near the top of a 2,425-foot (739 m) peak. Rugged mountain terrain and medieval fortifications, which once helped to preserve independence, attract three million tourists a year. The Sanmarinese, linked to Italy by language, ethnic stock, and treaty, are proud of their separate identity. They support themselves with farming, tourism, light industry, and the sale of postage stamps to collectors around the world.

Official name: *Republic of San Marino*
Area: *24 sq mi (61 sq km)*
Population: *23,000*
Capital: *San Marino (pop. 2,447)*
Ethnic groups: *Sanmarinese, Italian*
Language: *Italian*
Religious groups: *Roman Catholic*
Economy: *Agr: wheat, grapes, livestock. Ind: tourism, textiles, wine, olive oil, stamps, cement*
Currency: *Italian lira*

Vatican City

Behind a high stone wall on a hill in Rome lies the world's smallest independent nation. Vatican City is the headquarters for the Roman Catholic Church and the site of the world's largest church, St. Peter's Basilica. The Pope is the ruler of Vatican City and the spiritual leader of more than 800 million Roman Catholics in the world. Less than 500 people hold Vatican citizenship, but the state has its own coins, stamps, radio station, and newspaper, an army of 100 Swiss Guards, and a superb collection of art treasures. A 1929 treaty with Italy established the Vatican's independence.

Official name: *State of the Vatican City*
Area: *0.2 sq mi (0.4 sq km)*
Population: *830*
Ethnic groups: *Italian, other nationalities*
Language: *Italian, Latin*
Religious groups: *Roman Catholic*
Economy: *investments, contributions, tourist mementos, museum fees, stamps, publications*
Currency: *Vatican lira*

Malta

Malta's three major islands lie at the crossroads of the Mediterranean on some of the world's busiest shipping routes. Attracted by its strategic position and deep natural harbors, many nations have controlled Malta since ancient times. As a result, the Maltese people are a mixture of races and cultures.

Today independent and politically neutral, Malta takes advantage of its location. Shipbuilding and repair are major industries. A new drydock can handle modern supertankers.

Fresh water is scarce and the soil is thin, so farming in the low hills is limited, but a mild climate, prehistoric stone monuments, and historic sites make Malta a tourist's delight.

Official name: *Republic of Malta*
Area: *122 sq mi (316 sq km)*
Population: *350,000*
Capital: *Valletta (pop. 9,302)*
Ethnic groups: *Maltese (mixed Arab, Sicilian, Norman, Spanish, Italian, English)*
Language: *Maltese, English*
Religious groups: *Roman Catholic*
Economy: *Agr: vegetables, fruit, grains, livestock. Ind: tourism, shipbuilding, textiles, machinery*
Currency: *Maltese lira*

1 *Italy*

2 *Italy*

4 *Malta*

3 *Italy*

5 *Vatican City*

Italy

1 *The Roman Colosseum, an amphitheater that opened in* A.D. *80, saw fierce contests between gladiators or wild animals.*

2 *Once the arteries of a powerful maritime republic, Venice's canals are still vital— some 15 million tourists a year visit them.*

3 *Pasta just wouldn't be the same without parmesan cheese. Two million wheels of it come from the Parma region each year.*

Malta

4 *Deep natural harbors and a strategic location led to Malta's shipbuilding industry.*

Vatican City

5 *A Swiss Guard swears allegiance to the Pope, joining the elite force of 100 men that has guarded him since the early 1500s.*

CZECHOSLOVAKIA

SOVIET
UNION

GERMANY

LIECHTENSTEIN

*Lake
Constance*

Bregenz

Inn River

Krems

Danube River

Linz

Wels

Steyr

St. Polten

Vienna

Neusiedler
Lake

Salgotarjan

Miskolc

Nyiregyhaza

Oberndorf

Ipoly R.

Eger

Tisza River

Salzburg

AUSTRIA

Sopron

Gyor

Budapest

Debrecen

BAVARIAN ALPS

Kitzbuhel

DACHSTEIN

STYRIA

Leitha R.

Tatabanya

GREAT HUNGARIAN PLAIN

Innsbruck

Salzach R.

Enns River

Leoben

Szombathely

Veszprem

Szekesfehervar

Szolnok

SWITZERLAND

*Brenner
Pass*

+*Grossglockner*
12,461 FEET
3,798 METERS

Mur

Raab

Graz

Zalaegerszeg

Dunaujvaros

*Lake
Balaton*

Kecskemet

Koros River

Bekescsaba

CARINTHIA

Drau River

Raba River

HUNGARY

Hodmezovasarhely

ITALY

Villach

Klagenfurt

+*Triglav*
9,396 FEET
2,863 METERS

Maribor

Mura River

Kaposvar

Szekszard

Szeged

Subotica

ROMANIA

Drava River

SLOVENIA

Pecs

Danube River

Ljubljana

Sava River

Zagreb

JULIAN ALPS

GULF OF
TRIESTE

CROATIA

Osijek

VOJVODINA

Zrenjanin

Karlovac

Novi Sad

GULF OF
VENICE

Rijeka

Istria

Krk

Una River

Tisa River

Belgrade

Iron Gate
Dam

Pula

Gres

Banja Luka

Bosna River

Sava River

*Danube
River*

Pag

Tuzla

YUGOSLAVIA

SERBIA

ADRIATIC
SEA

*Dugi
Otok*

Zadar

Zenica

Sarajevo

BOSNIA & HERCEGOVINA

Kragujevac

Morava River

Sibenik

Split

Brac

Neretva River

Drina River

Nis

Vis

Hvar

Pec

Pristina

BULGARIA

Korcula

MONTENEGRO

Lastovo

Mljet

Dubrovnik

Ibar River

KOSOVO

Titograd

Bar

*Lake
Scutari*

Skopje

ALBANIA

MACEDONIA

Vardar River

Ohrid

Bitola

*Lake
Ohrid*

*Lake
Prespa*

GREECE

Modest in size today,
Austria and Hungary cre-
ated the great **Austro-
Hungarian Empire** in
1867. It encompassed
Czechoslovakia and
parts of Poland, Italy,
Yugoslavia, Romania,
and the Soviet Union.

The different national-
ities of the empire were
mostly interested in gaining their independence.
When World War I end-
ed in 1918, the empire
broke up and Austria and
Hungary shrank to small
republics. Yugoslavia is
now a federation of six
republics, but ethnic tensions threaten its unity.
Croatia and Slovenia are
demanding autonomy
and may seek secession.

| 0 | KILOMETERS | 125 |
| 0 | STATUTE MILES | 75 |

For map legend see page 21.

Austria

Mountains dominate Austria. The towering, snow-capped Alps cover nearly three-quarters of this small republic. Austrians regard their peaks as national assets. Rushing mountain streams generate hydroelectric power for factories, found mostly in the eastern lowlands. Thick forests of spruce and fir supply raw materials for lumber, pulp, and paper.

The tourist industry relies on striking mountain scenery and traditional Alpine villages to draw visitors in all seasons. More than 50 winter resorts such as Innsbruck and Kitzbühel cater to skiers. Strict laws protect parts of the Alps from overdevelopment and pollution. The government pays farmers to keep their land scenic.

Historically, Austria's location on heavily used trade routes gave it strategic importance. Mountain passes like Brenner Pass link Austria to countries to the north and south. The Danube River, a navigable waterway that crosses northern Austria, joins Western and Eastern Europe. By 1870, wars and alliances had made Austria the heart of the Austro-Hungarian Empire, a conglomerate nation of 50 million people. Its capital, Vienna, a center of science, art, and music, was noted for its gaiety. But after defeat in World War I, Austria was reduced to a fraction of the size of its former empire.

Today the Austrian constitution requires neutrality. Austria maintains peaceful, profitable relations with its neighbors, acting as a bridge between East and West. Many international agencies have headquarters in Vienna, a city still famed for classical music and imperial architecture—and for rich Viennese pastries.

Official name: *Republic of Austria*
Area: *32,377 sq mi (83,856 sq km)*
Population: *7,617,000*
Capital: *Vienna (pop. 1,531,346)*
Ethnic groups: *German*
Language: *German*
Religious groups: *Roman Catholic*
Economy: *Agr: livestock, grains, potatoes, sugar beets. Ind: machinery, iron, steel, tourism, chemicals, textiles, wood and paper products, mining*
Currency: *schilling*

Hungary

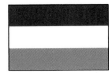

Hungarians feel isolated in their landlocked country. Unlike their Slavic and Germanic neighbors, they are Magyars, descendants of central Asian nomads who occupied the fertile Danube River basin more than a thousand years ago. This sense of being different has given Hungarians a strong cultural identity, which they held onto while often losing their freedom—to the Turks, Austrians, Germans, and, in 1947, to the Soviets.

In 1956 a popular uprising against Soviet control was brutally put down. After that, Hungary sought to forge its own way while not challenging the Soviet Union. Its brand of "goulash communism" (named for Hungary's traditional dish) promoted bold changes. These included limited private enterprise in small businesses and on farms, where about 20 percent of Hungarians produce enough food both to feed the country and to sell abroad.

In 1988 and 1989, as the Soviet government loosened its grip, Hungary's movement toward democracy speeded up. The Communist Party allowed the formation of other political parties and held free elections. The newly elected government plans to reform the ailing economy by, among other things, transferring most industries from government to private ownership.

Official name: *Republic of Hungary*
Area: *35,919 sq mi (93,030 sq km)*
Population: *10,569,000*
Capital: *Budapest (pop. 2,075,990)*
Ethnic groups: *Magyar*
Language: *Hungarian*
Religious groups: *Roman Catholic, Protestant*
Economy: *Agr: grains, potatoes, sugar beets, fruit, livestock. Ind: machinery, engineering, food processing, chemicals, textiles, metals, mining, wine*
Currency: *forint*

Yugoslavia

Ethnic rivalry is a characteristic of Yugoslav life. Six major ethnic groups are found here, along with several minorities. Most people belong to a larger group called Slavs. Yugoslavs speak three official languages, write in two alphabets (Latin and Cyrillic), and worship in three religions.

The country falls into several distinct regions. The island-studded coastal strip called Dalmatia is a popular tourist area. Farmers here grow olives, grapes, and plums in the mild climate. Inland, the Dinaric Alps run parallel to the coast, forming part of the mountainous terrain that covers about 75 percent of the country. Workers engage in forestry, stock farming, and fruit growing. Triglav, Yugoslavia's highest peak, dominates the rugged Julian Alps in the country's northwestern corner. Tourists flock to this region to enjoy winter sports. In the northeast, on fertile plains along the Danube River, farmers raise wheat, oats, and corn.

Over centuries, the Roman, Byzantine, Ottoman, and Austro-Hungarian Empires ruled parts of present-day Yugoslavia. In 1918, six territories formed a new kingdom that was later named Yugoslavia, meaning "land of the southern Slavs." During World War II the Germans forced the monarchy into exile. In 1946 Yugoslavia adopted a communist government and established itself as a federation of six republics.

Citizens of these republics have equal rights but very unequal levels of development, which aggravates ethnic differences. The northern republics benefited from rapid industrialization after the war. New jobs drew people from the countryside to the cities, where they enjoy well-stocked stores, television, and cars. The south remains underdeveloped and poor. An economic slowdown in the 1980s brought new demands for separation by some groups, leaving Yugoslavia vulnerable to the winds of revolution that began sweeping through Eastern Europe in 1989.

Official name: *Socialist Federal Republic of Yugoslavia*
Area: *98,766 sq mi (255,804 sq km)*
Population: *23,701,000*
Capital: *Belgrade (pop. 1,087,915)*
Ethnic groups: *Serb, Croat, Bosnian Muslim, Slovene, Albanian, Macedonian, Montenegrin*
Language: *Serbo-Croatian, Slovenian, Macedonian*
Religious groups: *Eastern Orthodox, Roman Catholic, Muslim*
Economy: *Agr: grains, sugar beets, potatoes, fruit, livestock. Ind: metals, machinery, motor vehicles, oil, textiles, wood products, food processing*
Currency: *Yugoslav dinar*

1 *Austria*

2 *Austria*

3 *Hungary*

4 *Yugoslavia*

Austria

1 *Steep, snow-shedding roofs protect houses huddled beneath the Dachstein Mountains of central Austria.*

2 *A Viennese pastry shop displays mouth-watering chocolate rolls, cakes, and other pastries for which the city is world famous.*

Hungary

3 *Dressed like one of his flock, a shepherd on the Great Hungarian Plain sports a traditional coat called a suba. His heavy felt hat can be used for drinking water.*

Yugoslavia

4 *Medieval fortifications surround old Dubrovnik, on the Dalmatian coast. Once a powerful city-state called Ragusa, the city today is a popular Adriatic resort.*

SOVIET UNION

A

HUNGARY

Satu Mare
Somes
Baia Mare
Suceava
Oradea
River
Cluj-Napoca
Tirgu Mures
Iasi
TRANSYLVANIA
Bacau
Arad
· Sighisoara
ROMANIA
Mures River
Sibiu
Olt River
Timisoara
Brasov
TRANSYLVANIAN ALPS
Galati
Resita
Buzau
Braila
Danube River Delta
Ploiesti
Tulcea
Pitesti
Iron Gate Dam
Bucharest
Craiova
Constanta
Vidin
Danube River
Ruse
YUGOSLAVIA
Tolbukhin
Iskur River
Pleven
Shumen
BULGARIA
Varna
Gabrovo
MOUNTAINS
BALKAN
Sliven
BLACK SEA
Sofia
Pernik
Valley of Roses
Stara Zagora
Burgas
Plovdiv
Maritsa River
Struma River
Tundzha River
RHODOPE MOUNTAINS
THRACE
Lake Scutari
Drin R.
ADRIATIC SEA
Shkoder
Drama
Komotini
Evros River
Tirana
Lake Ohrid
Serrai
Durres
Lake Prespa
Kavala
Elbasan
MACEDONIA
Thasos
ALBANIA
Korce
Veroia
Thessaloniki
Vlore
Vijose River
KHALKIDHIKI
Samothrace
Mount Olympus +
9,570 FEET
2,917 METERS
Lemnos
TURKEY
Corfu
Ioannina
PINDUS
Larisa
AEGEAN SEA
EPIRUS
· Volos
THESSALY
Lesbos
IONIAN SEA
GREECE
MTS.
Mitilini
IONIAN ISLANDS
Levkas
Agrinion
Delphi
Euboea
Chios
Cephalonia
Thebes
Zante
Patrai
Marathon
Samos
Olympia
Corinth
Athens
Andros
Piraeus
PELOPONNESUS
SPORADES
Siros
Mikonos
Kalamai
· Sparta
CYCLADES
Naxos
Kos
Milos
Cape Matapan
Rhodes
Kithira
Thira
DODECANESE
Rhodes
SEA OF CRETE
Karpathos
MEDITERRANEAN SEA
Khania
Iraklion
Knossos
CRETE

For map legend see page 21.

0 KILOMETERS 150
0 STATUTE MILES 100

Balkans is the name given to the countries of the **Balkan Peninsula** in southeastern Europe. The term applies to the countries on this map along with Yugoslavia and European Turkey.

Located at the crossroads of Asia, Europe, and Africa, the region has suffered many invasions and much internal conflict. With each conquest, political boundaries were redrawn—and often disputed again. From this, the word "balkanize" was coined, which means to break up a region.

Romania

When apple trees grew pears, proclaimed the Romanian dictator Nicolae Ceauşescu, reform would come to Romania. The scornful words prompted student protesters to hang pears on trees in Bucharest, Romania's capital. Tense drama exploded into bloody revolution in the final days of 1989, ending with the execution of Ceauşescu and his wife. The Romanian people ripped from their flags the communist emblem, the hated symbol of oppression. A new government promised to make reforms, but protesters again demanded democratic action.

Although Romania was a Soviet satellite, it tried to steer an independent course. Half its trade was with the West. Fertile plains stretch along Romania's western, eastern, and southern borders. Its forested mountains and central plateau contain deposits of oil and minerals.

But Ceauşescu's harsh measures for reducing the national debt impoverished the citizens. Fuel and farm produce were exported to help repay loans. People suffered from shortages of food, electricity, and gasoline. Especially cruel was a program to destroy villages and resettle the rural population in massive apartment buildings on agricultural-industrial complexes.

Since the 1950s, the government has emphasized heavy industries such as steel, chemicals, and machinery, but the country remains one of Europe's least industrial nations. About 30 percent of the work force still farms the land.

Romanian roots go back to the Romans who colonized the area in the second century, giving the country its name. Its language bears more resemblance to Italian and French than to the Slavic languages of most surrounding countries.

The Romanian heritage finds expression in traditional folk art and in music and dancing that enliven outdoor festivals. Vacationers from many countries have long enjoyed these festivities, as well as Romania's mountain scenery, sunny Black Sea resorts, and distinctive medieval churches with their fresco facades.

Official name: *Romania*
Area: *91,699 sq mi (237,500 sq km)*
Population: *23,153,000*
Capital: *Bucharest (met. pop. 1,989,823)*
Ethnic groups: *Romanian, Hungarian*
Language: *Romanian, Hungarian, German*
Religious groups: *Romanian Orthodox*
Economy: *Agr: corn, wheat, potatoes, sugar beets, oilseeds, livestock, fruit. Ind: machinery, oil, metals, mining, chemicals, lumber, textiles, food processing*
Currency: *leu*

Bulgaria

Most of the Western world's elegant perfumes are made in France, but chances are the rose oil that forms their base comes from the Valley of Roses in the heart of Bulgaria. Although dominated by mountains, Bulgaria manages to cultivate more than a third of its land. Wheat, corn, and sugar beets grow in the fertile valley that stretches from the Danube River south to the Balkan Mountains. Tobacco, cotton, and fruit thrive in the Maritsa River Valley, between the Balkan and Rhodope Mountains. Much of the produce is exported.

A communist country since the end of World War II, Bulgaria maintains strong ties with the Soviet Union that predate the rise of communism. The Bulgarian language sounds similar to Russian, and both use the Cyrillic alphabet. More important, though, Bulgaria has viewed the Russians as liberators since 1878, when the tsar's troops helped defeat the Ottoman Turks, who had ruled Bulgaria for 500 years. Voters in 1990 elected officials who remained communist but promised to make democratic reforms.

Bulgaria's government has done much to modernize the country. Small, private farms have been turned into huge collectives, where advances in farming techniques and greater use of machinery translate into higher productivity with fewer laborers. Accordingly, more and more Bulgarians are trading rural for urban life. About two-thirds of Bulgarians now live in towns or cities, primarily in Sofia, the capital.

Tourism plays an increasingly important role in Bulgaria's economy. While its resort areas on the Black Sea coast have long been popular with vacationers from Eastern European countries, Bulgaria has recently made an extra effort to attract Western tourists and their hard currency. Modern hotels look out on Black Sea beaches, and ski resorts deck mountain slopes. Bulgarians are careful to protect many national sites, ranging from a 2,300-year-old Thracian tomb to hundreds of nature reserves.

Official name: *People's Republic of Bulgaria*
Area: *42,823 sq mi (110,912 sq km)*
Population: *8,973,000*
Capital: *Sofia (pop. 1,114,759)*
Ethnic groups: *Bulgarian, Turk*
Language: *Bulgarian, Turkish*
Religious groups: *Eastern Orthodox, Muslim*
Economy: *Agr: grains, tobacco, fruit, vegetables, livestock, cotton, roses. Ind: machinery, electronics, chemicals, agricultural processing, metals, tourism*
Currency: *lev*

Albania

For nearly 50 years small, mountainous Albania mistrusted outside influence so much that it placed heavy restrictions on tourism, foreign news, and travel. While a United States passport allowed travelers easy access to many other European countries, the few Americans allowed to visit Albania were usually of Albanian descent. But in 1990 the government announced its wish to begin diplomatic relations with other countries and promised to let all Albanians apply for passports. Other reform measures, such as allowing people to own their homes, are expected to follow gradually.

With a long history of invasion and occupation by foreign powers, it's no wonder Albania values national independence. It became staunchly communist after driving out German forces in World War II, and it remains the most orthodox communist country in Europe.

About two-thirds of Albanians live in the countryside. Most work on collective farms along the coastal plain and in river valleys. Thanks to hillside terraces, irrigation, and land reclamation, farmland doubled in the years following the war. Albania also mines large deposits of chromite, in which it is a world leader.

The Albanian birthrate is high, and 60 percent of the people are under the age of 25. They benefit from steady improvements in education and health care. Nonetheless, the citizens of this formerly reclusive country endure the lowest standard of living in Europe.

Official name: *People's Socialist Republic of Albania*
Area: *11,100 sq mi (28,748 sq km)*
Population: *3,190,000*
Capital: *Tirana (pop. 215,857)*
Ethnic groups: *Albanian*
Language: *Albanian, Greek*
Religious groups: *Muslim, Eastern Orthodox*
Economy: *Agr: grains, vegetables, tobacco, fruit. Ind: mining, oil, food processing, textiles, lumber*
Currency: *lek*

Greece

The ideals of Western democracy were born in Greece 2,500 years ago, and the word "democracy" comes from the Greek for "power of the people." The ancient Greeks had other advanced ideas too. They thought that everything was made of small particles of matter called atoms, and that Earth revolved around the sun. Western civilization grew out of early Greek art, philosophy, and science.

Conquered by the Macedonians in 338 B.C., Greece suffered many centuries of foreign rule. Not until 1829 did it regain independence. In the 20th century the country was devastated, first by Nazi occupation, then by a bitter civil war. A conflict with Turkey over the island of Cyprus, begun in the 1950s, remains unresolved.

Greece is composed of a group of peninsulas and scattered islands. Mountains that cover about 80 percent of the country further separate regions from one another. The climate is typically Mediterranean, with hot, dry summers and mild, rainy winters. Almost half of the land is suitable for farming, and about a third of the population is employed in agriculture.

Tiny farmsteads, divided up among family descendants, make large-scale agricultural methods impossible. Because of strong family bonds, Greeks have often resisted government efforts to establish farm cooperatives, labor unions, and modern techniques. People who were left without land or jobs have had to seek work in other countries and send earnings home.

Greece's rate of industrial growth was among the highest in Europe from the 1940s to 1980. More than half the population now lives in cities. Companies making textiles, chemicals, and other products are concentrated around Athens, the capital, and its port, Piraeus. Air pollution has become a problem there.

The port of Thessaloniki, the largest city after Athens, is the shipping center in the north for the mining industry and for crops grown in Thessaly and Macedonia. Greece has one of the biggest shipping fleets in the world.

Tourism plays a large role in Greece's economy. Some eight million people a year visit the country, lured by its sunny climate, magnificent scenery, and antiquities such as the Athenian Parthenon. The Greek islands number nearly 2,000, many of them containing beach resorts and traditional fishing villages. On the largest island, Crete, stand the ruins of the great Minoan civilization, which predates the Golden Age of Greece by more than a thousand years.

Official name: *Hellenic Republic*
Area: *50,962 sq mi (131,990 sq km)*
Population: *10,031,000*
Capital: *Athens (pop. 885,737)*
Ethnic groups: *Greek*
Language: *Greek*
Religious groups: *Greek Orthodox*
Economy: *Agr: wheat, olives, tobacco, cotton, fruit, livestock. Ind: shipping, tourism, food processing, textiles, chemicals, metal products, minerals, oil*
Currency: *drachma*

1 *Greece*

2 *Greece*

3 *Bulgaria*

4 *Romania*

Greece

1 *A Greek Orthodox church clings to a cliff on the crescent-shaped island of Thíra in the Aegean Sea.*

2 *Greek* kefi—*high spirits*—*erupts in dancing near ancient Delphi, as villagers honor their patron saint, St. George.*

Bulgaria

3 *A rose picker displays a sample in the Valley of Roses. Bulgaria supplies 40 percent of the world's rose oil used in perfume.*

Romania

4 *The painted houses of a Transylvanian village, decorated with ornate wood carvings, are typical of this forest region.*

Asia

When Marco Polo returned to Italy from his 13th-century travels to Asia, people scoffed at the amazing tales he told. His descriptions of the continent—its size, the height of its mountains, its variety of peoples—seemed too fantastic to be real. But they were not greatly exaggerated. Largest of all the continents, Asia covers nearly one-third of the Earth's land surface and is home to more than half of its people in 40 countries. It stretches from the frozen wastes of the Arctic in the north to the sweltering rain forests of Indonesia, south of the Equator.

In the west, Asia's boundary with Europe is defined by a line mapmakers trace along the Ural Mountains, through the Caspian and Black Seas, and down the narrow straits that lead into the Mediterranean Sea. From there the Suez Canal runs into the Red Sea, and together they set off Asia from the African continent. About 6,000 miles (9,655 km) to the east, Asia ends in the island chains that arc into the Pacific Ocean. The Indian Ocean washes its southern shores.

Earth's highest point is found in Asia. From a central Asian hub, the continent's greatest mountain ranges radiate like the vanes of a pinwheel. To the southeast curves the Himalaya, the world's loftiest mountain realm. There Mount Everest soars 29,028 feet (8,848 m), surpassing all other peaks. The Kunlun Mountains stretch eastward; between these mountains and the Himalaya lies the high, vast Plateau of Tibet. To the north sweep the Tian Shan and the Altay Mountains, while the Hindu Kush angles off to the southwest. Asia's mountains and high plateaus have long been barriers to the movement of people and ideas.

Half a continent from Everest in the region known as the Middle East, the shore of the Dead Sea forms Asia's lowest point, 1,312 feet (400 m) below sea level. This salty inland sea drains the Jordan River, one of arid western Asia's life-giving streams. Rising in the mountains of Turkey, the Tigris and Euphrates Rivers flow into the Persian Gulf, supplying water to a wide, fertile plain between them that scholars call Mesopotamia, "the land between the rivers."

Here, some 55 centuries ago, the world's oldest civilization, the Sumerian, took shape. People learned to divert rivers for irrigation and began to harvest surplus food. This supported some people in non-farming jobs, and cities formed. Other civilizations arose, too, about 2500 B.C. along the Indus River, which flows through modern Pakistan, and 800 years later along China's Yellow River. Asian civilizations gave the world writing, the wheel, astronomy, mechanical printing, and Arabic numerals.

Asia also gave birth to all the world's major religions. Hinduism developed in India some 3,500 years ago and remains the primary religion there. Buddhism began in India and spread to East and Southeast Asia, where it is now practiced by many. From the Middle East came Judaism, Christianity, and Islam—three distinct religions that share common roots. Modern Judaism centers on Israel, created in 1948 as a homeland for the world's Jews. Christianity has the largest number of believers worldwide, but only about 10 percent live in Asia. Islam and Hinduism claim very nearly equal numbers of followers in Asia—about 700 million each.

Extreme heat, cold, and lack of water keep at least two-thirds of Asia unpopulated or only sparsely inhabited. Its northernmost expanses consist of bitter cold, treeless tundra where the subsoil is frozen all year. South of this stretches the taiga, a forest belt of hardy evergreens that can survive the long, cold winters and short summers. Vast grasslands called steppes cover much of central Asia. The steppes are the traditional home of herders, some of whom still live in portable shelters called *yurts*, or *gers*, and carry their belongings on two-humped camels.

Asia's high mountains and interior plateaus are mostly too dry and cold for human settlement. Interior deserts, such as the Taklimakan and the Gobi, are very thinly populated. In southern desert lands, including the Arabian Peninsula, people have settled along the coasts and at oases—areas made fertile by underground water sources that supply springs and wells. Tent-dwelling nomads still herd livestock in the open desert, though less than in the past.

Most of Asia's population clusters in lowlands along its rivers and coastlines. The valleys of three major rivers that rise in the Himalaya, the Indus, Ganges, and Brahmaputra, hold some of the greatest concentrations of people in the world. In China, the world's most populous country, people live chiefly along the Yellow

Peaks of the Himalaya, Earth's highest range

Wind-crested dunes in the Gobi, Mongolia

ARCTIC
OCEAN

ARCTIC CIRCLE

Taymyr
Peninsula

EUROPE

Siberia

URAL MOUNTAINS

Ob River

Yenisey River

Lena River

Amur River

Volga River

Irtysh River

ASIA

Lake Baykal
5,315 FEET
1,620 METERS
World's deepest lake

BLACK SEA

Anatolia

Caucasus Mts.

The Steppes

CASPIAN SEA

Altay Mts.

*Mongolian
Plateau*

Aral Sea

Gobi

Dead Sea
−1,312 FEET
−400 METERS

Zagros Mts.

Tian Shan

*Taklimakan
Desert*

Qilian Shan

Yellow River

*North
China
Plain*

Persian Gulf

Hindu Kush

Kunlun Mountains

Qin Ling

RED SEA

Arabian

*Plateau of
Tibet*

Yangtze River

Peninsula

Indus River

H
I
M
A
L
A
Y
A

Mt. Everest
29,028 FEET
8,848 METERS
World's highest point

TROPIC OF CANCER

Empty
Quarter

*Great
Indian
Desert*

Ganges River

Brahmaputra
River

Irrawaddy River

Taiwan

PACIFIC
OCEAN

ARABIAN
SEA

Deccan

Plateau

Philippines

BAY OF
BENGAL

Mekong River

SOUTH CHINA SEA

EQUATOR

Maldives

Sri Lanka

Malay Peninsula

Indonesia

INDIAN
OCEAN

TROPIC OF CAPRICORN

and Yangtze Rivers. Many Asian rivers, such as Southeast Asia's Mekong, provide new, fertile soil when annual floods recede and serve as important transportation routes.

Large numbers of Asians rely on the regular arrival of the summer rainy season. Yearly rains brought by monsoon winds drench South and Southeast Asia and China's southern regions. Farmers plant rice, Asia's most important food crop, in flooded fields and count on the rains to water crops of wheat, millet, and other grains. If the rains fail to arrive, thousands may starve.

Marco Polo had plenty of opportunity to learn about Asia. He spent 17 years in the service of the Mongol emperor of China, Kublai Khan. Starting with Kublai Khan's grandfather, Genghis, Mongols from the steppes of central Asia came closer than any other political power to controlling the whole continent. But Asia's incredible diversity of environments, ethnic groups, cultures, and languages has always made unification unlikely. In recent centuries, European powers carved up much of Asia into colonial empires to supply resources needed at home. Many of these countries have only gained independence since World War II, sometimes after years of war and human suffering.

Regardless of their current forms of government, Asian countries face many problems in common. Feeding a continually increasing population is the most pressing challenge. The continent as a whole has made much progress in growing food, but some countries experience severe shortages. Poverty and strife in rural areas force millions of Asians into already crowded cities. There they live in makeshift shelters without sanitation, the poorest of the poor.

Asia's natural resources, many so far untapped, remain its major strength and hope for the future. Wealth from the immense oil reserves in the Persian Gulf brings improved standards of living to many countries in that region. Hydroelectric power fueled by mighty Asian rivers bolsters the continent's energy supply. Nearly every mineral needed by modern industry can be found in the Asian earth. Powered by human resources, countries like Japan, Taiwan, Singapore, and Hong Kong have already made giant leaps into industry and modernization—but they still honor their Asian heritage.

Buddhist heads above an archway join Hindu statuary in the ancient Cambodian temple of Angkor Thom.

Facts About Asia

Area: *17,176,102 sq mi (44,485,900 sq km)
Population: *3,132,638,000
Highest Point: *Mount Everest, Nepal-Tibet, 29,028 ft (8,848 m) above sea level
Lowest Point: Dead Sea, Israel-Jordan, 1,312 ft (400 m) below sea level
Largest Country: *(by area)*
* U.S.S.R., excluding European U.S.S.R., 6,498,563 sq mi (16,831,200 sq km)
Largest Country: *(by population)*
* China 1,103,923,000
Largest Metropolitan Areas: *(by population)*

* Tokyo, Japan	30,395,000
Shanghai, China	12,550,000
Calcutta, India	11,830,000

Longest Rivers: *(mi and km)*

Yangtze (Chang Jiang)	3,964	6,380
Ob-Irtysh	3,362	5,410

Largest Lakes: *(sq mi and sq km)*

* Caspian Sea, Asia-Europe	143,244	371,000
Aral Sea, U.S.S.R.	15,444	40,000

Largest Desert: *(sq mi and sq km)*

Gobi, China-Mongolia	500,000	1,294,994

*World record

Glossary

Bedouin—a nomadic Arab of the desert.
Buddhism—a religion of Asia that grew from the teachings of Gautama Buddha in the 6th century B.C. He taught salvation through self-purification.
caste—a hereditary social class in Hinduism.
Christianity—a religion based on the teachings of Jesus Christ, who is believed to be the son of God.
dhow—an Arab boat with a triangular sail.
Hinduism—the major religion of India; it teaches righteous living to achieve a final union with Brahman, the supreme power of the universe.
Islam—a religious belief that Allah is the only God and that Muhammad is his Prophet.
Judaism—a religion developed by the ancient Hebrews that teaches belief in one God.
maharaja—a Hindu prince.
monsoon—a wind that produces dry and wet seasons in southern and eastern Asia.
mosque—an Islamic house of worship.
Muslim—a follower of Islam.
pagoda—a tower with several successive roofs, used as a temple or memorial in the Far East.
yurt—a circular tent of felt or animal skins used by nomads in central Asia; also called a ger in Mongolia.

0 KILOMETERS 600
0 STATUTE MILES 400
For map legend see page 21.

Covering half of Europe and half of Asia, the Soviet Union is the largest country in the world. From its European border it reaches across 11 time zones to an arctic island in the Bering Strait. Here the Soviet Union and the United States are only two miles (3 km) apart.

To the west of the Ural Mountains lies the densely populated European section of the Soviet Union that contains Moscow, the capital and chief city.

The Asian portion, the larger part of this huge country, includes Siberia with its vast uninhabited regions.

SWEDEN

NORWAY

BARENTS SEA

Franz Josef Land

ARCTIC OCEAN

BALTIC SEA

POLAND

Kaliningrad

RUSSIAN S.F.S.R
LATVIA
Tallinn

FINLAND

Murmansk

Novaya Zemlya

Severnaya Zemlya (North Land)

New Siberian Islands

LITHUANIA
Riga

ESTONIA

KARA SEA

Vilnius

Lake Ladoga

WHITE SEA

Leningrad

LAPTEV SEA

Lvov

Minsk

BYELORUSSIA

NORTHERN

Lake Onega

Arkhangelsk

Northern Dvina River

TAYMYR PENINSULA

Khatanga R.

MOLDAVIA

Volga R.

EUROPEAN

Kiev

UKRAINE

Dnieper River

Yaroslavl

Moscow

PLAIN

Vychegda R.

Pechora R.

Vorkuta

Kishinev

Krivoy Rog

Ryazan

Norilsk

Yenisey River

Verkhoyansk

Odessa

Kharkov

Don R.

Gorkiy

Voronezh

Kotuy River

CENTRAL SIBERIAN PLATEAU

Dnepropetrovsk

Penza

Kazan

Izhevsk

Ob River

Nadym

Lena River

Sevastopol
Sea of Azov

Donetsk

WEST SIBERIAN PLAIN

SIBERIA

BLACK SEA

Rostov

Saratov

Perm

URAL MOUNTAINS

RUSSIAN SOVIET FEDERATIVE SOCIALIST REPUBLIC

Krasnodar

Volgograd

Volga River

Kuybyshev

Nizhniy Tagil

Nizhnevartovsk

Lower Tunguska River

Yakutsk

TURKEY

Mount Elbrus 18,510 FEET 5,642 METERS Highest point in Europe

Volga-Don Canal

Ufa

Sverdlovsk

Irtysh River

Ob River

Astrakhan

Orenburg

SIBERIA

GEORGIA

Ural River

Magnitogorsk

Chelyabinsk

SOVIET UNION

Tbilisi

CAUCASUS MOUNTAINS

Tobol R.

Angara River

Ust Ilimsk

ARMENIA

Petropavlovsk

Lena River

Yerevan

Omsk

BAYKAL-AMUR MAINLINE R.R.

AZERBAIJAN

THE

Tomsk

Krasnoyarsk

Bratsk

Baku

STEPPES

Novosibirsk

Kemerovo

TRANS-SIBERIAN RAILROAD

CASPIAN SEA

Karaganda

Novokuznetsk

Lake Baykal

Aral Sea

KAZAKHSTAN

Barnaul

SAYAN MOUNTAINS

Ob River

Tom R.

Chita

Nukus

Syr Darya River

Lake Balkhash

Irkutsk

Shilka R.

TURKMENISTAN

KARA KUM DESERT

Amu Darya R.

Ulan Ude

IRAN

UZBEKISTAN

Argun R.

Ashkhabad

Boundary in dispute

Bukhara

MONGOLIA

Samarkand

Tashkent

Frunze

Alma Ata

Dushanbe

KIRGHIZIA

CHINA

TAJIKISTAN

Naryn R.

Communism Peak 24,590 FEET 7,495 METERS

AFGHANISTAN

UNITED STATES

CHUKCHI
SEA

Wrangel
Island

Bering Strait

AST SIBERIAN
SEA

Gulf of
Anadyr

Indigirka River

Kolyma River

ARCTIC CIRCLE

KOLYMA RANGE

BERING
SEA

Commander
Islands

Shelikhov
Gulf

Kamchatka
Peninsula

Oymyakon

Magadan

DZHUGDZHUR RANGE

Aldan River

Petropavlovsk
Kamchatskiy

SEA OF
OKHOTSK

Sakhalin
Island

Kuril Islands

Komsomolsk

Amur R.

Tatar Strait

Boundary in
dispute

Sovetskaya
Gavan

Amur R.

Khabarovsk

Ussuri R.

Blagoveshchensk

JAPAN

CHINA

PACIFIC
OCEAN

Vladivostok

SEA OF
JAPAN

NORTH
KOREA

Soviet Union

A thousand years ago, Viking ships headed eastward from Scandinavia. The Vikings were known as Rus. They followed wild rivers through deep forests, rivers we know today as the Volga and the Dnieper. They sailed south to the Caspian and the Black Seas, and set up trade routes to the Orient, building forts along the rivers. On the Dnieper, the Rus seized Kiev, a Slavic town, and made it a powerful state. This was the beginning of the nation to which they gave their name—Russia.

Today Russia is the dominant republic of the Soviet Union, a country that covers almost one-sixth of the land surface of Earth. After China and India, it is the world's most populous country and contains more than a hundred ethnic groups. These include Slavic peoples like the Russians and Ukrainians in the west; Lithuanians and Estonians along the Baltic Sea; Georgians and Azerbaijanis in the Caucasus Mountains; Uzbeks and Kazakhs, whose homes are on the borders with Afghanistan and China; native peoples of Siberia, such as Chukchis and Yakuts; and many more.

The political divisions of the Soviet Union are mostly based on these ethnic groupings. There are 15 major republics. The largest is the Russian Soviet Federative Socialist Republic. Armenia is the smallest. Most of the 15 republics are divided into smaller administrative regions. Sometimes the Soviet Union is called the Union of Soviet Socialist Republics, or U.S.S.R.

If you travel on the Volga today, everything you see is changed from the time of the Rus, except for one thing: As you go downriver, often the right bank is high and steep, the left bank low and flat. Many large cities, such as Volgograd, began long ago as settlements on the right bank, safe from floods and river raiders. On the high banks you can see old parts of these cities, golden domes of Russian Orthodox churches or small wooden houses. On the left bank there may be new high-rises, or beaches. In the countryside stand clusters of *dachas*, tiny cottages where city dwellers have gardens and spend vacations in the short summers.

Summer is precious in this country of generally long, hard winters. The greatest part of the Soviet Union lies farther north than any of the contiguous United States. Moscow is at the same latitude as Sitka, Alaska. Kiev is as far north as Newfoundland. And because the inland territory is so vast, the benefits of warm, moist, seaborne air reach very little of it.

Ukraine and Moldavia, part rolling steppe, part mountains, have a fairly mild climate. With their rich black soil, they are prime agricultural regions. In Ukraine are industrial cities like Donetsk, with 22 coal mines, and Krivoy Rog, with some of the country's largest steel mills.

On the Black Sea coast, sunshine and beaches attract millions of vacationers. Some cities are sheltered from cold, northern winds by the Caucasus Mountains, which reach from the Black Sea to the Caspian. Some people live in mountain villages so isolated that each has its own language. Others live in subtropical lowlands, with orange groves, vineyards, and tea plantations.

In Kazakhstan and the republics to the south, summers are warm and long, but dry. If you fly over parts of this region, you see great stretches of desert, with bright green patches where irrigation canals make it possible to grow rice, fruit, and especially cotton. The water comes chiefly from two rivers, the Amu Darya and the Syr Darya, that flow into the Aral Sea. Since ancient times, these rivers have been vital to the desert people, who say, to wish you good luck: "May there be much water in your life!"

But there is not much for the Aral Sea. Once it was bigger than Lake Michigan. For the last 30 years, so much water from the two rivers has been taken for irrigation that little is left when they reach the Aral, which has shrunk in volume by two-thirds. Fishing families who once lived on the shore of the sea now find the water's edge 20 miles (32 km) away. The government provides jobs for some by shipping frozen fish to a processing plant near the old fisheries.

The great rivers of Siberia, the Lena, the Ob, and the Angara-Yenisey system, originate in high mountain glaciers. The Angara flows through Lake Baykal, the world's oldest, deepest lake, with an area a little larger than the state of Maryland. On these rivers are some of the world's biggest hydroelectric stations, built to supply power to the coal and metal mines, oil and gas fields, lumber-processing plants, and cities of resource-rich Siberia.

Most of this region is permafrost. Expensive methods of construction are needed to ensure that, if the top layer of earth thaws, buildings don't sag or railroad tracks sink. In January, despite average temperatures of minus 16°F (-27°C), city life proceeds, children go to school, and workers stay at their jobs.

On the taiga and tundra, across Siberia to the edge of cities on the Pacific coast, many native peoples follow their traditional pursuits of hunting, fishing, and reindeer herding. But today they live in houses instead of tents made of reindeer skin, and often ride snowmobiles. Some are fur farmers and others work in the industries developed after the Russian Revolution of 1917.

In that year, under Vladimir Lenin, the Bolsheviks took power. The tsars had been overthrown, and the country became communist. Dark years of oppression and World War II followed under Joseph Stalin. Then, during a long stagnant period, the economy began to collapse, and leaders shut out Western ideas.

In 1985 Mikhail Gorbachev became head of the Communist Party—the nation's most powerful position. His program of *perestroika*, or restructuring, aims to bring new life to industry and agriculture by removing powers from the central government and letting people in the factories and on the farms make decisions. Gorbachev also introduced *glasnost*, or openness, that welcomes cooperation with other nations. Then, in 1990, in a step toward *demokratizatsia*—democratization—Gorbachev was elected President. With this move he will try to shift power from the party to the Soviet Constitution and the people's elected representatives. As leader of the world's largest country, Gorbachev faces some of the world's greatest challenges.

Official name: *Union of Soviet Socialist Republics*
Area: *8,649,538 sq mi (22,402,200 sq km)*
Population: *288,742,000*
Capital: *Moscow (met. pop. 9,390,000)*
Ethnic groups: *Russian, Ukrainian, Uzbek, other*
Language: *Russian, Ukrainian, many others*
Religious groups: *Russian Orthodox, Muslim*
Economy: *Agr: grains, potatoes, sugar beets, vegetables, fruit, tobacco, cotton, oilseeds, flax, livestock. Ind: machinery, mining, chemicals, oil, natural gas, metals, lumber, motor vehicles, textiles, fishing*
Currency: *ruble*

1 *Russian Republic, U.S.S.R.*

2 *Ukraine, U.S.S.R.*

Soviet Union

1 *St. Basil's Cathedral stands before the walls of the Kremlin in Moscow. Inside the Kremlin are tsarist palaces and churches, and offices of the Soviet government.*

2 *First graders of Odessa carry flowers for their teachers on the opening day of school.*

3 *A hunter on the Taymyr Peninsula sets out to find arctic foxes and wild reindeer.*

4 *Sturgeon eggs, carefully washed, strained, and salted, become caviar in Astrakhan, on the Volga River Delta.*

5 *A craftsman fashions jewelry from amber, fossilized pieces of resin that oozed from pine trees along the shores of the Baltic Sea 30 to 40 million years ago.*

3 *Siberia, U.S.S.R.*

4 *Russian Republic, U.S.S.R.*

5 *Lithuania, U.S.S.R.*

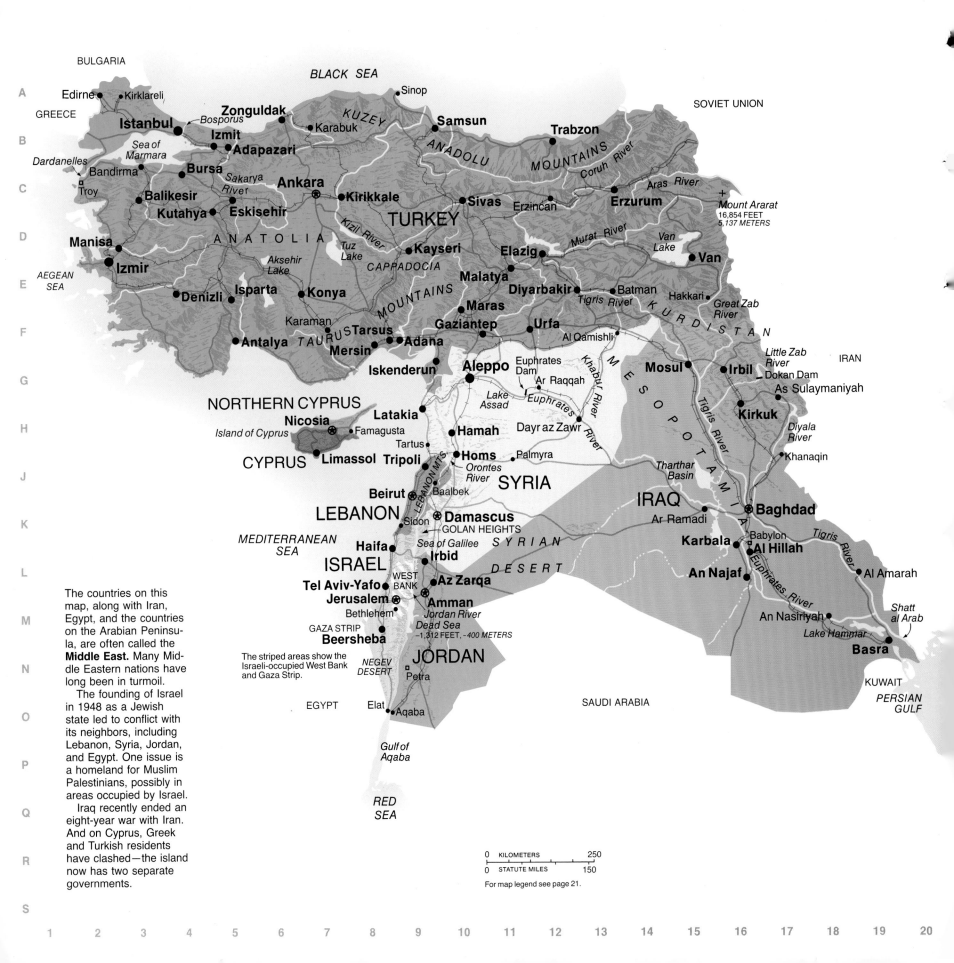

BULGARIA

BLACK SEA

SOVIET UNION

GREECE

Edirne • Kirklareli

Sinop

Zonguldak KUZEY

Samsun

Trabzon

Istanbul Bosporus

Izmit

Karabuk

ANADOLU

Adapazari

Sea of Marmara

MOUNTAINS

Coruh River

Dardanelles

Bursa Sakarya River

Aras River

Bandirma

Ankara

Kirikkale

Sivas

Erzincan

Erzurum

Mount Ararat
16,854 FEET
5,137 METERS

Troy

TURKEY

Balikesir

Kutahya **Eskisehir**

ANATOLIA

Tuz Lake

Kizil River

CAPPADOCIA

Kayseri

Murat River

Elazig

Van Lake

Manisa

Akshehir Lake

Diyarbakir

Batman

Hakkari

Van

Izmir

AEGEAN SEA

Malatya

Isparta

Konya

MOUNTAINS

Maras

Tigris River

KURDISTAN

Great Zab River

Denizli

Karaman

Gaziantep

Urfa

Al Qamishli

IRAN

Little Zab River

Antalya

TAURUS **Tarsus**

Adana

Euphrates Dam

Mosul

Irbil

Dokan Dam

Mersin

Ar Raqqah

Khabur River

M
E
S
O
P
O
T
A
M
I
A

As Sulaymaniyah

Iskenderun

Aleppo

Lake Assad

Euphrates

Tigris River

Kirkuk

NORTHERN CYPRUS

Latakia

Dayr az Zawr

Diyala River

Nicosia

Famagusta

Hamah

Island of Cyprus

Tartus

Khanaqin

CYPRUS

Limassol Tripoli

Homs

Palmyra

Tharthar Basin

LEBANON MTS.

Orontes River

SYRIA

Beirut

Baalbek

IRAQ

Baghdad

Ar Ramadi

Babylon

Tigris River

LEBANON

Sidon

Damascus

GOLAN HEIGHTS

SYRIAN

Karbala

Al Hillah

MEDITERRANEAN SEA

Haifa

Sea of Galilee

DESERT

An Najaf

Euphrates River

Al Amarah

ISRAEL

Irbid

Tel Aviv-Yafo

WEST BANK

Az Zarqa

Shatt al Arab

Jerusalem

Amman

An Nasiriyah

Bethlehem

Jordan River

Lake Hammar

GAZA STRIP

Dead Sea
−1,312 FEET, −400 METERS

Basra

Beersheba

JORDAN

KUWAIT

NEGEV DESERT

Petra

SAUDI ARABIA

PERSIAN GULF

EGYPT

Elat

Aqaba

RED SEA

Gulf of Aqaba

The countries on this map, along with Iran, Egypt, and the countries on the Arabian Peninsula, are often called the **Middle East.** Many Middle Eastern nations have long been in turmoil.

The founding of Israel in 1948 as a Jewish state led to conflict with its neighbors, including Lebanon, Syria, Jordan, and Egypt. One issue is a homeland for Muslim Palestinians, possibly in areas occupied by Israel.

Iraq recently ended an eight-year war with Iran. And on Cyprus, Greek and Turkish residents have clashed—the island now has two separate governments.

The striped areas show the Israeli-occupied West Bank and Gaza Strip.

0 KILOMETERS 250

0 STATUTE MILES 150

For map legend see page 21.

Turkey

East and West meet in Turkey, the country that bridges the continents of Asia and Europe. The European part of Turkey is a small peninsula of rolling grasslands in southeastern Europe. Across a series of waterways linking the Aegean and the Black Seas lies the Asian part of Turkey, a large, mountain-rimmed plateau called Anatolia.

Istanbul, Turkey's largest city, is the only city in the world on two continents. It occupies land on both sides of the Bosporus. Ferries and bridges connect its two halves. Once called Constantinople, Istanbul has been a major seaport for thousands of years.

More than half of Turkey's people are farmers. Many live in the mild coastal areas where they plant crops such as cotton, tobacco, citrus fruit, and nuts for export, and raise livestock. On the drier and colder plateau, farmers grow mostly wheat and barley for use at home. In mountainous eastern Turkey, farming is more difficult, although people grow grain in the valleys and raise Angora goats for their long, silky hair. Though Turkey has some oil deposits, it must import most of its petroleum needs.

Turkey's rich mineral resources of coal, chromite, copper, and iron, and its cotton crop support major industries. These employ many city dwellers and make Turkey one of the most industrialized countries in the Middle East.

East meets West in Turkey's culture and government as well. Formerly part of the Islamic Ottoman Empire, Turkey became a republic in 1923. The new leader, Kemal Atatürk, abolished many Islamic customs and brought in European ideas and technology. This set the stage for rapid modernization and the adoption of Western systems of law, education, and politics.

Official name: *Republic of Turkey*
Area: *300,948 sq mi (779,452 sq km)*
Population: *55,356,000*
Capital: *Ankara (met. pop. 2,235,035)*
Ethnic groups: *Turk, Kurd*
Language: *Turkish, Kurdish, Arabic*
Religious groups: *Sunni Muslim*
Economy: *Agr: cotton, tobacco, grains, sugar beets, fruit, nuts, livestock. Ind: textiles, food processing, minerals, steel, oil, construction, lumber, paper*
Currency: *Turkish lira*

Northern Cyprus

In 1983 Turkish Cypriots declared independence for the northern third of the island of Cyprus, severing all ties with the Greek-speaking majority in the south. Turkey alone recognizes this claim. Turkish aid and tourism bolster a struggling agricultural economy based mostly on citrus fruit and potatoes.

Official name: *Turkish Republic of Northern Cyprus*
Area: *1,295 sq mi (3,354 sq km)*
Population: *165,000*
Capital: *Nicosia (pop. 37,400)*

Cyprus

A delightful climate that allows a long growing season, golden sandy beaches, and archaeological sites spanning a rich history describe one face of the island nation of Cyprus. Its political climate shows a different one.

Fighting between the Greek-speaking Christian majority and Turkish-speaking Muslim minority has resulted in a divided country, with the capital, Nicosia, split in the process. Greek Cypriots control the south; there, agriculture, light industry, tourism, and generous doses of foreign aid sustain the economy.

Official name: *Republic of Cyprus*
Area: *2,277 sq mi (5,897 sq km)*
Population: *563,000*
Capital: *Nicosia (pop. 149,100)*

Lebanon

Tiny, strife-torn Lebanon was once a tourist paradise. Winter visitors could swim in the warm Mediterranean Sea, then ski the slopes of the Lebanon Mountains, all on the same day.

Beirut, the capital, was prosperous and cosmopolitan, the Paris of the Middle East. A center of international banking, trade, and education, Beirut had been a major port since the time of Phoenician traders, who sailed the Mediterranean 3,500 years ago.

Most of the Lebanese live in Beirut and other cities, mainly along the Mediterranean coast. Many are employed in Lebanon's major industries. Rural Lebanese are chiefly farmers. On the humid coastal plain they grow citrus fruit, olives, and grapes. Inland they plant vegetables, fruit, and grains in a fertile valley sheltered by two mountain ranges.

Although about 90 percent of Lebanon's people are Arab, about one-third of them are Christian. This makes Lebanon unique in the Middle East where most Arabs are Muslim. Since the 1970s, Lebanon's various Christian groups and several groups of Muslims, including Palestinian refugees, have been at war with each other. Many people have been killed in the turmoil, which has shattered Lebanon's economy and left its beautiful capital in ruin.

Official name: *Republic of Lebanon*
Area: *4,015 sq mi (10,400 sq km)*
Population: *3,301,000*
Capital: *Beirut (met. pop. 1,100,000)*
Ethnic groups: *Arab, Armenian*
Language: *Arabic, French*
Religious groups: *Muslim, Christian*
Economy: *Agr: fruit, wheat, corn, barley, potatoes, tobacco, olives, onions. Ind: banking, food processing, textiles, cement, oil, chemicals, jewelry, metals*
Currency: *Lebanese pound*

Syria

The roots of civilization in Syria reach far back into time. People have lived inside the walls of Damascus, its capital and major center of trade, since 2500 B.C., making it one of the oldest continuously occupied cities in the world.

Behind a narrow, fertile plain along the Mediterranean Sea rise mountain ranges that run south along Lebanon's eastern border. Damascus and other cities lie on a plain east of these mountains. Syria's industry is centered here, and most Syrians live here or on the coast.

Despite their rich urban heritage, many Syrians are farmers. Along the coast they grow citrus fruit and vegetables. In the arid land east of the cities they live in river valleys, using the water to irrigate fields of barley, wheat, and cotton. In the Syrian Desert, small groups of nomads herd flocks of sheep and goats among the sparse vegetation.

The Euphrates River, an ancient source of fertile land, holds great promise for Syria's future. In 1978, a dam built in the north created 50-mile-long (80 km) Lake Assad. When the irrigation system is operating fully, Syrians may have twice as much farmland as they do now. The dam is designed to provide abundant hydroelectric power, an important source of energy since Syria lacks great oil reserves.

Predominantly Arab and Muslim, Syria does not recognize Israel, its neighbor to the southwest, as a legitimate state. In recent decades, Syria and Israel have fought several wars as well as intervening in Lebanon's civil war.

Official name: *Syrian Arab Republic*
Area: *71,044 sq mi (184,004 sq km)*
Population: *12,080,000*
Capital: *Damascus (met. pop. 1,219,448)*
Ethnic groups: *Arab, Kurd, Armenian*
Language: *Arabic, Kurdish, Armenian*
Religious groups: *Sunni Muslim, Christian*
Economy: *Agr: cotton, fruit, grains, tobacco, livestock. Ind: textiles, food processing, phosphates, oil*
Currency: *Syrian pound*

Iraq

Tall, stately date palms laden with clusters of sweet fruit would have been a familiar sight to Adam and Eve in the biblical Garden of Eden. Scholars locate Eden near the port of Basra in southern Iraq. Here date palms line the banks of the Tigris and Euphrates Rivers where they join to form the Shatt al Arab waterway.

More than 4,000 years ago, the Sumerians built the world's first known cities on the Tigris-Euphrates plain. The rivers provided irrigation for crops that would support urban settlement. Most of Iraq's people still live on the plain, many clustered in Baghdad, the capital, and other cities. Iraq has the world's second largest oil reserves, and oil income has turned Baghdad into a modern center of government and industry.

Desert covers southwestern Iraq, the traditional home of nomadic Bedouin herders, though many have now joined settled farmers and herders on the plain. Kurds inhabit the mountainous region that stretches from northern Iraq into neighboring countries. Non-Arab Muslims, the Kurds have long fought the Arab Iraqis for the independence of their homeland, Kurdistan.

For most of the 1980s, Iraqis also battled their Iranian neighbors for control of the Shatt al Arab waterway in the south, with its access to oil fields, refineries, and shipping terminals. They waged bloody battles that cost billions of dollars and thousands of lives. Now that the fighting has ceased, Iraq can rechannel some of its oil income to improve its most ancient asset, the fertile lands of the Tigris-Euphrates plain.

Official name: *Republic of Iraq*
Area: *169,235 sq mi (438,317 sq km)*
Population: *18,074,000*
Capital: *Baghdad (met. pop. 3,844,608)*
Ethnic groups: *Arab, Kurd*
Language: *Arabic, Kurdish*
Religious groups: *Shia Muslim, Sunni Muslim*
Economy: *Agr: vegetables, wheat, barley, dates, rice, cotton, livestock. Ind: oil, textiles, cement*
Currency: *Iraqi dinar*

Israel

What's prickly on the outside and sweet on the inside? A cactus fruit that Israelis call a sabra—the name they also give Jewish people born in Israel. With the creation of modern Israel in 1948, many Jews returned to their historic homeland, lost when the Romans exiled their ancestors some 1,900 years ago. Today, sabras make up about half the population of Israel.

Aside from the fertile Mediterranean coast, most of Israel is desert. To expand farmland, Israelis have mastered water management. One project pipes fresh water from the Sea of Galilee to irrigate *kibbutzim* (collective farms with assets owned in common) and *moshavim* (cooperative farms with some private ownership) as far south as the Negev Desert.

Israel's well-educated and chiefly urban work force competes worldwide in high-technology industries. But diamond cutting and polishing, centered in the city of Tel Aviv-Yafo, ranks as the most profitable industry, contributing a third of the nation's export income.

For centuries other native-born inhabitants of the area, the Muslim Arabs, have regarded the land called Palestine as *their* homeland. They, too, revere ancient sites in Jerusalem, as do Jews and Christians. Though Palestinians now officially accept Israel's right to exist, they condemn its occupation of land seized from several Arab nations in 1967. Two peoples coveting one historic homeland—this is the dilemma that has led to years of warfare in the Middle East.

Official name: *State of Israel*
Area: *8,473 sq mi (21,946 sq km)*
Occupied territories: 2,416 sq mi (6,258 sq km)
Population: *4,480,000 (Occupied terr: 1,611,000)*
Capital: *Jerusalem (pop. 457,700)*
Ethnic groups: *Jewish, Arab*
Language: *Hebrew, Arabic*
Religious groups: *Jewish, Muslim (mostly Sunni)*
Economy: *Agr: citrus and other fruit, vegetables, cotton, livestock. Ind: food processing, diamond cutting, textiles, chemicals, machinery, electronics*
Currency: *new Israeli shekel*

Jordan

Dressed for a military parade, Jordan's king sports a shiny silver dagger, a symbol of the country's legendary Desert Patrol. Today only a few camelback patrols police Jordan's eastern desert, where they once settled disputes among the tent-dwelling Bedouin, who herd livestock. Their way of life and the Bedouin's are still much admired in Jordan.

Jordan's meager farmland lies in the valley of the Jordan River, where vegetables, fruit, and grain grow in irrigated fields. Minerals from the salty Dead Sea and other sites are made into fertilizer at a plant in Aqaba, Jordan's only port.

Jordan exports experts, it is said. Since 1962, the education-conscious country has started four major universities, including one in Amman, the capital. Many graduates obtain jobs in the oil-rich Persian Gulf states; the earnings they send home greatly aid Jordan's economy.

Following the 1948-49 war with Israel, Jordan controlled the West Bank of the Jordan River, home of Muslim Palestinians, until Israel occupied it in 1967. Now close to a million Palestinian refugees live in Jordan. Jordan has renounced claims to the West Bank, but the issue of a Palestinian homeland there remains unresolved.

Official name: *Hashemite Kingdom of Jordan*
Area: *35,467 sq mi (91,860 sq km)*
Population: *2,956,000*
Capital: *Amman (pop. 812,500)*
Ethnic groups: *Arab*
Language: *Arabic*
Religious groups: *Sunni Muslim, Christian*
Economy: *Agr: vegetables, fruit, olive oil, wheat, livestock. Ind: chemicals, phosphates, potash*
Currency: *Jordanian dinar*

1 *Turkey*

2 *Turkey*

Turkey

1 *In Istanbul, the only city to straddle two continents, the domes and minarets of the Süleymaniye Mosque overlook waterways that separate Europe from Asia (in the far background).*

2 *Women of Turkey's Anatolia region weave a traditional rug with bold, geometric patterns. Turkish rugs have long been prized around the world.*

1 *Israel*

2 *Israel*

Israel

1 *A devout Jew prays at the Western Wall in Jerusalem, a city sacred to Jews, Christians, and Muslims. The Wall is all that remains of a temple destroyed in* A.D. *70.*

2 *Source of life in a dry land, the Jordan River winds through green orchards and gray fields of cotton on a kibbutz, an Israeli collective farm.*

Jordan

3 *Jordanian women tend thriving cucumber plants in a plastic hothouse. Modern techniques yield big harvests from Jordan's scant fertile land.*

3 *Jordan*

4 *Lebanon*

5 *Iraq*

Lebanon

4 *An antiaircraft gun becomes a jungle gym for children in Beirut. Discarded shells on the ground speak of the dangers of life in Lebanon's war-torn capital.*

Iraq

5 *In the ancient city of Baghdad, domed mosques share the skyline with modern structures built by Iraq's oil wealth.*

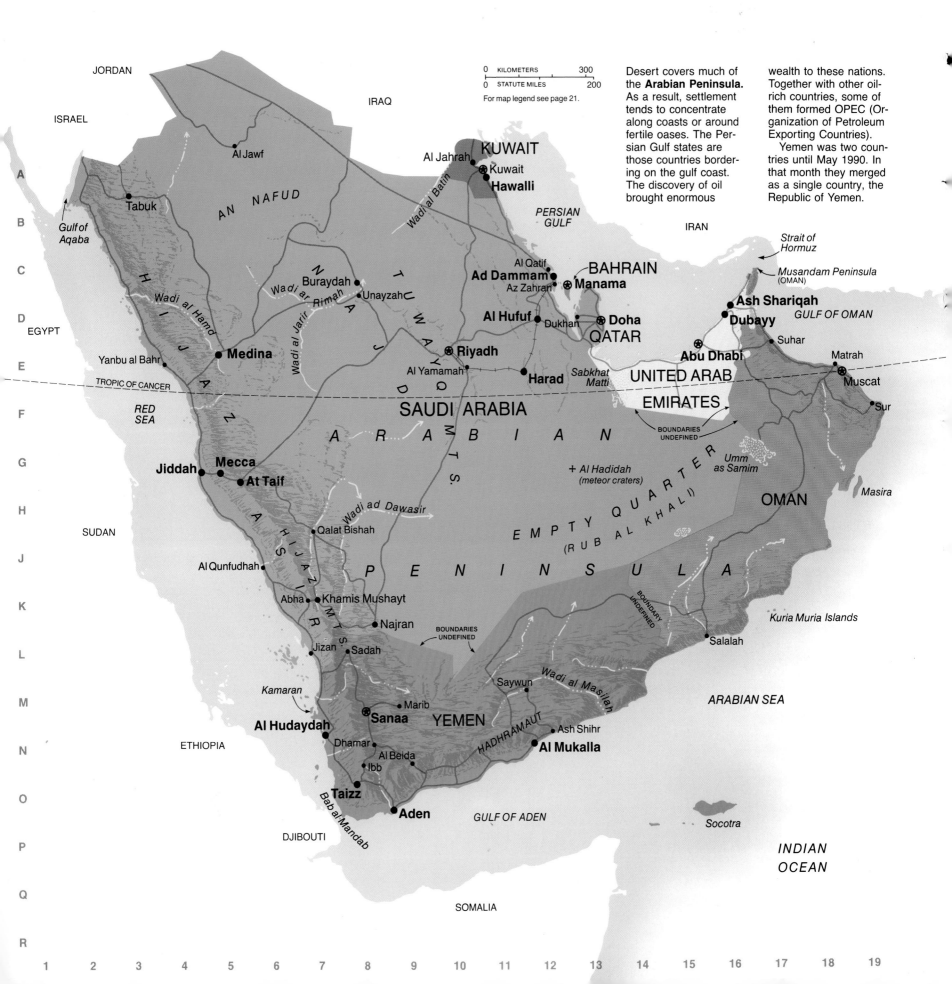

JORDAN

ISRAEL

IRAQ

EGYPT

SUDAN

ETHIOPIA

DJIBOUTI

SOMALIA

Desert covers much of the **Arabian Peninsula.** As a result, settlement tends to concentrate along coasts or around fertile oases. The Persian Gulf states are those countries bordering on the gulf coast. The discovery of oil brought enormous wealth to these nations. Together with other oil-rich countries, some of them formed OPEC (Organization of Petroleum Exporting Countries).

Yemen was two countries until May 1990. In that month they merged as a single country, the Republic of Yemen.

KILOMETERS
0   300
STATUTE MILES
0   200
For map legend see page 21.

A

B

C

D

E

F

G

H

J

K

L

M

N

O

P

Q

R

Al Jawf

Tabuk

Gulf of Aqaba

AN NAFUD

Wadi al Batin

KUWAIT
Al Jahrah
⊗ Kuwait
Hawalli

PERSIAN GULF

IRAN

Strait of Hormuz

Musandam Peninsula (OMAN)

Buraydah
Wadi ar Rimah
Unayzah

Al Qatif
Az Zahran
Ad Dammam ⊗ **Manama**
BAHRAIN

Ash Shariqah
Dubayy
Suhar
GULF OF OMAN

N
A
J
D

Al Hufuf Dukhan
Doha
QATAR

⊗ **Abu Dhabi**

Matrah
⊗ Muscat

Yanbu al Bahr

Wadi al Hamd

Medina

Wadi al Jarir

TROPIC OF CANCER

RED SEA

H
I
J
A
Z

T
U
W
A
Y
Q

⊗ **Riyadh**
Al Yamamah

D
A
H
N
A

Harad

Sabkhat Matti

UNITED ARAB
EMIRATES

Sur

SAUDI ARABIA

BOUNDARIES UNDEFINED

Jiddah **Mecca**
At Taif

A
R
A
B
I
A
N

+ Al Hadidah
(meteor craters)

Umm as Samim

OMAN

Masira

H
I
J
A
Z

M
T
S.

Wadi ad Dawasir

Qalat Bishah

E M P T Y   Q U A R T E R
(R U B   A L   K H A L I)

Al Qunfudhah

P
E
N
I
N
S
U
L
A

BOUNDARY
UNDEFINED

Kuria Muria Islands

Abha **Khamis Mushayt**

A
S
I
R

Najran

BOUNDARIES
UNDEFINED

Salalah

Jizan
Sadah

M
T
S.

Kamaran

Saywun
Wadi al Masilah

ARABIAN SEA

Al Hudaydah
Dhamar

Marib
⊗ **Sanaa**   **YEMEN**

HADHRAMAUT
Ash Shihr
Al Mukalla

Al Beida
Ibb

Taizz

Bab al Mandab

Aden   *GULF OF ADEN*

Socotra

INDIAN OCEAN

1 2 3 4 5 6 7 8 9 10 11 12 13 14 15 16 17 18 19

Saudi Arabia

For more than 13 centuries, Muslims all over the world have turned to face western Arabia five times a day. They are directing prayers to the Kaaba in Mecca, Islam's holiest city and birthplace of the Prophet Muhammad. Faithful Muslims hope to make the required hajj, or pilgrimage, to Mecca at least once in their lives.

During those centuries much of the region's income came from pilgrims who visited Mecca and Medina, Muhammad's burial place. Today, Saudi Arabia's riches come from its east: A quarter of the world's known oil reserves lie on the Persian Gulf and in the eastern desert.

Desert covers most of Saudi Arabia, harshest in the southeast's sparsely populated Empty Quarter. The country has no rivers or permanent bodies of water. Rainfall irrigates fertile croplands in the southwest, while seasonal wadis or oases provide water for farming elsewhere. For millennia, nomadic Bedouin herders have brought their livestock to graze at desert oases fringed with date palms. Riyadh, the country's capital, sits amid a large oasis.

The modern kingdom of Saudi Arabia did not exist until 1932, six years before the first major oil strike was made. Ibn Saud, who had spent nearly 25 years uniting the warring tribes of the Arabian Peninsula, became its first king.

Oil money propelled Saudi Arabia into the modern world, providing funds for new schools, hospitals, towns, ports, and factories. Yet the country remains a firm guardian of conservative Islamic life. Women cannot board a plane or check into a hotel room without permission from a male relative, and anyone renouncing the Islamic faith risks the death penalty.

Official name: *Kingdom of Saudi Arabia*
Area: *830,000 sq mi (2,149,690 sq km)*
Population: *14,733,000*
Capital: *Riyadh (met. pop. 1,200,000)*
Ethnic groups: *Arab*
Language: *Arabic*
Religious groups: *Sunni Muslim, Shia Muslim*
Economy: *Agr: wheat, dates, livestock. Ind: oil, petrochemicals, cement, steel, construction, fertilizer*
Currency: *Saudi riyal*

Kuwait

When a Kuwaiti couple get married, they receive the blessings of their families and more than $7,000 from the Kuwaiti government. Marriage bonuses are only one of the many benefits that oil money brings to citizens of this desert nation at the head of the Persian Gulf. Others include free education, and subsidized health care, housing, food, electricity, and telephone service. Foreign workers receive some of the same benefits.

Before oil was discovered in 1938, the Kuwaiti economy relied on pearling, fishing, and trading. Lack of water limited cultivation to a few oases. Kuwait now has large facilities for distilling salt water, which enables crops to be grown and provides water for industry and for the personal use of the mostly urban population.

Official name: *State of Kuwait*
Area: *6,880 sq mi (17,818 sq km)*
Population: *2,090,000*
Capital: *Kuwait (pop. 44,335)*
Ethnic groups: *Arab, South Asian, Iranian*
Language: *Arabic, English*
Religious groups: *Sunni Muslim, Shia Muslim*
Economy: *Ind: oil, petrochemicals, desalination, food processing, salt, construction, fishing*
Currency: *Kuwaiti dinar*

Bahrain

One of the first countries on the Persian Gulf to strike oil may be the first to run out. Bahrain discovered oil in 1932 and soon was transformed from an archipelago of pearl divers to a significant producer of crude oil and natural gas. Of the 35 sand-covered islands that form the emirate of Bahrain, only 6 are inhabited. Causeways link Bahrain Island, the largest and most heavily populated, with two other islands and with the mainland of Saudi Arabia.

Since their oil reserves may be gone by the year 2000, Bahrainis are developing other industries. Manama, the capital, has become an international banking center, with many foreign banks recycling the gulf region's oil money. Aluminum processing, shipbuilding and repairs, a duty-free port, and satellite communications may also help to ensure a bright future.

Official name: *State of Bahrain*
Area: *267 sq mi (691 sq km)*
Population: *467,000*
Capital: *Manama (pop. 108,684)*
Ethnic groups: *Arab, Asian, Iranian*
Language: *Arabic*
Religious groups: *Shia Muslim, Sunni Muslim*
Economy: *Agr: fruit, vegetables. Ind: oil and oil refining, aluminum, banking, ship repair, fishing*
Currency: *Bahraini dinar*

Qatar

A Qatari who wants to complain to the government can go straight to the top. The emir, or ruler, of Qatar will meet in person with any citizen. He makes decisions in consultation with his advisers and within the strict code of Islamic law followed there. Life in this country of stony desert jutting out into the Persian Gulf is still guided by tradition, more so than in some gulf coast countries where oil exports have also brought new prosperity. Qatari women remain heavily veiled. Until recently they were forbidden to drive, even though luxury cars have long been available in Qatar.

Former pursuits of pearl diving and camel herding have given way to jobs in the oil and natural gas industries. Qatar relies on workers from Iran, India, and Pakistan to fill many of these jobs but seeks to replace them with educated, trained Qatari citizens. Today only about a quarter of the population is native Qatari.

Official name: *State of Qatar*
Area: *4,247 sq mi (11,000 sq km)*
Population: *437,000*
Capital: *Doha (pop. 217,294)*
Ethnic groups: *Arab, Indian, Pakistani, Iranian*
Language: *Arabic*
Religious groups: *Sunni Muslim*
Economy: *Ind: oil, fertilizer, petrochemicals, steel, cement, fishing*
Currency: *Qatari riyal*

United Arab Emirates

In the dusty haze of dawn in Sharjah, one of the United Arab Emirates, young boys race their grumbling camels along a six-mile desert course. No betting occurs at these popular contests. It is forbidden by Islamic law in this federation of seven states, each ruled by an emir, or hereditary chieftain.

The discovery of oil in 1958 brought tremendous change to the emirates. Oil derricks drill along a coast once renowned for piracy. Oil money builds roads, ports, schools, and hospitals, and helps expand agricultural land.

When it comes to oil wealth, not all emirates were created equal. Abu Dhabi, which includes the capital, and Dubayy, another trade center, are the wealthiest, with the highest revenues.

Most of the population lives in towns that bear the same names as the emirates. For lack of citizens to fill all the jobs, foreigners form about 85 percent of the work force.

Official name: *United Arab Emirates*
Area: *32,278 sq mi (83,600 sq km)*
Population: *1,698,000*
Capital: *Abu Dhabi (pop. 242,975)*
Ethnic groups: *Arab, Indian, Pakistani, Iranian*
Language: *Arabic*
Religious groups: *Sunni Muslim, Shia Muslim*
Economy: *Agr: dates, alfalfa, vegetables. Ind: oil, fishing, petrochemicals, aluminum, cement*
Currency: *U.A.E. dirham*

Oman

Qaboos, the sultan's son, was dismayed. Oil had been found in Oman in 1964, but six years later life was little changed. Oman had once had a rich seafaring trade based on sail-driven dhows, but that had declined in the 20th century. Most Omanis now farmed, herded, or fished and had no education or health care. So Qaboos took matters into his own hands: He overthrew his father and became sultan himself.

Today, Oman has more than 350 primary schools instead of only three, and 47 hospitals instead of only one, but it remains largely rural. Isolated villages on the Musandam Peninsula overlook the strategic Strait of Hormuz that funnels oil-laden tankers into the Arabian Sea. Fertile areas on Oman's north coast produce mostly dates and on the south coast, livestock.

Mountains in the north and a barren inland plateau complete the picture. Besides oil, great promise lies with an expanding copper industry and the building of deep-water ports.

Official name: *Sultanate of Oman*
Area: *82,030 sq mi (212,457 sq km)*
Population: *1,420,000*
Capital: *Muscat (met. pop. 50,000)*
Ethnic groups: *Arab, Baluchi, Indian*
Language: *Arabic*
Religious groups: *Ibadhi Muslim, Sunni Muslim*
Economy: *Agr: fruit, dates, grains, cattle, camels. Ind: oil, natural gas, copper, cement, fishing*
Currency: *Omani rial*

Yemen

Arabia Felix, "happy Arabia," the ancient Romans called this region, famed for its rich trade in the precious resins, frankincense and myrrh. Legend says the Queen of Sheba ruled part of it as a wealthy kingdom more than 2,500 years ago. Yemen's capital, the walled city of Sanaa, was once a crossroads for camel caravans bearing goods from as far away as China.

The northern part of Yemen has the greatest share of natural advantages on the Arabian Peninsula. Here high mountains trap the yearly rains. Farmers sow fertile fields in valleys and on terraced hillsides. They grow grains and *qat*, the shrubby plant whose leaves are chewed for their narcotic effect.

By contrast, the south has very little fertile land. Even so, nearly half of the work force is involved in agriculture, growing grains and dates, and raising livestock. The south's economic life centers on the port of Aden, strategically located near the entrance to the Red Sea. A refinery at Aden processes imported crude oil.

From the 1960s to 1990 Yemen was two countries known as the Yemen Arab Republic and the People's Democratic Republic of Yemen. The latter had a socialist government. In May 1990, they united under one flag, fulfilling the old Arab saying, "All Yemen is one."

Official name: *Republic of Yemen*
Area: *203,850 sq mi (527,968 sq km)*
Population: *9,446,000*
Capital: *Sanaa (pop. 427,185)*
Ethnic groups: *Arab*
Language: *Arabic*
Religious groups: *Shia Muslim, Sunni Muslim*
Economy: *Agr: grains, qat, cotton, coffee, fruit, vegetables, livestock. Ind: oil, textiles, leather*
Currency: *Yemeni rial and dinar*

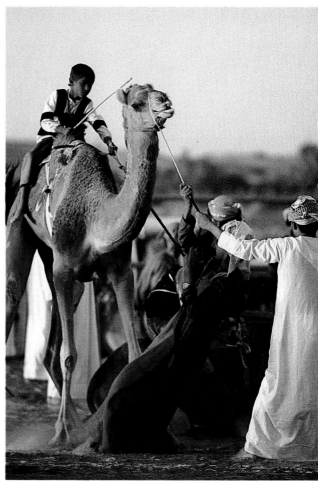

1 *United Arab Emirates*

United Arab Emirates

1 *Bedouin keepers haul a balky camel toward the starting line for a race in Sharjah, one of the seven states that make up the United Arab Emirates.*

Saudi Arabia

2 *A swirl of Muslim pilgrims circles the Kaaba—Islam's holiest shrine—in Mecca. Thousands come here each year to make the hajj, a pilgrimage aspired to at least once in a devout Muslim's life. Founded by the Prophet Muhammad in the seventh century, Islam is one of the most widely practiced religions in Asia.*

2 *Saudi Arabia*

1 *Oman*

2 *Saudi Arabia*

3 *Saudi Arabia*

Oman

1 *A fisherman hauls his catch from coastal waters. Oil industry jobs have lured Omani fishermen away from the sea.*

Saudi Arabia

2 *A lonely outpost in the Arabian desert, a derrick drills for oil in the vast Empty Quarter. One of the world's largest oil fields lies under its shifting sands.*

3 *Brightly dressed girls swing on a beach at Jiddah. In a few years they will don the veil still worn for modesty by most Saudi women.*

4 *Kuwait*

5 *Yemen*

Kuwait

4 *'Vette for Sale: Fast, expensive cars sell quickly in Kuwait city, where oil wealth provides for the luxuries of life as well as its necessities.*

Yemen

5 *An ilb tree stands beside the frankincense trail. The southern part of the Arabian Peninsula supplied frankincense and myrrh to the ancient world.*

For map legend see page 21.

0 KILOMETERS 300
0 STATUTE MILES 200

Landlocked Afghanistan long served as a buffer between Russia and the lands of the British Empire, which included Pakistan. Formerly part of British India, Pakistan was created as a separate Muslim country when India gained independence in 1947.

The Soviet invasion of Afghanistan in 1979 reminded the world of that country's strategic location and sent millions of its people fleeing as refugees, mostly to Pakistan.

Iran, to the west of these countries, has a Middle Eastern orientation and for eight years waged war with its western neighbor, Iraq.

SOVIET UNION

Lake Urmia

Khvoy

TURKEY

Tabriz

Ardabil

CASPIAN SEA

Orumiyeh

AZERBAIJAN

Bandar-e Anzali

Atrak River

SOVIET UNION

Pyandz River

Amu Darya R.

Pamir R.

Feyzabad

CHINA

Rasht

Bojnurd

Zanjan

Bandar-e Torkeman

Quchan

Mazar-e Sharif

HINDU KUSH

Chitral

K2 (Godwin Austen)
28,250 FEET
8,611 METERS

Qazvin

Baghlan

KARAKORAM RANGE

Sanandaj

Mt. Demavend
18,606 FEET
5,671 METERS

Mashhad

Meymaneh

Charikar

KASHMIR

Tehran

ELBURZ MOUNTAINS

Hamadan

Torbat-e Heydariyeh

PAROPAMISUS RANGE

Kabul

Mardan

Bakhtaran

Qom

DASHT-E KAVIR
(Salt Desert)

Herat

Harirud River

Indus River

FRONTIER

Area claimed by India

IRAQ

Arak

Kashan

Khyber Pass

Islamabad

Rawalpindi

Dezful

ZAGROS

IRAN

Birjand

Ghazni

Peshawar

AFGHANISTAN

NORTH-WEST

Gujrat

Sialkot

Karun River

Esfahan

DASHT-E LUT

Farah River

Qandahar

Dera Ismail Khan

Sargodha

PUNJAB

Gujranwala

Ahvaz

Yazd

Helmand River

Faisalabad

Lahore

Khorramshahr

MOUNTAINS

Zabol

DASHT-E MARGO

Zhob River

Ravi River

Okara

Abadan

Persepolis

Kerman

RIGESTAN

Quetta

Multan

Sutlej River

KUWAIT

Shiraz

Zahedan

Dera Ghazi Khan

Bahawalpur

INDIA

SAUDI ARABIA

Bushehr

Bam

CHAGAI HILLS

PAKISTAN

Persian Gulf

BAHRAIN

Bandar-e Abbas

BALUCHISTAN

Sukkur

GREAT INDIAN DESERT

QATAR

Strait of Hormuz

CENTRAL MAKRAN RANGE

SIND

Chah Bahar

Gulf of Oman

Hyderabad

UNITED ARAB EMIRATES

Karachi

Indus River

TROPIC OF CANCER

OMAN

ARABIAN SEA

INDIAN OCEAN

Iran

The stern face of a gray-bearded man dressed in black appeared often in the news in the 1980s. He was the Ayatollah Khomeini, a Muslim religious leader who inspired a revolution in Iran, replacing the monarchy of the shah with a republic based on the teachings of Islam.

Iran consists of a high inland plateau covered with gravel desert and salt flats and rimmed by mountains. Most people live in the mountainous north and northwest and on the fertile plain bordering the Caspian Sea. At least a third of Iran's cropland must be irrigated. Since ancient times, Iranians have used hand-dug underground canals called *qanats* to tap groundwater and carry it many miles to irrigate farmland. Grains are the chief crops. Sheep, tended by nomads, provide wool for finely woven carpets, known as "Persian" from Iran's former name, Persia.

Iran's people differ from those of other Middle Eastern countries in that they are mostly Persians, not Arabs, descended from Aryan peoples who migrated from central Asia long ago. Most of them are Shia Muslims. The Shia disagree in certain religious interpretations with the Sunni, who form the Muslim majority worldwide.

The discovery of oil in Iran dates back to 1908. In the 1960s and 1970s, the shah used oil income to modernize his backward agricultural country and expand industry, but there was growing discontent. Conservative Muslims complained that his values came from Western countries, not from the Koran, Islam's holy book.

The shah's regime collapsed in 1979, and Khomeini became the head of a religious form of government called a theocracy. Under Khomeini, Iran promoted the Islamic Revolution, often through acts of violence and terrorism.

In 1980 neighboring Iraq, taking advantage of Iran's weakened state and seeking to recover certain rights in the strategic Shatt al Arab waterway, attacked Iran. The war lasted eight years, disrupted agriculture and oil production, and took hundreds of thousands of lives.

Khomeini died in 1989. Iran's new government appears to be less militant. Yet, while the country tries to rebuild its damaged economy, the rest of the world waits to see whether the fervor of the Khomeini years is over.

Official name: *Islamic Republic of Iran*
Area: *636,296 sq mi (1,648,000 sq km)*
Population: *53,867,000*
Capital: *Tehran (met. pop. 6,022,029)*
Ethnic groups: *Persian, Azeri Turk, Kurd, other*
Language: *Persian, Turkic languages, Kurdish*
Religious groups: *Shia Muslim, Sunni Muslim*
Economy: *Agr: wheat, barley, rice, sugar, cotton, dates, grapes, sheep, goats, tea, tobacco, pistachios. Ind: oil, petrochemicals, textiles, cement, carpets*
Currency: *Iranian rial*

Afghanistan

Known as the crossroads of central Asia, Afghanistan has been invaded throughout its history. Successive groups have sought to attach this strategic, landlocked territory to their empires or to penetrate through the Khyber Pass to lands beyond. Those who came—Persians, Greeks, Arabs, and Mongols among them—left settlers who added to Afghanistan's ethnic diversity.

Afghanistan is covered with mountains or desert. A plain in the north provides good farmland. Most Afghans are subsistence farmers and herders, members of a variety of tribal and ethnic groups. Less that 25 percent of them can read, but there are plans to improve education.

In Afghanistan, tribal and ethnic loyalties come first, which makes national unity a problem. But when the Soviet Union sent troops to Afghanistan in 1979 to support the failing Marxist government there, they met fierce resistance from Muslim guerrillas known as *mujahidin*—holy warriors—united by their religious beliefs.

During the ten years of Soviet occupation, millions of Afghans fled to neighboring Pakistan and Iran or to the West. Thousands more left their bombed-out villages and crowded into Kabul, the capital. With Soviet troops now gone, Afghanistan faces a huge rebuilding task.

Official name: *Republic of Afghanistan*
Area: *251,773 sq mi (652,090 sq km)*
Population: *14,825,000*
Capital: *Kabul (pop. 1,127,417)*
Ethnic groups: *Pathan, Tajik, Uzbek, Hazara*
Language: *Pashtu, Dari (Persian), many others*
Religious groups: *Sunni Muslim, Shia Muslim*
Economy: *Agr: livestock, wheat, fruit, nuts. Ind: textiles, soap, furniture, shoes, cement, carpets*
Currency: *afghani*

Pakistan

The cradle of one of the world's oldest civilizations forms the heartland of modern Pakistan. About 4,500 years ago, planned cities with household water supplies and public sewer systems flourished on the Indus River Plain. Today that plain is the agricultural center of Pakistan, a Muslim nation created when India was partitioned in 1947. The Islamic faith unites the Pakistani people, who are otherwise divided by differences in language and cultural heritage.

Towering mountains arc through northern and western Pakistan. K2 (Godwin Austen), the world's second highest peak, rises 28,250 feet (8,611 m) in the Karakoram Range. Desert covers the southeast region, while a dry tableland ridged with low mountains spans the southwest.

About half of Pakistan's people are farmers. Wheat, the main food crop, and cotton, an important export crop and the basis for a growing textile industry, benefit from an extensive irrigation system. Much manufacturing is centered in Karachi, a populous port on the Arabian Sea.

During the 1980s, the Soviet occupation of neighboring Afghanistan sent millions of refugees through mountain passes into Pakistan's North-West Frontier Province. There, groups of Pathans, the province's fierce warriors, offered traditional Muslim and tribal hospitality to their kinsmen from across the border.

Official name: *Islamic Republic of Pakistan*
Area: *307,374 sq mi (796,095 sq km)*
Population: *110,407,000*
Capital: *Islamabad (met. pop. 204,364)*
Ethnic groups: *Punjabi, Sindhi, Pathan, Baluchi*
Language: *Urdu, Punjabi, Sindhi, Pashtu*
Religious groups: *Sunni Muslim, Shia Muslim*
Economy: *Agr: wheat, rice, cotton, sugarcane. Ind: textiles, steel, food processing, cement, fertilizer, oil and natural gas*
Currency: *Pakistan rupee*

1 *Afghanistan*

Afghanistan

1 *Two women of Kabul wear the billowy* chadri *that screens face and body from public gaze. The veil is voluntary in Afghanistan, where many women now wear Western dress.*

Iran

2 *Tehran clings to the southern slopes of the snow-dusted Elburz Mountains. Modern buildings here in the northern part of the capital give way to old bazaars and twisted lanes in the south.*

2 *Iran*

3 *Pakistan*

4 *Pakistan*

Pakistan

3 *Afghan children receive religious instruction at a makeshift school in western Pakistan. Pakistan took in many refugees when the Soviet Union occupied Afghanistan.*

4 *Bobbing in rowboat-like howdahs, women and children of western Pakistan ride camels to a wedding in traditional style.*

5 *Young women return the gaze of bystanders from a bus in Lahore. Many women travel freely and unveiled in Pakistan's large cities.*

5 *Pakistan*

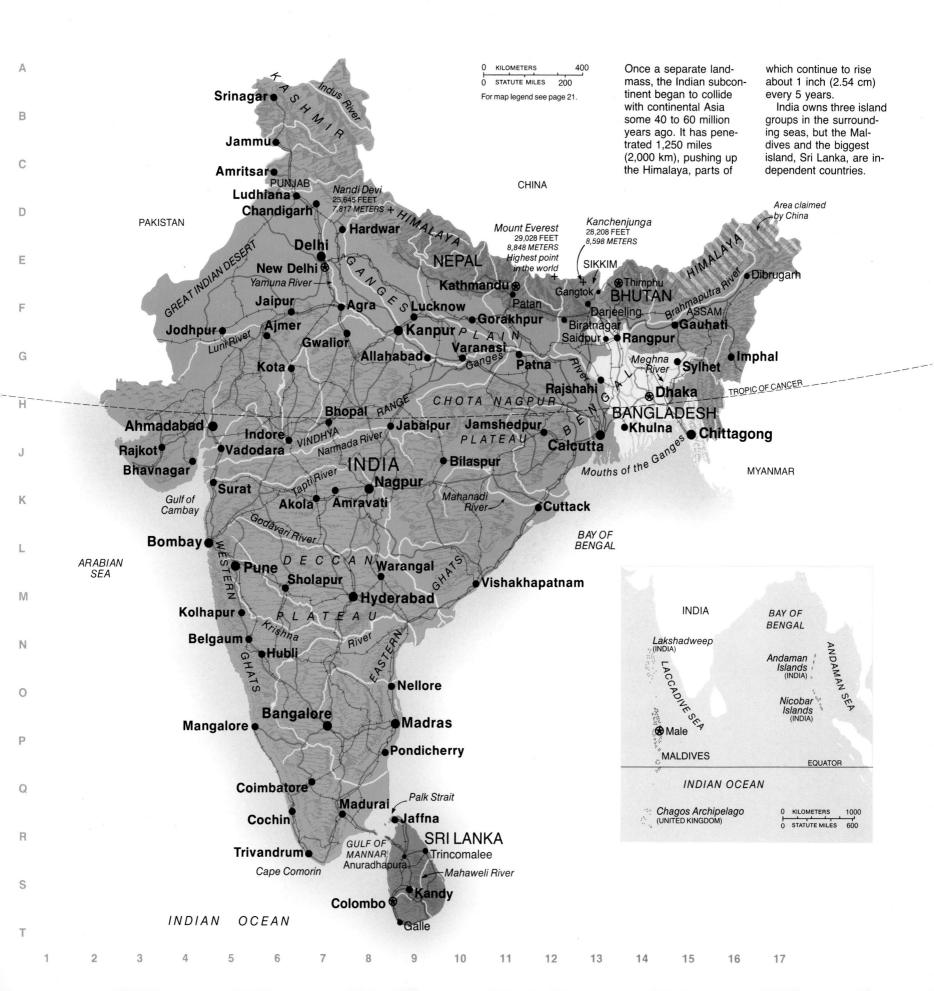

A B C D E F G H J K L M N O P Q R S T

1 2 3 4 5 6 7 8 9 10 11 12 13 14 15 16 17

Srinagar

Jammu

Amritsar

Ludhiana
Chandigarh

PUNJAB

KASHMIR

Indus River

Nandi Devi
25,645 FEET
7,817 METERS +

HIMALAYA

CHINA

Hardwar

Delhi

PAKISTAN

GREAT INDIAN DESERT

New Delhi ⊕
Yamuna River

Mount Everest
29,028 FEET
8,848 METERS
Highest point
in the world
+

Kanchenjunga
28,208 FEET
8,598 METERS

Area claimed
by China

Jaipur

Agra

Lucknow

NEPAL

Kathmandu ⊕

Patan

SIKKIM

Gangtok

⊕ Thimphu

BHUTAN

Darjeeling

Brahmaputra River

ASSAM

Dibrugarh

Jodhpur

Ajmer

Gwalior

Kanpur

P L A I N

Gorakhpur

Biratnagar
Saidpur

Rangpur

Gauhati

Lunr River

GANGES

Imphal

Kota

Allahabad

Varanasi
Ganges

Patna

River

Meghna
River

Sylhet

Rajshahi

Dhaka

BANGLADESH

BENGAL

TROPIC OF CANCER

Ahmadabad

Bhopal

RANGE

CHOTA NAGPUR

Jabalpur

Jamshedpur
PLATEAU

Khulna

Chittagong

Indore

VINDHYA

Narmada River

Calcutta

Rajkot

Vadodara

INDIA

Bilaspur

Mouths of the Ganges

MYANMAR

Bhavnagar

Surat

Tapti River

Nagpur

*Gulf of
Cambay*

Akola

Amravati

*Mahanadi
River*

Cuttack

Godavari River

BAY OF
BENGAL

Bombay

WESTERN

DECCAN

Warangal

Vishakhapatnam

*ARABIAN
SEA*

Pune

Sholapur

GHATS

Kolhapur

Hyderabad

PLATEAU

Krishna

Belgaum

River

Hubli

EASTERN

Nellore

GHATS

Bangalore

Madras

Mangalore

Pondicherry

Coimbatore

Madurai

Cochin

Palk Strait

Jaffna

SRI LANKA

Trivandrum

*GULF OF
MANNAR*

Trincomalee

Anuradhapura

Mahaweli River

Cape Comorin

Colombo ⊕

Kandy

Galle

INDIAN OCEAN

Once a separate land-
mass, the Indian subcon-
tinent began to collide
with continental Asia
some 40 to 60 million
years ago. It has pene-
trated 1,250 miles
(2,000 km), pushing up
the Himalaya, parts of

which continue to rise
about 1 inch (2.54 cm)
every 5 years.
India owns three island
groups in the surround-
ing seas, but the Mal-
dives and the biggest
island, Sri Lanka, are independent countries.

0 KILOMETERS 400
0 STATUTE MILES 200
For map legend see page 21.

INDIA

BAY OF
BENGAL

Lakshadweep
(INDIA)

*Andaman
Islands*
(INDIA)

ANDAMAN SEA

LACCADIVE SEA

*Nicobar
Islands*
(INDIA)

⊕ Male

MALDIVES

EQUATOR

INDIAN OCEAN

Chagos Archipelago
(UNITED KINGDOM)

0 KILOMETERS 1000
0 STATUTE MILES 600

India

From the high wall of the Himalaya to the tip of Cape Comorin, the subcontinent of India reveals an enormous diversity of peoples, languages, and physical terrain. Tibetan-speaking herdsmen tend yaks and sheep in the western Himalaya. Hindi-speaking farmers live in mud-walled villages on the Ganges Plain. From Gypsies in the western desert to fishermen on the southwest coast, people converse in different languages. Hindi is the national one, but 14 other major languages exist.

India's population adds up to more than 835 million—second in size only to China. Nearly 40 percent of these people live on the fertile Ganges Plain. To the south stretches the Deccan Plateau, a central highland bordered by mountain ranges that drop to narrow coastal plains.

In this polyglot country, English serves as the chief language of government and business. This is a heritage from the years before 1947 when India was part of the far-flung British Empire and prized for its textiles, jute, indigo, spices, and land taxes. The British were the last of a number of conquerors.

Aryan herders from central Asia arrived about 1500 B.C. Their religion blended with practices of the local people to form Hinduism, which is followed by about 80 percent of Indians. Hinduism supports the organization of society into groups called castes. A person is born into a caste, which traditionally defines occupation, the groups one can eat with, and the groups into which one can marry. Groups with a very low status, such as latrine cleaners, were formerly called untouchables. The caste system still operates in India, although modern law makes discrimination illegal.

There are about 90 million Muslims in India, despite the fact that millions left in 1947, when the separate Muslim nation of Pakistan was partitioned off at the time of India's independence. Millions of Hindus and Sikhs also fled into India from the two areas designated as Pakistan, producing one of the largest migrations of people in history—and one of the bloodiest, as Muslims and non-Muslims slaughtered each other.

More than 7 out of 10 Indians live in villages, and farming supports about two-thirds of the work force. Much of the land is fertile, but most farmers own merely a few acres and many none at all. They cannot afford fertilizer, good seed, or machinery, and have to rely on the annual monsoon rains to provide water for their crops.

At least half of all Indians live in grinding poverty. In crowded cities, squatters' shacks spring up to house landless migrants from the countryside. More than eleven million people jam Calcutta, India's largest metropolitan area, and Bombay is not far behind. Industry is important in the cities. Cotton textiles are a major export, with huge factories located in Bombay. Calcutta manufactures jute, and the iron and steel mills of nearby Jamshedpur rank among Asia's largest. India also has a strong electronics industry.

With an electorate of about 400 million people, India is the world's largest democracy. Politicians campaign briskly in rural areas, where villagers who cannot read learn to recognize the different political parties by their symbols. Literacy is only 36 percent, but the government is trying to remedy this through village schools.

Hindus and Muslims still clash in India, as do Hindus and Sikhs, members of a militant offshoot of Hinduism, many of whom want their own independent state. Violence, poverty, and a skyrocketing population that by the year 2000 may exceed one billion provide the most serious challenges to the future of this diverse country.

Official name: *Republic of India*
Area: *1,269,346 sq mi (3,287,590 sq km)*
Population: *835,035,000*
Capital: *New Delhi (pop. 273,036)*
Ethnic groups: *Indo-Aryan, Dravidian*
Language: *Hindi, English, many other languages*
Religious groups: *Hindu, Sunni Muslim, other*
Economy: *Agr: rice, wheat, legumes, oilseeds, cotton, jute, sugarcane, rubber, tobacco, tea, coffee. Ind: textiles, food processing, steel, machinery, motor vehicles, electronics, cement, chemicals, mining, gems*
Currency: *Indian rupee*

Nepal

Nestled under the eaves of the lofty Himalaya, landlocked Nepal forms a steep staircase to Earth's highest mountain realm. Along its border with India, a flat region called the Terai lies only about 250 feet (75 m) above sea level. To the north, swift rivers lash the lower ranges of the Himalaya, shaping fertile valleys. On Nepal's border with China stand eight of the world's highest peaks, with Everest topping the rest.

The average per capita income in Nepal is only $160 a year. About 90 percent of the people are subsistence farmers. They plant grain and tend livestock in the central region and the Terai, where most Nepalese live. Yak herders inhabit the northern high mountain zone.

Nepal is the world's only official Hindu country, but Buddhism flourishes there as well. Temples and monuments of both faiths abound, especially in the Kathmandu Valley, site of the capital, Kathmandu. Festivals of either religion draw the whole community to celebrate.

Wood provides 70 percent of the country's fuel, and deforestation is rampant. Rapid population growth also drives farmers up mountain slopes to clear new fields. When the slopes are stripped of trees, erosion results, destroying fields and clogging rivers with mud. Villagers are planting new trees, and hydroelectric power may one day provide an energy alternative.

Official name: *Kingdom of Nepal*
Area: *54,362 sq mi (140,797 sq km)*
Population: *18,700,000*
Capital: *Kathmandu (pop. 235,160)*
Ethnic groups: *Indo-Nepalese, Tibeto-Nepalese*
Language: *Nepali*
Religious groups: *Hindu, Buddhist*
Economy: *Agr: rice, corn, wheat, sugarcane, oilseeds, jute, livestock. Ind: tourism, textiles, cement*
Currency: *Nepalese rupee*

Bhutan

Money is new to the Bhutanese, as are roads and tourists. After centuries of self-imposed isolation under the rule of Buddhist monks, the tiny Himalayan Kingdom of Bhutan, the Land of the Thunder Dragon, is entering the modern world slowly and cautiously.

Most Bhutanese grow grain and raise livestock on remote mountain slopes and in valleys cut by rivers flowing north to south. Fortress-like *dzongs*, massive stone religious and administrative centers, dominate the valleys. Above the tree line, herders pasture yaks in the summer. In southern Bhutan, farmers cultivate rice and fruit amid tropical vegetation.

Bhutan is ruled by a king under a special treaty with India that provides defense and foreign policy advice. To protect its cultural traditions, Bhutan limits tourists to a few thousand a year.

Official name: *Kingdom of Bhutan*
Area: *18,147 sq mi (47,000 sq km)*
Population: *1,534,000*
Capital: *Thimphu (pop. 15,000)*
Ethnic groups: *Bhotia, Nepalese*
Language: *Dzongkha (a Tibetan dialect), Nepali*
Religious groups: *Mahayana Buddhist, Hindu*
Economy: *Agr: grains, potatoes, fruit, cardamom. Ind: cement, chemicals, food processing, lumber*
Currency: *ngultrum*

Bangladesh

Water defines Bangladesh, the mostly flat delta country born of the silt carried by three major river systems: the Ganges, the Brahmaputra, and the Meghna. At the Bay of Bengal the rivers drop their remaining load. It spreads out in lacy fingers of land at the edge of the huge river delta.

The rivers constantly shift course, and annual monsoon rains flood their banks. This compels rural Bangladeshis—about 85 percent of the population—to build their houses on mounds of earth and raise them further on mud platforms. Boats provide most transportation; roads often wash out or break off at the river's edge.

Fertile soil, the country's chief resource, and ample water enable Bangladeshi farmers to harvest as many as three rice crops a year. This is seldom enough, though, to feed the inhabitants of the world's most densely populated agricultural nation. Farmers earn money by planting jute, Bangladesh's chief export. Cash crops of tea grow in hilly regions in the east.

The rainy season is a crucial time. Raging monsoon floods often combine with runoff from deforested slopes upriver in Nepal and northern India to drown the land, causing thousands of deaths and leaving millions of people homeless. At monsoon's end, cyclones may strike, followed by deadly tidal waves that surge up from the Bay of Bengal. When the rains come late, poor harvests cause widespread hunger.

Bangladesh was formerly East Pakistan, half of a two-part nation split off from India in 1947; West Pakistan lay about 1,000 miles (1,600 km) away. The two had little in common besides the Muslim faith, and the East fought a civil war to gain independence in 1971. Bangladesh depends on foreign aid for survival. Its leaders strive against huge odds to improve the agricultural economy and to provide health, education, and employment for its ever-growing population.

Official name: *People's Republic of Bangladesh*
Area: *55,598 sq mi (143,998 sq km)*
Population: *114,718,000*
Capital: *Dhaka (met. pop. 3,458,602)*
Ethnic groups: *Bengali*
Language: *Bengali*
Religious groups: *Sunni Muslim, Hindu*
Economy: *Agr: rice, jute, tea, sugarcane. Ind: textiles, fertilizer, steel, food processing, shrimp, leather*
Currency: *taka*

Maldives

The Maldives, an archipelago in the Indian Ocean about 400 miles (644 km) southwest of India, consists of more than a thousand small coral islands. They form 19 atolls—groups of islands encircling a lagoon. Only 200 or so of the islands are inhabited. The original Maldivians probably arrived there from southern India and Sri Lanka several thousand years ago.

The islands' position on major sea routes brought traders of many nationalities. Legend says one traveler, a Muslim holy man, converted the people to Islam, now the sole religion.

Many Maldivians are poor and fish for a living, casting from boats for tuna. Some of the catch, when boiled and smoked, becomes "Maldive fish," a delicacy exported to Japan, India, and Sri Lanka. Tourism also brings in revenue. The government rents out some 60 islands as resorts—visited mostly by Europeans and Japanese drawn to the white sand beaches, colorful coral formations, and abundant marine life.

Official name: *Republic of Maldives*
Area: *115 sq mi (298 sq km)*
Population: *211,000*
Capital: *Male (pop. 46,334)*
Ethnic groups: *Maldivian*
Language: *Divehi*
Religious groups: *Sunni Muslim*
Economy: *Agr: coconuts, grains, root crops, vegetables, fruit. Ind: fishing, tourism, shipping, clothing*
Currency: *Maldivian rufiyaa*

Sri Lanka

Sri Lanka has had various names over the centuries. Arab traders called this spice-growing island off the southeastern tip of India Serendib. This led to the word "serendipity," which means finding something valuable or pleasant by accident.

The moist, green highlands of Sri Lanka's southern interior *are* pleasant—and valuable, too. Tea, introduced by the British, who called the island Ceylon, flourishes there on well-tended plantations. Sri Lanka is the second largest tea exporter in the world. India comes first.

Flat or gently rolling plains cover the rest of Sri Lanka. Coconut and rubber plantations sprawl across the moist areas of the southwest. Spices are still cultivated but are now less important to the economy. Rice, the chief food crop, grows all over but must often be irrigated.

Pleasant aspects of Sri Lanka besides are its beautiful parks that protect elephants and other wildlife. Inland, spectacular Buddhist monuments reflect the faith of 70 percent of the population. Nearly 9 out of 10 Sri Lankans can read, an extremely high literacy rate for Asia.

But Sri Lanka also has its dark side. For the last seven years, the Hindu Tamil minority has been engaged in a civil war with the Buddhist Sinhalese majority. The Tamils claim discrimination and demand an independent Tamil homeland. Thousands on both sides have lost their lives in the fighting. India, mindful of the sympathies of the 50 million Tamils in its southernmost state, sent troops to try to disarm the Sri Lankan Tamils, but they were later withdrawn.

Official name: *Democratic Socialist Republic of Sri Lanka*
Area: *25,332 sq mi (65,610 sq km)*
Population: *16,881,000*
Capital: *Colombo (met. pop. 683,000)*
Ethnic groups: *Sinhalese, Tamil, Moor*
Language: *Sinhala, Tamil, English*
Religious groups: *Theravada Buddhist, Hindu*
Economy: *Agr: rice, tea, coconuts, rubber, sugarcane, livestock. Ind: textiles, cement, gems*
Currency: *Sri Lankan rupee*

India

1 *In royal splendor, the former Maharaja of Banaras leads a procession during a religious festival. Banaras, a holy city on the Ganges, draws millions of faithful Hindus who come to bathe in the sacred waters. The city's official name is Varanasi, but it is known to most people as Banaras.*

India

1 *Trucks, carts, bicycles, and rickshas vie for space on a crowded Delhi street. The old city and the capital, New Delhi, together form India's third largest urban area.*

2 *Village girls swing and sing to celebrate the coming of the monsoon season. Most Indian farmers depend on the regular arrival of the rains to water their crops.*

Sri Lanka

3 *A stroll along an ancient reservoir takes these children of Anuradhapura to school. Their town was once the capital of Sinhalese kings.*

Nepal

4 *To curb erosion on this mountain slope, a young boy plants pine seedlings near Kathmandu. Nepalese now replenish forests cleared for farmland, firewood, and fodder.*

Bangladesh

5 *Bundles of jute, the country's main export, sail upstream from the Ganges Delta. Rivers transport goods and people in this watery land.*

1 *India*

2 *India*

3 *Sri Lanka*

4 *Nepal*

5 *Bangladesh*

China occupies the heart of the **Far East,** which is a name given to the regions of eastern and southeastern Asia.

Home to one-fifth of Earth's people, China overshadows two tiny territories: Portugal's Macau and the United Kingdom's Hong Kong. Both are scheduled to become part of China by the end of this century.

Taiwan is a part of China, but has its own government, formed by Nationalist Chinese who fled the mainland in 1949 after the communist takeover.

cold

SOVIET UNION

Hovsgol Lake

Uvs Lake

Youyi Feng
14,350 FEET
4,374 METERS

Hovd

Uliastay

• Darhan

Orhon River

• Choybalsan

MANCHURIA

• Qiqihar

Songhua River

• Harbin

GREATER KHINGAN RANGE

Amur River

⊛ Ulan Bator (Ulaanbaatar)

Herlen River

Changchun

• Jilin

Altay

Bayanhongor

MONGOLIA

Saynshand

Liao River

Shenyang

• Fushun

NORTH KOREA

Shihezi

ALTAY MOUNTAINS

INNER MONGOLIA

Anshan

• Dandong

Kashi

Urumqi

TIAN SHAN

GOBI

Beijing

Baotou

Hohhot

Dalian

Shache

XINJIANG

Turpan Depression
-505 FEET
-154 METERS

Datong

Tianjin

Tangshan

SOUTH KOREA

TAKLIMAKAN DESERT

Tarim River

Lop Nur Lake

Yumen

Great Wall

Yinchuan

NORTH

Shijiazhuang

AFGHANI-STAN

Jiayuguan

Yellow River

Taiyuan

CHINA

Qingdao

PAKISTAN

KUNLUN MOUNTAINS

Muztag
25,340 FEET
7,723 METERS

Qinghai Lake

PLAIN

Jinan

YELLOW SEA

Area claimed by India

Xining

Luoyang

Grand Canal

Golmud

Lanzhou

Zhengzhou

INDIA

PLATEAU OF TIBET

Xi'an

Huainan

Wuxi

Yangtze

TIBET

Yellow River

Nanjing

Shanghai

Yangtze River

QIN LING

Suzhou

Indus R.

Salween River

Mekong River

Wuhan

Hangzhou

Ningbo

Brahmaputra River

Chengdu

Dongting Lake

Poyang Lake

EAST CHINA SEA

NEPAL

HIMALAYA

Lhasa

Chongqing

Nanchang

Xigaze

Changsha

Fuzhou

Formosa Strait

Mount Everest
29,028 FEET
8,848 METERS
Highest point in the world

BHUTAN

INDIA

Hengyang

Taipei

Guiyang

Taichung

TAIWAN

Kunming

Guilin

Xiamen

Tainan

Shantou

Kaohsiung

TROPIC OF CANCER

Guangzhou

PACIFIC OCEAN

MYANMAR

Nanning

Xi River

HONG KONG (UNITED KINGDOM)

MACAU (PORTUGAL)

Victoria

LAOS

VIETNAM

Gulf of Tonkin

Haikou

SOUTH CHINA SEA

HAINAN

0   KILOMETERS   500

0   STATUTE MILES   300

For map legend see page 21.

Mongolia

Genghis Khan, ruler of the Mongols, led an army of swift, fierce horsemen out of central Asia around A.D. 1200 and founded an empire that would one day stretch from Korea to the Danube. Today, Mongolia is about twice the size of Texas, a high, dry plateau situated between China and the Soviet Union. Until recent times nearly all Mongolians were nomads who rode horseback to herd sheep and lived in round tents called *gers* or *yurts*. Camels and yaks provided transport for trade.

Mongolia was a Chinese province known as Outer Mongolia for more than 200 years. It declared itself the Mongolian People's Republic in 1924. Its communist government began modernizing the economy with help from the Soviet Union. Mining for coal and copper now rivals animal husbandry in importance. A quarter of the people live in Ulan Bator, the capital. Trucks and motorbikes are replacing camels and horses, and former nomads now live on big state farms with television in their tents.

Official name: *Mongolian People's Republic*
Area: *604,250 sq mi (1,565,000 sq km)*
Population: *2,125,000*
Capital: *Ulan Bator (pop. 511,100)*
Ethnic groups: *Mongolian, Kazakh*
Language: *Khalkha Mongolian*
Religious groups: *Lamaistic Buddhist. (Government discourages religion.)*
Economy: *Agr: livestock, wheat, oats, barley, hay. Ind: animal products, building materials, mining*
Currency: *tugrik*

China

The Great Wall of China, snaking from the Yellow Sea to the desert lands of the west, was the Chinese Empire's defense against invaders from the north. Begun more than 2,200 years ago, it was rebuilt over the centuries. On its other borders, China was already protected by nature's barriers: seas, tropical forests, the world's highest mountains, and a vast desert.

For 4,000 years, the Chinese shunned outside influence and built a great civilization in the country they called the Middle Kingdom. Foreign influence in politics, economics, and technology began to encroach in the mid-19th century, and in the 20th century China took its place as one of the world's great powers.

More than a billion people live in China—more than four times as many as in the United States, although China is only slightly bigger. Because much of the country is covered with mountains, arid steppe, or desert, 90 percent of the people crowd into the low-lying eastern third of China. Many cities such as the capital, Beijing, and Shanghai, China's largest city, hold millions of people, but most Chinese live in the countryside. Beijing is a northern city and Mandarin, a northern tongue, is the national language.

Chinese civilization began in the north along the Yellow River, or Huang He in Chinese. The population is still densest in fertile valleys where great rivers cross China. About 70 percent of Chinese farm the land. In the north today they grow wheat for steamed bread and noodles. The Yangtze River, China's longest waterway, flows 3,964 miles (6,380 km) from the Tibetan border to the East China Sea. Its Chinese name, Chang Jiang, means simply "long river." It roughly divides the dry, cool north from the warm, moist south. The south is called "China's rice bowl" because it supplies the whole country with its staple food, rice.

China's cold northeast, sometimes called Manchuria, has large deposits of oil, coal, and iron, as well as great forests for timber. Industry is strong there and the people enjoy the highest standard of living in China.

Western China consists of two regions rich in minerals and resources that together make up about one-third of China's territory. Most people belong to ethnic minorities. Xinjiang, a region of mountains and deserts, is inhabited chiefly by central Asian peoples who are Muslims. Tibet, just to the south on the world's highest plateau, is often called "the roof of the world." Tibetans are devout Buddhists. All told,

China has 55 ethnic minorities, many with their own customs, dress, and languages. The majority group are known as the Han Chinese.

China was ruled by emperors until this century. A single family called a dynasty would hold power until it weakened and was overthrown. Then a new leader would declare himself emperor and start a new dynasty. Around 500 B.C., a philosopher named Confucius created a social philosophy that taught the Chinese to respect authority and seek harmony within the family and the nation. This way of thinking prevailed throughout most of China's long history.

In the 19th century European powers broke through China's isolation. Seeking trade in tea, silk, porcelain, and ivory, they introduced opium, which undermined Chinese society. By superior military power they forced the Chinese to let them set up enclaves along the coast.

In 1911, Chinese revolutionaries overthrew the last emperor and made China a republic. The new Nationalist Party government tried to unite China but failed. A Chinese Communist Party was formed in the 1920s, and after World War II civil war escalated between the two. In 1949 the Communists routed the Nationalists and established the People's Republic of China under Mao Zedong. The Nationalists fled to the island of Taiwan and set up a rival government. China is still trying to induce Taiwan to return to the control of the Beijing government.

In an attempt to modernize China, the Communists completely changed the way people lived. All land was claimed by the government. Peasants were organized into communes and women joined the work force. Floods and famine, China's eternal scourges, were eased by new dams and improved agriculture. Many plans went wrong, though, and the cost of economic progress was lack of freedom. When Mao Zedong died in 1976, a new government brought reforms and there were signs that China was becoming a more open society. But efforts to control and modernize such an enormous population seem to cause China's governments to seesaw between oppression and freedom.

Official name: *People's Republic of China*
Area: *3,705,407 sq mi (9,596,961 sq km)*
Population: *1,103,923,000*
Capital: *Beijing (pop. 5,970,000; met. pop. 9,750,000)*
Ethnic groups: *Han Chinese, 55 minorities*
Language: *Mandarin Chinese, many others*
Religious groups: *Confucian, Buddhist, Taoist*
Economy: *Agr: rice, wheat, corn, other grains, oilseeds, fruit, vegetables, sugarcane, cotton, livestock. Ind: steel, iron, coal, machinery, electronics, textiles, chemicals, food processing, paper, oil, fishing*
Currency: *yuan*

Taiwan

Two governments claim to rule China: The Communist Party government on the mainland and the Nationalist Party government on the island of Taiwan, which its leaders call the Republic of China. Neither government, in fact, has any control over the other's territory, yet both agree that Taiwan is a province of China.

Communists overthrew the Nationalist government in China in 1949. More than one million refugees fled to Taiwan. Their leaders set up the Nationalist government there, hoping to regain control of the mainland. Until 1971 Taiwan represented China in international affairs. That year the United Nations recognized the People's Republic of China instead.

Dynamic Taiwan, humming with industry, lies about 100 miles (160 km) off China's east coast. It has one of the world's great trading economies, with many exports going to the United States. Most people live modern lives in Taiwan's crowded cities, but farmers also grow enough food to create a surplus for export. A rich Chinese culture reflects centuries of immigration of the Taiwanese people from China.

Taiwan's political future depends on its relations with the mainland. So far it has refused China's invitations to join the People's Republic.

Official name: *Taiwan*
Area: *13,900 sq mi (36,000 sq km)*
Population: *19,980,000*
Capital: *Taipei (pop. 2,637,100)*
Ethnic groups: *Taiwanese, Chinese*
Language: *Mandarin Chinese, Taiwanese, Hakka*
Religious groups: *Buddhist, Confucian, Taoist*
Economy: *Agr: sugarcane, rice, vegetables, fruit. Ind: machinery, electronics, textiles, plastics, food processing, plywood, cement, shipbuilding*
Currency: *new Taiwan dollar*

Macau

Macau, a tiny territory on China's south coast, has been a Portuguese trading center since 1557. Gambling has long been an important source of income, but today Macau relies also on tourism and the manufacture of textiles, fireworks, and many other goods for export. Most of its food comes from China. The capital city's architecture, customs, and official language are Portuguese, but most of its people are Chinese. In 1999, Portugal will give Macau back to China.

Official name: *Macau*
Area: *6.5 sq mi (16.9 sq km)*
Population: *434,300*
Capital: *Macau*

Hong Kong

Machinery whirs and business bustles around the clock. Hong Kong never sleeps. One of the world's greatest trading centers, the small British colony on China's south coast handles more international trade than all of China through its deep, modern harbor. Banks, offices, and shops crowd its tall buildings.

Though Hong Kong is administered by a British governor, nearly all its 5.7 million people are Chinese. It is one of the most densely populated places on Earth. With little farmland, it must import most of its food and water from China.

The colony consists of several adjacent areas: The United Kingdom forced China to give up Hong Kong Island in 1842, then took another island and Kowloon Peninsula on the mainland in 1860. In 1898 the British leased a neighboring area called the New Territories for 99 years.

The United Kingdom has agreed to give the whole colony back to China in 1997 when the lease expires. Hong Kong's people were not consulted about their future, but the government of China has promised to let them keep their capitalist system and free way of life for 50 years.

Official name: *Hong Kong*
Area: *403 sq mi (1,045 sq km)*
Population: *5,709,000*
Capital: *Victoria (pop. 633,138)*
Ethnic groups: *Chinese*
Language: *Chinese, English*
Religious groups: *Buddhist, Confucian, Taoist*
Economy: *Agr: rice, vegetables, livestock. Ind: textiles, electronics, finance, trade, tourism, shipping*
Currency: *Hong Kong dollar*

China

1 *Winding nearly 4,000 miles (6,437 km) from east coast to western desert, the Great Wall, begun more than 22 centuries ago, guarded ancient China's northern border.*

2 *Silkworms seek vacant compartments in a cocoon "condo." When settled, they spin the strong filaments used in thread and fabric.*

3 *Shoulder-harnessed trackers pull a junk upstream against the Yangtze's current.*

4 *China's largest city and major seaport, Shanghai is home to 12.5 million people.*

5 *Toy trucks destined for the United States take shape on assembly lines in one of China's Special Economic Zones. Low taxes and other bargains draw foreign investors.*

1 *China*

2 *China*

3 *China*

4 *China*

5 *China*

1 *China*

China

1 *Horses graze beneath the Potala, the former palace of the Dalai Lama in Lhasa, Tibet. The Buddhist leader fled to India in 1959 after China crushed a Tibetan revolt.*

Hong Kong

2 *Night-lit skyscrapers illumine Hong Kong's thriving business district. Its magnificent harbor has made it one of the Far East's most successful trading centers.*

Mongolia

3 *A Mongolian horse breeder poses proudly with his stock. Mounted on swift steeds, his forebears conquered much of Asia in the 13th century.*

4 *Round felt tents called yurts or gers house nomad families. Nowadays, many nomads settle down in urban areas.*

2 *Hong Kong*

3 *Mongolia*

4 *Mongolia*

0 KILOMETERS 250
0 STATUTE MILES 150
For map legend see page 21.

North and South Korea share a peninsula that for more than a thousand years held a unified country. Japan controlled Korea from 1910 until the end of World War II. Japan's defeat resulted in the north-south division that endures today.

Across the Korea Strait sprawls the 2,000-mile-long (3,220 km) archipelago of Japan, industrial giant of the Far East. Most of Japan's people share the same ethnic background, and this island nation shows a unique degree of cultural unity.

SOVIET UNION

HOKKAIDO

Teshio River
KITAMI MTS.
Asahikawa
Ishikari River
Sapporo
Kushiro
Tomakomai
HIDAKA RANGE
Hakodate
Uchiura Bay

Tsugaru Strait

CHINA
Paektu 9,003 FEET 2,744 METERS
Tuman River
Najin
Chongjin
Manpo
Yalu River
Kimchaek
Sinuiju
NANGNIM MOUNTAINS
Taedong River
Hamhung
Hungnam

NORTH KOREA

Aomori
Hachinohe

Akita
Morioka
Kitakami River

HONSHU
OU RANGE

Pyongyang
Korea Bay
Wonsan
Nampo
Haeju
Kosong
Sokcho
TAEBAEK
Seoul
Chunchon
Inchon
Wonju
Suwon
Han River
MTS.

Sado
Yamagata
Ishinomaki
Niigata
Sendai
Shinano River
Iwaki
ABUKUMA MTS.

JAPAN

SOUTH KOREA

YELLOW SEA
Chongju
Naktong River
Taejon
Chonju
Pohang
Taegu
Ulsan
Kwangju
Masan
Mokpo
Yosu
Pusan

SEA OF JAPAN
Oki Islands

Toyama
Kanazawa
Nagano
Utsunomiya
MIKUNI RANGE
Maebashi
RYOHAKU MTS.
Wakasa Bay
Lake Biwa
Gifu
AKAISHI RANGE
Tokyo
Yokohama
Mount Fuji 12,388 FEET 3,776 METERS

PACIFIC OCEAN

CHUGOKU MTS.
Kyoto
Himeji
Nagoya
Okayama
Kobe
Shizuoka
Hiroshima
Osaka
Hamamatsu
STRAIT
Tshushima Islands
Sakai
KOREA
Takamatsu
Inland Sea
Wakayama
Cheju
Cheju Island
Kitakyushu
Suo Sea
Matsuyama
MTS.
Fukuoka
Sasebo
Beppu
Oita
Kochi
SHIKOKU
Goto Retto
Kumamoto
KYUSHU MTS.
SHIKOKU
Nagasaki
Mount Aso 5,223 FEET 1,592 METERS

EAST CHINA SEA

PHILIPPINE SEA

Miyazaki
Kagoshima
KYUSHU

Osumi Islands

RYUKYU ISLANDS

Tokara Islands

Amami Islands
Naze

Okinawa Islands
ISLANDS

Okinawa
Naha

RYUKYU

Sakishima Islands

PHILIPPINE SEA

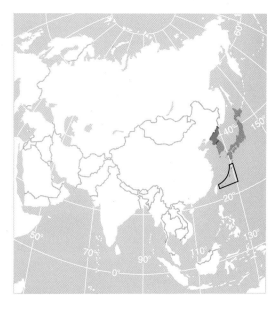

North Korea

The Korean peninsula stands as a buffer between Japan and China. Japan controlled it from 1910 to the end of World War II. The Japanese defeat resulted in a division—meant to be temporary—that endures today. North Korea, occupied at that time by Soviet troops, became a communist state, and U. S.-occupied South Korea became a constitutional democracy.

North Korea has abundant natural resources of coal and iron ore but little farmland because three-fourths of its mountainous terrain is forested. Even so about half of North Koreans are farmers, organized into large collectives and state farms. Industry, a major income earner, employs more than a third of the work force.

North Korea pours much of its income into military expansion. Troops of its army, fifth largest in the world, stand poised along the border with South Korea. In 1950 the army invaded, launching the three-year Korean War.

Official name: *Democratic People's Republic of Korea*
Area: *46,540 sq mi (120,538 sq km)*
Population: *22,521,000*
Capital: *Pyongyang (pop. 1,500,000)*
Ethnic groups: *Korean*
Language: *Korean*
Religious groups: *Buddhist, Confucian, Chondogyo. (Government discourages religion.)*
Economy: *Agr: rice, corn, vegetables. Ind: machinery, chemicals, mining, metals, textiles, cement*
Currency: *North Korean won*

South Korea

For centuries the Korean peninsula was a single kingdom called Choson—Land of the Morning Calm. In 1945 Korea lost its unity. A country in which all the people spoke the same language and belonged to the same ethnic group was divided into North and South Korea; five years later they were at war.

South Korea occupies the lower 45 percent of the rugged Korean peninsula. Forested mountains cover the country's central region, rising to their highest in the east. Lowlands stretch along the south and west coasts, where most people live. A humid climate often allows two crops a year. People of both Koreas eat rice daily with their national dish, *kimchi*, a fiery mixture of cabbage, white radish, and red pepper.

South Korea encourages free enterprise and attracts many foreign investors. In the past 30 years the country has had strong economic growth. Much industry is centered around Seoul, the capital, a mere 25 miles (40 km) from the heavily patrolled border with North Korea.

Official name: *Republic of Korea*
Area: *38,230 sq mi (99,016 sq km)*
Population: *43,093,000*
Capital: *Seoul (pop. 9,639,110)*
Ethnic groups: *Korean*
Language: *Korean*
Religious groups: *Buddhist, Christian, Confucian*
Economy: *Agr: grains, vegetables, fruit. Ind: textiles, steel, electronics, ships, motor vehicles, fishing*
Currency: *South Korean won*

Japan

Pop a tape into your VCR, turn on your TV, play a cassette on your boom box, boot your computer, or snap a picture with your camera. Each time you do one of these things, chances are you are using a product made in Japan. In little more than a hundred years, Japan has transformed itself from an isolated, feudal island empire to one of the world's leading manufacturers of electronic goods, cars, and ships.

This industrial miracle has been accomplished in a country that crowds 123 million people into a space about the size of California. Japan's four major and many smaller islands are spread out in a 2,000-mile-long (3,220 km) arc, but the extremely steep, forested terrain tends to limit settlement to the narrow coastal plains and riv-

er valleys. Most crowded is the area from Kobe to Tokyo on southern Honshu. Over 50 percent of the people live there, more than 30 million in the Tokyo metropolitan area alone.

Japan is dangerously earthquake-prone. It experiences more than 10,000 tremors a year. Hundreds of volcanoes, at least 40 of them active, rise on the Japanese landscape. The most famous is Japan's highest mountain and national symbol, Mount Fuji, an almost perfect cone.

Japan has few mineral resources and must import fuel and nearly all the raw materials it needs for industry. Less than one-fifth of the land is suitable for cultivation. Remarkably, Japanese farmers grow about three-fourths of the country's food. They use technologies such as mechanization, irrigation, and chemical fertilizers, and have developed improved varieties of rice, the main food crop. Japan's fishing fleet, one of the largest in the world, provides another staple of the Japanese diet.

The country's chief resources are its people and a culture that allows for change. Early in its history, Japan borrowed heavily from China, adopting Chinese writing as well as ideas about art, music, and religion, especially Buddhism. Most Japanese today observe Buddhism along with Shintoism, Japan's own ancient religion.

Two centuries of isolation under the rule of military governors called shoguns ended in the 1860s. Japan sought out Western ideas and technologies in order to modernize the country and establish Japanese industry. The desire for raw materials spurred Japan to conquer countries in the Pacific and fueled its militancy in World War II. Japan emerged from defeat to become within a few decades an industrial giant.

Japanese life today blends the old with the new. The ancient sport of sumo wrestling is almost as popular as American-style *beisuboru*, or baseball. Centuries-old forms of drama called No and Kabuki thrive alongside one of the world's largest film industries. And no matter how busy their lives or how crowded their cities, Japanese seek inspiration in nature's beauty and simplicity, an aspect of their Shinto heritage.

Official name: *Japan*
Area: *145,875 sq mi (377,815 sq km)*
Population: *123,200,000*
Capital: *Tokyo (pop. 11,829,000; met. pop. 30,394,532)*
Ethnic groups: *Japanese*
Language: *Japanese*
Religious groups: *Shinto, Buddhist*
Economy: *Agr: rice, sugar, wheat, vegetables, fruit. Ind: metals, machinery, electrical products, electronics, motor vehicles, textiles, chemicals, cement, fishing, shipbuilding*
Currency: *yen*

1 *Japan*

2 *Japan*

3 *Japan*

4 *Japan*

Japan

1 *The snowcapped cone of Mount Fuji rises above the haze on Honshu. The volcano is sacred to members of the Fujiko sect, who seek harmony with its pure shape.*

2 *A computerized locator map in this Honda helps a driver navigate city streets. Japan exports about four million cars each year.*

3 *A monk rakes pebbles in a Zen garden near Kyoto. In this form of Buddhism, doing such a simple, mechanical task can bring the mind enlightenment.*

4 *Aspiring sumo wrestlers try to topple a professional who probably outweighs each boy six to one. Though popular, the ancient sport has lost many fans to baseball.*

South Korea

5 *The heavy traffic of modern Seoul circles the city's old South Gate. One in four South Koreans now lives in the teeming capital.*

6 *The workday may last 16 hours in a Seoul sweatshop. Low wages helped build South Korea's textile industry but keep its workers struggling to make ends meet.*

5 *South Korea*

6 *South Korea*

A B C D E F G H J K L M N O P Q R S T U

1 2 3 4 5 6 7 8 9 10 11 12 13 14 15 16 17 18

+ *Hkakabo Razi*
19,296 FEET
5,881 METERS

0 KILOMETERS 300
0 STATUTE MILES 200
For map legend see page 21.

These countries, together with West Malaysia, were long known as **Indochina** because of their ancient ties to India and China. All except Thailand have known European domination.

Myanmar, formerly called Burma, was part of British India and later a crown colony until independence in 1947.

France controlled Vietnam, Cambodia, and Laos for many years until the 1950s. The three have known little respite from war in recent times.

INDIA

CHINA

KUMON RANGE

Chindwin River

Irrawaddy River

• Myitkyina

TROPIC OF CANCER

BANGLADESH

• Ha Giang
• Lao Cai

Red River

Lashio •

CHIN HILLS

Monywa • **Mandalay**

Thai Nguyen

Myingyan •
Pagan •

Kaladan R.

Taunggyi

Salween River

Hanoi ⊗

Haiphong
Nam Dinh

• Dien Bien

Gulf of Tonkin

Sittwe

MYANMAR
(BURMA)

TANEN RANGE

Mekong River

Thanh Hoa

• Louangphrabang

Vinh

Ramree Island

ARAKAN RANGE

• Toungoo

Cheduba Island

Prome •

Chiang Mai

LUANG PRABANG RANGE

• Xaignabouri

LAOS

A N N A M   C O R D I L L E R A

BAY
OF
BENGAL

Henzada •

Pegu

Lampang •

Nan River

Vientiane ⊗

Udon Thani •

Bassein

**Yangon
(Rangoon)** ⊗

Tak •
• Phitsanulok

**Khon
Kaen**

Savannakhet •

Hue

Irrawaddy River Delta

Mawlamyine

Ping River

THAILAND

Da Nang
Da Nang

Gulf of Martaban

Nakhon
Sawan •

Ubon
Ratchathani •

Pakxe •

VIETNAM

Ye •

Preparis

Chao Phraya River →

Nakhon
Ratchasima •

• Quang Ngai

*Great Coco
Little Coco*

Tavoy •

DANGREK RANGE

Play Cu •

Qui Nhon

BILAUKTAUNG RANGE

Bangkok ⊗

CAMBODIA

*CENTRAL
HIGHLANDS*

Andaman
Islands
(INDIA)

*ANDAMAN
SEA*

• Chon Buri

□ Angkor

Tonle Sap

Buon Me Thuot •

Mergui •

Phet
Buri •

Battambang •

*CARDAMOM
MTS*

Kompong Chhnang •

Da Lat

Nha Trang

Cam Ranh

Kompong Cham •

Phnom Penh ⊗

Bien Hoa

• Phan Thiet

Chumphon •

Takeo •

Ho Chi Minh City

Kompong Som •

Long Xuyen

My Tho

*Gulf of
Thailand*

Rach Gia

Can Tho

*INDIAN
OCEAN*

Mergui Archipelago

Surat Thani •

ISTHMUS of Kra

*Ca Mau
Peninsula*

Bac
Lieu •

*Mekong River
Delta*

*MALAY
PENINSULA*

**Nakhon Si
Thammarat**

SOUTH CHINA SEA

Phuket •

*Phuket
Island*

Songkhla •

Hat Yai
Yala •
• Narathiwat

MALAYSIA

Myanmar

Until 1989 Myanmar was known as Burma, a name that referred only to the Burmans, the nation's largest ethnic group. But many other groups share this country, the largest on the Southeast Asian mainland, so its name was changed to one that the people use for their country.

A horseshoe of mountains and a high plateau rim Myanmar, shutting it in on three sides. Through the center flows the Irrawaddy River, the country's 1,240-mile-long (1,995 km) lifeline, providing transportation and fertile soil. Two-thirds of the population lives in the Irrawaddy Valley; the delta yields abundant crops of rice, one of the country's main exports. Yangon (Rangoon), the capital, also serves as the major port.

Myanmar has ample mineral deposits and forests that provide 75 percent of the world's teak, but the economy suffers from poor planning and a thriving black market. Rebel groups, too, have fought for decades to gain independence or to protect an illegal opium trade. Such problems keep Myanmar one of Asia's poorest countries.

Official name: *Union of Myanmar (Burma)*
Area: *261,218 sq mi (676,552 sq km)*
Population: *40,804,000*
Capital: *Yangon (Rangoon) (pop. 2,458,712)*
Ethnic groups: *Myanmar (Burman, Shan, Karen)*
Language: *Myanmar (Burmese), Shan, Karen*
Religious groups: *Theravada Buddhist*
Economy: *Agr: rice, legumes, oilseeds, sugarcane, peanuts. Ind: food processing, textiles, teak, mining*
Currency: *kyat*

Thailand

Thailand is shaped like an elephant's head. Mountains in the north and west form the long forehead. A dry eastern plateau marks the ear. The mouth cuts into the fertile central plain, the country's "rice bowl," while the trunk snakes down the narrow tin-rich peninsula that connects Thailand with Malaysia.

Established as a kingdom in the 13th century, the country was named Siam in 1782. Unlike its Southeast Asian neighbors, Siam was never ruled by a Western country. In 1939 it changed its name to Thailand—"land of the free."

Most Thai are farmers who live in villages where the *wat*, or Buddhist temple, is the social and religious focus for the community. Many young Thai men shave their heads and eyebrows and don yellow robes for at least several months of life as a Buddhist monk.

Thailand is prosperous. Bangkok, the capital, chief port, and industrial center, is the site of the shrine-filled Grand Palace, which helps bring in valuable tourist income. But Thailand faces many problems. Despite crop-substitution programs, illegal opium poppies are still grown in the hills. On the peninsula, a Muslim minority is pressing for independence. And refugees stream in from Cambodia, Laos, and Vietnam, seeking asylum from communist regimes.

Official name: *Kingdom of Thailand*
Area: *198,457 sq mi (514,000 sq km)*
Population: *55,552,000*
Capital: *Bangkok (met. pop. 5,609,352)*
Ethnic groups: *Thai, Chinese*
Language: *Thai*
Religious groups: *Theravada Buddhist*
Economy: *Agr: rice, sugarcane, corn, rubber, cassava, pineapples. Ind: tourism, textiles, tin, fishing*
Currency: *baht*

Laos

Geographically, politically, and economically, Laos is truly a land caught in the middle. Five countries hem in this landlocked nation covered with mountains and rain forest. During the Vietnam War, North Vietnamese Communists used Laos as a supply route to South Vietnam. With no railroads or access to the sea, Laos depends on Thailand and Vietnam to help get its exports to market.

About half the population is ethnic Lao. Most live in villages on the fertile floodplain of the Mekong River and its tributaries, which also form the main transportation network. Nearly all Lao are farmers who grow sticky rice. Tribal peoples such as the Hmong live in the highlands, supplementing their income from slash-and-burn agriculture by planting opium poppies.

Laos has known little peace since its independence from France in 1953. Two decades of civil war ended in 1975 with a communist takeover aided by North Vietnam. Many people, especially the Hmong, have fled the country.

Official name: *Lao People's Democratic Republic*
Area: *91,429 sq mi (236,800 sq km)*
Population: *3,936,000*
Capital: *Vientiane (pop. 377,409)*
Ethnic groups: *Lao, tribal Thai, Hmong*
Language: *Lao*
Religious groups: *Theravada Buddhist, tribal*
Economy: *Agr: rice, corn, vegetables, fruit, coffee, cotton. Ind: tin, gypsum, lumber, electricity, fishing*
Currency: *new kip*

Cambodia

A large fertile basin watered by the Mekong River system forms the heart of Cambodia. The basin also contains Tonle Sap, a lake that quadruples in size during the rainy season. The annual flooding enriches the soil with sediment, and farmers plant rice. Mountains and forested hills surround the basin on three sides.

Nine out of ten Cambodians are Khmer, descendants of a people who controlled Southeast Asia from the 9th to the 13th century. The Khmer built magnificent stone and brick temples at Angkor. Angkor lies now in partial ruin, victim of the invading forest and of nearly ceaseless civil wars since 1970. Cambodia suffered greatly under a radical communist regime that destroyed the economy and caused the deaths of more than a million people. Hundreds of thousands fled to refugee camps in Thailand. The survivors struggle to rebuild their lives while fighting rages on in the countryside.

Official name: *Cambodia*
Area: *69,898 sq mi (181,035 sq km)*
Population: *6,838,000*
Capital: *Phnom Penh (met. pop. 700,000)*
Ethnic groups: *Khmer, Chinese*
Language: *Khmer*
Religious groups: *Theravada Buddhist*
Economy: *Agr: rice, rubber, corn, cassava, pepper. Ind: rice milling, textiles, fishing, lumber, cement*
Currency: *riel*

Vietnam

Vietnamese describe their country as "two rice baskets dangling from opposite ends of a carrying pole." In the north lies the fertile delta of the Red River. Dikes and irrigation channels enable its farmers to harvest two crops of rice each year. The south contains the wide, swampy delta of the Mekong River, one of the world's most productive rice-growing areas. The "pole" is the Annam Cordillera, a mountain chain covering two-thirds of the country. To the east of that range lies a narrow coastal plain.

The Vietnamese, who came from China more than 2,000 years ago, remained in the north for centuries. There Vietnamese culture took shape with many Chinese influences, including Buddhism. Gradually the Vietnamese moved south.

Vietnam was controlled by France for about 70 years before nationalists drove the French out in 1954. Independence resulted in a divided country. Communist North Vietnam's desire to control non-communist South Vietnam led to the ten-year-long Vietnam War. More than three million United States troops were sent to help fight the Communists. Saigon, the capital of South Vietnam, fell to the North in 1975. All of Vietnam was united under a communist government based in Hanoi, the North's capital, and Saigon was renamed Ho Chi Minh City.

Today, a unified Vietnam bears the scars of war. Millions of people have fled, many by boat. Soviet aid bolsters an economy plagued by food shortages. The government has tried, often unsuccessfully, to relocate people in new farming areas in the Central Highlands. Bombing damaged much of the North's heavy industry, now rebuilt; power shortages everywhere prevent factories from operating fully. Ho Chi Minh City fares better than Hanoi. With more consumer goods available, many sent from Vietnamese overseas, it has a burgeoning market economy.

Throughout Vietnam, people celebrate the three-day holiday of Tet, the lunar new year, with fireworks, flowers, and feasts.

Official name: *Socialist Republic of Vietnam*
Area: *127,242 sq mi (329,556 sq km)*
Population: *66,821,000*
Capital: *Hanoi (pop. 2,674,400)*
Ethnic groups: *Vietnamese*
Language: *Vietnamese*
Religious groups: *Mahayana Buddhist, Taoist*
Economy: *Agr: rice, rubber, fruit, vegetables, corn, sugarcane. Ind: food processing, oil, cement, metals, chemicals, paper, machinery, textiles, fishing*
Currency: *dong*

1 *Myanmar*

2 *Laos*

3 *Vietnam*

4 *Thailand*

5 *Cambodia*

Myanmar

1 *Worth nearly its weight in gold, Shwe Dagon Pagoda in Yangon glistens with 90 million dollars' worth of the metal. Legend says eight hairs of the Buddha rest within.*

Laos

2 *Laotians pan for gold in the mud of the Mekong River. The small amounts extracted provide farmers with extra income.*

Vietnam

3 *Imposing buildings and tree-lined boulevards give Hanoi a French air. The French controlled Vietnam for some 70 years.*

Thailand

4 *Before dawn, a tapper slits a rubber tree to start the flow of latex into a cup below. The sap runs heaviest early in the day.*

Cambodia

5 *Making one of the 2,000 gestures she needs to qualify, this student of Khmer ballet hopes to join the national dance troupe.*

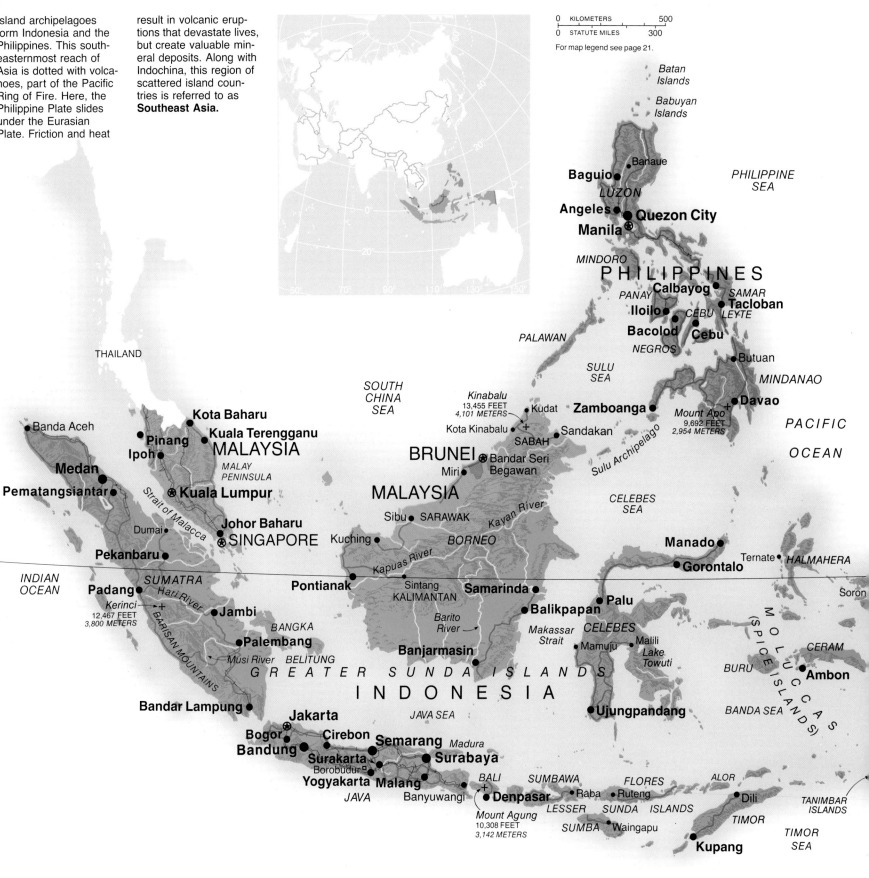

Island archipelagoes form Indonesia and the Philippines. This south-easternmost reach of Asia is dotted with volca-noes, part of the Pacific Ring of Fire. Here, the Philippine Plate slides under the Eurasian Plate. Friction and heat result in volcanic erup-tions that devastate lives, but create valuable min-eral deposits. Along with Indochina, this region of scattered island coun-tries is referred to as **Southeast Asia.**

For map legend see page 21.

0   KILOMETERS   500
0   STATUTE MILES   300

Batan Islands

Babuyan Islands

PHILIPPINE SEA

• Banaue

Baguio •

LUZON

Angeles •

Manila ⊗   ● **Quezon City**

MINDORO

PHILIPPINES

Calbayog •

PANAY   *SAMAR*

Iloilo •   **Tacloban**

CEBU LEYTE

Bacolod •   **Cebu**

PALAWAN   *NEGROS*   • Butuan

SULU SEA   *MINDANAO*

SOUTH CHINA SEA

Kinabalu 13,455 FEET 4,101 METERS   • Kudat

Kota Kinabalu +   **Zamboanga** ●   Mount Apo 9,692 FEET 2,954 METERS   ● **Davao**

SABAH   • Sandakan   *PACIFIC OCEAN*

Sulu Archipelago

THAILAND

• Banda Aceh

Kota Baharu •

Pinang •   **Kuala Terengganu**

Ipoh •   **MALAYSIA**   *MALAY PENINSULA*

Medan •   **BRUNEI**   ⊗ Bandar Seri Begawan   *CELEBES SEA*

Pematangsiantar •   ⊗ **Kuala Lumpur**   Miri •   **MALAYSIA**

Dumai •   **Johor Baharu** •   Sibu •   *SARAWAK*   Kayan River   **Manado** ●

Pekanbaru •   ⊗ **SINGAPORE**   Kuching •   *BORNEO*   Ternate • *HALMAHERA*

INDIAN OCEAN   *SUMATRA*   Kapuas River   **Gorontalo** ●

Padang •   Hari River   **Pontianak**   Sintang   *KALIMANTAN*   **Samarinda** ●   **Palu** ●

Kerinci 12,467 FEET 3,800 METERS   +   **Jambi** •   **Balikpapan** ●

BARISAN MOUNTAINS   *BANGKA*   Barito River   *CELEBES*   Malili •   *M O L U C C A S   (S P I C E   I S L A N D S)*

Palembang •   Makassar Strait   Lake Towuti   *CERAM*

Musi River   *BELITUNG*   Mamuju •   *BURU*   **Ambon** ●

G R E A T E R   S U N D A   I S L A N D S   **Banjarmasin** ●   *BANDA SEA*

Bandar Lampung •   I N D O N E S I A   **Ujungpandang** ●

Jakarta   *JAVA SEA*

Bogor ⊗   **Cirebon**   Soron

Bandung   **Semarang** *Madura*

Surakarta   **Surabaya**   *BALI*   *SUMBAWA*   *FLORES*   *ALOR*

Borobudur ▫   *SUMBA WA*   • Dili

Yogyakarta   **Malang**   Raba •   • Ruteng   *TANIMBAR ISLANDS*

JAVA   Banyuwangi   ● **Denpasar**   *LESSER   SUNDA   ISLANDS*   *TIMOR*

Mount Agung 10,308 FEET 3,142 METERS   *SUMBA*   • Waingapu   *TIMOR SEA*

Kupang ●

A B C D E F G H J K L M N O P Q R S

1 2 3 4 5 6 7 8 9 10 11 12 13 14 15 16 17 18 19 20

Philippines

Described as "a piece of Latin America in the Pacific," the Philippines is unique in Southeast Asia. This sprawling archipelago encompasses 7,100 islands spread over 500,000 square miles (1,295,000 sq km). Claimed for Spain in 1521 by Ferdinand Magellan and named after King Philip II, the Philippines spent 333 years as a Spanish colony. Because of this heritage, about 85 percent of the people are Roman Catholic. The hub of many small towns is a typically Spanish central square dominated by a church.

The islands are tropical and mountainous with narrow coastal plains. They lie at the mercy of nature's often destructive forces. Typhoon season can bring storms packing winds of 185 miles an hour (298 kmph). Volcanoes erupt, creating havoc, and earthquakes followed by huge waves Filipinos call *malaking alon* take many lives.

The archipelago's first inhabitants are thought to have crossed by land bridges from mainland Asia some 30,000 years ago. Later, groups of Malays, ancestors of most modern Filipinos, arrived by boat in a succession of migrations. One group of Malays, the Ifugao, built extensive, irrigated rice terraces on Luzon like those still cultivated there.

Today about 700 islands are inhabited. Most people live on Luzon or Mindanao, which make up two-thirds of the country. Agriculture, fishing, and forestry employ about half the work force. The Philippines is the largest exporter of coconuts and coconut oil. The products of its vast but dangerously depleted hardwood forests are major exports, too; Philippine mahogany is famous throughout the world. Industry, centered around Manila, the capital, employs about 10 percent of the working population.

Filipino is the official language, but English is widely spoken and is used in all the schools. The United States controlled the Philippines from 1898 until the Japanese occupation in World War II. In 1946 the Philippines set up a U. S.-inspired democratic system. Many present leaders, including President Corazon Aquino, received their higher education in the United States. In 1986, Aquino peacefully forced out dictator Ferdinand Marcos, signaling a return to democracy and a commitment to reducing the wide gap between the country's rich and poor.

Official name: *Republic of the Philippines*
Area: *115,831 sq mi (300,000 sq km)*
Population: *64,907,000*
Capital: *Manila (pop. 1,728,441)*
Ethnic groups: *Malay*
Language: *Filipino, English*
Religious groups: *Roman Catholic, Muslim*
Economy: *Agr: rice, corn, coconuts, sugarcane, fruit. Ind: food processing, textiles, chemicals, wood products, electronics, minerals, oil refining, fishing*
Currency: *Philippine peso*

Malaysia

Malaysia owes much of its economic success to some rubber seeds that a 19th-century British explorer smuggled out of Brazil. The British took some seedlings to their protectorate on the Malay Peninsula and established rubber plantations there in the 1890s. Today, Malaysia is the world's leading producer of natural rubber.

Only half of Malaysia occupies the lower peninsula. The other half lies 400 miles (644 km) across the South China Sea on the island of Borneo. Both sections have mountainous interiors and swampy coastal plains. Heat and abundant rainfall promote dense rain-forest vegetation, including about a thousand varieties of orchids.

Nearly half of the people are Malays who came from southern China about 4,000 years ago. The majority of Malays today farm or fish for a living. In the 19th century, the British recruited Indian workers to work on the rubber plantations, where most of their descendants have stayed. Chinese also came to mine tin, another of Malaysia's exports. Many Chinese took their earnings from tin and started businesses in the cities. Tribal groups such as the Iban live in the rain forests of East Malaysia.

An independent federation since 1963, Malaysia is booming. Industry is centered around densely populated Kuala Lumpur, the capital. A literate work force and low wages attract foreign investors, but the government encourages Malay business ownership. Rich in resources including timber and petroleum, Malaysia holds enormous economic promise.

Official name: *Malaysia*
Area: *127,317 sq mi (329,749 sq km)*
Population: *17,407,000*
Capital: *Kuala Lumpur (pop. 1,000,000)*
Ethnic groups: *Malay, Chinese, Indian, other*
Language: *Malay, many other languages*
Religious groups: *Muslim, Buddhist, Hindu*
Economy: *Agr: rubber, oil palm, rice, cacao, pepper. Ind: electronics, oil, tin, textiles, lumber, fishing*
Currency: *ringgit or Malaysian dollar*

Singapore

Located off the tip of the Malay Peninsula, the tiny country of Singapore is made up of 58 islands. The country, chief island, and capital are all called Singapore. Established by the British in 1819 on the site of a Malay fishing village, Singapore was valued for its deep-water harbor and strategic position along the narrow sea routes connecting the Indian and Pacific Oceans. It quickly became an important free port and entrepôt—a distribution center—for goods traveling between Asia and the West.

Since independence in 1965, Singapore has concentrated on industrial development. The people are prosperous by Asian standards. In this densely populated country, most of them live in high-rise apartments built by the government, complete with shopping centers and recreation facilities. Lacking much farmland,

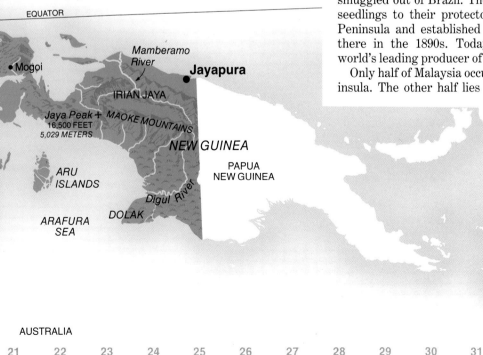

EQUATOR

Mogoi
Mamberamo River
Jayapura
IRIAN JAYA
Jaya Peak 16,500 FEET 5,029 METERS
MAOKE MOUNTAINS
NEW GUINEA
ARU ISLANDS
PAPUA NEW GUINEA
Digul River
DOLAK
ARAFURA SEA
AUSTRALIA
21 22 23 24 25 26 27 28 29 30 31 32

Singapore must import most of its food and even its water, which is piped in from Malaysia.

Official name: *Republic of Singapore*
Area: *239 sq mi (618 sq km)*
Population: *2,681,000*
Capital: *Singapore*
Ethnic groups: *Chinese, Malay, Indian*
Language: *English, Malay, Chinese, Tamil*
Religious groups: *Buddhist, Muslim, Hindu*
Economy: *Agr: poultry, vegetables, fruit, orchids. Ind: oil refining, electronics, shipbuilding, finance*
Currency: *Singapore dollar*

Brunei

The Sultan of Brunei rules his tiny Islamic kingdom with a firm hand, but most people don't seem to mind. Wealth from oil and natural gas provides Brunei's citizens with free education and medical care, and low-cost housing, fuel, and food.

Brunei consists of two separate wedges of land in northern Borneo. Most people live along the coast near the offshore oil fields or in the capital, Bandar Seri Begawan. Like other towns and villages in the swampy lowlands, part of the capital is built on stilts. Most Bruneians work for the government or in the oil industry. The country must import the bulk of its food. Beef comes from an Australian cattle ranch Brunei owns, which is larger than Brunei itself.

Official name: *State of Brunei Darussalam*
Area: *2,226 sq mi (5,765 sq km)*
Population: *257,000*
Capital: *Bandar Seri Begawan (pop. 50,500)*
Ethnic groups: *Malay, Chinese, other*
Language: *Malay, English, Chinese*
Religious groups: *Sunni Muslim, Buddhist*
Economy: *Agr: rice, cassava, fruit, vegetables. Ind: oil, natural gas, construction, fishing*
Currency: *Brunei dollar*

Indonesia

"Unity in diversity" is the national motto of Indonesia. Some 300 ethnic groups speaking more than 250 languages inhabit this 13,677-island equatorial archipelago that extends for 3,200 miles (5,150 km). Indonesia has the largest population in the world after China, India, the Soviet Union, and the United States.

Less than half of the mountainous islands are inhabited. Sixty percent of the huge population lives on Java, an island about the size of Alabama. Java also contains most of the archipelago's active volcanoes, whose ash often creates fertile farmland. Rain forest and swamps cover much of neighboring Sumatra, a site of rich offshore deposits of oil and natural gas.

The Moluccas, known as the Spice Islands, have supplied the world with cloves, nutmeg, and pepper for centuries. Drawn by the spice trade, Portuguese, Spanish, British, and Dutch adventurers sailed to Indonesia in the 1500s. The Dutch eventually controlled most of the islands as a colony. Independence came in 1949.

Irian Jaya occupies the western half of the island of New Guinea. Only decades ago, headhunting and cannibalism were practiced by the tribes living among its remote rain forests. Irian Jaya and Kalimantan today are Indonesia's frontier, with valuable mineral resources, vast stands of hardwoods, and spare land for resettling people from overcrowded islands.

Many centuries ago, rival Buddhist and Hindu kingdoms vied for control of the archipelago with its vital waterways that link the Pacific and Indian Oceans. Later, Muslim traders brought Islam, which spread throughout the islands except for Bali. Today Indonesia has more followers of Islam than any other country.

On Bali, Hindu beliefs still hold fast. Combined with spirit and ancestor worship, they guide all aspects of life. Here and on Java, graceful dancers perform the precise movements of ancient dances to the exotic strains of a gamelan orchestra. Instruments include metal gongs, drums, and the xylophonelike *gambang*.

Most Indonesians farm, growing rice and other food crops on small plots of land. They also work on plantations that supply cash crops such as rubber. Indonesia's high birthrate puts pressure on the land that sends millions to cities like Jakarta, the capital, on densely packed Java. There many live in makeshift housing and earn a meager living selling food or operating foot-driven pedicabs. Indonesia's hope rests on its vast mineral resources, many of them untapped, to create jobs for its growing population.

Official name: *Republic of Indonesia*
Area: *741,101 sq mi (1,919,443 sq km)*
Population: *184,583,000*
Capital: *Jakarta (met. pop. 7,600,000)*
Ethnic groups: *Some 300 groups, mostly Malay*
Language: *Bahasa Indonesia, Javanese, other*
Religious groups: *Muslim*
Economy: *Agr: rice, cassava, corn, oil palm, rubber, cacao, coffee, sugarcane, coconuts, tea, tobacco. Ind: oil, natural gas, lumber, minerals, textiles, fishing*
Currency: *rupiah*

1 *Philippines*

2 *Philippines*

3 *Philippines*

Philippines

1 *Flooded terraces on Luzon provide ample rice harvests thanks to the "green revolution." This agricultural research program produced high-yield varieties of grain.*

2 *In a sterile environment, workers assemble circuits at a factory in Manila. The delicate components are then shipped to foreign electronics firms.*

3 *This 11-year-old boy mines gold in the hills of Mindanao. Laws prohibiting child labor are often ignored by poor Filipinos.*

1 *Malaysia*

2 *Singapore*

3 *Singapore*

4 *Indonesia*

5 *Indonesia*

6 *Indonesia*

Malaysia

1 *An orangutan, a "person of the forest" in Malay, seems to ponder its future. Protected by law, orangutans still face hunting, and destruction of their rain forest habitat.*

Singapore

2 *The luxury goods of the world await shoppers at Singapore's Lucky Plaza, where duty-free imports draw local people and tourists alike.*

3 *Fast-food, Singapore style: Street hawkers like these have been moved into Food Centers, where they conform to strict laws of cleanliness, a modern trademark.*

Indonesia

4 *Children in a Java village gather to watch cartoons on a TV set provided by the government. The country's only channel broadcasts about five or six hours a day.*

5 *A Buddha gazes out over the temple complex of Borobudur in central Java. In 1983 an international team completed restoration of the ninth-century monument.*

6 *In the remote highland jungles of Irian Jaya, a Dani tribesman uses friction to start a fire with dried grasses.*

Africa

Until the 19th century, most of Africa was a mystery to the Western world. Its impenetrable forests, rivers blocked by falls, vast deserts, and diseases had stymied explorers' attempts to penetrate the interior. Little was known about the hundreds of different groups of people who lived south of the Sahara in communities ranging from small villages to sprawling kingdoms. Nor was it guessed that, some four million years ago, our earliest ancestors took their first upright steps in Africa's heartland. Africa, home of the lion and elephant, the tall Watusi and diminutive Pygmy, the longest river and largest desert, was also the birthplace of humanity.

Africa is a huge continent, second in size only to Asia, but it has few of the geographical features found on other continents. Its coastline has a relatively small number of inlets and peninsulas. Most of the continent consists of a large, high plateau that drops steeply to narrow coastal plains. Few mountain regions mark Africa, and those that do, like the Atlas Mountains in the northwest, are small ranges compared to those on other continents or are isolated volcanic mountains, such as Mount Kilimanjaro. In addition, Africa's major rivers follow very irregular courses. Africa's unique geological history explains these features.

On a map of the world, Africa's west coast and South America's east coast look as if they could fit together. That's because they once did. In Earth's early days, the continents formed a single supercontinent called Pangaea. Africa lay at the center of the southern part, known as Gondwana. Some 180 million years ago Gondwana broke away from Pangaea. Later, continent-size chunks broke off from Gondwana and drifted away on tectonic plates. Some pieces collided with other plates and crumpled along their edges, forming long mountain chains. The African Plate moved very little, so it has no collision-caused ranges like the Andes or the Himalaya.

Sharp land drops called escarpments formed at the continent's edges where the other plates broke away. At the same time, Africa's rivers, which had once emptied into vast inland seas and lakes, carved new channels as lakes and rivers drained toward the new coasts. Rivers such as the Nile, the Niger, and the Zambezi changed their courses, sometimes drastically.

The Great Rift Valley is a currently active plate tectonics zone. Cracks in the Earth's crust here are pulling apart, forming wide rift valleys. Erosion has uncovered fossils buried for millions of years. At Olduvai Gorge and other sites, archaeologists have found the remains of ancestral humans and other long-extinct species.

Africa is centered on the Equator. A large part of the land is desert. The Kalahari and Namib Deserts blanket much of southern Africa; in the north the Sahara, Earth's largest desert, covers more than a quarter of the continent. The desert is chiefly the domain of nomadic herders. Settlement is possible, though, around oases.

Severe droughts and unwise land use are expanding the Sahara about three miles (5 km) a year into the Sahel, the arid region of short grasses on the Sahara's southern border. In the 1980s, the shrinking Sahel was the site of extreme human misery. Millions of people starved or became refugees, and nomads' herds died.

In contrast to the desert countries, central African countries along the Equator are among the wettest places on Earth. Here rain falls nearly every day on dense rain forests. Away from the urbanized coast, the forest remains sparsely settled. In West Africa, however, high populations and long settlement have greatly changed the environment.

Between forest and desert lie savanna grasslands, home to wildebeests, zebras, lions, and other animals. In East Africa, the rapidly growing human population is encroaching on the savanna, placing many species in danger. To save its wildlife, some African nations are setting aside huge tracts of land for national parks. Much of the Serengeti Plain in Kenya and Tanzania is now a wildlife sanctuary. But poachers still endanger the survival of elephants and rhinoceroses, which they kill for their valuable tusks and horns.

Culturally and historically, there are two Africas, roughly divided by the Sahara. In ancient times, the Egyptian Empire spread civilization along the Nile. Later, North African people were influenced by the Greek and Roman Mediterranean civilizations. In the seventh century, an Arab invasion swept across the region. Today the Islamic religion is the most important influence in North African society, and Arabic is

Tanzania's snowcapped Mount Kilimanjaro

Victoria Falls on the Zambezi River

EUROPE

MEDITERRANEAN SEA

ATLAS MOUNTAINS

ASIA

Nile

TROPIC OF CANCER

Ahaggar
Mountains

Tibesti
Mountains

Libyan Desert

Nubian
Desert

RED SEA

S A H A R A

Lake Assal
512 FEET
−156 METERS
Lowest point in
Africa

Cape Verde Islands

Senegal
River

Niger River

S A H E L

Lake Chad

ETHIOPIAN

GULF OF ADEN

S U D A N

HIGHLANDS

AFRICA

Zaire (Congo) River

INDIAN
OCEAN

EQUATOR

Lake Victoria

Congo
Basin

Great Rift Valley

Mount Kilimanjaro
19,340 FEET
5,895 METERS
Highest point in
Africa

ATLANTIC
OCEAN

Lake
Tanganyika

Seychelles

St. Helena

Lake Malawi

Comoro
Islands

Zambezi River

MOZAMBIQUE CHANNEL

Namib Desert

Victoria Falls

Madagascar

TROPIC OF CAPRICORN

Kalahari
Desert

Orange River

Cape of Good Hope

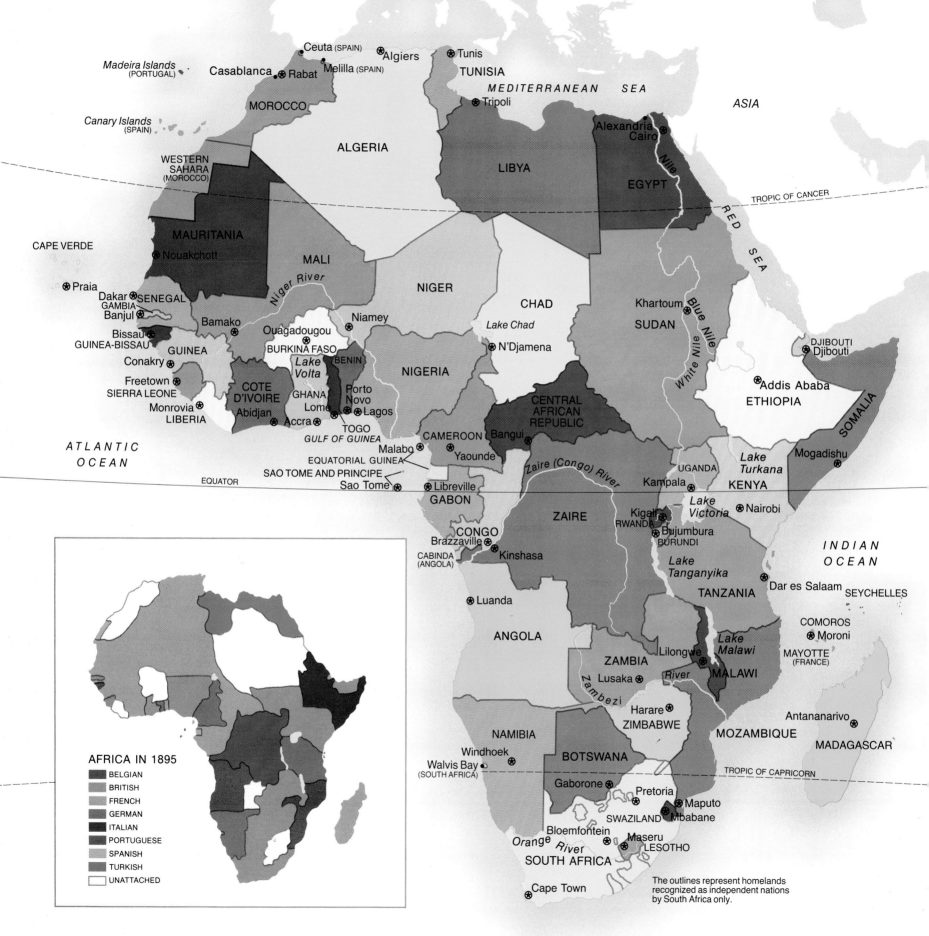

EUROPE

Ceuta (SPAIN)
⊗ Algiers
⊗ Tunis
TUNISIA
MEDITERRANEAN SEA
Madeira Islands (PORTUGAL)
Casablanca ⊗ Rabat
Melilla (SPAIN)
⦿ Tripoli
ASIA
MOROCCO
ALGERIA
LIBYA
Alexandria
Cairo
Canary Islands (SPAIN)
WESTERN SAHARA (MOROCCO)
EGYPT
Nile
TROPIC OF CANCER

CAPE VERDE
MAURITANIA
⊗ Nouakchott
MALI
NIGER
CHAD
Khartoum
RED SEA

⊗ Praia
Dakar ⊗ SENEGAL
GAMBIA
Banjul
Niger River
Niamey
Lake Chad
SUDAN
Blue Nile
DJIBOUTI ⊗ Djibouti
Bissau ⊗
GUINEA-BISSAU
GUINEA
Bamako
Ouagadougou
BURKINA FASO
BENIN
⊗ N'Djamena
NIGERIA
White Nile
⊗ Addis Ababa
ETHIOPIA
Conakry ⊗
Lake Volta
Freetown ⊗
SIERRA LEONE
COTE D'IVOIRE
GHANA
Lome
Porto Novo
CENTRAL AFRICAN REPUBLIC
SOMALIA
Monrovia ⊗
LIBERIA
Abidjan
Accra
⊗ Lagos
TOGO
CAMEROON ⊗ Bangui
Mogadishu

ATLANTIC OCEAN
GULF OF GUINEA
Malabo ⊗
EQUATORIAL GUINEA
⊗ Yaounde
Zaire (Congo) River
UGANDA
Lake Turkana

SAO TOME AND PRINCIPE
Kampala ⊗
KENYA
EQUATOR
Sao Tome ⊗ Libreville
GABON
ZAIRE
Kigali
RWANDA
Lake Victoria
⊗ Nairobi
INDIAN OCEAN
CONGO
Brazzaville ⊗
⊗ Bujumbura
BURUNDI
Kinshasa
Lake Tanganyika
CABINDA (ANGOLA)
TANZANIA
⊗ Luanda
Dar es Salaam
SEYCHELLES

ANGOLA
COMOROS
⊗ Moroni
ZAMBIA
Lilongwe
Lake Malawi
MAYOTTE (FRANCE)
Lusaka ⊗
River
MALAWI
Zambezi
Harare ⊗
Antananarivo ⊗
NAMIBIA
ZIMBABWE
MOZAMBIQUE
MADAGASCAR
Windhoek ⊗
BOTSWANA
Walvis Bay (SOUTH AFRICA)
TROPIC OF CAPRICORN
Gaborone ⊗
Pretoria
⊗ Maputo
SWAZILAND
Mbabane
Bloemfontein
Maseru
Orange River
LESOTHO
SOUTH AFRICA
⊗ Cape Town

The outlines represent homelands recognized as independent nations by South Africa only.

AFRICA IN 1895
- ▮ BELGIAN
- ▮ BRITISH
- ▮ FRENCH
- ▮ GERMAN
- ▮ ITALIAN
- ▮ PORTUGUESE
- ▮ SPANISH
- ▮ TURKISH
- ▯ UNATTACHED

the primary language. The area is commonly grouped with Middle Eastern Arabic countries.

South of the Sahara lies a land of tremendous human diversity, where hundreds of black ethnic groups live, many with different languages and cultures. Traditional beliefs have been overlaid with Muslim and Christian ones, but many Africans still practice traditional religions that emphasize the power of ancestors and of spirits that inhabit the natural world.

Great kingdoms and empires developed here thousands of years ago. By the 14th century Timbuktu was a thriving center of commerce and Islamic learning in West Africa. Zimbabwe flourished as a political and trading center in the southeast. Ruins uncovered there contained coins from China and beads from India.

Extensive contact with Europeans began in the 1440s, when Portuguese sailors began exploring Africa's west coast. Soon, slaves became a major item of trade. Over the next three centuries more than 25 million Africans, most of them captured in raids by other Africans, were sold into slavery. By the late 1800s, European colonization was in full swing. In 1885 European leaders carved the entire continent into colonies, setting borders without regard to ethnic boundaries. Those decisions still haunt Africa, even though most African countries won independence in the 1960s. In recent years, civil wars have taken an enormous toll in human lives.

Today, poverty plagues much of Africa. The continent includes 21 of the world's 29 poorest countries. Most people depend on farming for survival. Diseases such as malaria, sleeping sickness, and AIDS attack millions, and malnutrition continues to be a major problem.

African countries are striving to improve health, education, and agricultural development. Many are overly dependent on a single cash crop or commodity whose value may fluctuate and are seeking to diversify their economies. There are other signs, too, of change. In South Africa, where the government policy of apartheid has long made discrimination against nonwhites legal, black Africans are winning new rights. And Namibia, the last black colony, celebrated its independence in 1990 with the establishment of a multiparty system—a promising omen for Africa's political future.

A mountain of ivory tusks confiscated by Kenyan officials in 1989 represents 1,500 elephants killed by poachers.

Facts About Africa

Area: 11,687,187 sq mi (30,269,680 sq km)
Population: 646,389,000
Highest Point: Mount Kilimanjaro, Tanzania, 19,340 ft (5,895 m) above sea level
Lowest Point: Lake Assal, Djibouti, 512 ft (156 m) below sea level
Largest Country: *(by area)* Sudan 967,500 sq mi (2,505,813 sq km)
Largest Country: *(by population)* Nigeria 115,316,000
Largest Metropolitan Areas: *(by population)*

Cairo, Egypt	9,080,000
Alexandria, Egypt	3,280,000
Kinshasa, Zaïre	2,990,000

Longest Rivers: *(mi and km)*

* Nile	4,145	6,671
Zaïre (Congo)	2,900	4,667
Niger	2,590	4,169

Largest Desert: *(sq mi and sq km)*

* Sahara	3,500,000	9,064,958

Largest Lakes: *(sq mi and sq km)*

Victoria	26,834	69,500
Tanganyika	12,703	32,900

*World record

Glossary

apartheid—a government policy of racial segregation and discrimination in South Africa.

cacao—a tropical tree bearing seeds called cacao or cocoa beans, used to make cocoa and chocolate.

CFA franc—currency of the Communauté Financière Africaine (African Financial Community); worth half a French franc.

drought—a long period without rain.

griot—an oral historian, a singer-storyteller.

homeland—an area set aside for a people of a particular national, racial, or cultural origin.

nomads—usually herders, who travel from place to place seeking supplies of food and water.

poach—to capture or kill wild animals illegally.

Pygmies—groups of central African peoples who usually stand less than five feet tall.

rift valley—a trough-shaped valley formed when the Earth's crust sinks between parallel faults.

Sahel—the semiarid grassland directly south of the Sahara in western and central Africa.

savanna—a tropical grassland with scattered trees.

Sudan—the largest country in Africa, in the northeast; also the name given by Arabs to the region in north-central Africa between the Sahara and the equatorial forests. It includes the Sahel.

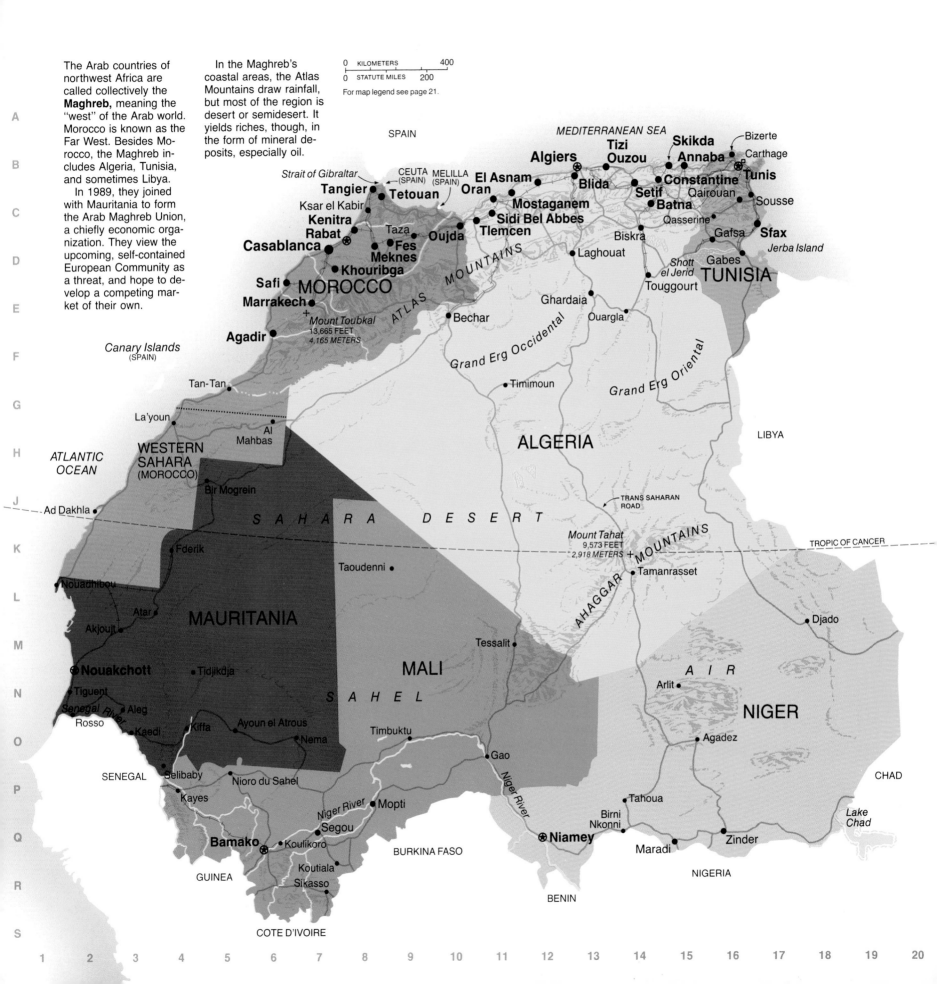

The Arab countries of northwest Africa are called collectively the **Maghreb,** meaning the "west" of the Arab world. Morocco is known as the Far West. Besides Morocco, the Maghreb includes Algeria, Tunisia, and sometimes Libya.

In 1989, they joined with Mauritania to form the Arab Maghreb Union, a chiefly economic organization. They view the upcoming, self-contained European Community as a threat, and hope to develop a competing market of their own.

In the Maghreb's coastal areas, the Atlas Mountains draw rainfall, but most of the region is desert or semidesert. It yields riches, though, in the form of mineral deposits, especially oil.

KILOMETERS 400
STATUTE MILES 200
For map legend see page 21.

SPAIN

MEDITERRANEAN SEA

Bizerte
Carthage
Skikda
Annaba
Algiers
Tizi Ouzou
Tunis
El Asnam
Blida
Constantine
Setif
Qairouan
Oran
Batna
Sousse
Mostaganem
Sidi Bel Abbes
Qasserine
Sfax
Tlemcen
Biskra
Gafsa
Jerba Island
Laghouat
Gabes
Shott el Jerid
TUNISIA
Touggourt

Strait of Gibraltar
CEUTA (SPAIN) MELILLA (SPAIN)
Tangier
Tetouan
Ksar el Kabir
Kenitra
Rabat
Taza
Oujda
Casablanca
Fes
Meknes
Khouribga
MOROCCO
Safi
Marrakech
+ Mount Toubkal
13,665 FEET
4,165 METERS
Agadir

Ghardaia
Ouargla
Bechar

ATLAS MOUNTAINS

Canary Islands
(SPAIN)

Grand Erg Occidental

Grand Erg Oriental

Tan-Tan

Timimoun

La'youn
Al Mahbas

LIBYA

ALGERIA

ATLANTIC OCEAN

WESTERN SAHARA (MOROCCO)

Bir Mogrein

Ad Dakhla

SAHARA   DESERT

TRANS SAHARAN ROAD

Fderik

Mount Tahat
9,573 FEET
2,918 METERS +

TROPIC OF CANCER

Taoudenni

AHAGGAR MOUNTAINS

Tamanrasset

Nouadhibou

Djado

Atar
MAURITANIA
Akjoujt

Tessalit

A I R

Nouakchott

Arlit

Tidjikdja

MALI

Tiguent
SAHEL

NIGER

Senegal River
Aleg
Rosso
Kaedi
Kiffa
Ayoun el Atrous
Nema

Timbuktu

Agadez

Gao

SENEGAL
Selibaby
Nioro du Sahel
Kayes

Niger River

Tahoua
Birni Nkonni

Zinder

CHAD

Lake Chad

Niger River
Mopti
Segou
Bamako
Koulikoro
Sikasso
Koutiala

Niamey

Maradi

BURKINA FASO

NIGERIA

GUINEA

BENIN

COTE D'IVOIRE

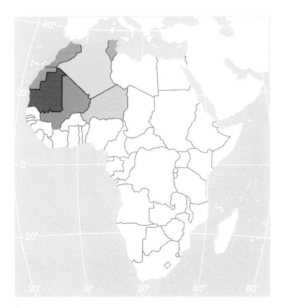

The discovery of phosphates in the desert region of **Western Sahara** (formerly Spanish Sahara) to the southwest, helped fuel a costly war between Morocco and the Polisario, a guerrilla organization fighting for Western Saharan independence. Morocco has claimed sovereignty over this onetime Spanish colony, and Moroccan troops have occupied much of the region since 1976. The King of Morocco and Polisario leaders have agreed to put the matter to a vote. It remains to be seen whether this area of nomadic herders will vote for independence or choose to stay permanently part of Morocco.

Official name: *Kingdom of Morocco*
Area: *275,117 sq mi (712,550 sq km)*
Population: *25,792,000*
Capital: *Rabat (pop. 893,042)*
Ethnic groups: *Arab, Berber, Moor*
Language: *Arabic, Berber, French*
Religious groups: *Sunni Muslim*
Economy: *Agr: livestock, wheat, barley, fruit, sugar beets, vegetables, olives. Ind: phosphates, food processing, textiles, tourism, leather, fishing*
Currency: *Moroccan dirham*

Algeria

There's a strong French flavor to Algeria. People in its cities speak French as well as Arabic. Vintners in its coastal hills produce fine wines, and French dishes are enjoyed along with local favorites such as couscous, a savory stew of semolina and lamb.

From 1834 to 1962 Algeria was a possession of France. A French elite owned much of the farmland and ran business and government. The legendary French Foreign Legion patrolled the Sahara. In 1954 a bloody civil war erupted. When it ended in 1962, Algeria had won independence, but it lost many of its professionals and skilled workers as more than a million French citizens fled back to France.

Huge deposits of oil and natural gas helped revive its economy. Refineries, iron and steel mills, textile factories, and a vehicle assembly plant now place Algeria among the most developed Arab countries. But the rush to fill better-paying city jobs and falling oil prices also spelled trouble. Algiers, the capital, and other cities suffer unemployment and housing shortages, and the outskirts swell with *bidonvilles*, shantytowns where many migrant rural families dwell.

Most Algerians live along the coastal plain, a fertile strip that slopes up to a northern range of the Atlas Mountains. South of this range lie high plateaus, home to herders of sheep and goats. Beyond the Saharan Atlas Mountains stretches the barren desert that blankets more than 85 percent of the country.

Official name: *Democratic and Popular Republic of Algeria*
Area: *919,595 sq mi (2,381,741 sq km)*
Population: *24,946,000*
Capital: *Algiers (pop. 1,483,000)*
Ethnic groups: *Arab, Berber*
Language: *Arabic, Berber, French*
Religious groups: *Sunni Muslim*
Economy: *Agr: wheat, barley, fruit, olives, vegetables, livestock. Ind: iron, steel, oil, natural gas, mining, motor vehicles, cement, textiles, wine, chemicals*
Currency: *Algerian dinar*

Tunisia

Smallest and northernmost of the North African countries, Tunisia has an extensive coastline along the Mediterranean Sea. More than two million visitors a year come to resorts on these sunny shores. Tourism makes a significant contribution to the country's income.

Besides tourism, Tunisia's economy relies on oil, mining, and agriculture. Dates grow in isolated areas including the desert, but most farming takes place in the country's fertile northern half. Olive groves flourish along the east coast, and Tunisia is a leading exporter of olive oil.

Strategically located at the Strait of Sicily, Tunisia controlled many of the major trade routes of the ancient world. The Carthaginian Empire was founded here some 2,800 years ago. Rome grew into a powerful rival empire and, in 146 B.C., completely destroyed Carthage.

Governed by France from 1881 to 1956, Tunisia after independence adopted a progressive outlook. Under the leadership of Habib Bourguiba, whose poor health forced his retirement in 1987, women were freed from the veil and won the right to vote. The new government faces a growing fundamentalist Islamic movement.

Official name: *Republic of Tunisia*
Area: *63,170 sq mi (163,610 sq km)*
Population: *7,916,000*
Capital: *Tunis (pop. 596,654)*
Ethnic groups: *Arab*
Language: *Arabic, French*
Religious groups: *Sunni Muslim*
Economy: *Agr: wheat, barley, olives, grapes, citrus fruit, dates, vegetables. Ind: phosphates, oil, tourism, cement, steel, textiles, food processing, fishing*
Currency: *Tunisian dinar*

Morocco

Africa draws closest to Europe at Morocco's northern tip. Spain lies only nine miles (14 km) away, across the Strait of Gibraltar, yet Morocco is a world as well as a continent apart. In the teeming main square of Marrakech, vendors in hooded robes called djellabas offer wares made of tooled leather or copper and brass. Dentists advertise their trade with samples of extracted molars. Snake charmers and fire-eaters vie for attention.

From fertile plains along the Atlantic coast, Morocco's terrain rises to the Atlas Mountains, snowcapped in winter. Beyond stretches the Sahara. Originally inhabited by Berbers, whose descendants still herd and farm in the highlands, Morocco was invaded by Arabs in the seventh century. The following century, an alliance of Arabs and Berbers conquered Spain. Their descendants, known as Moors, ruled parts of the Iberian Peninsula until finally driven out in 1492 by a Christian campaign. Spain and Portugal seized lands in northern Morocco, and Spain still controls the coastal towns of Ceuta and Melilla.

Today about half of Moroccans live by farming, chiefly on the Atlantic plains. Fishing off the Atlantic coast is also important. But Morocco's economy relies most heavily on its mineral resources. With the world's largest known phosphate reserves, it has become the leading exporter of phosphate rock. Casablanca, the largest city and chief port, handles most export trade, and is also the main industrial center.

Mauritania

An orbiting camera over West Africa in 1987 recorded a huge dust cloud heading across the Atlantic— the topsoil of Mauritania, blowing away in the hot winds of the Sahara.

For centuries nomads herded livestock in the Sahel, the semiarid grassland that runs across the country's southern region. But the land was overgrazed and stripped of trees for fuel. Mauritanians now plant trees and irrigate crops in the south, but the nation lies defenseless against droughts and the steady advance of the Sahara.

Refugees jam camps of tents and cardboard shacks, their animals dead and farmlands exhausted. Nouakchott, the capital since 1960 when this French colony won independence, was built for a few thousand residents but now holds 350,000. Coastal fishing and mining offer the greatest promise for this stricken country.

Official name: *Islamic Republic of Mauritania*
Area: *397,955 sq mi (1,030,700 sq km)*
Population: *1,969,000*
Capital: *Nouakchott (met. pop. 350,000)*
Ethnic groups: *Moor, Fulani, Wolof, other*
Language: *Arabic, French, Fula, Wolof, other*
Religious groups: *Sunni Muslim*
Economy: *Agr: livestock, millet, vegetables, dates, gum arabic. Ind: fishing, iron ore, gypsum*
Currency: *ouguiya*

Mali

In the 11th century, Tuareg nomads founded a seasonal camp at a West African oasis. From this camp grew Timbuktu, a caravan post trading in gold, salt, and slaves. Also a center of Islamic learning, it became the pearl of the Mali and Songhai Empires that ruled from the 13th to the 16th century. European adventurers, lured by tales of its splendor, found Timbuktu in the 1800s—a dusty, run-down town, its glory broken by raids and changing trade routes.

Droughts in the Sahel today plague Mali, a country of small farmers and nomadic herders. Particularly severe droughts in the 1970s forced many of the Tuareg nomads to settle in towns. Mali stretches north into the Sahara, but the Niger River waters the nation's best croplands in the southern region, where most of the people live. Cotton rules a farm-based economy, and sugarcane and peanuts are also grown as cash crops. Fishing is centered around Segou and Mopti, northeast of the capital, Bamako.

Mali lacks a seacoast; steamboats on the Niger, a few roads, and a single railroad link it to neighboring nations. Formerly a colony called French Sudan, Mali has taken back its old, imperial name. It gained full independence in 1960.

Official name: *Republic of Mali*
Area: *478,841 sq mi (1,240,192 sq km)*
Population: *8,918,000*
Capital: *Bamako (pop. 404,000)*
Ethnic groups: *Bambara, Fulani, Tuareg, other*
Language: *French, Bambara, Fula, other*
Religious groups: *Sunni Muslim, traditional*
Economy: *Agr: millet, rice, corn, cotton, peanuts, sugarcane, livestock. Ind: food processing, fishing*
Currency: *CFA franc*

Niger

The landlocked nation of Niger is shaped somewhat like a fish, its tail pointing toward the Atlantic Ocean hundreds of miles away. The country's northern half reaches into the searing Sahara. Much of the south is part of the Sahel, a thirsty belt along the desert's edge where droughts periodically turn sparse grasslands to dust and wipe out nomadic herders' cattle, goats, and sheep.

A five-year drought struck in 1968; by the time the June-to-September rains returned, 90 percent of the livestock had died. Thousands of people had fled to neighboring countries or crowded into Niger's few cities in search of food and jobs. Niger is one of the hottest places on Earth. The heat can soar above 120°F (49°C) and evaporate rain before it hits the ground.

Nine out of ten people live on the southern edge of Niger, where most herd livestock or tend crops such as peanuts, sorghum, and millet. Niger's mountains yield uranium, an important export. In the tail of the fish, the Niger River that gave the country its name also gives it its best farmland. Here villagers raise rice, cotton, and other crops. Once a French colony, Niger won independence in 1960.

Official name: *Republic of Niger*
Area: *489,191 sq mi (1,267,000 sq km)*
Population: *7,448,000*
Capital: *Niamey (met. pop. 360,000)*
Ethnic groups: *Hausa, Djerma-Songhai, Fulani*
Language: *French, Hausa, Djerma, Fula, other*
Religious groups: *Sunni Muslim*
Economy: *Agr: grains, cassava, peanuts, cotton, cowpeas, livestock. Ind: uranium, cement, textiles*
Currency: *CFA franc*

1 *Tunisia*

Tunisia

1 *Modern buildings flank a divided avenue in Tunisia's capital, Tunis. Trees shade traditional market stalls that line the center of the avenue.*

Niger

2 *Young Wodaabe herdsmen use elaborate makeup and facial contortions to charm girls. The courtship rituals of these nomads of the Sahel are centuries old.*

3 *Women near Tahoua file past a steeply sloped field of crops. Rainfall here is so sparse that farmers may have to plant 100 seeds for every one that sprouts.*

2 *Niger*

3 *Niger*

Morocco

1 *In crowded Fes only one street is open to motor traffic. People use mules to carry goods through narrow passageways.*

2 *Gleaming brass and copper brighten a corner in a suq, or marketplace, in Marrakech. Many Moroccan women veil their faces when going out in public.*

Mauritania

3 *Villagers shovel encroaching desert dunes away from their schoolhouse. Caused partly by deforestation, creeping sands have buried whole towns in the Sahel region.*

Mali

4 *Made entirely of mud bricks, a mosque looms like a fortress near Timbuktu. Protruding studs help workmen scale the walls when the surface needs repair.*

Algeria

5 *Traders haggle over sheep in the marketplace at Ghardaia, a desert town known for centuries for this "stock exchange."*

1 *Morocco*

2 *Morocco*

3 *Mauritania*

4 *Mali*

5 *Algeria*

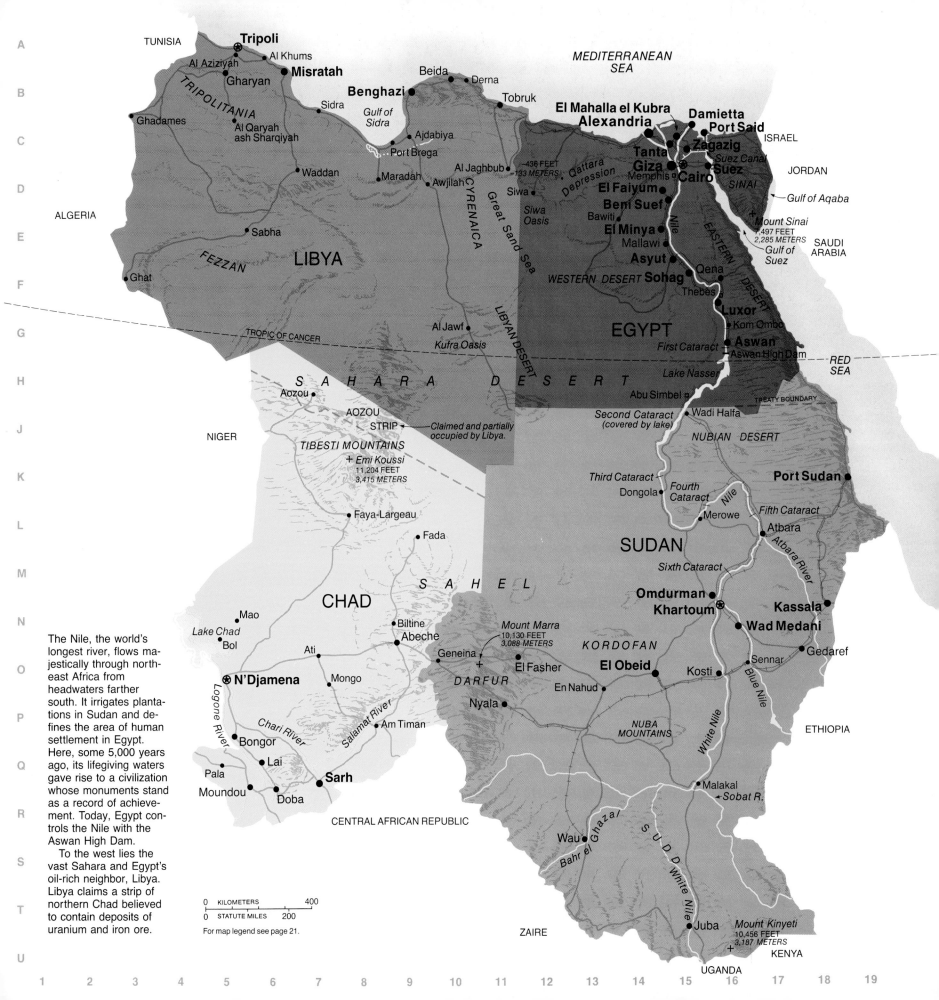

A
B
C
D
E
F
G
H
J
K
L
M
N
O
P
Q
R
S
T
U

1 2 3 4 5 6 7 8 9 10 11 12 13 14 15 16 17 18 19

TUNISIA

Tripoli ⊗

MEDITERRANEAN
SEA

Al Khums

Al Aziziyah

Gharyan   **Misratah**   Beida   Derna

TRIPOLITANIA   **Benghazi** •   Tobruk

Ghadames   **El Mahalla el Kubra**   **Damietta**
                                                                                       Alexandria   **Port Said**
        Al Qaryah   Gulf of   ISRAEL
        ash Sharqiyah   Sidra   **Tanta**   **Zagazig**
                                                          Ajdabiya   **Giza**   **Suez**   Suez Canal
                                                                                          -436 FEET Qattara   **Cairo** ⊗   JORDAN
        Waddan   Port Brega   -133 METERS Depression Memphis   SINAI
                                                     Al Jaghbub   **El Faiyum**   Gulf of Aqaba
ALGERIA   Maradah   Awjilah   Siwa   Mount Sinai
                                                                                          Beni Suef   + 7,497 FEET
                                                          C   Siwa   Bawiti   2,285 METERS SAUDI
                                          Y   Oasis   Gulf of ARABIA
        Sabha   R   **El Minya**   Suez
                                          E   Mallawi
        FEZZAN   N   Great Sand Sea   **Asyut**
                                          A   WESTERN DESERT **Sohag**   Qena
Ghat •   I   Thebes
                                          C   **Luxor**
                                          A   Kom Ombo
                                                    Al Jawf •   LIBYAN DESERT   **EGYPT**   **Aswan**
        TROPIC OF CANCER   Kufra Oasis   First Cataract Aswan High Dam   RED
                                                                                                                          SEA
                                                                                    Lake Nasser
                    S A H A R A   D E S E R T
        Aozou •   Abu Simbel •   TREATY BOUNDARY

NIGER   AOZOU
               STRIP ← Claimed and partially   Second Cataract   • Wadi Halfa
                        occupied by Libya.   (covered by lake)
        TIBESTI MOUNTAINS   NUBIAN DESERT
        + Emi Koussi
          11,204 FEET   **Port Sudan** •
          3,415 METERS   Third Cataract •   Fifth Cataract
                                              Dongola • Fourth   Nile
        Faya-Largeau •   Cataract • Merowe   Atbara
                              Fada •   • **Kassala**
                                                          SUDAN   Atbara River
                                                    Sixth Cataract
        CHAD   S A H E L   **Omdurman**
                                          Biltine •   **Khartoum** ⊗
        Mao •   Abeche •   Mount Marra   **Wad Medani**
Lake Chad   Geneina 10,130 FEET   Gedaref •
        Bol •   Ati •   ← 3,088 METERS KORDOFAN   Sennar •
                    Mongo •   El Fasher •   **El Obeid** • Kosti •
        ⊗ **N'Djamena**   DARFUR   En Nahud •   Blue Nile
                                          Nyala •   NUBA
Logone River   MOUNTAINS   ETHIOPIA
        Bongor •   Chari River Salamat River   White Nile
        Lai •   • Am Timan
Pala •   Malakal •
Moundou •   Doba • **Sarh**   Sobat R.
                                                                    Bahr el Ghazal   S
CENTRAL AFRICAN REPUBLIC   Wau •   U
                                                                              D D
                                                                                          White Nile
                                                                                          Juba • Mount Kinyeti
                                                                                                  10,456 FEET
        ZAIRE   3,187 METERS
                                                                    UGANDA   +
                                                                                          KENYA

The Nile, the world's
longest river, flows ma-
jestically through north-
east Africa from
headwaters farther
south. It irrigates plantations in Sudan and de-
fines the area of human
settlement in Egypt.
Here, some 5,000 years
ago, its lifegiving waters
gave rise to a civilization
whose monuments stand
as a record of achieve-
ment. Today, Egypt con-
trols the Nile with the
Aswan High Dam.

To the west lies the
vast Sahara and Egypt's
oil-rich neighbor, Libya.
Libya claims a strip of
northern Chad believed
to contain deposits of
uranium and iron ore.

0   KILOMETERS   400
0   STATUTE MILES   200

For map legend see page 21.

Libya

Part of the world's largest desert, the Sahara, dominates Libya. In a country bigger than Alaska, only two strips of land 50 miles (80 km) wide along the Mediterranean Sea receive enough rainfall for farming. One fertile region surrounds Tripoli, the capital, in the northwest, while the other includes the city of Benghazi in the northeast. Most Libyans live in these coastal lowlands. Between them, the desert comes right to the sea at the Gulf of Sidra.

At one time, farmers in the north produced enough food to make the country self-sufficient, but with the discovery of oil in 1959, many people left farming for higher-paying oil-field jobs. Despite lower oil prices in recent years, petroleum remains a mainstay of Libya's economy.

During spring and fall, hot, dust-laden winds known as ghiblis blow from the desert. When the ghibli blows, temperatures in coastal centers can reach 110°F (43°C). There are no permanent rivers in Libya, only watercourses called wadis that fill during infrequent rain showers. Even within the desert, though, huge underground reservoirs of water have been found. The Libyan government is using some of its oil money to build a pipeline hundreds of miles long that will carry water from the desert to coastal cities and agricultural projects.

Libya has a young population: More than half its people are under 18 years old. Most are of Arab or Berber descent, but groups of Tuaregs, a nomadic people, herd goats and camels in the desert, and Tebu tribesmen live in the Tibesti Mountains. Since 1969 Col. Muammar Qaddafi has ruled Libya through a socialist government.

Official name: *Socialist People's Libyan Arab Jamahiriya*
Area: *679,362 sq mi (1,759,540 sq km)*
Population: *4,080,000*
Capital: *Tripoli (met. pop. 990,697)*
Ethnic groups: *Arab, Berber*
Language: *Arabic, Berber*
Religious groups: *Sunni Muslim*
Economy: *Agr: wheat, barley, olives, vegetables, fruit, livestock. Ind: oil, food processing, textiles*
Currency: *Libyan dinar*

Egypt

Egypt was known in ancient times for its engineering wonders. Beginning about 2650 B.C., stone masons and laborers built huge pyramids on the western bank of the Nile. They were tombs for Egypt's rulers. In the largest, the Great Pyramid of Cheops, some 2 million stones averaging more than 2.5 tons each (2.3 metric tons) were hauled into place.

In the 1960s, Egyptian and Soviet engineers constructed a modern wonder: the Aswan High Dam on the Nile, 364 feet (111 m) high and 2.3 miles (3.7 km) wide. Lake Nasser, stretching behind the dam from Egypt into Sudan, is the largest freshwater lake in either country. The High Dam tamed the Nile's annual floods and provided a year-round supply of water for irrigation and hydroelectric power. Though the dam has blocked the flow of alluvial silt that once enriched the soil, its benefits are considerable.

An ancient Greek historian called Egypt "the gift of the Nile," because the river is Egypt's lifeblood. The Nile Valley and its delta, which make up about 4 percent of Egypt's land, support most of the country's agriculture and 99 percent of its population. In the Western Desert that covers two-thirds of the country, rain has not fallen in some areas for years. But underground water reservoirs are being explored, and in fertile oases date palms grow.

Along the Nile, cotton, sugarcane, fruit, and vegetables are cultivated for export. Fellahin—peasant farmers—raise food crops such as corn and rice, as well as sheep and goats. Farm families usually live in houses made of mud bricks that have been dried in the sun.

Life for most Egyptians is hard, with poverty the norm. One reason is that the country's population is growing faster than its economy. In the past Egypt was able to grow enough food to support its people. But even with the irrigation provided by the High Dam, the nation must now import more than half its food. Unemployment is rife, and Cairo, Egypt's capital and the largest city in Africa, has serious housing problems. Many people live in tomb cities on the outskirts of Cairo and some even in shacks on rooftops.

Industry is concentrated in Cairo and in Alexandria, the chief port and second largest city. Cairo's prestige in the Arab world, eroded by the signing of a peace treaty with Israel in 1979, is growing again, and the city remains an important center of Muslim tradition and culture.

Official name: *Arab Republic of Egypt*
Area: *386,662 sq mi (1,001,449 sq km)*
Population: *54,778,000*
Capital: *Cairo (pop. 5,875,000; met. pop. 9,080,000)*
Ethnic groups: *Egyptian*
Language: *Arabic*
Religious groups: *Sunni Muslim, Coptic Christian*
Economy: *Agr: corn, rice, wheat, cotton, sugarcane, vegetables, citrus fruit, livestock. Ind: food processing, textiles, tourism, oil, fertilizers, cement, fishing*
Currency: *Egyptian pound*

Chad

The Sahara already covers nearly all of Chad's mountainous northern half. Now the desert is slowly moving south into the semiarid Sahel region where nomads graze cattle, bringing with it famine and desolation. Chad's only good agricultural land lies in the south, around Lake Chad and between the Chari and Lagone Rivers. Here farmers raise livestock, food crops, and cash crops of cotton on small farms. Lions, elephants, and leopards living in the wooded savanna are major tourist attractions.

The people of Chad are among the world's poorest. The country has few roads and no railroad, and there is little manufacturing. Even the capital, N'Djamena, does not have a daily newspaper. Civil war between the Muslim north, supported by Libya, and the non-Muslim south has devastated Chad's frail economy.

Official name: *Republic of Chad*
Area: *495,755 sq mi (1,284,000 sq km)*
Population: *4,949,000*
Capital: *N'Djamena (pop. 402,000)*
Ethnic groups: *Sara, many others*
Language: *French, Arabic, African languages*
Religious groups: *Muslim, traditional, Christian*
Economy: *Agr: millet, sorghum, peanuts, cassava, yams, dates, cotton, livestock. Ind: textiles, fishing*
Currency: *CFA franc*

Sudan

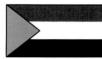

The next time you toast a marshmallow or pop a gumdrop in your mouth, you may be eating a bit of Sudan. Gooey goodies such as these contain gum arabic, the sticky sap of the acacia tree that grows in Sudan, the largest and most diverse country in Africa. More than 50 different ethnic groups live within its borders, which encompass savannas, deserts, mountains, and rain forests.

In the south lies the Sudd, one of the world's largest swamps. It drains into the White Nile, which joins the Blue Nile at Khartoum, the capital, to form the main course of the Nile. Farmers grow cotton, an important export crop, in the irrigated region between the two rivers. Sugarcane grows between the Sudd and Khartoum on one of the world's largest sugar plantations.

The Sahara covers the northern third of Sudan. Here Arab nomads chiefly raise camels and goats. Hills along the Red Sea trap enough rain to nourish pastures where Beja nomads graze camels and flocks of sheep.

Most Sudanese are small farmers, living off sorghum and millet crops. Women use stones to grind the grains into a flour from which they make a flat bread. This is eaten with a spicy vegetable soup that may also contain meat or eggs.

Sudan has plenty of good farmland. Yet millions in the south face starvation because farming has been disrupted by a civil war between the mostly Arab central government located in the north and the black Africans who live in the south. Drought, political instability, and the arrival of floods of refugees from war-torn neighboring countries have made matters worse.

The different cultures that make up Sudan meet in town markets called suqs, where Arab merchants sell clothing and imported goods, while tribal people peddle food and handicrafts. Old and new customs also mix in Sudan. Members of the Nuer tribe, their faces and bodies covered with ritual scars, work the country's oil fields, using the money they earn to buy cows to increase the size of their traditional herds.

Official name: *Republic of the Sudan*
Area: *967,500 sq mi (2,505,813 sq km)*
Population: *24,484,000*
Capital: *Khartoum (pop. 476,218)*
Ethnic groups: *Arab, Nilotic groups, Beja, other*
Language: *Arabic, African languages, English*
Religious groups: *Muslim, traditional, Christian*
Economy: *Agr: sorghum, millet, wheat, cotton, gum arabic, sesame, peanuts, sugarcane, livestock. Ind: food processing, textiles, oil, cement, mining, fishing*
Currency: *Sudanese pound*

Egypt

1 *Pyramids rise from the sands of the Sahara at Giza. These huge stone structures were built about 4,500 years ago as tombs for the kings of Egypt.*

2 *Boys guide straw-laden donkeys through palm-shaded fields in the Nile Valley.*

3 *Cairo, Africa's largest city, already contains more than 9 million people in its greater metropolitan area. That number may reach 30 million by the 21st century.*

Chad

4 *A goatherd drives his flock across the Sahara. About half of Chad is desert.*

Libya

5 *At a factory in Gharyan, workers turn out ceramic tableware.*

Sudan

6 *Forehead scars of a woman carrying a water pot identify her as one of the Mondari people. Many different ethnic groups inhabit Sudan, Africa's largest country.*

1 *Egypt*

2 *Egypt*

3 *Egypt*

5 *Libya*

4 *Chad*

6 *Sudan*

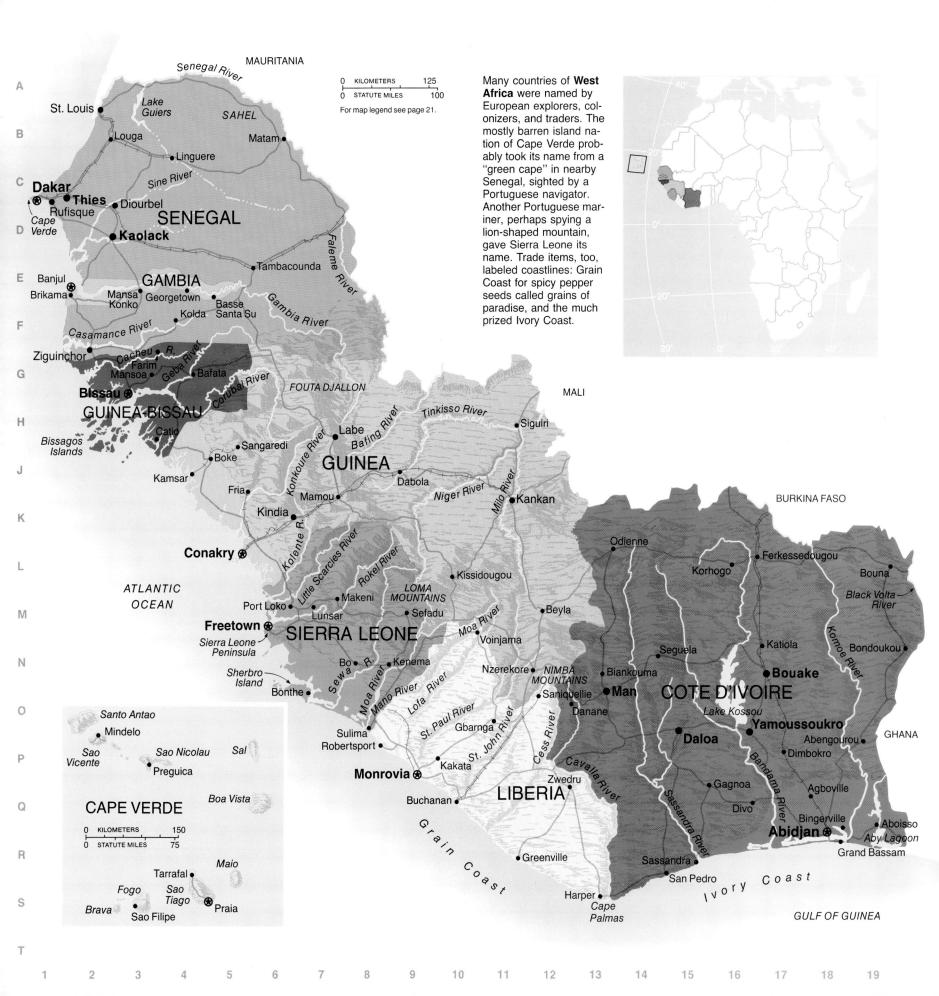

MAURITANIA

KILOMETERS 125
STATUTE MILES 100

For map legend see page 21.

Many countries of **West Africa** were named by European explorers, colonizers, and traders. The mostly barren island nation of Cape Verde probably took its name from a "green cape" in nearby Senegal, sighted by a Portuguese navigator. Another Portuguese mariner, perhaps spying a lion-shaped mountain, gave Sierra Leone its name. Trade items, too, labeled coastlines: Grain Coast for spicy pepper seeds called grains of paradise, and the much prized Ivory Coast.

Senegal River

St. Louis
Lake Guiers
SAHEL
Louga
Matam
Linguere
Sine River
Dakar
Thies
Rufisque
Diourbel
SENEGAL
Cape Verde
Kaolack
Tambacounda
Faleme River

Banjul
Brikama
GAMBIA
Mansa Konko
Georgetown
Basse Santa Su
Kolda
Gambia River

Casamance River
Ziguinchor
Cacheu R.
Farim
Mansoa
Geba River
Bafata
Corubal River
FOUTA DJALLON
MALI
Bissau
GUINEA-BISSAU

Bissagos Islands
Catio
Sangaredi
Labe
Bafing River
Tinkisso River
Siguiri
Boke
Kamsar
Fria
Konkoure River
GUINEA
Dabola
Niger River
Milo River
Kankan
Mamou
Kindia
Kolente R.

BURKINA FASO

Odienne
Ferkessedougou
Korhogo
Bouna
Black Volta River

ATLANTIC OCEAN

Conakry
Little Scarcies River
Rokel River
Kissidougou
LOMA MOUNTAINS
Beyla
Port Loko
Makeni
Lunsar
Sefadu
Moa River
Voinjama
Freetown
Sierra Leone Peninsula
SIERRA LEONE
Bo R.
Kenema
Nzerekore
NIMBA MOUNTAINS
Biankouma
Man
COTE D'IVOIRE
Seguela
Katiola
Komoe River
Bondoukou
Sewa R.
Moa River
Mano River
Lofa River
Saniquellie
Danane
Lake Kossou
Bouake
Sherbro Island
Bonthe
Sulima
St. Paul River
Gbarnga
St. John River
Cess River
Yamoussoukro
Daloa
Abengourou
GHANA
Robertsport
Kakata
Cavalla River
Sassandra River
Bandama River
Dimbokro
Monrovia
LIBERIA
Zwedru
Gagnoa
Divo
Agboville
Buchanan
Bingerville
Abidjan
Aboisso
Aby Lagoon
Grand Bassam
Greenville
Sassandra
San Pedro
Ivory Coast
Grain Coast
Harper
Cape Palmas
GULF OF GUINEA

Santo Antao
Mindelo
Sao Nicolau
Sal
Sao Vicente
Preguica
Boa Vista

CAPE VERDE

KILOMETERS 150
STATUTE MILES 75

Maio
Tarrafal
Fogo
Sao Tiago
Praia
Brava
Sao Filipe

Cape Verde

Drought has defined Cape Verde from the time of its first Portuguese settlement in 1462 to the present. An independent country since 1975, this chain of 15 volcanic islands 400 miles (644 km) west of Senegal is mostly barren and mountainous, with cliffs dropping to the sea. A nearly continuous drought that began in 1968 cut crop yields by 90 percent and sent thousands of people abroad in search of work.

Of those who remain, many continue to farm. Others have found jobs as fishermen, salt miners, or laborers digging water wells, planting drought-resistant trees, and building dams to conserve rainwater.

Most poor countries can't afford such projects. But Cape Verde receives aid from many foreign governments as well as money sent home by Cape Verdeans living abroad.

Official name: *Republic of Cape Verde*
Area: *1,557 sq mi (4,033 sq km)*
Population: *368,000*
Capital: *Praia (pop. 57,748)*
Ethnic groups: *Creole, African*
Language: *Portuguese, Crioulo*
Religious groups: *Roman Catholic*
Economy: *Agr: corn, beans, sweet potatoes, sugarcane, cassava, bananas, coffee. Ind: fishing, salt*
Currency: *Cape Verde escudo*

Senegal

In Senegal, local singer-storytellers called *griots* tell tales of history and tradition. They are keepers of the cultural heritage in this land of low, rolling plains—a land occupied for centuries by France before Senegal achieved independence in 1960.

The French favored Senegal above their other colonies, making Dakar the headquarters for their West African empire. Today Dakar is Senegal's capital and one of the leading ports in Africa, well equipped to handle supertankers and other large oceangoing ships.

French roots hold fast in Senegal. French is the official language and many French citizens hold key jobs in commerce and industry. Still, the nation retains its African character. Most Senegalese speak a native language called Wolof. Most farm or raise cattle, sheep, and goats.

Senegal benefits from a sizable amount of industry, chiefly in food processing, textiles, and chemicals, with factories centered around Dakar. It also has successful fishing, tourism, and phosphate mining operations. But it suffers from disastrous droughts. When these occur, crops fail, including the chief export crop, peanuts. With the help of foreign aid, Senegal and neighboring countries hope to solve the water-shortage problem by building irrigation canals and damming rivers.

In 1981 Senegal instituted a multiparty system of government—one of a growing number of African countries to follow this political route.

Official name: *Republic of Senegal*
Area: *75,955 sq mi (196,722 sq km)*
Population: *7,171,000*
Capital: *Dakar (met. pop. 1,200,000)*
Ethnic groups: *Wolof, Fulani, Serer, other*
Language: *French, Wolof, other African languages*
Religious groups: *Sunni Muslim*
Economy: *Agr: grains, peanuts, cassava, cotton, livestock. Ind: fishing, textiles, chemicals, mining*
Currency: *CFA franc*

The Gambia

A narrow ribbon of land 200 miles (322 km) long, The Gambia snakes into the western edge of the African continent. Except for its coastline, this country is entirely surrounded by Senegal, with which it shares many ethnic and religious ties. A former British colony, The Gambia gained independence in 1965.

In 1889 Great Britain and France fixed the country's unusual boundaries, which follow the Gambia River as it winds through dense mangrove swamps and grass-covered flats. Back from the river lie rolling savanna lands, where Gambians grow upland crops such as the nation's principal cash crop, peanuts.

Saltwater and freshwater fishing bring in additional income, as does tourism. But most Gambians live in poverty, struggling against drought and insect infestation to raise enough corn, rice, and millet to feed themselves. Life expectancy here is low, only 35 years.

Official name: *Republic of The Gambia*
Area: *4,361 sq mi (11,295 sq km)*
Population: *835,000*
Capital: *Banjul (pop. 49,181)*
Ethnic groups: *Malinke, Fulani, Wolof, Jola*
Language: *English, Mandinka, Fula, Wolof*
Religious groups: *Sunni Muslim*
Economy: *Agr: grains, peanuts, cotton, livestock. Ind: food processing, tourism, textiles, fishing*
Currency: *dalasi*

Guinea-Bissau

Small groups of courageous villagers spearheaded the struggle for liberation in Guinea-Bissau in the early 1960s. Scrambling through thickets and rice fields, they battled the well-equipped army of their Portuguese colonial rulers. Soon thousands of their countrymen joined them in a war that would last more than ten years.

The Portuguese fought hard to keep this land with its navigable rivers, its tropical rain forests, its many coastal islands where coconut palms grow. They had done little to develop it, though. When they finally gave it up, they left ruined crops and widespread poverty.

The country's new socialist leaders tried to rebuild the economy, but Guinea-Bissau remains poor. Nearly three-quarters of the people grow only enough food for themselves. Many live in straw huts with thatched roofs.

On the coast, the Balante grow rice in irrigated paddies. In the interior, the Malinke farm and the nomadic Fulani raise livestock. Their herds survive despite the presence of the tsetse fly, which transmits a disease called nagana to animals—and sleeping sickness to humans.

More people may turn to fishing in the future: Fish and shellfish abound off the coast and in the deep estuaries along the shore.

Official name: *Republic of Guinea-Bissau*
Area: *13,948 sq mi (36,125 sq km)*
Population: *966,000*
Capital: *Bissau (pop. 109,214)*
Ethnic groups: *Balante, Fulani, Malinke, other*
Language: *Portuguese, Crioulo, African languages*
Religious groups: *traditional, Muslim*
Economy: *Agr: rice, oil palm, root crops, peanuts, coconuts, fruit. Ind: food processing, fishing, lumber*
Currency: *Guinea-Bissau peso*

Guinea

The Fouta Djallon region—high plateaus cut by rivers, deep valleys, and plunging waterfalls—helps Guinea earn its reputation for scenic beauty. The country is a treasure-house of natural resources, including one-third of the world's bauxite. Huge deposits of iron ore lie in the mountains near the Liberian border. Most of the land is well-watered and fertile.

Despite these resources, Guinea remains poor and undeveloped. More than 80 percent of its people make a bare living from farming. In the swampy soil along the coast, they grow staple crops of cassava and rice, and in upland valleys, vegetables and fruit. Herders on the Fouta Djallon plateau and eastern savanna graze small, humpless cattle called N'dama. On the forested hills of the southeast farmers grow cash crops of coffee.

Guinea's first leader after independence from France in 1958 was a dictator, Ahmed Sekou Touré. "We prefer poverty in liberty to wealth in slavery," he proclaimed. During most of Touré's 25-year regime, the country turned its back on the West and on policies that might have helped to develop its resources. Many people were imprisoned for their political beliefs. Nearly two million fled abroad. Since Touré's death in 1984, a new government has improved foreign relations and tried to speed up development.

Official name: *Republic of Guinea*
Area: *94,926 sq mi (245,857 sq km)*
Population: *7,086,000*
Capital: *Conakry (met. pop. 1,110,000)*
Ethnic groups: *Fulani, Malinke, Susu, 15 others*
Language: *French, African languages*
Religious groups: *Muslim, traditional*
Economy: *Agr: cassava, rice, fruit, vegetables, oil palm, peanuts, coffee. Ind: bauxite, diamonds*
Currency: *Guinea franc*

Sierra Leone

A 15th-century Portuguese explorer gave this West African region its name: Sierra Leone, meaning "lion mountain," maybe because of the lionlike shape of a mountain on the Sierra Leone Peninsula. Here, in 1787, British philanthropists established Freetown as a settlement for liberated slaves. After the British government outlawed slavery in 1807, it made Sierra Leone a colony. British Navy ships patrolled the coast, intercepting slave ships bound for the New World. Freetown became a refuge for thousands of former slaves.

The descendants of those slaves, the Creoles, today make up barely 2 percent of the population of the now independent nation, but their mother tongue, Krio, is spoken throughout the country. The Creoles once were prominent in Sierra Leone's political and commercial life. Since independence in 1961, leaders from larger ethnic groups have replaced them.

More and more of Sierra Leone's people are moving to cities in search of jobs. But almost three-quarters still live in rural areas, from the coastal belt of beaches and swampland to the inland forests, plains, and mountains. Crop yields are low, so many farmers work part of the year as miners. Diamond mining is particularly important to the economy. On the coast, fishermen in a fleet of 2,500 canoes catch about 65,000 tons (59,000 metric tons) of fish a year. Women traders called mammies handle the local fish marketing and act as moneylenders.

Official name: *Republic of Sierra Leone*
Area: *27,699 sq mi (71,740 sq km)*
Population: *4,064,000*
Capital: *Freetown (met. pop. 469,776)*
Ethnic groups: *Mende, Temne, Creole, other*
Language: *English, Krio, Mende, Temne*
Religious groups: *traditional, Muslim*
Economy: *Agr: rice, cassava, cacao, coffee, oil palm, livestock. Ind: diamonds, rutile, bauxite, fishing*
Currency: *leone*

Liberia

Freed black slaves left the United States in the early 1800s to found a new nation in West Africa. They settled along a sandy coastline dotted with lagoons and bordered by thick rain forest. Here the newcomers mingled with local fishermen, farmers, and traders. Liberia became Africa's first independent republic in 1847, with a constitution modeled after that of the United States and a capital named after President Monroe.

Descendants of the American settlers make up 5 percent of Liberia's population today. These Americo-Liberians once ran the country and many remain in government, but a revolt in 1980 brought a purely African group to power.

A quarter of Liberians live in the Monrovia urban area. Many of the rest live in villages scattered throughout the forests. The women farm cassava, rice, fruit, and vegetables for family use, while the men grow coffee and cacao for sale. Liberia's economy relies chiefly on the export of rubber, iron ore from deposits in the Nimba Mountains and other ranges, and timber from its extensive forests.

Official name: *Republic of Liberia*
Area: *43,000 sq mi (111,369 sq km)*
Population: *2,476,000*
Capital: *Monrovia (pop. 421,058)*
Ethnic groups: *Kpelle, Bassa, Grebo, other*
Language: *English, many African languages*
Religious groups: *traditional, Muslim, Christian*
Economy: *Agr: rice, cassava, rubber, oil palm, coffee, cacao. Ind: iron ore, diamonds, lumber, fishing*
Currency: *Liberian dollar*

Côte d'Ivoire

A century ago, Abidjan was a sleepy coastal fishing village of about 700 people. Today 1.4 million Ivoirians live and work in this cosmopolitan city with its high-rise office buildings and wide avenues. It remains the seat of government‡ although Yamoussoukro some 137 miles (220 km) northwest has been designated the new capital.

Abidjan continues to grow. Each year roughly 10,000 people, mainly farmers from the dry northern savanna, move to the city. They seek work in government and in the automobile-assembly plant, aluminum factory, and small manufacturing firms. But many Ivoirians live in traditional villages of grass-covered huts scattered throughout the humid, forested southern half of the country, the economic heartland. Some grow export crops such as cacao and coffee that provide income for the developing nation.

Félix Houphouët-Boigny, president after independence was gained from France in 1960, increased economic growth by encouraging foreign investment, improving farming methods, and expanding the range of exports.

Côte d'Ivoire, known in English as the Ivory Coast, takes its name from the elephant ivory trade that began in the 1400s and flourished through the late 1800s and early 1900s. Today ivory trade is illegal, and the nation protects its elephants and other wildlife in game reserves.

Official name: *Republic of Côte d'Ivoire*
Area: *124,504 sq mi (322,463 sq km)*
Population: *12,097,000*
Capital: *Abidjan (met. pop. 1,423,323)*
Ethnic groups: *More than 60 groups*
Language: *French, African languages*
Religious groups: *traditional, Muslim, Christian*
Economy: *Agr: yams, cassava, rice, corn, millet, cacao, coffee, oil palm, fruit, cotton, rubber, sugarcane. Ind: food processing, lumber, oil refining, textiles*
Currency: *CFA franc*

Côte d'Ivoire

1 *With daggers drawn to heighten the drama, dancers of the Dan ethnic group toss a young girl back and forth. Girls selected to learn the ritual acrobatic dances begin training at the age of four. The government hopes to preserve such customs while melding some 60 ethnic groups into one nation.*

1 *Côte d'Ivoire*

1 *Sierra Leone*

2 *Senegal*

Sierra Leone

1 *At an open-air market in Freetown, many women run their own small businesses, selling goods and foodstuffs.*

Senegal

2 *Window-shopping in Senegal's capital, Dakar, elegantly dressed women study the latest fashions from Paris.*

3 *Spacious boulevards and plazas mark Dakar. Founded as a colonial outpost in 1857, today it blends French chic with African zest.*

3 *Senegal*

5 *Cape Verde*

The Gambia

4 *A boat on the Gambia River takes on a cargo of peanuts. The river is a national lifeline, The Gambia's main avenue of trade, travel, and communication.*

Cape Verde

5 *Islanders gather fresh coconuts to eke out food supplies. Thin soil and frequent droughts limit farming; Cape Verdeans import much of their food.*

4 *The Gambia*

The Gold Coast, Europeans called Ghana. Copious amounts of the precious metal, mined or panned from rivers, were once carried overland to the Mediterranean. The Portuguese exploited the West African sea route in the 15th century, trading goods for gold with local African nations. They built a great castle called Elmina (from "the mine") that warded off competitors for nearly a century.

Elmina became a staging post for the human trade between the 16th and 19th centuries that gave the Slave Coast its name. This region was a center for the West African slave trade.

0 KILOMETERS 250
0 STATUTE MILES 150

For map legend see page 21.

Burkina Faso

In 1984 Upper Volta chose a new name, Burkina Faso, which, loosely translated, means "land of honest men" in the local languages. The country's main ethnic group is called the Mossi.

The nation is one of the poorest in the world. Ninety percent of the families scratch out a living growing sorghum, millet, and corn, or raising livestock. One in ten people can read. One in four children goes to school.

Burkina Faso lies on an inland plateau cut by three major south-flowing rivers. Part of the northern region is in the arid Sahel. All over the country, too much grazing and cultivation have changed already poor land into semidesert. Droughts cause food shortages and even famine. Each year about 500,000 Burkinabe leave home to find seasonal work in countries to the south.

Some hope for Burkina Faso lies in its mineral deposits, especially manganese in the northeast. But mining requires roads and railways, both inadequate in this struggling nation.

Official name: *Burkina Faso*
Area: *105,869 sq mi (274,200 sq km)*
Population: *8,707,000*
Capital: *Ouagadougou (pop. 441,515)*
Ethnic groups: *More than 50 groups, including Mossi, Mande, Fulani, Lobi, Bobo*
Language: *French, African languages*
Religious groups: *traditional, Muslim, Christian*
Economy: *Agr: grains, livestock, peanuts, cotton, shea nuts, sesame. Ind: food processing, textiles*
Currency: *CFA franc*

Ghana

Ghana's local chieftains oversee festivals marking birth and death, puberty, marriage, and harvest. By doing so they hope to preserve traditional Ghanaian culture despite the pressures of modernization.

In 1957 Ghana became the first black African colony to win its independence, a symbol of hope for all of Africa. Rich in gold and diamonds, in fertile land, and in waters teeming with fish, the new nation's future seemed bright, especially with a visionary leader like Kwame Nkrumah.

Ghana had only one harbor: Nkrumah built a second, modern port at Tema. Ghana needed more electricity: Nkrumah raised the giant Akosombo Dam on the Volta River, creating a steady source of energy and the world's largest artificial lake—3,500 square miles (9,065 sq km) in area. But Nkrumah gradually transformed his government into a dictatorship. Unwise spending and mismanagement led to economic and political chaos. A military coup toppled him in 1966, but the situation has improved little under seven succeeding regimes.

Today a quarter of the people live in poverty, in areas ranging from the dry rolling northern savanna to the humid forests of the southwest. Most Ghanaians farm, using simple tools to raise their own food on small plots. About one-fourth of the population works in the forest belt to produce cocoa beans, Ghana's largest export.

Official name: *Republic of Ghana*
Area: *92,100 sq mi (238,537 sq km)*
Population: *14,566,000*
Capital: *Accra (pop. 964,879)*
Ethnic groups: *Ashanti, Ewe, Fante, Ga, other*
Language: *English, Akan, Dagomba, Ewe, Ga*
Religious groups: *traditional, Christian, Muslim*
Economy: *Agr: cassava, yams, corn, sorghum, millet, rice, plantains, cacao, cotton, coffee. Ind: mining, lumber, fishing, food processing, aluminum*
Currency: *cedi*

Togo

Long and narrow, measuring only 100 miles (160 km) across at its widest, Togo stretches 360 miles (580 km) north from the Gulf of Guinea. Highlands extend southwest to northeast through grassy plains, where coffee, cacao, and cotton are raised. Forests of teak, mahogany, and bamboo grow on southern plateaus.

Togo's main ethnic group, the Ewe, live near the coast, where French colonial rule provided schooling and jobs until independence in 1960. Today many Ewe farm, the traditional livelihood of most Togolese; some are merchants or government workers. Southern Togolese also mine phosphates, an ingredient of fertilizers and the country's leading export.

The hill people of the north include the Kabye, whose ancestors settled northern Togo from the West African savanna. Skilled farmers, they cultivate millet, sorghum, and beans for food, and peanuts as a cash crop.

Official name: *Republic of Togo*
Area: *21,925 sq mi (56,785 sq km)*
Population: *3,449,000*
Capital: *Lomé (pop. 229,400)*
Ethnic groups: *37 groups, including Ewe, Kabye*
Language: *French, Ewe, Kabye, Dagomba*
Religious groups: *traditional, Christian, Muslim*
Economy: *Agr: cassava, yams, corn, sorghum, millet, beans, livestock, coffee, cacao, cotton, peanuts, oil palm. Ind: phosphates, food processing, textiles*
Currency: *CFA franc*

Benin

Formerly called Dahomey, Benin established its national palm-oil trade in the 1800s under an African kingdom of that name. Later a French colony, it won independence in 1960.

Benin has fertile soil and some forest cover; a grassy landscape reaches nearly to its seacoast. In lagoon villages on the marshy southern shore, fishermen and their families live in bamboo huts built on stilts, and children ferry to school in dugout canoes. Beyond the lagoons, on a fertile plateau, farmers clear the land to grow crops for their own use, and cotton and oil palms for income. Herders of cattle and sheep live in the Atakora Mountains of the northwest.

Under French rule, many citizens attended school, but today there are not enough skilled jobs for these people. Recently the communist government renounced Marxism and now hopes to expand private enterprise.

Official name: *Republic of Benin*
Area: *43,484 sq mi (112,622 sq km)*
Population: *4,664,000*
Capital: *Porto Novo, official (pop. 144,000) Cotonou, de facto (pop. 383,250)*
Ethnic groups: *Fon, Adja, Yoruba, Bariba, other*
Language: *French, Fon, other African languages*
Religious groups: *traditional, Christian, Muslim*
Economy: *Agr: cassava, yams, corn, beans, sorghum, peanuts, cotton, oil palm. Ind: food, textiles*
Currency: *CFA franc*

Nigeria

One of every four black Africans is Nigerian. Known as the giant of West Africa, Nigeria has more people than any other country on the continent. With its high birthrate it may soon become the world's fourth most populous nation after China, India, and the Soviet Union.

Nigeria is also an economic giant in Africa, with rich deposits of natural gas and oil. The discovery of oil in the 1950s generated enormous income. Nigeria's leaders invested much of this wealth in roads, railways, and schools, as well as in manufacturing and communications systems. In recent years the nation has relied on oil for 90 percent of its export earnings, which makes it vulnerable to the rise and fall of world oil prices.

Urban life has a long history here. Some cities, such as Kano, a Muslim cultural center in the north, and Ibadan, a regional capital in the south, date back several centuries. Others grew up during the oil boom, when people moved from country to city in search of jobs. Today, about a quarter of Nigeria's people are city dwellers. Lagos, the capital, has more than four and a half million residents. The city spreads from the mainland to four islands, all joined by bridges.

Many Nigerians, however, dwell in mud-and-thatch huts in small villages, where they farm, fish, or herd. Their loyalties to extended family and to village are strong. So are their ethnic allegiances. More than 300 ethnic groups live in Nigeria. The variety of languages, customs, artistic traditions, and styles of dress give the nation its great cultural richness.

The largest groups include the Hausa and Fulani, who dominate the broad expanse of the sandy northern plains bordering the Sahara. Though the region receives little rain, these people manage to grow sorghum, millet, peanuts, and cotton, and to raise livestock.

Other major groups are the Yoruba of the southwest and the Ibo of the southeast. Nigeria's moist southern regions support dense tropical forest—much of which southern farmers have cleared to plant cacao, rubber, and oil palm trees. On the coast, amid a maze of creeks and lagoons, people grow coconut and oil palms.

After achieving independence from British colonial rule in 1960, Nigeria divided sharply along ethnic and regional lines. A bitter and bloody civil war erupted in 1967 when the Ibo formed the Republic of Biafra along the southeastern coast. About a million civilians died, primarily from starvation, before the war ended in 1970. Nigeria's present leaders continue to struggle for stability and unity among the nation's diverse peoples.

Official name: *Federal Republic of Nigeria*
Area: *356,669 sq mi (923,768 sq km)*
Population: *115,316,000*
Capital: *Lagos (met. pop. 4,710,000)*
Ethnic groups: *More than 300 groups*
Language: *English, Hausa, Ibo, Yoruba*
Religious groups: *Muslim, Christian, traditional*
Economy: *Agr: yams, cassava, sorghum, millet, corn, rice, cacao, peanuts, oil palm, rubber, cotton, livestock. Ind: oil, natural gas, minerals, steel, textiles, food processing, lumber, car assembly, fishing*
Currency: *naira*

Cameroon

Diverse lands and peoples meet in Cameroon. The landscape ranges from coastal rain forest to inland savanna, from palm-lined beaches to mountain forests. The people include about 200 ethnic groups, many with their own arts, traditions, and languages.

The most dominant group economically are the Bamileke of the western mountains, who grow coffee for export. They also hold about 70 percent of the nation's professional jobs. On the northern and central savannas, farmers raise millet, peanuts, and rice; nearby the Fulani herd horses, cattle, sheep, and goats.

Isolated bands of Pygmies hunt small game and birds, and gather food in the southeastern forests. On the southern coastal plain live the Douala, for whom the nation's major port is named. Considered the coastal elite, they are the most educated people in the country.

Oil production and manufacturing have boosted steady economic growth in recent years, but agriculture remains the chief source of income. Varied crops grow on the lush hillsides of Cameroon Mountain. At 13,451 feet (4,100 m), this volcano is the highest mountain in West Africa and one of the wettest places on Earth, receiving more than 30 feet (9 m) of rain a year.

Official name: *Republic of Cameroon*
Area: *183,569 sq mi (475,442 sq km)*
Population: *10,817,000*
Capital: *Yaoundé (pop. 653,670)*
Ethnic groups: *About 200 groups*
Language: *French, English, African languages*
Religious groups: *Christian, traditional, Muslim*
Economy: *Agr: root crops, grains, cacao, coffee, cotton, bananas, rubber, oil palm, sugarcane, livestock. Ind: agricultural processing, oil, lumber, aluminum*
Currency: *CFA franc*

1 *Benin*

2 *Nigeria*

3 *Burkina Faso*

4 *Ghana*

Benin

1 *Wooden pilings hold bamboo houses above the high tide mark in Ganvié, a village built on a tidal lagoon near Cotonou. Canoes are used for fishing and ferrying.*

Nigeria

2 *Known as the "go-slow," rush hour clogs a street in Lagos. Some four and a half million people crowd Nigeria's capital.*

Burkina Faso

3 *Bella tribesmen go to great lengths to protect themselves from desert sun; their white head wraps reflect sunlight. Cotton veils shield faces from windblown sand.*

Ghana

4 *Country women near Sunyani fill pots and pails with water for the day's chores. Missionaries helped build the village well.*

Cameroon

5 *Cupped in a volcanic crater, Lake Bambili is slowly drying up, like the already swampy lake beyond. Someday this volcanic soil will be fertile farmland.*

5 *Cameroon*

Through **Equatorial Africa,** from the shores of the Gulf of Guinea to Zaïre's eastern border, runs a broad belt of tropical rain forest. Rainfall that ranges from 60 to 400 inches (152 to 1,016 cm) a year sustains luxuriant growth. In densely populated coastal areas, the forest has been cleared for cultivation of commercial and food crops. But in the Zaïre (Congo) River basin and other interior regions, poorer soil and dense vegetation have kept population numbers down. It is estimated that two-thirds of Zaïre's valuable forest ecosystem remains intact.

For map legend see page 21.

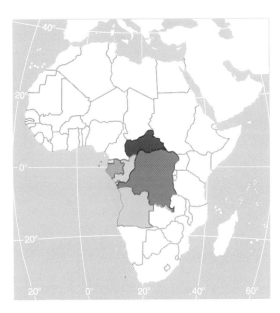

São Tomé and Príncipe

Off the west coast of Equatorial Africa two volcanic islands rise from the sea, São Tomé and smaller Príncipe. A former Portuguese colony, the mountainous islands and several islets were united as an independent country in 1975.

Close to 90 percent of the people dwell on São Tomé, where they farm or fish for tuna and shark. The country specializes in cacao and other cash crops that flourish here—so much so that it has to import most of its food.

Official name: *Democratic Republic of São Tomé and Príncipe*
Area: *372 sq mi (964 sq km)*
Population: *121,000*
Capital: *São Tomé (pop. 40,000)*
Ethnic groups: *mixed African, Portuguese-African*
Language: *Portuguese*
Religious groups: *Roman Catholic*
Economy: *Agr: cacao, coconuts, coffee, oil palm, bananas. Ind: food processing, textiles, soap, fishing*
Currency: *dobra*

Gabon

Dense equatorial forest, lush with more than 3,000 species of vegetation, blankets most of Gabon. The huge okoumé tree, used for making plywood, once supplied much of the nation's income. Now oil does, though forestry is still important. Rich deposits of iron ore, manganese, and uranium also help to give Gabon the highest per capita income in tropical Africa.

The government allocates a lot of money to roads, railways, and large agricultural projects such as banana and oil-palm plantations. Many Gabonese don't benefit from these programs. Half the people live in villages on the coast or along the rivers, where they grow cassava, yams, and taro on small family plots.

Gabon is known to many as the onetime home of Albert Schweitzer, the Nobel Prize-winning physician and philosopher who founded a missionary hospital near Lambaréné in 1913.

Official name: *Gabonese Republic*
Area: *103,347 sq mi (267,667 sq km)*
Population: *1,132,000*
Capital: *Libreville (pop. 251,400)*
Ethnic groups: *about 40 Bantu groups*
Language: *French, Fang, other Bantu languages*
Religious groups: *Christian, traditional*
Economy: *Agr: root crops, bananas, cacao, coffee, oil palm. Ind: oil, lumber, mining, food processing*
Currency: *CFA franc*

Central African Republic

At the heart of Africa lies the Central African Republic. Most of this landlocked nation consists of a rolling plateau of grassland drained by two river systems, one flowing north, the other flowing south. The country's southwestern corner dips into Africa's rain-forest belt; its northeastern tip is semidesert. Along the rivers and scattered across the countryside lives a sparse population of 80 ethnic groups.

Since winning independence from France in 1960, Central Africans have suffered political instability and economic hardship. One ruler declared himself emperor and made a fortune at the country's expense before being deposed.

Today, four out of five people farm. Many grow food crops on small plots. Others raise cotton for export or labor on European-owned coffee plantations. Some workers mine diamonds, but deposits of uranium remain unexploited.

Official name: *Central African Republic*
Area: *240,535 sq mi (622,984 sq km)*
Population: *2,806,000*
Capital: *Bangui (pop. 473,817)*
Ethnic groups: *80 groups, including Banda, Baya*
Language: *French, Sango*
Religious groups: *traditional, Christian*
Economy: *Agr: cassava, yams, peanuts, millet, sorghum, corn, rice, bananas, livestock, cotton, coffee, sesame, tobacco. Ind: diamonds, lumber, textiles*
Currency: *CFA franc*

Equatorial Guinea

Violent storms often strike Equatorial Guinea, lashing the rain forest of Río Muni, its mainland region, and battering the shores of its five islands. Political storms, too, struck the nation after it won independence from Spain in 1968. The first ruler of the new republic ruined its economy and created a reign of terror, killing or exiling a third of the people. He was overthrown in 1979, but economic recovery is slow.

Today nearly all workers in this poor country are farmers. Some grow cacao, the major export crop, on the boot-shaped island of Bioko. Here and on the less fertile mainland, where most Equatorial Guineans live, small-scale farmers grow coffee. Lumbermen harvest trees for plywood from the thick tropical woodlands.

Official name: *Republic of Equatorial Guinea*
Area: *10,831 sq mi (28,051 sq km)*
Population: *353,000*
Capital: *Malabo (pop. 34,980)*
Ethnic groups: *Fang, Bubi*
Language: *Spanish, Fang, Bubi, other*
Religious groups: *Roman Catholic*
Economy: *Agr: yams, cassava, bananas, cacao, coffee, oil palm, livestock. Ind: lumber, fishing*
Currency: *CFA franc*

Congo

The northern part of Congo is a world of green intensity. Dense vine thickets and tropical trees create a thick blanket of vegetation.

Most Congolese live south of this deeply forested region, in the coastal plains and river valleys between the capital, Brazzaville, and the sea. Here lie most of the country's farmlands and industries. About a third of the people are farmers, populating the thousands of small settlements clustered along the Congo River and its tributaries. Many plant cassava, fruit, and peanuts on family plots or tend cash crops such as sugarcane on modern plantations.

The nation's city dwellers hold jobs in government, commerce, or industry. Most live in Brazzaville on the Congo, or in the port city of Pointe Noire, linked to the capital by the Congo-Ocean Railway. This railroad and the Congo's many waterways make the nation central Africa's door to the Atlantic for trade and transport. Though lumber provides the country with a steady income, oil has driven its economy since rich offshore oilfields began to produce in 1978.

Official name: *People's Republic of the Congo*
Area: *132,047 sq mi (342,000 sq km)*
Population: *2,228,000*
Capital: *Brazzaville (pop. 596,200)*
Ethnic groups: *BaKongo, Teke, Mboshi, Sangha*
Language: *French, Lingala, Kikongo, other*
Religious groups: *traditional, Christian*
Economy: *Agr: cassava, other root crops, fruit, sugarcane, peanuts, corn, rice, livestock, oil palm, coffee, cacao. Ind: oil, lumber, food processing, mining*
Currency: *CFA franc*

Zaïre

In the deep tropical forest of Zaïre, a haunting yodel at times breaks the shady silence and resonates for a while among the trees. It is the song of Pygmy women who make their home in the rain forest of this hot, humid region. The Pygmies' ancestors in prehistoric times settled the land that is now Zaïre.

Zaïre is a huge country lying at the heart of the Zaïre River basin. It is 75 times the size of Belgium, its former ruler, which granted Zaïre independence in 1960. Central Africa's largest nation in population as well as land area, Zaïre counts more than 200 ethnic groups among its diverse peoples.

Many of Zaïre's people are poor farmers. They live in houses of mud bricks or dried mud and sticks in villages that hold from a few dozen to a few hundred people. There they grow cassava, corn, and rice, and some catch fish in the rivers. More and more Zaïrians are moving to Kinshasa, the capital, and other big cities to look for jobs. Most can't find work and end up living in crowded squatters' villages outside the cities.

Zaïre has the potential for great wealth. Some of the world's largest reserves of copper, cobalt, and diamonds are found in the south. The Zaïre River system also offers rich promise for transportation and hydroelectric power. And, with farmland ranging from tropical lowlands to cool, dry highlands, Zaïre can grow valuable cash crops of coffee, oil palm, rubber, tea, and cotton.

Since independence, however, civil war, corruption, and mismanagement have devastated the economy. Falling export earnings and rising import prices have made matters worse. Zaïre plans to aid its economy by developing new in-

dustry and by improving its inadequate road, railway, and river transportation network.

Official name: *Republic of Zaïre*
Area: *905,568 sq mi (2,345,409 sq km)*
Population: *34,853,000*
Capital: *Kinshasa (met. pop. 2,990,000)*
Ethnic groups: *More than 200 groups, mostly Bantu*
Language: *French, many African languages*
Religious groups: *Christian, traditional*
Economy: *Agr: cassava, bananas, root crops, corn, peanuts, rice, coffee, oil palm, rubber, tea, cotton. Ind: mining, food processing, textiles, cement, oil*
Currency: *zaïre*

Angola

More than 20 years of war have made life harsh for Angolans. The country is well endowed with rich farmland and valuable minerals, such as diamonds, iron ore, and copper. War has disrupted the economy and devastated the land, from the narrow coastal plain to the hilly central plateau, the nation's breadbasket.

The conflict began in the 1960s, when three rebel groups fought for independence from the Portuguese. When Portugal finally withdrew in 1975, one group seized power. Fierce fighting continues between this ruling Marxist party and the other rebels. Today few Angolans—most of them farmers, herders, traders, or miners—escape the effects of war.

War has slowed mining, blocked roads and railways, and, in places, brought farming to a halt. Coffee plantations lie abandoned. Farming families are unable to grow the corn, cassava, and other food crops they live on. Many have moved to the *musseques*, the poor shantytowns surrounding urban centers.

Once a major exporter of several cash crops, Angola now exports less and imports most of its food. One bright spot in the economy is oil. Big reserves lie off the shore of Cabinda, a forested sliver of land separated from the rest of Angola by a strip of coastal territory belonging to Zaïre.

Official name: *People's Republic of Angola*
Area: *481,354 sq mi (1,246,700 sq km)*
Population: *8,534,000*
Capital: *Luanda (met. pop. 1,200,000)*
Ethnic groups: *Ovimbundu, Kimbundu, other*
Language: *Portuguese, Bantu languages*
Religious groups: *traditional, Christian*
Economy: *Agr: cassava, corn, millet, bananas, sugarcane, vegetables, sweet potatoes, coffee, cotton, sisal. Ind: oil, mining, food processing, textiles*
Currency: *kwanza*

1 *Angola*

Angola

1 *The swift Cuanza River rushes over a scenic waterfall. A dam on the Cuanza southeast of the capital, Luanda, produces one-third of Angola's hydroelectric power.*

2 *Drillers work on an oil rig off the Cabinda coast, where Angola is developing a rich petroleum field.*

2 *Angola*

1 *Zaïre*

2 *Zaïre*

3 *Zaïre*

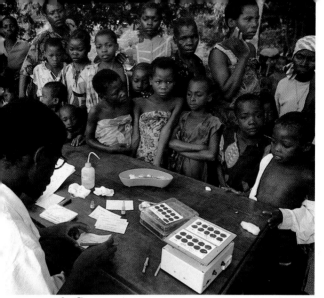

4 *Congo*

Zaïre

1 *In the Ituri Forest, seminomadic Efe Pygmy women cook while men prepare to hunt. When the clan moves, women build new huts of saplings and leaves.*

2 *Tidy mud houses with thatched roofs give a storybook look to Luotu, a farming village on the Equator south of Beni.*

3 *Balancing amid rapids on the Zaïre River, an Enya tribesman prepares to place a trumpet-shaped fish trap.*

Congo

4 *At Brazzaville, children line up to have blood tests for parasitic infections. Health programs fight tropical diseases such as sleeping sickness and malaria.*

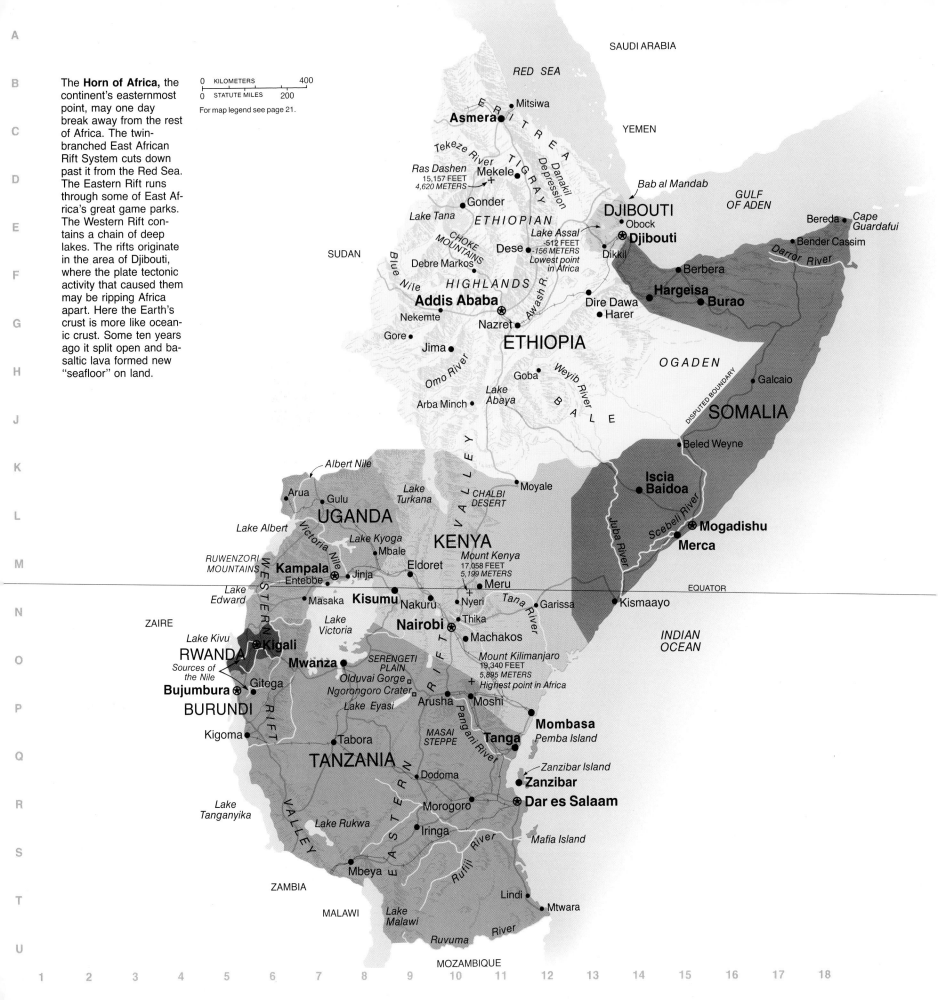

The **Horn of Africa,** the continent's easternmost point, may one day break away from the rest of Africa. The twin-branched East African Rift System cuts down past it from the Red Sea. The Eastern Rift runs through some of East Africa's great game parks. The Western Rift contains a chain of deep lakes. The rifts originate in the area of Djibouti, where the plate tectonic activity that caused them may be ripping Africa apart. Here the Earth's crust is more like oceanic crust. Some ten years ago it split open and basaltic lava formed new "seafloor" on land.

KILOMETERS 0 — 400
STATUTE MILES 0 — 200
For map legend see page 21.

SAUDI ARABIA
RED SEA
YEMEN

ERITREA
Mitsiwa
Asmera
Tekeze River
TIGRAY
Danakil Depression
Bab al Mandab
GULF OF ADEN
Cape Guardafui
Bereda
Ras Dashen
15,157 FEET
4,620 METERS
Mekele
DJIBOUTI
Obock
Bender Cassim
Darror River
Gonder
Lake Tana
ETHIOPIAN
Lake Assal
-512 FEET
-156 METERS
Lowest point in Africa
Djibouti
Dikkil
Berbera
SUDAN
Blue Nile
CHOKE MOUNTAINS
Debre Markos
Dese
HIGHLANDS
Dire Dawa
Hargeisa
Burao
Addis Ababa
Awash R.
Harer
Nekemte
Nazret
Gore
Jima
ETHIOPIA
OGADEN
Omo River
Goba
Weyib River
Galcaio
Arba Minch
Lake Abaya
BALE
DISPUTED BOUNDARY
SOMALIA

Albert Nile
Beled Weyne
Arua
Gulu
Lake Turkana
Moyale
Iscia Baidoa
CHALBI DESERT
UGANDA
KENYA
Scebeli River
Mogadishu
Lake Albert
RUWENZORI MOUNTAINS
Lake Kyoga
Mbale
Mount Kenya
17,058 FEET
5,199 METERS
Juba River
Merca
Victoria Nile
Eldoret
Kampala
Jinja
Meru
EQUATOR
Lake Edward
Entebbe
Masaka
Kisumu
Nakuru
Nyeri
Tana River
Garissa
ZAIRE
Lake Victoria
Thika
Machakos
Kismaayo
INDIAN OCEAN
Kigali
Lake Kivu
RWANDA
Mwanza
SERENGETI PLAIN
Sources of the Nile
Olduvai Gorge
Mount Kilimanjaro
19,340 FEET
5,895 METERS
Highest point in Africa
Bujumbura
Gitega
Ngorongoro Crater
Arusha
Moshi
BURUNDI
Lake Eyasi
Mombasa
Kigoma
Tabora
MASAI STEPPE
Pemba Island
Tanga
WESTERN RIFT VALLEY
Zanzibar Island
TANZANIA
Dodoma
Zanzibar
Lake Tanganyika
Morogoro
Dar es Salaam
Iringa
Mafia Island
Lake Rukwa
EASTERN RIFT VALLEY
Rufiji River
ZAMBIA
Mbeya
Lindi
Lake Malawi
Mtwara
MALAWI
Ruvuma River
MOZAMBIQUE
Pangani River

For more than 2,000 years emperors and kings ruled Ethiopia. In 1974, military officers overthrew Emperor Haile Selassi and founded a socialist government. Strife now plagues the nation as its northern provinces, Eritrea and Tigray, wage civil war against the government.

Official name: *People's Democratic Republic of Ethiopia*
Area: *471,778 sq mi (1,221,900 sq km)*
Population: *49,763,000*
Capital: *Addis Ababa (pop. 1,464,901)*
Ethnic groups: *Oromo, Amhara, Tigre, other*
Language: *Amharic, Orominga, Tigrinya, Arabic*
Religious groups: *Ethiopian Orthodox, Muslim, traditional*
Economy: *Agr: grains, legumes, coffee, oilseeds, livestock. Ind: textiles, food processing, oil refining*
Currency: *birr*

Ethiopia

Famine brought Ethiopia to world attention in the 1980s, when devastating drought struck the land. Fields once rich in crops turned to seas of dust. Nearly eight million people faced starvation, many of them children. Despite food aid, more than one million Ethiopians died. Today famine stalks the countryside again.

Were it not for recurring drought, poor crop management, and a long-running war that drains government resources, Ethiopia might be one of the most prosperous agricultural countries in Africa. Its land varies from hot lowlands to rugged mountains reaching above 15,000 feet (4,570 m). Two-thirds of the country is made up of a high, temperate, fertile plateau, where most Ethiopians live and farm. A range of crops can thrive in this diverse terrain, including the coffee bush, which grows wild in the rain forest of the southwestern highlands. Ethiopia is thought to be the original home of coffee, and this crop has become its chief export.

The plateau is split by the Great Rift Valley, a 4,000-mile-long (6,437 km) scar that slices through eastern Africa. Earthquakes often shake the valley. On its floor have been found some of the oldest fossils of early humans— bones four million years old, believed even older than those found at Olduvai Gorge in Tanzania.

Ethiopia's recorded history is long, too. It is one of the world's oldest independent countries. Today it has some 70 ethnic groups. Most of its people are Christian or Muslim.

Djibouti

One of the hottest, driest spots on Earth, Djibouti is a land of rocky desert dotted with salt lakes and rare patches of pastureland. Its location, wrapped around a natural harbor at the southern end of the Red Sea, has made its capital, also called Djibouti, an international port crucial to the country's economy. Half the population lives in the port city; the rest are nomadic herders of sheep, goats, and camels.

Official name: *Republic of Djibouti*
Area: *8,958 sq mi (23,200 sq km)*
Population: *394,000*
Capital: *Djibouti (pop. 200,000)*
Ethnic groups: *Somali (Issas), Afar, French, Arab*
Language: *French, Somali, Afar, Arabic*
Religious groups: *Sunni Muslim*
Economy: *transshipment, livestock, vegetables*
Currency: *Djibouti franc*

Somalia

Most people in Somalia belong to one ethnic group and share a common descent and culture. They believe that places with large Somali populations, including parts of Djibouti and Kenya, and Ogaden in Ethiopia, should belong to Somalia. Somalis have fought unsuccessfully to gain these territories.

Two-thirds of Somalia's workers are nomadic herders on the dry scrubby plateaus. Droughts from time to time wipe out large parts of their livestock. The best farmland lies in the south between the Juba and Scebeli Rivers. Farmers grow food crops and raise bananas for export.

Official name: *Somali Democratic Republic*
Area: *246,201 sq mi (637,657 sq km)*
Population: *8,248,000*
Capital: *Mogadishu (pop. 500,000)*
Ethnic groups: *Somali*
Language: *Somali, Arabic*
Religious groups: *Sunni Muslim*
Economy: *Agr: grains, sugarcane, livestock, bananas. Ind: sugar, hides, textiles, oil refining*
Currency: *Somali shilling*

Uganda

"The pearl of Africa," Winston Churchill called this green land of mountains, lakes, and wild animals. That was in colonial days, before the civil war that raged for two decades.

Uganda draws together people from many different linguistic and cultural backgrounds. Most trace their roots to one of 40 ethnic groups who have lived in this region for hundreds of years, farming the fertile plateau and uplands.

The plateau lies just north of Lake Victoria, the world's third largest lake, and is rimmed by mountains in the east and west. In the far west, the sharp white tops of the Ruwenzori Range, known as the Mountains of the Moon, soar up to 16,763 feet (5,109 m). Like their forebears, most Ugandans still raise food crops and livestock— in the east on mountain slopes, in the southwest, and on Lake Victoria's shores.

Uganda's future seemed bright at independence in 1962. Cash crops earned money for schools, hospitals, and roads. But in 1971, Idi Amin Dada rose to power and instituted a reign of terror. The following years brought violence, fear, and economic ruin. Uganda's present government seeks to restore peace, but economic recovery has been slow. Now the country faces a new threat: AIDS. Thousands have died from it.

Official name: *Republic of Uganda*
Area: *91,134 sq mi (236,036 sq km)*
Population: *17,008,000*
Capital: *Kampala (pop. 458,423)*
Ethnic groups: *40 groups: Bantu, Nilotic, other*
Language: *English, KiSwahili, Luganda*
Religious groups: *Christian, traditional*
Economy: *Agr: plantains, cassava, sweet potatoes, grains, coffee, cotton, tea, sugarcane, tobacco, livestock. Ind: food processing, textiles, cement, fishing*
Currency: *Uganda shilling*

Kenya

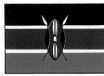

The world as it was in the beginning. That is how people describe the great grasslands and plains of Kenya, which still teem with huge herds of wild animals despite heavy poaching in recent years. In the mid-1900s, the government set aside 6 million acres (2.4 million ha) to protect its lions, elephants, rhinoceroses, and other wildlife. Today, 15 national parks and 23 game reserves, besides Indian Ocean beaches, make tourism a vital industry.

Kenya, though poor, is East Africa's most prosperous country. Good farmland is found only in the southwestern highlands, which occupy barely 10 percent of the land. Here, amid drought, farmers struggle to grow enough crops to feed the nation. They raise corn and other food, as well as cash crops of coffee, tea, sisal, and pyrethrum, used to make pesticides. About 75 percent of the people crowd within this small area. The dry inland plain that extends across 60 percent of Kenya is only sparsely inhabited by nomadic herders of cattle and camels.

Most Kenyans descend from Africans, but many coastal people have Arab roots. Of the 32 ethnic groups that live in Kenya, the largest and most dominant is the Kikuyu. The country has the world's fastest growing population; many families have six or more children. This booming growth hinders Kenya's economic progress, creating unemployment as well as land shortages that threaten the nation's parklands.

Official name: *Republic of Kenya*
Area: *224,961 sq mi (582,646 sq km)*
Population: *24,097,000*
Capital: *Nairobi (pop. 1,162,189)*
Ethnic groups: *Kikuyu, Luhya, Luo, Kamba, Kalenjin, Kisii, Meru, other*
Language: *English, KiSwahili, Kikuyu, other*
Religious groups: *traditional, Christian*
Economy: *Agr: grains, cassava, sugarcane, fruit, coffee, tea, sisal, pyrethrum, cotton, livestock. Ind: tourism, food processing, oil refining, cement*
Currency: *Kenya shilling*

Rwanda

In the steep, grassy hills of this tiny nation, one is rarely out of sight of people. Rwanda, one of Africa's most densely populated countries, has more than a thousand people sharing each square mile of farmland. Some 90 percent of Rwandans work plots that dot the hillsides. They raise export crops of coffee and tea—also vegetables and grains, though barely enough to feed their growing numbers.

Of the three ethnic groups in Rwanda, the Hutu, the Tutsi, and the Pygmy Twa, the Hutu make up 85 percent of the population. Farmers by tradition, they were dominated for centuries by the Tutsi, a tall, lanky, cattle-herding people who migrated to the region about 500 years ago from the Horn of Africa. In 1959, the Hutu rose up and seized power from the Tutsi. Since then conditions have remained relatively stable.

Official name: *Republic of Rwanda*
Area: *10,169 sq mi (26,338 sq km)*
Population: *6,989,000*
Capital: *Kigali (pop. 117,749)*
Ethnic groups: *Hutu, Tutsi, Twa*
Language: *Kinyarwanda, French, KiSwahili*
Religious groups: *Christian, traditional*
Economy: *Agr: bananas, root crops, grains, livestock, coffee, tea, pyrethrum. Ind: tin, other mining*
Currency: *Rwanda franc*

Burundi

Like neighboring Rwanda, Burundi is a small, densely populated, landlocked nation. Ethnic conflict often flashes through these rolling highlands to the northeast of Lake Tanganyika. Since independence from Belgium in 1962, surges of violence have erupted between the minority Tutsi and the majority Hutu. The worst clash occurred in 1972, when more than 100,000 Hutu were killed. Though outnumbered by the Hutu six to one, the Tutsi control the government, army, and businesses.

Burundi has a pleasant climate but hardly any flat land. Most people live on family farms in clusters of huts that sit atop the many hills. From these farms come enough bananas, vegetables, and other food crops to feed the people and small crops of coffee, tea, and cotton for export. The country has deposits of nickel and other ores, which it plans to mine.

Official name: *Republic of Burundi*
Area: *10,747 sq mi (27,834 sq km)*
Population: *5,456,000*
Capital: *Bujumbura (pop. 172,201)*
Ethnic groups: *Hutu, Tutsi, Twa*
Language: *Kirundi, French, KiSwahili*
Religious groups: *Christian, traditional*
Economy: *Agr: bananas, root crops, grains, livestock, coffee, tea, cotton. Ind: textiles, hides*
Currency: *Burundi franc*

Tanzania

Tanzania shows the many faces of Africa within the bounds of a single nation. It encompasses the varied physical terrain of a continent—wide, lion-colored plains and snowcapped mountains, coastal beaches and highland lakes. It also embraces more than 120 ethnic groups and a spectrum of religions, from Christianity and Islam to traditional African beliefs.

No single ethnic group dominates the country. One group, though small, is known worldwide: the nomadic Masai, some of whom still herd humped cattle in the grassy northern plains. The mighty Serengeti and other great game parks draw tourists eager to see the elephants, lions, giraffes, and immense herds of gazelles, wildebeests, and zebras.

One of Africa's most stable nations, Tanzania was created in 1964 when mainland Tanganyika joined with the island state of Zanzibar. From this union came the name TAN-ZAN-IA. Soon after, under the presidency of Julius Nyerere, the country launched a program of African socialism called *ujamaa*, which translates as "family-hood" in KiSwahili.

Most Tanzanians live in far-flung homesteads and villages near the country's borders—on the narrow coastal plain, on lake shores, and on fertile mountain slopes, such as those of Mount Kilimanjaro. Few inhabit the interior, a desolate plateau covering much of the country.

Through ujamaa the government encouraged people to live and farm together, sharing work, resources, health care, and schooling. Under the program, the nation's literacy rate jumped from 28 percent in 1967 to nearly 80 percent in 1985. Life expectancy rose from 38 years to 52.

But farm production fell short of government hopes. Most farmers still grow only enough food crops for their own use, and, in spite of their efforts, food is a leading import. In very fertile areas, some farmers grow export crops of coffee, cotton, tea, and on Zanzibar, cloves.

Official name: *United Republic of Tanzania*
Area: *364,900 sq mi (945,087 sq km)*
Population: *26,343,000*
Capital: *Dar es Salaam (pop. 1,096,000)*
Ethnic groups: *More than 120 groups, mostly Bantu, including Sukuma, Makonde, Chaga, Nyamwezi*
Language: *KiSwahili, English, African languages*
Religious groups: *traditional, Christian, Muslim*
Economy: *Agr: cassava, grains, vegetables, fruit, coffee, cotton, tea, sisal, tobacco, cloves, cashew nuts. Ind: food processing, textiles, oil refining, tourism*
Currency: *Tanzanian shilling*

1 *Tanzania*

Tanzania

1 *A mother cheetah and four cubs enjoy a protected life in a national park on the Serengeti Plain. Outside such preserves, their chances of survival would be slim.*

2 *Young Masai women gather to celebrate the birth of a child in a village near the rim of Ngorongoro Crater. Some 15,000 Masai herders live in this area.*

2 *Tanzania*

1 *Somalia*

2 *Uganda*

Somalia

1 *Nomads share in milking a camel. Desert life depends on camels; they supply milk, meat, hides, and wool, and are prized as pack or riding animals.*

Uganda

2 *City workers catch their buses during Kampala's afternoon rush hour. Many commute from the countryside, where they grow crops to supplement their salaries.*

Ethiopia

3 *Flat-topped acacia trees provide shade for cattle grazing on government grasslands. Peasant families have the right to farm 25 acres (10 ha) on nationalized rural lands.*

3 *Ethiopia*

4 *Rwanda*

5 *Kenya*

Rwanda

4 *A mountain gorilla munches wild celery in the Virunga Mountains west of Kigali. Fewer than 600 members of this endangered subspecies survive in the wild.*

Kenya

5 *Nairobi's high-rise city-center serves as the commercial and communications hub of East Africa.*

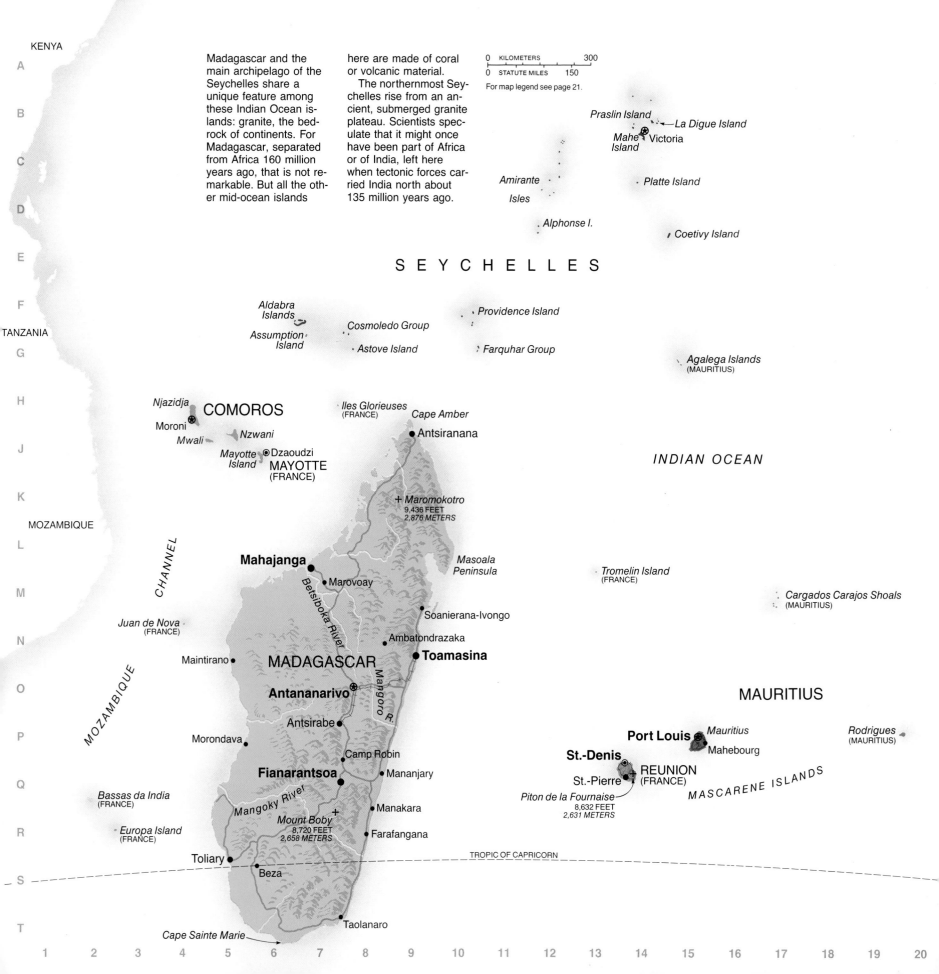

SOMALIA

KENYA

Madagascar and the main archipelago of the Seychelles share a unique feature among these Indian Ocean islands: granite, the bedrock of continents. For Madagascar, separated from Africa 160 million years ago, that is not remarkable. But all the other mid-ocean islands here are made of coral or volcanic material.

The northernmost Seychelles rise from an ancient, submerged granite plateau. Scientists speculate that it might once have been part of Africa or of India, left here when tectonic forces carried India north about 135 million years ago.

0   KILOMETERS   300
0   STATUTE MILES   150
For map legend see page 21.

Praslin Island
La Digue Island
Mahe Island ⊛ Victoria

Amirante Isles

Platte Island

Alphonse I.

Coetivy Island

S E Y C H E L L E S

TANZANIA

Aldabra Islands
Providence Island
Cosmoledo Group
Assumption Island
Astove Island
Farquhar Group

Agalega Islands
(MAURITIUS)

MOZAMBIQUE

Njazidja
COMOROS
Moroni ⊛
Mwali *Nzwani*
Mayotte Island ⊚ Dzaoudzi
MAYOTTE
(FRANCE)

Iles Glorieuses
(FRANCE)
Cape Amber
● Antsiranana

INDIAN OCEAN

+ *Maromokotro*
9,436 FEET
2,876 METERS

CHANNEL

Mahajanga ●
● Marovoay

Masoala Peninsula

Tromelin Island
(FRANCE)

Cargados Carajos Shoals
(MAURITIUS)

Juan de Nova
(FRANCE)

Betsiboka River

● Soanierana-Ivongo

Maintirano ●
MADAGASCAR
● Ambatondrazaka
Toamasina

MOZAMBIQUE

Antananarivo ⊛

Mangoro R.

MAURITIUS

● Antsirabe

Morondava ●

Camp Robin ●

Port Louis ● *Mauritius*
Mahebourg
St.-Denis ●
St.-Pierre ● REUNION
(FRANCE)
Piton de la Fournaise
8,632 FEET
2,631 METERS

Rodrigues
(MAURITIUS)

Bassas da India
(FRANCE)

Fianarantsoa ●
● Mananjary

Mangoky River

MASCARENE ISLANDS

● Manakara

Europa Island
(FRANCE)

Mount Boby
8,720 FEET
2,658 METERS

● Farafangana

TROPIC OF CAPRICORN

Toliary ●
Beza ●

● Taolanaro

Cape Sainte Marie

Comoros

Early travelers called the Comoros "Islands of the Moon," because of the magical gleam of moonlight on their shores. Mostly mountainous and volcanic, the three main islands of the Comoros support tropical vegetation but few crops. They lie between Africa and Madagascar in the Mozambique Channel of the Indian Ocean.

Most Comorans share Arab, African, and Malagasy origins, practice the Islamic religion, and speak a Swahili dialect. Their traditional dwellings are made of banana and coconut leaves or of lava cemented with sand and chalk.

Almost all Comorans farm. Many raise food crops, but yields are poor and the country must import more than half its food. Occupying much of the scarce land are foreign-owned plantations that cultivate cash crops: vanilla, cloves, copra, and plants that provide oils for perfume. The country is the leading producer of ylang-ylang.

The Comoros formerly belonged to France but declared its independence in 1975. Since then it has faced poverty despite foreign aid and has suffered from turbulent politics.

Official name: *Federal Islamic Republic of the Comoros*
Area: *719 sq mi (1,862 sq km)*
Population: *444,000*
Capital: *Moroni (pop. 17,267)*
Ethnic groups: *Comoran (Bantu, Arab, Malagasy)*
Language: *Arabic, French, Shaafi Islam (Swahili)*
Religious groups: *Sunni Muslim*
Economy: *Agr: cassava, rice, corn, yams, bananas, coconuts, vanilla, cloves, ylang-ylang. Ind: perfume*
Currency: *Comoran franc*

Mayotte

Coral reefs surround this tropical island in the Comoro archipelago. The reefs enclose a large lagoon, whose sheltered waters protect shipping and Mayotte's new lobster and shrimp industry. Vanilla, coffee, coconuts, and plants such as the ylang-ylang tree, used to make perfume, grow in the volcanic island's fertile soil.

In 1975, Mayotte chose to remain linked to France when the rest of the Comoro Islands declared independence. The Comoran government still claims Mayotte as part of its territory.

Official name: *Territorial Collectivity of Mayotte*
Area: *144 sq mi (373 sq km)*
Population: *69,000*
Capital: *Dzaoudzi (pop. 5,675)*

Madagascar

Earth's fourth largest island after Greenland, New Guinea, and Borneo, Madagascar lies 250 miles (400 km) east of the African coast. A high central plateau rises steeply from the narrow, densely populated east coast, then slopes gradually down to the drier grasslands of the western plains.

Madagascar was under French control before independence in 1960. The Malagasy, as the inhabitants are called, are Afro-Asian. They are thought to descend from Indonesian seafarers who migrated to Madagascar 1,500 to 2,000 years ago, possibly by way of Africa. Later groups, too, arrived from Asia and Africa. Some Malagasy look more Asian, others more African, but all speak the same language, Malagasy.

The central highlands are home to the largest, most powerful group, the Merina, who once ruled Madagascar. Here they and the Betsileo cultivate rice, the island's chief staple, and work in government and commerce in urban areas. The second largest group, the Betsimisaraka, live on the east coast, where they raise valuable export crops of coffee, vanilla, and cloves.

Once part of the African mainland, the island of Madagascar broke away about 160 million years ago. Its plants and animals, isolated from outside species, evolved into unique varieties, including some 40 species of lemurs, 200 species of butterflies, half the world's chameleon species, and 1,000 types of orchids. Since humans arrived, many species have become extinct.

Today Madagascar faces environmental disaster. After centuries of misuse, four-fifths of the island is bare and eroded, burned over by the Malagasy who must farm and herd to survive. Rain washes the red clay soil downhill to rivers that carry it far out to sea. Only a fraction of the island's forests remains. Madagascar's leaders are taking steps toward conservation. They realize that halting the damage is vital to the economy—and to the survival of the island once called "the naturalist's promised land."

Official name: *Democratic Republic of Madagascar*
Area: *226,658 sq mi (587,041 sq km)*
Population: *11,602,000*
Capital: *Antananarivo (pop. 662,585)*
Ethnic groups: *Merina, Betsimisaraka, other*
Language: *French, Malagasy*
Religious groups: *traditional, Christian*
Economy: *Agr: rice, cassava, bananas, beans, livestock, coffee, vanilla, cloves, sugarcane, peanuts, sisal. Ind: food processing, textiles, mining, fishing*
Currency: *Malagasy franc*

Seychelles

Isolated in the Indian Ocean, the islands of Seychelles have evolved a variety of unique species, such as the jellyfish plant, whose fruit with winged seeds resembles a jellyfish, and the *coco-de-mer*, a giant palm bearing a nut that weighs up to 40 pounds (18 kg).

The nation of Seychelles is made up of more than 90 widely scattered islands. It includes about 40 large granite islands with high green peaks and some 50 small coral islets, flat and uninhabited. Ninety percent of the people live on Mahé, the largest island, which is also the site of the capital, Victoria.

Uninhabited until the mid-1700s, Seychelles was ruled first by the French, then by the British, and gained independence in 1976. Most Seychellois have mixed African, European, and Asian ancestry. On the larger islands they grow coconuts and cinnamon, the chief cash crops. Fish is important, too, as a food and an industry. The plant and animal life draw tourists, as do the clear seas, white beaches, and tropical climate.

Official name: *Republic of Seychelles*
Area: *175 sq mi (453 sq km)*
Population: *68,000*
Capital: *Victoria (met. pop. 23,334)*
Ethnic groups: *Creole*
Language: *Creole, English, French*
Religious groups: *Roman Catholic*
Economy: *Agr: coconuts, bananas, cinnamon, vanilla, tea. Ind: tourism, food processing, fishing*
Currency: *Seychelles rupee*

Réunion

Often called the twin sister of Mauritius, nearby Réunion shares its sugar-based economy, volcanic origin, and climate, but sugar production lags far behind its sister island. Réunion has less favorable conditions. Level farmland is scarce, and torrential rains strip the soil from steep slopes. Volcanoes dominate the landscape; Piton de la Fournaise erupts almost every year.

Réunion's population traces its descent to French settlers, African slaves, and Asian laborers. Once a French colony, the island became a French overseas department in 1946.

Official name: *Department of Réunion*
Area: *969 sq mi (2,510 sq km)*
Population: *585,000*
Capital: *Saint-Denis (pop. 126,323)*
Ethnic groups: *mixed French, African, Malagasy, Chinese, Pakistani, Indian*
Language: *French, Creole*
Religious groups: *Roman Catholic*
Economy: *Agr: sugarcane, corn, cassava, fruit, vegetables, vanilla, tea. Ind: rum, perfume oils, tourism*
Currency: *French franc*

Mauritius

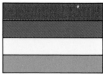

The smell of molasses pervades this oyster-shaped volcanic island in the Indian Ocean. Cane sugar and its by-products, rum and molasses, have dominated the economy of Mauritius for more than a century. Of late, export processing—the making of export goods such as clothing from imported material—and tourism have gained importance. But sugar still reigns.

Coral reefs surround the island, which has natural harbors and fine beaches. From the coast, the land rises to misty central plateaus rimmed by dramatic black peaks. Rodrigues Island and two island groups are dependencies.

Mauritius averages more than 1,300 people per square mile. The Creoles descend from African slaves and Europeans, but most islanders trace their roots to Indians who came to work the cane fields after slavery was abolished.

Official name: *Mauritius*
Area: *788 sq mi (2,040 sq km)*
Population: *1,121,000*
Capital: *Port Louis (pop. 136,323)*
Ethnic groups: *Indo-Mauritian, Creole*
Language: *English, Creole, Hindi, Urdu*
Religious groups: *Hindu, Roman Catholic, Muslim*
Economy: *Agr: sugarcane, tea, tobacco. Ind: food processing, textiles, tourism, electronics, jewelry*
Currency: *Mauritian rupee*

1 *Madagascar*

2 *Seychelles*

3 *Mauritius*

4 *Réunion*

Madagascar

1 *Vendors offer a variety of goods, including clothes, rice, and French-style bread, a colonial legacy, at a market in Camp Robin.*

Seychelles

2 *With wooden spears, weekend fishermen on La Digue Island search for octopuses, which they can sell for extra cash.*

Mauritius

3 *Pins, skewers, and hooks pierce a Tamil penitent during a Hindu religious ceremony called Cavadee. Many inhabitants of Mauritius trace their ancestry to India.*

Réunion

4 *Flares and lava flows attract tourists and scientists as Réunion's only active volcano, Piton de la Fournaise, puts on one of its frequent displays of natural fireworks.*

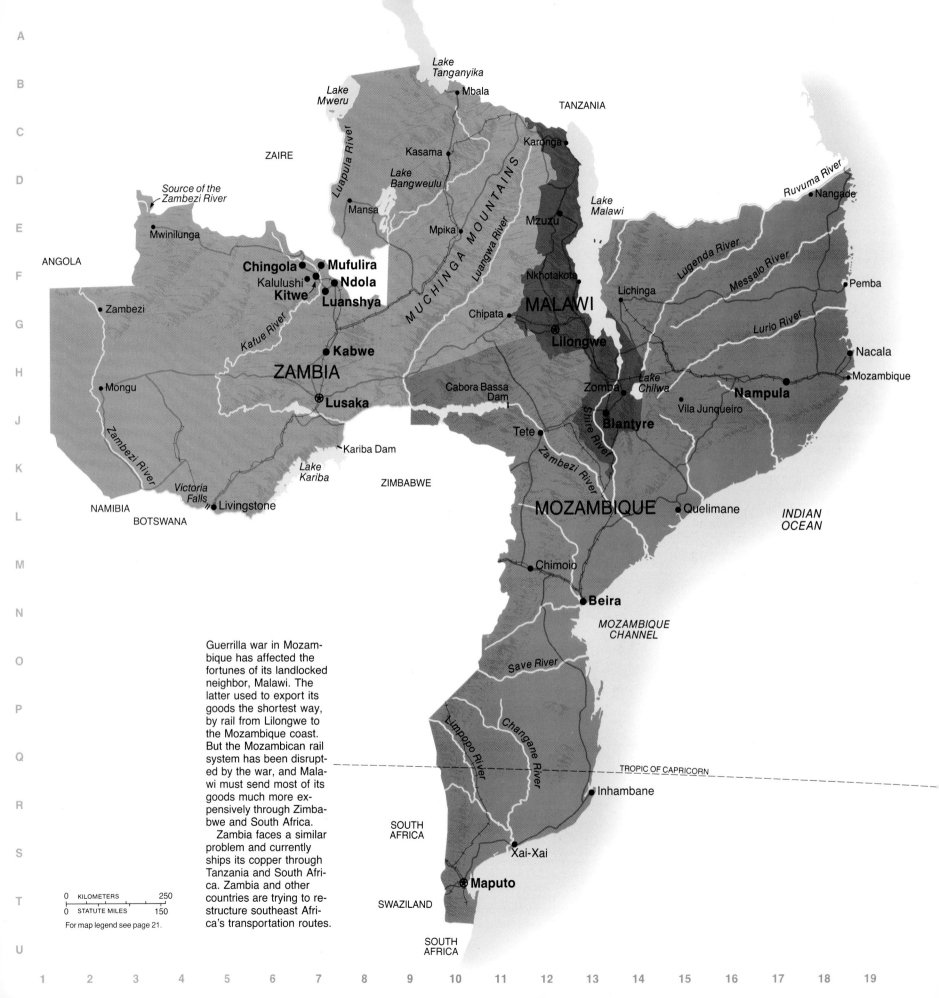

A

B

C

D

E

F

G

H

J

K

L

M

N

O

P

Q

R

S

T

U

1 2 3 4 5 6 7 8 9 10 11 12 13 14 15 16 17 18 19

Lake Tanganyika

Lake Mweru

● Mbala

TANZANIA

ZAIRE

Luapula River

Kasama ●

Lake Bangweulu

Karonga ●

Ruvuma River

Nangade ●

Source of the Zambezi River

Mansa ●

Mpika ●

Mzuzu ●

Lake Malawi

Lugenda River

Messalo River

Mwinilunga ●

ANGOLA

Chingola ● ● **Mufulira**
Kalulushi ● ● **Ndola**
Kitwe ● **Luanshya**

Luangwa River

Nkhotakota ●

Lichinga ●

Pemba ●

Zambezi ●

Kafue River

MUCHINGA MOUNTAINS

Chipata ●

MALAWI

⊛ **Lilongwe**

Nacala ●

● **Kabwe**

Nampula

Mongu ●

ZAMBIA

⊛ **Lusaka**

Cabora Bassa Dam

Zomba ●

Lake Chilwa

Vila Junqueiro ●

Lurio River

Mozambique ●

Zambezi River

Tete ● ● **Blantyre**

Kariba Dam

Lake Kariba

ZIMBABWE

Shire River

Victoria Falls
● Livingstone

Zambezi River

MOZAMBIQUE

Quelimane ●

INDIAN OCEAN

NAMIBIA

BOTSWANA

Chimoio ●

● **Beira**

MOZAMBIQUE CHANNEL

Guerrilla war in Mozam-
bique has affected the
fortunes of its landlocked
neighbor, Malawi. The
latter used to export its
goods the shortest way,
by rail from Lilongwe to
the Mozambique coast.
But the Mozambican rail
system has been disrupt-
ed by the war, and Mala-
wi must send most of its
goods much more ex-
pensively through Zimba-
bwe and South Africa.
    Zambia faces a similar
problem and currently
ships its copper through
Tanzania and South Afri-
ca. Zambia and other
countries are trying to re-
structure southeast Afri-
ca's transportation routes.

Save River

Limpopo River

Changane River

Inhambane ●

TROPIC OF CAPRICORN

SOUTH AFRICA

Xai-Xai ●

0 KILOMETERS 250
0 STATUTE MILES 150

For map legend see page 21.

⊛ **Maputo**

SWAZILAND

SOUTH AFRICA

The government now encourages city dwellers to return to farming. It also supports the growing of export crops such as tobacco and coffee and the large-scale farming of fish in the Kafue and Zambezi Rivers and in Lake Kariba.

Official name: *Republic of Zambia*
Area: *290,586 sq mi (752,614 sq km)*
Population: *8,148,000*
Capital: *Lusaka (met. pop. 818,994)*
Ethnic groups: *More than 70 groups, mainly Bantu*
Language: *English, many Bantu languages*
Religious groups: *Christian, traditional*
Economy: *Agr: corn, millet, cassava, sugarcane, cotton, peanuts, tobacco, coffee. Ind: mining, food processing, textiles, chemicals, cement, fishing*
Currency: *Zambian kwacha*

Mozambique

Mozambique forms a Y 1,556 miles (2,504 km) long on the southeast coast of Africa. The Zambezi River splits the nation. In the south, a broad coastal plain gives way to grassy plateaus in the west. North of the river, a narrow shoreline yields to low plateaus and rugged highlands cloaked in tropical vegetation.

War, too, divides the country. Mozambique won independence from Portuguese rule in 1975. Since then rebels supported by South Africa have waged guerrilla war against Mozambique's socialist government. As many as 600,000 people have died in the conflict, including 100,000 civilians killed by the rebels. More than a million Mozambicans have fled, seeking refuge in neighboring countries. Half of those who remain face severe food shortages and survive on food supplied by other countries. Drought or flooding have laid waste the family plots that feed most Mozambicans.

For foreign income, Mozambique has always relied on fees paid by nearby landlocked nations that use its railroads and ports. Since 1981, guerrillas have disrupted these transport routes by blowing up bridges and rails, so this source of income has diminished. In the country's fertile north-central provinces, cash crops once grew in abundance: coconuts, cotton, tea, and the leading export, cashews. Now much of the land lies fallow and deserted.

Mozambique has great potential for wealth, with good farmland and large mineral deposits. One of the world's largest dams, the Cabora Bassa on the Zambezi River, supplies electricity and water for irrigation. Lake Malawi and the Indian Ocean offer rich fishing opportunities. (Shrimp already is an important export.) During their long rule, the Portuguese exploited the nation's natural resources but left its economy underdeveloped. Their departure caused the exodus, too, of most skilled managers and technicians. War and natural calamities have since hindered Mozambique's rebuilding process.

Zambia

Some say that Zambia was born with a copper spoon in its mouth. Along the nation's border with Zaïre runs a "copperbelt" that holds one of the world's richest copper deposits.

Though mining provides jobs and government income, farming remains the backbone of Zambia's economy. Grassy plateaus offer fertile farmland. Water resources are plentiful. The Luangwa and Kafue Rivers run like blue threads through the landscape, crossing two large national parks that are home to leopards, elephants, and other wildlife. The great Zambezi River forms the border with Zimbabwe. On its way east, the river spills over mile-wide Victoria Falls, cascading 354 feet (108 m) into a misty gorge. Downstream, the river enters manmade Lake Kariba, formed by the huge Kariba Dam and power station, a major energy source.

Seven out of ten Zambian workers are farmers. Most tend their own land, using hand hoes to cultivate corn and other food crops on village plots. Others work on the big foreign-owned farms along the railroad lines between Kabwe and Livingstone, where they grow cash crops such as corn, cotton, peanuts, and tobacco.

Each year, hundreds of Zambians leave this way of life to seek better jobs and housing in the cities. The nation has become highly urbanized. More than half its people are crowded into the copperbelt cities and the capital, Lusaka.

Zambia's economy has suffered from a decline in world copper prices that began in the 1970s.

Malawi

The widespread burning of grass to plant crops turns Malawi into a land of fire each October. Agriculture dominates the economy of this small country. Farmers raise rice on the hot, humid shores of Lake Malawi, which forms the landlocked nation's eastern border and occupies a fifth of its territory. The sparkling lake, famed for its sandy beaches, is home to hundreds of fish species. From the lake the land rises steeply to cooler plateaus where tobacco thrives, an important export crop. Another is tea, grown on mountain slopes to the south.

Ninety percent of all Malawians till small plots of farmland near their mud-hut villages. Many of them are members of large families of nine or ten people. In a country with few natural resources and little industry, population growth is a major problem. Jobs are scarce. Many thousands of men seek work in South Africa, Zambia, and Zimbabwe, while the women stay home to raise food for their families.

Malawi also suffers under the burden of some half a million refugees from the guerrilla war in neighboring Mozambique. Malawi itself has remained peaceful and politically stable since gaining independence from the British in 1964.

Official name: *Republic of Malawi*
Area: *45,747 sq mi (118,484 sq km)*
Population: *8,737,000*
Capital: *Lilongwe (pop. 186,800)*
Ethnic groups: *Chewa, Nyanja, Tumbuka, Yao*
Language: *Chichewa, English, other African*
Religious groups: *Christian, traditional, Muslim*
Economy: *Agr: corn, root crops, sugarcane, tobacco, tea, peanuts, cotton. Ind: food processing, fishing*
Currency: *Malawi kwacha*

Official name: *People's Republic of Mozambique*
Area: *308,642 sq mi (799,380 sq km)*
Population: *15,248,000*
Capital: *Maputo (met. pop. 1,006,765)*
Ethnic groups: *Makua, Tsonga, Malawi, Shona*
Language: *Portuguese, many African languages*
Religious groups: *traditional, Christian, Muslim*
Economy: *Agr: cassava, coconuts, corn, sorghum, peanuts, bananas, cashews, sugarcane, cotton, tea, sisal. Ind: food processing, mining, textiles, shrimp*
Currency: *metical*

1 *Mozambique*

2 *Malawi*

3 *Malawi*

4 *Malawi*

5 *Zambia*

Mozambique

1 *Villagers near Nangade sway to the rhythmic accompaniment of wooden drums.*

Malawi

2 *A fisherman shaves on the shore of Lake Malawi. The lake's many fish include unique species of colorful cichlids, prized worldwide as aquarium fish.*

3 *Highland timber plantations await harvesting. To conserve trees, Malawians turn wood into charcoal, a slow-burning fuel.*

4 *In a forest near Lilongwe, a woman searches for fallen branches. Cutting live timber for firewood is against the law.*

Zambia

5 *A Luangwa Valley woman's traditional stone fireplace makes a fuel-efficient stove.*

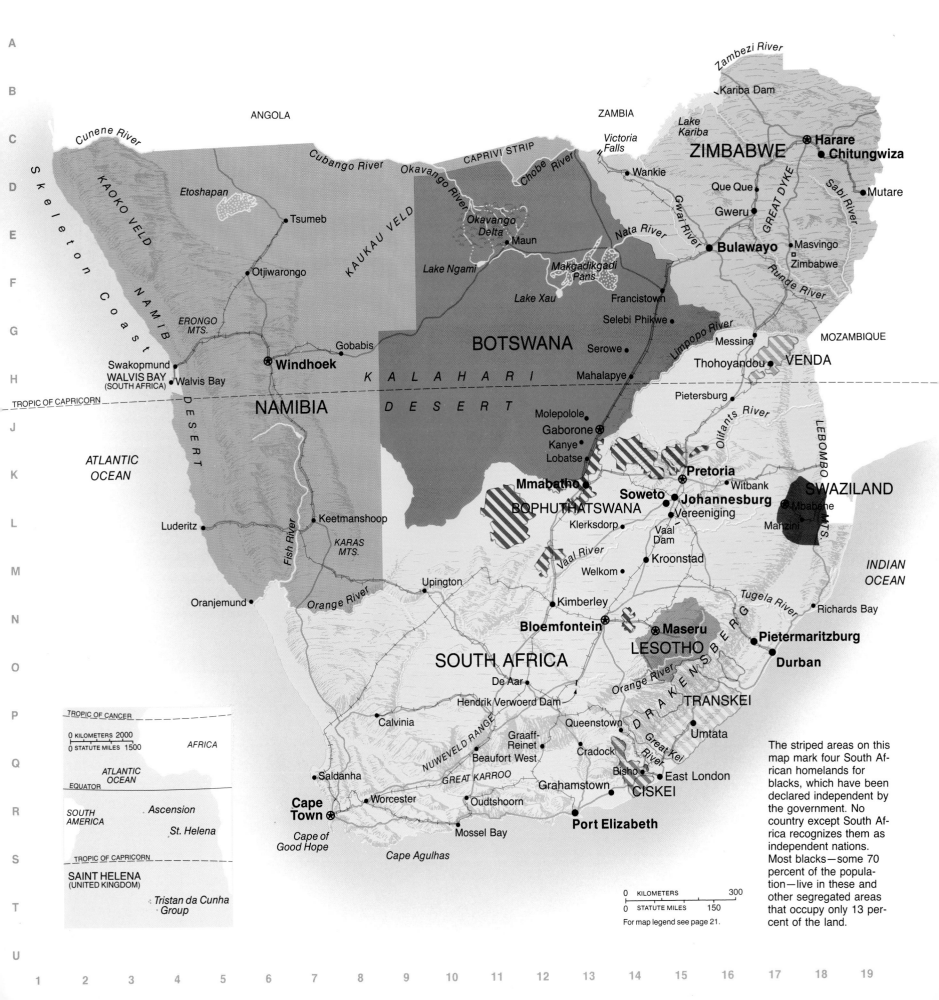

A
B
C
D
E
F
G
H
J
K
L
M
N
O
P
Q
R
S
T
U

1 2 3 4 5 6 7 8 9 10 11 12 13 14 15 16 17 18 19

Zambezi River

ANGOLA

Cunene River

Cubango River

ZAMBIA

Okavango River

CAPRIVI STRIP

Chobe River

Kariba Dam

Lake Kariba

Victoria Falls

ZIMBABWE

⊛ **Harare**
● **Chitungwiza**

Etoshapan

● Tsumeb

KAOKO VELD

Okavango Delta

● Maun

Nata River

Wankie ●

Que Que ●

Gweru ●

GREAT DYKE

Sabi River

● Mutare

Skeleton Coast

NAMIB

● Otjiwarongo

KAUKAU VELD

Lake Ngami

Makgadikgadi Pans

Lake Xau

Francistown ●

Bulawayo ●

Masvingo ●

□ Zimbabwe

Runde River

ERONGO MTS.

● Gobabis

Selebi Phikwe ●

MOZAMBIQUE

Swakopmund
WALVIS BAY
(SOUTH AFRICA)
● Walvis Bay

⊛ **Windhoek**

BOTSWANA

Serowe ●

Limpopo River

Messina ●

K A L A H A R I

Mahalapye ●

Thohoyandou ●

VENDA

TROPIC OF CAPRICORN

NAMIBIA

D E S E R T

Pietersburg ●

Olifants River

Molepolole ●

Gaborone ⊛

Kanye ●

Lobatse ●

ATLANTIC
OCEAN

Mmabatho ●

Pretoria ⊛

Witbank ●

SWAZILAND

DESERT

Fish River

Luderitz ●

Keetmanshoop ●

KARAS MTS.

BOPHUTHATSWANA

Soweto
Johannesburg

Vereeniging ●

● Mbabane

Manzini ●

LEBOMBO MTS.

Klerksdorp ●

Vaal River

Vaal Dam

Kroonstad ●

Oranjemund ●

Orange River

Upington ●

Welkom ●

INDIAN
OCEAN

Kimberley ●

Bloemfontein ⊛

⊛ **Maseru**

LESOTHO

Tugela River

● Richards Bay

Pietermaritzburg

SOUTH AFRICA

De Aar ●

Hendrik Verwoerd Dam

DRAKENSBERG

Orange River

TRANSKEI

Durban

TROPIC OF CANCER

0 KILOMETERS 2000
0 STATUTE MILES 1500

AFRICA

Calvinia ●

NUWEVELD RANGE

Queenstown ●

Great Kei River

Umtata ●

ATLANTIC
OCEAN

EQUATOR

SOUTH
AMERICA

Ascension

St. Helena

Graaff-Reinet ●

Beaufort West ●

Cradock ●

GREAT KARROO

Bisho ●

CISKEI

East London ●

TROPIC OF CAPRICORN

SAINT HELENA
(UNITED KINGDOM)

Tristan da Cunha Group

Saldanha ●

Worcester ●

Cape Town ⊛

Oudtshoorn ●

Grahamstown ●

Port Elizabeth

Cape of Good Hope

Mossel Bay ●

Cape Agulhas

0 KILOMETERS 300
0 STATUTE MILES 150

For map legend see page 21.

The striped areas on this map mark four South African homelands for blacks, which have been declared independent by the government. No country except South Africa recognizes them as independent nations. Most blacks—some 70 percent of the population—live in these and other segregated areas that occupy only 13 percent of the land.

Namibia

In the language of the Nama, *namib* means "the land without people." Namibia's sparse population, which includes the Nama and nine other ethnic groups, inhabits a harsh land. The Namib Desert, a narrow ribbon of towering dunes and rock outcrops extends along the Atlantic coast. Inland, desert sands rise to a plateau of patchy grassland where herders vie for scarce grazing range. The east belongs to the sand and scrub of the Kalahari Desert.

Namibia was ruled for 74 years by South Africa, despite a long rebellion by black nationalist groups and criticism from the United Nations. In 1990 Namibia became a democracy and elected as its first president Sam Nujoma, a leader of the 23-year guerrilla war against South African rule. Nujoma's government seeks to heal ethnic divisions with a strong multiparty system and to encourage agriculture and Namibia's fishing and mining industries. Large deposits of diamonds, uranium, and other minerals promise a bright future for Africa's newest nation.

Official name: *Namibia*
Area: *318,261 sq mi (824,292 sq km)*
Population: *1,817,000*
Capital: *Windhoek (pop. 110,000)*
Ethnic groups: *Ovambo and others, white, mixed*
Language: *English, Afrikaans, African, German*
Religious groups: *Christian, traditional*
Economy: *Agr: livestock, grains. Ind: mining (diamonds, uranium, other ores), meat packing, fishing*
Currency: *South African rand*

Botswana

Botswana's national emblem has a one-word motto: "Pula." Rain. There is never enough of it. The rolling red sands and low thorny scrub of the Kalahari Desert cover most of this country. From May to October, the sun bakes the land to dust. Droughts strike often, with searing sun and hot winds. It is sometimes many years before the rains fall again.

Botswana has a flourishing democracy and little strife. Poor at independence in 1966, it now has one of Africa's fastest growing economies. The discovery of diamonds in 1967 fueled its growth. At heart, though, this remains a cattle country. Most people make a living through farming and livestock. Because crop yields are often low, thousands of men migrate to South Africa and Zimbabwe to work mines and farms.

Northern Botswana holds the great inland delta of the Okavango River, a fertile, watery world of shifting streams and abundant wildlife. Rising in the west, the river fans out across a vast marshland before being swallowed by the sands of the Kalahari, the Land of Thirst.

Official name: *Republic of Botswana*
Area: *231,805 sq mi (600,372 sq km)*
Population: *1,241,000*
Capital: *Gaborone (pop. 94,705)*
Ethnic groups: *Batswana, Kalanga, Basarwa*
Language: *English, seTswana, other African*
Religious groups: *traditional, Christian*
Economy: *Agr: corn, sorghum, millet, beans, livestock. Ind: mining, meat packing, tourism*
Currency: *pula*

Zimbabwe

An ancient hilltop city gave this nation its name, which means "house of stone." Built between the 8th and 15th centuries in southeastern Zimbabwe, the massive stone citadel was the center of a flourishing gold trade for the Shona people. Most of Zimbabwe occupies a high, rolling plateau studded with rock outcrops. At its core lies the Great Dyke, a geological formation that holds rich deposits of gold, silver, chromite, and other minerals.

The Ndebele warrior people, arriving from South Africa in the 1830s, conquered the Shona. The abundant natural resources also brought white settlers, the cause of a turbulent history. For more than 80 years a tiny white minority controlled the country, then called Rhodesia. When white leaders declared the nation independent from the United Kingdom in 1965, guerrilla war ensued, as blacks fought for a government based on majority rule. The United Nations imposed sanctions forbidding trade with Rhodesia. In 1980 the white government gave in, and Zimbabwe was born.

Most Zimbabweans depend on farming for a living. But nearly half the country, including the best farmland, still belongs to whites, who own large commercial farms that produce tobacco, wheat, and other export crops. The government is trying to redistribute land, but progress has been slow. Zimbabwe is also one of the major manufacturing nations in Africa.

Famous for its beauty, Zimbabwe has national parks with herds of elephants, zebras, lions, and hippos, and in the west are the spectacular Victoria Falls, whose African name translates as "the smoke that thunders."

Official name: *Republic of Zimbabwe*
Area: *150,804 sq mi (390,580 sq km)*
Population: *10,119,000*
Capital: *Harare (pop. 681,000)*
Ethnic groups: *Shona, Ndebele*
Language: *English, Shona, SiNdebele*
Religious groups: *traditional, Christian*
Economy: *Agr: corn, millet, wheat, tobacco, cotton, sugarcane, soybeans, coffee, tea, cattle. Ind: mining, food processing, metals, textiles, chemicals, wood*
Currency: *Zimbabwe dollar*

South Africa

South Africa occupies a huge swath of land at the continent's southernmost tip, where the Atlantic and Indian Oceans meet. Few African nations have such a range of terrain. At the heart of South Africa sprawls a vast inland plateau, much of it prairielike. A string of mountain ranges including the Drakensberg skirts the east and south. Desert dominates the west.

Africa's wealthiest nation, South Africa has enormous mineral deposits: gold, diamonds, chromite, platinum, and coal. The income from these minerals has generated cities, industrial centers, huge cattle and sheep ranches, and mechanized farms. Orchards cloak rolling hills, and there are great fields of corn, wheat, and sugarcane. Johannesburg, center of gold mining, is South Africa's largest urban area, followed by Cape Town, one of three capitals.

For all its wealth and beauty, South Africa is a

troubled land, riven by *apartheid*—the name given to the policy of racial segregation enforced by the white-minority government. The word means "apartness." Under apartheid, blacks have virtually no political rights, though they outnumber whites five to one. They cannot freely choose where they live or work or go to school. Good land and good jobs are reserved for whites. So are most other economic and political advantages. The policy has brought fierce rebellion at home and condemnation from abroad.

Apartheid was created by Afrikaners—South Africans descended from Dutch settlers—who came to power in 1948 after years of British domination. The Afrikaners divided South Africans into four major groups and governed each by a separate set of laws. These groups are whites, coloreds (people of mixed race), Asians, and Africans. The last group, the largest by far, numbers more than 25 million.

Under its policy of separateness, the government established racially based states or "homelands," one for each of the ten major black ethnic groups. It set aside only 13 percent of the nation's total area for black Africans and forced many blacks to move to these scattered fragments of rural land. Here the poor soil makes it hard to raise sufficient crops and livestock. With no natural resources and few jobs, the homelands are islands of poverty in an otherwise prosperous nation.

Four homelands have been declared independent countries by the South African government: **Transkei** on the Indian Ocean in 1976; a collection of seven separate enclaves called **Bophuthatswana** in 1977; **Venda** in the far north in 1979; and **Ciskei**, a small wedge of dry land in the south, in 1981. Only South Africa recognizes the four homelands as independent countries.

Today most black South Africans live in these homelands or in townships, huge segregated suburbs and shantytowns on the outskirts of cities. Both homelands and townships serve as pools of cheap labor, which keep South Africa's mines, industries, and commercial farms going.

Beginning early in the 1900s, black South Africans founded the African National Congress (ANC) and other groups, aiming to achieve majority rule in South Africa. The ANC's efforts have included strikes and demonstrations, often brutally suppressed by the South African police. Thousands of blacks have died in the clashes. Many have been imprisoned, including Nelson Mandela, the best known leader of the ANC and a symbol of black resistance. There has been conflict also between rival black groups.

In 1990, Mandela was released from prison by South Africa's newly elected president, F. W. de Klerk. In sweeping reforms, de Klerk repealed many of the laws upon which apartheid is based and lifted a longstanding ban on black political groups. In so doing, he set the country on a new course. Apartheid will not be dismantled overnight. The road to a nonracial, democratic South Africa will likely be long and arduous.

Official name: *Republic of South Africa*
Area: *471,445 sq mi (1,221,037 sq km)*
Population: *38,509,000*
Capital: *Pretoria, administrative (pop. 443,059)*
   Cape Town, legislative (pop. 776,617)
   Bloemfontein, judicial (pop. 104,381)
Ethnic groups: *black, white, mixed, Asian*
Language: *Afrikaans, English, Bantu languages*
Religious groups: *Christian, Hindu, Muslim*
Economy: *Agr: corn, wheat, sugarcane, tobacco, fruit, cattle, sheep. Ind: gold, diamonds, iron, coal, and other mining, steel, machinery, motor vehicles, chemicals, textiles, food processing, fishing*
Currency: *South African rand*

Swaziland

A king called the Ngwenyama, or Lion, rules this mountainous nation, one of Africa's three remaining monarchies, the others being Lesotho and Morocco. Almost surrounded by South Africa, tiny, landlocked Swaziland fits like a handkerchief in the breast pocket of its giant neighbor, and is tightly bound to its economy. More than 95 percent of Swazi imports come from South Africa or travel through it.

Swaziland has valuable deposits of coal and diamonds, large forests, and well-watered farmland, but the king and his subjects reap few benefits from this wealth. They own less than two-thirds of their nation's land. The rest belongs to Europeans, who mine all the minerals and raise most of the export crops: sugarcane, citrus fruit, and timber grown on plantations.

Most Swazis are farmers who raise corn and cattle on lands that suffer from erosion and overgrazing. The people regard their animals as prize possessions and measures of their wealth.

Official name: *Kingdom of Swaziland*
Area: *6,704 sq mi (17,364 sq km)*
Population: *763,000*
Capital: *Mbabane (pop. 38,636)*
Ethnic groups: *Swazi, Zulu*
Language: *English, siSwati*
Religious groups: *Christian, traditional*
Economy: *Agr: corn, rice, livestock, sugarcane, cotton, fruit. Ind: food processing, wood pulp, mining*
Currency: *lilangeni*

Lesotho

The name Lesotho means "place of the Sotho tribe" to the Basotho, the people of this country. High plateaus and spectacular snow-clad mountains cover most of this tiny kingdom that is entirely surrounded by South Africa. Lesotho has few resources and little farmland—just a narrow strip in the western lowlands, where most people live. The land suffers from erosion and overgrazing by cattle and by sheep and goats raised for their wool and mohair.

Though Lesotho is strongly opposed to South Africa's racial policies, it relies heavily on its neighbor for trade and jobs. About a third of Basotho men leave their country for three to nine months a year to work in South Africa, chiefly in the gold and coal mines. These miners earn as much as ten times the wage of their countrymen who remain on the farm at home.

Under way is a project that may change Lesotho's economy: four dams that will catch the flow from the Orange River and its tributaries and divert it to the north for sale to South Africa.

Official name: *Kingdom of Lesotho*
Area: *11,720 sq mi (30,355 sq km)*
Population: *1,724,000*
Capital: *Maseru (pop. 45,000)*
Ethnic groups: *Basotho*
Language: *Sesotho, English*
Religious groups: *Christian, traditional*
Economy: *Agr: corn, sorghum, wheat, legumes, fruit, livestock. Ind: tourism, wool, mohair*
Currency: *loti*

St. Helena

The British colony of St. Helena is a tiny volcanic island in the Atlantic Ocean 1,200 miles (1,930 km) from Africa. Its main claim to fame is that French emperor Napoleon Bonaparte lived in exile there from 1815 until his death in 1821.

Though barren land covers much of St. Helena, it has diverse plant life, including 40 unique species. The islanders fish, raise livestock and crops on the scarce arable land, and make lace or wood carvings, which they sell to passengers on ships that stop at Jamestown, the only village.

The colony includes the Tristan da Cunha island group and Ascension Island, famous as a nesting ground for sea turtles and sooty terns.

Official name: *St. Helena*
Area: *158 sq mi (410 sq km)*
Population: *7,000*
Capital: *Jamestown (pop. 1,413)*

1 *Namibia*

2 *Namibia*

Namibia

1 *Like a great sand sea, the 1,300-mile-long (2,100 km) Namib Desert covers all of Namibia's shoreline and extends into neighboring Angola and South Africa.*

2 *Uncut diamonds mined near Oranjemund range in color from blue-white to pink to chartreuse. Such gem-quality diamonds are a leading Namibian export.*

1 *Lesotho*

Lesotho

1 *Toting saddle and baggage, a miner arrives home on a visit from his job in South Africa. Many men of Lesotho seek work there because jobs are scarce at home.*

Botswana

2 *Water-lily pads up to 16 inches (40 cm) across cover a lagoon in the Okavango River Delta. This inland swamp is a refuge for hippos, crocodiles, and other wildlife.*

2 *Botswana*

3 *South Africa*

4 *South Africa*

South Africa

3 *In a gold mine near Johannesburg, miners drill holes for explosives. Although the races work side by side, white miners usually hold better-paying supervisory jobs.*

4 *Balancing her heavy load, a Zulu woman carries home a bucket of precious water from a distant well.*

Zimbabwe

5 *Shaking off its colonial past, Zimbabwe (formerly Rhodesia) has changed its capital's name from Salisbury to Harare. Renamed avenues now honor African heroes.*

5 *Zimbabwe*

Oceania

Nothing on Earth is bigger than the Pacific Ocean. It covers a third of the globe, more than all the land areas lumped together. It reaches from the Arctic Ocean to Antarctica and includes 21 seas within its borders. At its widest, near the Equator, the Pacific Ocean extends more than 11,000 miles (17,700 km)—almost halfway around the world. It touches every continent but Europe and Africa.

The Pacific is also the world's deepest ocean, with an average depth of 12,925 feet (3,940 m). The deepest point, Challenger Deep in the Mariana Trench, lies 35,812 feet down (10,915 m)—nearly 7 miles (11 km) below the surface.

More than 25,000 islands (not counting the many islands of Japan, the Philippines, and Indonesia) are spread across the Pacific. They range in size from Australia's 2,966,153 square miles (7,682,300 sq km) to tiny reefs and atolls that barely rise above the waves. This part of the world is known as Oceania.

Oceania's high islands have greater resources than its low ones. Many high islands are volcanic, made up of mountains tall enough to wring out moisture from offshore breezes. As rain, the moisture provides abundant water for plants or crops to grow in the rich volcanic soil. High islands such as New Zealand, Tahiti, and Hawaii can support heavily concentrated populations because of their large size and varied resources. Many high islands also have copper, nickel, gold, and other valuable mineral deposits.

By contrast, many of the low islands are covered only with thin, sandy soil and suffer from periodic droughts. Only small, widely scattered groups of people can live on them. Very often they depend on fish from the sea and on coconuts or coconut products for a livelihood.

Most of the low islands are atolls—coral islands surrounding a lagoon. Corals are the hardened limestone skeletons of countless tiny sea creatures called coral polyps. Most atolls begin as volcanic islands fringed with coral reefs. As the land wears away or sinks beneath the sea, the polyps continue to build up the reef until it breaks the surface. Such islands are sometimes swamped in a storm. Many are uninhabited.

Geographers divide Oceania into four regions. Melanesia means "black islands." Melanesians generally are short, with dark skin and frizzy hair, much like Australia's Aborigines. Micronesia means "little islands" and Polynesia means "many islands." The people of these regions usually are lighter skinned and taller than Melanesians. Most have some white or Asian ancestors in their family trees. Australia and New Zealand, settled largely by British colonists, have predominantly white populations.

Most Pacific islands lie in the tropics and so are warm year-round and have adequate rainfall. Much of Australia, on the other hand, is hot and dry. The Murray-Darling is its only major river. Australia's climate is partly the result of its size and position on the Tropic of Capricorn. Here a globe-circling high-pressure system—a belt of warm, dry air—keeps the interior dry.

Facts About Oceania

Population: 26,456,000
Largest Country: Australia, area 2,966,153 sq mi (7,682,300 sq km); pop. 16,820,000
Highest Point: Mount Wilhelm, Papua New Guinea, 14,793 ft (4,509 m) above sea level.
Lowest Point: Lake Eyre, Australia, 52 ft (16 m) below sea level
Largest Metropolitan Area: Sydney, pop. 3,790,000
Longest River: Murray-Darling, Australia, 2,310 mi (3,717 km)
Longest Reef: *Great Barrier Reef, Australia, 1,250 mi (2,012 km)
Largest Lake: Eyre 3,600 sq mi (9,324 sq km)

*World record

Glossary

archipelago—a group or chain of islands.
atoll—a ring of coral islands encircling a lagoon.
the Commonwealth—a voluntary association of independent countries that maintains ties of friendship, cooperation, and assistance. The British monarch is the symbolic head.
copra—dried coconut meat that yields oil.
coral—hardened skeletons of tiny marine animals, called coral polyps, which form reefs and islands.
outback—the remote backcountry of Australia.
pidgin—simplified speech consisting of words adapted from other languages; used between people who speak different languages.
taro—a plant raised throughout the tropics for its edible, starchy root.

Mount Cook, tallest mountain in New Zealand

Desert oaks in Australia's Simpson Desert

Great Barrier Reef off Australia's northeast coast

TROPIC OF CANCER

Hawaiian Islands

Mariana
Islands

M I C R O N E S I A

Marshall
Islands

P O L Y N E S I A

Caroline Islands

Gilbert Islands

EQUATOR

PACIFIC

OCEAN

Phoenix
Islands

Line Islands

M E L A N E S I A

New Guinea

Solomon
Islands

Tuvalu

Tokelau Islands

Great Barrier Reef

CORAL SEA

Vanuatu

Samoa
Islands

Fiji Islands

Cook Islands

Great Dividing Range

AUSTRALIA

New Caledonia

Tonga
Islands

Society
Islands

INDIAN
OCEAN

Great
Sandy
Desert

Macdonnell
Ranges

Central Lowlands

Great
Artesian
Basin

TROPIC OF CAPRICORN

Tubuai
Islands

Western Plateau

Great
Victoria
Desert

Lake Eyre
−52 FEET
−16 METERS
Lowest point in
Australia

Darling River

Murray River

+ Mt. Kosciusko
7,310 FEET
2,228 METERS
Highest point in
Australia

TASMAN
SEA

New Zealand

Southern Alps

Mt. Cook
12,349 FEET
3,764 METERS

Chatham Islands

Tasmania

Auckland Islands

ANTARCTIC CIRCLE

A N T A R C T I C A

PAPUA
NEW GUINEA

Torres Strait

ARAFURA SEA

Darwin

*ARNHEM
LAND*

TIMOR SEA

Cape York
Peninsula

*GULF OF
CARPENTARIA*

*CORAL
SEA*

Katherine

*KIMBERLEY
PLATEAU*

*Victoria
River*

*Nicholson
River*

Cairns

Derby

*Fitzroy
River*

*INDIAN
OCEAN*

Halls
Creek

*TANAMI
DESERT*

*NORTHERN
TERRITORY*

Tennant Creek

GREAT

Townsville

GREAT BARRIER REEF

Port Hedland

*GREAT
SANDY
DESERT*

Mount Isa

DIVIDING

*Barrow
Island*

Lake
Mackay

MACDONNELL RANGES

TROPIC OF CAPRICORN

Lake
Disappointment

Ashburton River

Alice Springs

Sandringham Station

QUEENSLAND

RANGE

Rockhampton

*Shark
Bay*

*WESTERN
AUSTRALIA*

GIBSON DESERT

Ayers Rock

*SIMPSON
DESERT*

*GREAT

ARTESIAN

Gladstone

Lake
Carnegie

AUSTRALIA

BASIN*

Lake
Eyre

Brisbane

Toowoomba

**Gold
Coast**

Geraldton

GREAT VICTORIA DESERT

*SOUTH
AUSTRALIA*

Lake
Frome

Darling River

DIVIDING RANGE

Kalgoorlie

Lake
Torrens

NEW SOUTH WALES

Newcastle

Lake
Gairdner

Broken Hill

Lachlan River

GREAT

Sydney

Perth

Port Pirie

Murray River

Wollongong

Esperance

GREAT AUSTRALIAN BIGHT

Wagga
Wagga

Canberra

Albany

Adelaide

AUSTRALIAN ALPS

*AUSTRALIAN CAPITAL
TERRITORY*

Spencer Gulf

Bendigo

VICTORIA

Mount Kosciusko
7,310 FEET
2,228 METERS
*Highest point
in Australia*

Kangaroo Island

Ballarat

Geelong

Melbourne

Australia. The word
comes from *australis,* the
Latin word for southern,
and refers to the world's
sixth largest country but
smallest continent. Aus-
tralia is a dry continent.
Moisture brought by Pa-
cific winds falls mostly
along the east coast. As

moisture-laden air rises
over the Great Dividing
Range, it condenses and
falls as rain or snow.
   Although Australia is
geologically old, New
Zealand, to the east, is
young. It has active vol-
canoes, as well as gey-
sers and hot springs.

Bass Strait

TASMAN SEA

Marrawah

Launceston

0   KILOMETERS   500
0   STATUTE MILES   300

For map legend see page 21.

TASMANIA

Hobart

A B C D E F G H J K L M N O P Q

1 2 3 4 5 6 7 8 9 10 11 12 13 14 15 16 17 18 19

Australia

Australia is the only country to occupy an entire continent. And because all of it lies south of the Equator, people sometimes call it Down Under. It is an ancient land whose highlands have been worn down into broad plains and plateaus. The longest and highest mountain chain, the Great Dividing Range, runs the entire length of the east coast and reaches its greatest height—7,310 feet (2,228 m)—on top of Mount Kosciusko.

Australia is a thinly populated land. It is also prosperous, thanks to productive farms, extensive sheep and cattle ranches, and large deposits of coal, bauxite, iron ore, gold, and other minerals. Most Australians live about as well as Americans and Canadians do. More than 80 percent of the nation's 16.8 million people live in large, modern cities located mostly along the southeast coast. Here the climate is moderate, rain is reliable, and the soil is fertile.

West of the Great Dividing Range lies a region of wheat farms and livestock ranches. And farther west spread the great plains and deserts of central and western Australia—the outback, as Australians call it. Here, amid the sparse vegetation, blistering heat, and dust sprawl enormous sheep and cattle ranches, called stations. One of them in South Australia covers more than 12,000 square miles (31,080 sq km). In the great empty reaches of the outback, children get their lessons by mail and radio, doctors visit their patients by plane, and stockmen use helicopters to help round up cattle.

Australia's long isolation from other continents has given it many unusual animals; these include kangaroos, koalas, wombats and wallabies—marsupials that carry their young in pouches. The dingo, a wild dog, roams the outback, and the duck-billed platypus, a mammal hatched from an egg, swims the rivers.

Extending off the Queensland coast for 1,250 miles (2,012 km) is the Great Barrier Reef. Built by tiny coral polyps over millions of years, it is the biggest structure ever built by living creatures and is home to 1,500 species of fish, 400 corals, and countless other marine animals.

Australia's earliest inhabitants, the Aborigines, came from Asia via Indonesia about 40,000 years ago. Today most of them live in poverty, outcasts in their own land. Capt. James Cook claimed the continent for England about 200 years ago. It remained a British colony until winning independence in 1901. Today Australia is a self-governing member of the Commonwealth. The country is made up of six states, one of which is the island of Tasmania. It also has two federal territories: Northern Territory and the Australian Capital Territory, which contains the capital city, Canberra.

Official name: *Commonwealth of Australia*
Area: *2,966,153 sq mi (7,682,300 sq km)*
Population: *16,820,000*
Capital: *Canberra (pop. 273,600)*
Ethnic groups: *European, Asian, Aborigine*
Language: *English*
Religious groups: *Protestant, Roman Catholic*
Economy: *Agr: livestock, wheat, sugarcane, barley, fruit, vegetables, cotton. Ind: iron, coal, other mining, wool, oil, food processing, machinery, motor vehicles, chemicals, textiles, electronics, tourism*
Currency: *Australian dollar*

New Zealand

"God's own country," an early prime minister called New Zealand. He referred to the island nation's spectacular scenery, lush pastures, mild climate, and pristine beaches. Though only about the size of the British Isles, New Zealand's two main islands enjoy all the geographical diversity of an entire continent.

North Island, where three-quarters of the nation's three million or so people live, has fertile fields, as well as active volcanoes, geysers, and a major ski resort amid snow-clad mountains. Near the middle of the island, Lake Taupo is famous for its trout. Auckland, the island's largest city, presides as a center of commerce and manufacturing for textiles and wood products. The nation's capital, Wellington, lies near Cook Strait, which separates the two islands.

South Island is a land of mountains and forests and glaciers and lakes. The Southern Alps, rising abruptly from the sea, create spectacular fjords and waterfalls along the southwest coast. New Zealand's highest mountain, Mount Cook, rises 12,349 feet (3,764 m) above sea level. On fertile plains and pastures along the east coast, New Zealanders grow cereal grains and graze immense flocks of sheep and herds of cattle. The world's largest exporter of lamb and dairy products, New Zealand ranks third behind Australia and the Soviet Union as a producer of wool.

Most New Zealanders are descendants of 19th-century British settlers or of Maori explorers who arrived from Polynesia about a thousand years ago.

Official name: *New Zealand*
Area: *103,883 sq mi (269,057 sq km)*
Population: *3,372,000*
Capital: *Wellington (pop. 137,495)*
Ethnic groups: *European, Maori, Pacific Islander*
Language: *English, Maori*
Religious groups: *Protestant, Roman Catholic*
Economy: *Agr: livestock, fodder, fruit, vegetables. Ind: food processing, wool, wood and paper products, metals, textiles, chemicals, motor vehicles, fishing*
Currency: *New Zealand dollar*

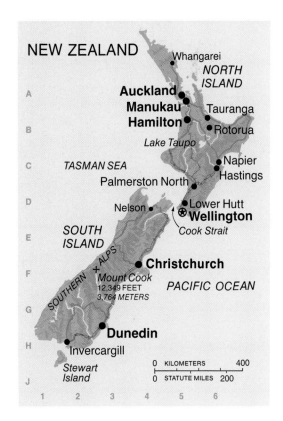

Australia

1 *Soap, soda pop, and spears combine old and new ways of life in the north. Father and daughter have just visited a truck that supplies their Aboriginal village.*

2 *Oscar the camel noses into a lesson transmitted by two-way radio to a girl living at Sandringham Station, an isolated cattle ranch in Queensland.*

3 *Ferryboats churn the waters of Sydney Harbor in an annual Ferrython race. The finish line lies beyond the light, scalloped domes of the city's Opera House.*

4 *A koala youngster hitches a ride from its mother. Australia's isolation from other continents helped produce koalas, kangaroos, and other pouched marsupials.*

New Zealand

5 *Workers check sliced kiwifruit at a cannery on North Island. The fuzzy fruit takes its name from the flightless kiwi, New Zealand's national bird.*

6 *A Maori boy, his face decorated with a felt-tip pen, recalls the custom of tattooing—a warrior's reward for bravery in battle.*

1 *Australia*

3 *Australia*

2 *Australia*

5 *New Zealand*

4 *Australia*

6 *New Zealand*

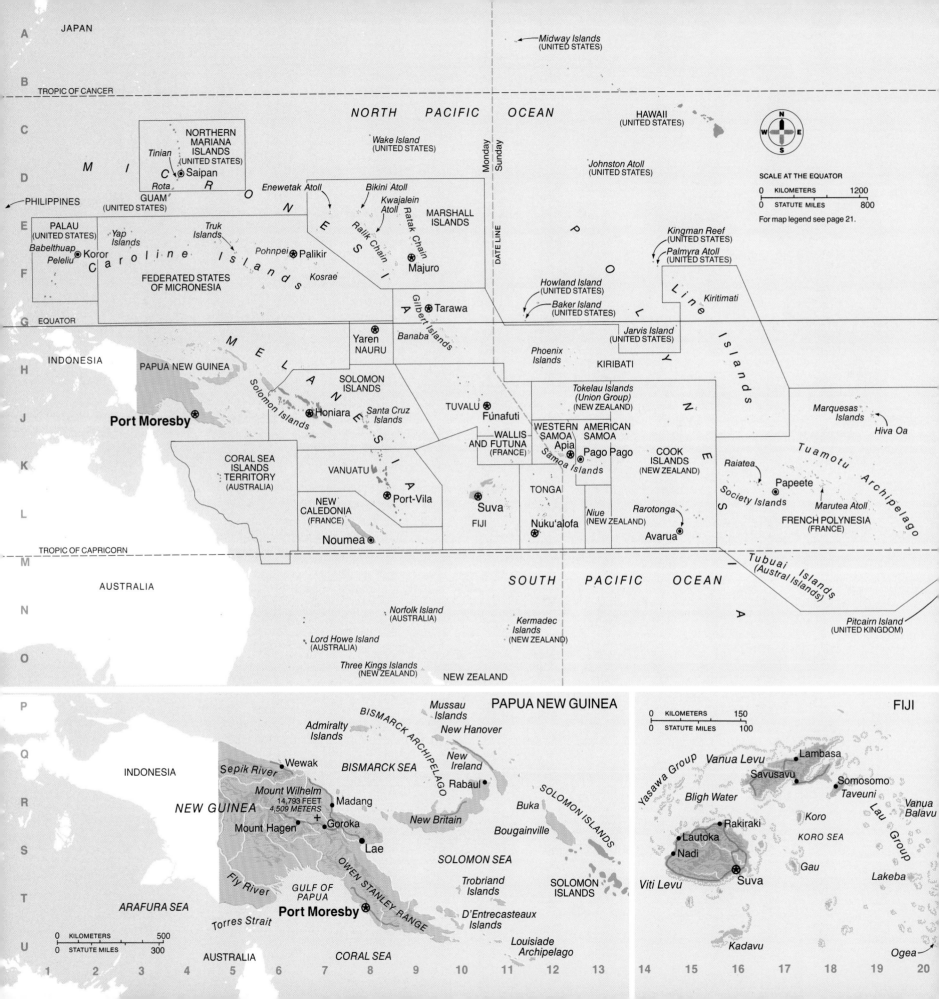

Main map (Oceania / Pacific):

A JAPAN

Midway Islands (UNITED STATES)

B TROPIC OF CANCER

NORTH PACIFIC OCEAN

HAWAII (UNITED STATES)

C

Wake Island (UNITED STATES)

NORTHERN MARIANA ISLANDS (UNITED STATES)

Tinian

Johnston Atoll (UNITED STATES)

SCALE AT THE EQUATOR

D Rota

Saipan

M I C R O N E S I A

GUAM (UNITED STATES)

Enewetak Atoll

Bikini Atoll

Kwajalein Atoll

MARSHALL ISLANDS

Monday | Sunday

0 KILOMETERS 1200
0 STATUTE MILES 800

For map legend see page 21.

PHILIPPINES

E PALAU (UNITED STATES)

Yap Islands

Truk Islands

Ralik Chain

Ratak Chain

Kingman Reef (UNITED STATES)

DATE LINE

P O L Y N E S I A

Babelthuap

Koror

Caroline Islands

Pohnpei

Palikir

Palmyra Atoll (UNITED STATES)

Peleliu

FEDERATED STATES OF MICRONESIA

Kosrae

Majuro

Howland Island (UNITED STATES)

Line Islands

Kiritimati

F

G EQUATOR

Gilbert Islands

Tarawa

Baker Island (UNITED STATES)

Jarvis Island (UNITED STATES)

Yaren NAURU

Banaba

Phoenix Islands

KIRIBATI

H INDONESIA

PAPUA NEW GUINEA

M E L A N E S I A

Solomon Islands

SOLOMON ISLANDS

Santa Cruz Islands

Marquesas Islands

Hiva Oa

J Port Moresby

Honiara

TUVALU

Funafuti

Tokelau Islands (Union Group) (NEW ZEALAND)

WESTERN SAMOA

AMERICAN SAMOA

Raiatea

Tuamotu Archipelago

K CORAL SEA ISLANDS TERRITORY (AUSTRALIA)

VANUATU

WALLIS AND FUTUNA (FRANCE)

Apia

Pago Pago

Samoa Islands

COOK ISLANDS (NEW ZEALAND)

Society Islands

Papeete

Marutea Atoll

L

NEW CALEDONIA (FRANCE)

Port-Vila

Suva

TONGA

Nuku'alofa

FIJI

Niue (NEW ZEALAND)

Rarotonga

Avarua

FRENCH POLYNESIA (FRANCE)

Noumea

M TROPIC OF CAPRICORN

Tubuai Islands (Austral Islands)

N AUSTRALIA

SOUTH PACIFIC OCEAN

Norfolk Island (AUSTRALIA)

Kermadec Islands (NEW ZEALAND)

Pitcairn Island (UNITED KINGDOM)

O

Lord Howe Island (AUSTRALIA)

Three Kings Islands (NEW ZEALAND)

NEW ZEALAND

Inset map: PAPUA NEW GUINEA

P

Mussau Islands

BISMARCK ARCHIPELAGO

Q Admiralty Islands

Wewak

New Hanover

BISMARCK SEA

New Ireland

INDONESIA

Sepik River

R NEW GUINEA

Mount Wilhelm 14,793 FEET 4,509 METERS

Madang

Rabaul

New Britain

Buka

SOLOMON ISLANDS

Mount Hagen

Goroka

S

Lae

Bougainville

Fly River

OWEN STANLEY RANGE

GULF OF PAPUA

SOLOMON SEA

Trobriand Islands

SOLOMON ISLANDS

T ARAFURA SEA

Port Moresby

D'Entrecasteaux Islands

0 KILOMETERS 500
0 STATUTE MILES 300

Torres Strait

Louisiade Archipelago

U AUSTRALIA

CORAL SEA

Inset map: FIJI

0 KILOMETERS 150
0 STATUTE MILES 100

Yasawa Group

Vanua Levu

Lambasa

Savusavu

Somosomo

Taveuni

Vanua Balavu

Bligh Water

Koro

Lau Group

Rakiraki

KORO SEA

Lautoka

Nadi

Gau

Lakeba

Viti Levu

Suva

Kadavu

Ogea

1 2 3 4 5 6 7 8 9 10 11 12 13 14 15 16 17 18 19 20

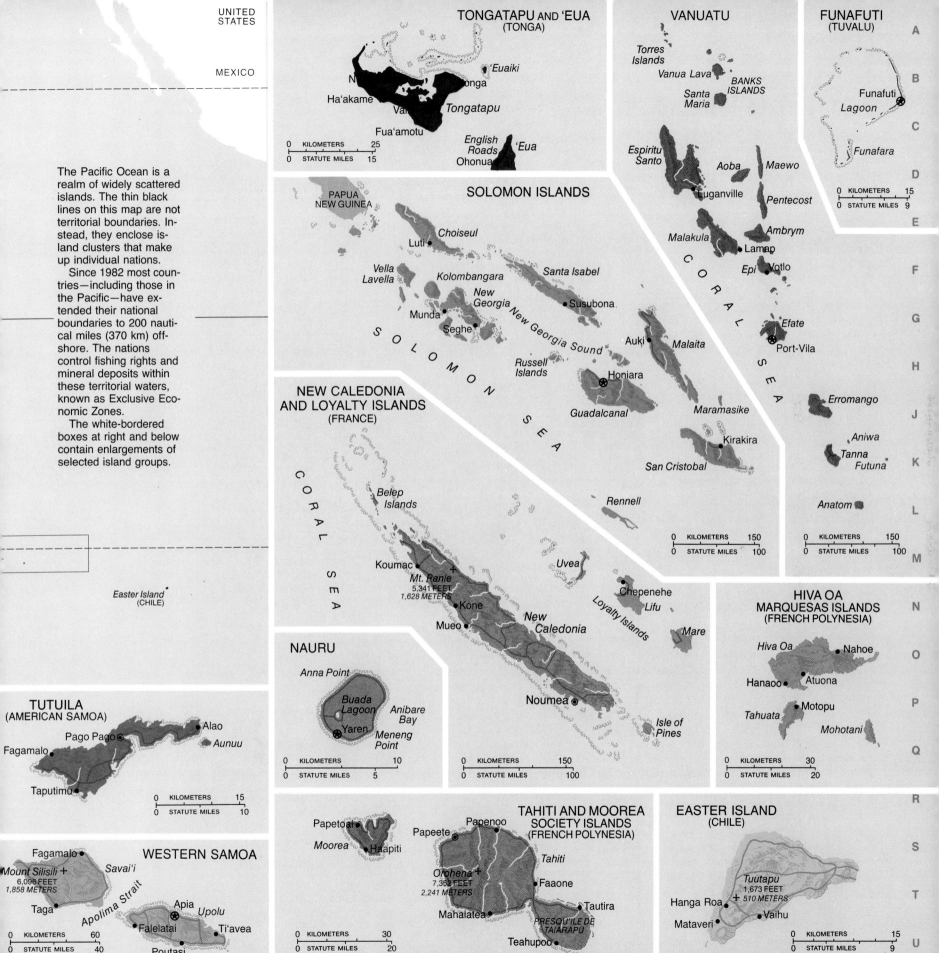

UNITED
STATES

MEXICO

The Pacific Ocean is a realm of widely scattered islands. The thin black lines on this map are not territorial boundaries. Instead, they enclose island clusters that make up individual nations.

Since 1982 most countries—including those in the Pacific—have extended their national boundaries to 200 nautical miles (370 km) offshore. The nations control fishing rights and mineral deposits within these territorial waters, known as Exclusive Economic Zones.

The white-bordered boxes at right and below contain enlargements of selected island groups.

Easter Island
(CHILE)

TONGATAPU AND 'EUA (TONGA)

'Euaiki

...onga

Ha'akame

Va...

Tongatapu

Fua'amotu

English Roads

'Eua

Ohonua

0 KILOMETERS 25
0 STATUTE MILES 15

VANUATU

Torres Islands

Vanua Lava

Santa Maria

BANKS ISLANDS

Espiritu Santo

Aoba

Maewo

Luganville

Pentecost

Malakula

Ambrym

Lamap

Epi

Votlo

C O R A L

Efate

Port-Vila

Erromango

Aniwa

Tanna

Futuna

S E A

Anatom

0 KILOMETERS 150
0 STATUTE MILES 100

FUNAFUTI (TUVALU)

Funafuti

Lagoon

Funafara

0 KILOMETERS 15
0 STATUTE MILES 9

SOLOMON ISLANDS

PAPUA NEW GUINEA

Choiseul

Luti

Vella Lavella

Kolombangara

Santa Isabel

New Georgia

Susubona

Munda

Seghe

New Georgia Sound

Auki

Malaita

Russell Islands

Honiara

S O L O M O N   S E A

Guadalcanal

Maramasike

Kirakira

San Cristobal

Rennell

0 KILOMETERS 150
0 STATUTE MILES 100

NEW CALEDONIA AND LOYALTY ISLANDS (FRANCE)

Belep Islands

C O R A L

S E A

Koumac

Mt. Panie
5,341 FEET
1,628 METERS

Kone

Mueo

New Caledonia

Uvea

Chepenehe

Lifu

Loyalty Islands

Mare

Noumea

Isle of Pines

0 KILOMETERS 150
0 STATUTE MILES 100

NAURU

Anna Point

Buada Lagoon

Anibare Bay

Yaren

Meneng Point

0 KILOMETERS 10
0 STATUTE MILES 5

HIVA OA MARQUESAS ISLANDS (FRENCH POLYNESIA)

Hiva Oa

Nahoe

Hanaoo

Atuona

Tahuata

Motopu

Mohotani

0 KILOMETERS 30
0 STATUTE MILES 20

TUTUILA (AMERICAN SAMOA)

Alao

Pago Pago

Aunuu

Fagamalo

Taputimu

0 KILOMETERS 15
0 STATUTE MILES 10

WESTERN SAMOA

Fagamalo

Mount Silisili +
6,096 FEET
1,858 METERS

Savai'i

Taga

Apolima Strait

Apia

Falelatai

Upolu

Ti'avea

Poutasi

0 KILOMETERS 60
0 STATUTE MILES 40

TAHITI AND MOOREA SOCIETY ISLANDS (FRENCH POLYNESIA)

Papetoai

Moorea

Haapiti

Papeete

Papenoo

Tahiti

Orohena +
7,352 FEET
2,241 METERS

Faaone

Mahaiatea

Tautira

PRESQU'ILE DE TAIARAPU

Teahupoo

0 KILOMETERS 30
0 STATUTE MILES 20

EASTER ISLAND (CHILE)

Tuutapu
1,673 FEET
+ 510 METERS

Hanga Roa

Vaihu

Mataveri

0 KILOMETERS 15
0 STATUTE MILES 9

21   22   23   24   25   26   27   28   29   30   31   32   33   34   35   36   37   38   39   40

Northern Mariana Islands

This string of 14 islands—some large, some small—forms a 500-mile-long (805 km) arc in the western Pacific Ocean. The northernmost islands, small and volcanic, are mostly uninhabited. At the southern end of the chain, Saipan, Tinian, and Rota are the largest, most populated islands in the Northern Mariana group.

During World War II these onetime Japanese strongholds suffered some of the fiercest fighting in the Pacific. After the war the United States took over their administration as part of the U. S. Trust Territory of the Pacific Islands.

In 1978 the Northern Marianas became self-governing, but with continued ties to the United States. The islanders enjoy some rights and privileges of U. S. citizenship. Most of them are Chamorros, people of mixed Micronesian and Spanish ancestry. Many of them work for the government or in the booming tourist trade.

Official name: *Commonwealth of the Northern Mariana Islands*
Area: *184 sq mi (477 sq km)*
Population: *21,200*
Capital: *Saipan (pop. 17,182)*
Ethnic groups: *Chamorro, Micronesian*
Language: *English, Chamorro*
Religious groups: *Roman Catholic*
Economy: *Agr: coconuts, fruit, vegetables, cattle, pigs. Ind: tourism, copra, handicrafts, fishing*
Currency: *U. S. dollar*

United States Territories

A handful of territories belonging to the United States dots the blue Pacific—islands scattered from **Midway** in the north to **American Samoa** in the south, from **Palmyra Atoll** in the east to **Guam** in the west. These holdings range in size from 209-square-mile (541 sq km) Guam, a volcanic island rising 1,332 feet (406 m) above sea level, to **Howland Island,** a mile-and-a-half-long (2.4 km) coral strip that barely pokes above the waves.

Baker, Howland, and **Jarvis Islands,** as well as Palmyra Atoll and **Kingman Reef,** are uninhabited. Scientists visit them from time to time to study seabirds and marine life. During World War II some of them served as military bases or staging areas. Palmyra, a collection of about 50 islets, is covered with dense growths of coconut and other trees. In the 1800s Howland, Baker, and Jarvis Islands were mined for guano, bird droppings used as fertilizer.

U. S. military forces maintain bases on islands such as **Johnston Atoll,** the site of high-altitude nuclear tests during the 1950s and 1960s. The Navy administers the Midway Islands, scene of a World War II naval battle that turned the tide of war against Japan. And the Air Force is in charge of **Wake Island,** three coral islets clustered around a lagoon. Once used as a refueling stop for transpacific flights, Wake is now a weather station and a small military base.

Guam and American Samoa, the most heavily populated of the U. S. Pacific islands, are self-governing territories. Their people, most of them island natives, are U. S. citizens and enjoy modern conveniences from shopping malls to discotheques, cars to television sets. Fishing, fish processing, tourism, and subsistence crops of coconuts, sweet potatoes, bananas, and corn are the mainstays of American Samoa's economy. On Guam, most islanders earn salaries from jobs in stores or on U. S. military installations.

Palau

Westernmost of the Caroline Islands, Palau stands on the threshold of independence. It remains the last island group under United States administration in what was once the far-flung U. S. Trust Territory of the Pacific Islands.

Some 200 islands make up Palau, which is sometimes called Belau. In hopes of eventual independence, a new capital is planned for mountainous Babelthuap, largest of the islands. The present capital, Koror, is a cinder-block and tin-roof town of about 8,100 people on the nearby island of the same name. Tourism and U. S. aid are the chief sources of income for the islands.

Palau is famed as a scuba diver's paradise. Many of its green-clad limestone islands, surrounded by reefs and translucent water, bulge from the sea like mushroom caps. On some islands, shrimp and jellyfish live in marine lakes fed by seeping seawater. And the wreckage of World War II, rusting ships and airplanes, rests in sapphire lagoons. On one island, Peleliu, more than 13,000 people died as U. S. Marines struggled to wrest the island from Japan.

Official name: *Palau*
Area: *177 sq mi (458 sq km)*
Population: *14,000*
Capital: *Koror (pop. 8,100)*
Ethnic groups: *Palauan*
Language: *Palauan, English*
Religious groups: *Roman Catholic*
Economy: *Agr: coconuts, cassava, sweet potatoes. Ind: tourism, handicrafts, fishing*
Currency: *U. S. dollar*

Federated States of Micronesia

The Federated States of Micronesia celebrated a big event in 1986: It became one of the world's newest self-governing countries. It has its own government, and in 1989 it dedicated a brand-new capital, Palikir, on the island of Pohnpei (or Ponape, as it used to be called). The federation also has its own courts, its own flag, even its own states—island clusters named Yap, Truk (recently renamed Chuuk), Pohnpei, and Kosrae.

But the new country also has problems. It is very small. The total land area, about four times the size of Washington, D. C., is broken into some 600 tropical islands and atolls scattered across 1,800 miles (2,900 km) of open ocean. This gives the islanders wonderful vistas of sea and sky, but makes communications difficult and provides few natural resources.

Thus the islands have little industry besides tourism and are heavily dependent on aid from the United States. To keep U. S. aid flowing after independence, the Federated States has signed a compact of free association that allows the U. S. to set up military bases in the event of an emergency. Most of the nation's 102,000 people either work for the government or grow coconuts, cassava, and sweet potatoes.

Official name: *Federated States of Micronesia*
Area: *271 sq mi (702 sq km)*
Population: *102,000*
Capital: *Palikir (pop. 9,000)*
Ethnic groups: *Micronesian, Polynesian*
Language: *English, indigenous languages*
Religious groups: *Protestant, Roman Catholic*
Economy: *Agr: coconuts, cassava, sweet potatoes, fruit, pigs, poultry. Ind: copra, tourism, fishing*
Currency: *U. S. dollar*

Marshall Islands

Paradise lost. That's the story of the Marshall Islands, a double chain of low-lying atolls and islands reaching some 800 miles (1,285 km) across the western Pacific Ocean. Governed by the United States since the end of World War II, islanders in 1986 became a self-governing nation in free association with the United States—and largely supported by continuing U. S. aid.

The Marshall Islands are best known for two of their remotest atolls, Bikini and Enewetak (Eniwetok). Between 1946 and 1958 the atolls were rocked by 66 nuclear blasts. One of them was more powerful than the combined power of all the explosives ever used in war. Enewetak islanders have since returned to their palm-shaded atoll, but Bikini is still too radioactive. Today most Bikinians live on a distant island, far from the palm-fringed lagoon of their old home.

Kwajalein, the world's largest atoll, has a lagoon that has become a target for unarmed missiles launched from California. It is also the site of a large, modern U. S. Army base. And in Majuro, the capital, some leaders hope to turn a few islands into income-producing dumps for household trash shipped from the U. S.

Official name: *Republic of the Marshall Islands*
Area: *70 sq mi (181 sq km)*
Population: *42,000*
Capital: *Majuro (pop. 12,800)*
Ethnic groups: *Micronesian*
Language: *English, Malayo-Polynesian*
Religious groups: *Christian*
Economy: *Agr: coconuts, taro, fruit, pigs, poultry. Ind: tourism, copra, fishing, handicrafts*
Currency: *U. S. dollar*

Nauru

They used to call it Pleasant Island. Now, thanks to the sale of phosphates, it's also one of the richest nations on Earth. The citizens of the eight-square-mile (21 sq km) island near the Equator have an average income of $20,000 a year.

Most Nauruans live in ranch-style houses that use solar energy. They drive new cars and powerboats, and play golf. To shop, they jet to Australia or Hawaii or Europe. Nauruans pay no taxes. Food, schools, houses, and health care are available free or at rock-bottom prices. Some Nauruans work for the government, which hires foreigners to mine the phosphates that make up much of the island. But soon the fertilizer deposits will give out, so Nauru is investing in money-making properties overseas.

Meantime success has created another problem: Rich, imported food has made many islanders obese—and subject to heart diseases.

Official name: *Republic of Nauru*
Area: *8 sq mi (21 sq km)*
Population: *8,042*
Capital: *Yaren*
Ethnic groups: *Nauruan, other Pacific Islanders*
Language: *Nauruan, English*
Religious groups: *Protestant, Roman Catholic*
Economy: *Agr: coconuts. Ind: phosphates, finance*
Currency: *Australian dollar*

Kiribati

It's spelled Kiribati but you pronounce it Kiribas, and until 1979, when this former British colony became independent, it was known as the Gilbert Islands. Made up of 33 coral atolls and islands, the nation straddles the Equator and sprawls across a Pacific Ocean area almost two-thirds the size of the 48 United States. If lumped together, the land area of its scattered islands would total only 277 square miles (717 sq km).

Most of Kiribati's islands are low-lying and studded with palm and pandanus trees. Islanders fish, harvest coconuts, and grow bananas, taro, breadfruit, and papaya. One island, Banaba, or Ocean Island, earned income through exports of phosphate. But now the deposits are exhausted and the citizens of Kiribati rely on aid from Australia, New Zealand, and the United Kingdom. The island of Tarawa, where Kiribati's capital is, was the scene of some of the bloodiest fighting in the Pacific during World War II.

Official name: *Republic of Kiribati*
Area: *277 sq mi (717 sq km)*
Population: *69,000*
Capital: *Tarawa (pop. 21,393)*
Ethnic groups: *Micronesian*
Language: *English, Gilbertese*
Religious groups: *Roman Catholic, Protestant*
Economy: *Agr: coconuts, root crops, vegetables, fruit, pigs, poultry. Ind: fishing, copra, handicrafts*
Currency: *Australian dollar*

Papua New Guinea

Papua New Guinea occupies the eastern half of New Guinea, the world's second largest island (after Greenland). An Australian territory until it won independence in 1975, the country today numbers about four million people. The capital, Port Moresby, is a major shipping center for coffee, cocoa, copra, coconut oil, and timber, and is home to about 145,000 people. Offshore islands include Bougainville, site of a huge copper mine that, when operating, brings in nearly half the nation's income.

Papua New Guinea is a rugged, tropical country swept by monsoon rains and covered with thick rain forests. Here live the brilliant birds of paradise and a butterfly with an 11-inch (28 cm) wingspread. The nation's southwestern low-lands include one of the world's largest swamps, and giant crocodiles called *pukpuks*.

Inland rise the central highlands, a tangle of volcanic peaks and sharp limestone ridges nearly 15,000 feet (4,570 m) high. In places the terrain is so jagged that explorers called it "broken bottle country." In valleys and forests tucked amid the crags lived tribes unknown to the outside world or even to each other until the 1930s.

Some tribes practiced head-hunting. Others were cannibals. All led traditional lives, hunting, gathering, raising pigs, and cultivating plots of taro and yams. Many now have taken up modern trappings such as T-shirts, radios, plastic beads, and dancing for tourists. Even today some highland villages can be reached only on foot or by air. Although few paved roads connect the nation's towns and villages, more than 400 airstrips serve the backcountry.

Altogether, Papua New Guinea's people speak more than 700 languages. Many speak pidgin English, or a variation called "police motu," and refer to their monarch, Queen Elizabeth II, as "Misis Kwin." For although Papua New Guinea is an independent nation, it is also a member of the Commonwealth.

Official name: *Papua New Guinea*
Area: *178,260 sq mi (461,691 sq km)*
Population: *3,905,000*
Capital: *Port Moresby (met. pop. 145,300)*
Ethnic groups: *Papuan, Melanesian*
Language: *English, Papuan and Melanesian languages, pidgin English*
Religious groups: *Christian, traditional*
Economy: *Agr: coconuts, root crops, cacao, coffee, oil palm, pigs. Ind: copper, gold, lumber, fishing*
Currency: *kina*

Solomon Islands

When the fighting was over, 25,000 men—mostly Japanese and American troops—lay dead. And the ocean floor east of Guadalcanal, largest of the Solomon Islands, was so littered with sunken ships that the area became known as "Iron Bottom Sound."

Today, the guns of war are silent. But the wreckage of World War II still rusts on many of the beaches of this nation, a British protectorate until it won independence in 1978.

The Solomons got their name from a wily Spanish explorer who sought to recruit settlers by linking the islands to the fabled riches of King Solomon. The islands themselves form a twin chain of volcanic peaks and low-lying atolls in the Solomon Sea. The six biggest islands are rugged, with razor-backed ridges slashed by deep valleys and matted with dense forests. Equatorial rains drench them much of the year.

Most of the islanders are Melanesians. Many live along the shore in thatched grass houses. They harvest crops of coconuts for themselves and for export. From the coconuts comes copra, the dried meat that provides oil for cooking and for making soap and candles. The islanders also sell fish, timber, and seashells used for buttons. They speak some 80 different languages, and they also speak pidgin English.

Honiara, the capital and largest city, is on the island of Guadalcanal.

Official name: *Solomon Islands*
Area: *10,985 sq mi (28,450 sq km)*
Population: *324,000*
Capital: *Honiara (pop. 30,499)*
Ethnic groups: *Melanesian*
Language: *English, Melanesian languages*
Religious groups: *Protestant, Roman Catholic*
Economy: *Agr: coconuts, taro, oil palm, cacao, rice, fruit, vegetables. Ind: fishing, lumber, copra*
Currency: *Solomon Islands dollar*

Tuvalu

Tuvalu. In the local tongue the word means "eight standing together." Although this nation (until 1978 a British colony known as the Ellice Islands) consists of nine atolls and islands, only eight of them are inhabited. Altogether their land area totals a sixth the size of Washington, D. C., and no land rises more than 15 feet (4.5 m) above sea level. Tuvalu's capital lies on the island of Funafuti.

Most of the coral islands encircle lagoons and are shaded by coconut palms and breadfruit and pandanus trees. The islanders live in thatched houses, and fish and cultivate their gardens for a living. The country exports copra and handicrafts, but most of its income is derived from selling coins and stamps to collectors, and from aid sent by foreign nations, including other members of the Commonwealth.

Official name: *Tuvalu*
Area: *10 sq mi (26 sq km)*
Population: *9,000*
Capital: *Funafuti (pop. 2,810)*
Ethnic groups: *Polynesian*
Language: *Tuvaluan, English*
Religious groups: *Protestant*
Economy: *coconuts (copra), fishing, stamps, coins*
Currency: *Tuvaluan and Australian dollars*

Western Samoa

"Home is the sailor, home from the sea. . . ." So read the words on the mountaintop tomb of Robert Louis Stevenson, author of *Treasure Island* and other tales of adventure. He died nearly a century ago on his beloved island of Upolu, one of the two largest reef-fringed, volcanic islands in Western Samoa. His house still stands near Apia, the capital and only major town of this South Sea island nation.

The words on Stevenson's grave are fitting. For, according to legend, it was from these islands that the Samoans launched their giant, double-hulled canoes more than a thousand years ago and began to spread their Polynesian culture across the unexplored Pacific.

Today, Western Samoa, unlike the neighboring islands of American Samoa, still clings to traditional Polynesian ways. Most of its 182,000 people live along the shore in *fales*, palm-thatched shelters with no walls. They live in large family groups presided over by a *matai*, or chief, and fish and raise pigs and chickens, as well as crops of coconuts, bananas, and taro.

Official name: *Independent State of Western Samoa*
Area: *1,093 sq mi (2,831 sq km)*
Population: *182,000*
Capital: *Apia (met. pop. 33,170)*
Ethnic groups: *Samoan*
Language: *Samoan, English*
Religious groups: *Protestant, Roman Catholic*
Economy: *Agr: coconuts, taro, bananas, papayas. Ind: lumber, tourism, food processing, fishing*
Currency: *tala*

Vanuatu

Most of Vanuatu's people live in thatched houses, as they always have. They raise pigs and cultivate taro, yams, and bananas for themselves. To earn money they export copra, cocoa, beef, and timber cut from tropical rain forests.

Once known as New Hebrides, Vanuatu was ruled jointly by Britain and France until 1980. That year the Y-shaped string of 80 coral and volcanic islands became an independent nation. Its capital, Port-Vila, is a whitewashed town of about 14,000 people on the island of Efate. It is also a tax haven. Some 70 banks shelter millions of dollars sent from Hong Kong, Singapore, and other overseas money centers.

But traditional beliefs still shape life on these South Pacific islands. On the island of Tanna, for example, one group of people awaits the second coming of John Frum. The group belongs to a cargo cult. They believe in a god who will someday return to their island, bringing gifts of trucks, jeeps, radios, and other goods the way American soldiers did in World War II. They have built piers to receive the cargoes.

And on Pentecost Island, young "land divers" hurl themselves from towers up to 90 feet (27 m) high to assure a good yam harvest. Vines tied to the divers' ankles break their fall.

Official name: *Republic of Vanuatu*
Area: *5,699 sq mi (14,760 sq km)*
Population: *160,000*
Capital: *Port-Vila (pop. 14,184)*
Ethnic groups: *Melanesian, French*
Language: *Bislama, English, French*
Religious groups: *Protestant, Roman Catholic*
Economy: *Agr: coconuts, taro, yams, fruit, cacao, coffee, livestock. Ind: tourism, foods, fishing, lumber*
Currency: *vatu*

Fiji

In Fiji they tell the legend of a fisherman who one day caught an eel. The eel, fearing for its life, pleaded to be put back in the water. The fisherman obliged and, in return, he and his descendants were granted the ability to walk barefoot across hot stones without burning their feet. To this day Fijian fire walkers entertain tourists by strolling unharmed across hot stones—feats that defy scientific explanation.

Fiji is a nation of some 320 islands in the South Pacific Ocean, only about 105 of which are inhabited. Some are volcanic peaks rising abruptly out of the ocean. Others are coral strips or flat, sandy isles. In size the islands range from mere rocks to 4,010-square-mile (10,386 sq km) Viti Levu, largest of the group's two main islands.

Most of Fiji's 754,000 people live near the coast on Viti Levu. Here, too, stands the nation's capital, Suva, a busy metropolis that combines colorful parks and gardens with Indian, Melanesian, and European architectural styles.

Native Fijians, a mixture of Melanesian and Polynesian, are slightly outnumbered by the descendants of workers brought from India in the late 1800s and early 1900s to work on sugarcane plantations. Today, as businessmen, farmers, doctors, lawyers, and teachers, Indians control much of Fiji's economy, while native islanders own most of the land. The situation has led to tension between the two groups and in 1987 led to the takeover of the government by Fijians.

A British colony from 1874 until it achieved independence in 1970, Fiji once was known as the Cannibal Islands. Today it is a sunny, tropical republic where visitors can relax on white, sandy beaches and be assured of a warm *Ni sa bula*—Welcome.

Official name: *Republic of Fiji*
Area: *7,056 sq mi (18,274 sq km)*
Population: *754,000*
Capital: *Suva (pop. 69,481)*
Ethnic groups: *Indian, Fijian*
Language: *English, Fijian, Hindi*
Religious groups: *Christian, Hindu*
Economy: *Agr: sugarcane, coconuts, cassava, rice, ginger. Ind: tourism, gold mining, fishing, lumber*
Currency: *Fiji dollar*

Tonga

When Capt. James Cook, the English navigator, visited Tonga in 1773 and 1777 he was so cordially welcomed he named this cluster of 170 South Sea islands the "Friendly Islands." Little did he know the local chiefs planned to kill him. But Cook sailed away unaware of his narrow escape, and the island nation, ruled a thousand years by Polynesian kings, later became a British protectorate.

Today Tonga is again an independent kingdom, the only monarchy remaining in all of Polynesia. It is also a member of the Commonwealth. Nearly two-thirds of the people live on Tongatapu, Tonga's largest island and site of its capital, Nuku'alofa.

Many of Tonga's islands are fertile and have plenty of rainfall. Some are forest covered. Low-lying islands are made of coral; higher ones are volcanic, some with active volcanoes.

Most Tongans live in small villages, where they raise pigs and grow their own fruit and vegetables. They also fish and earn money by harvesting coconuts, vanilla beans, and bananas for sale overseas.

Official name: *Kingdom of Tonga*
Area: *270 sq mi (699 sq km)*
Population: *100,000*
Capital: *Nuku'alofa (met. pop. 28,899)*
Ethnic groups: *Tongan*
Language: *Tongan, English*
Religious groups: *Protestant, Roman Catholic*
Economy: *Agr: coconuts, yams, taro, vegetables, bananas, vanilla, spices. Ind: tourism, fishing*
Currency: *pa'anga*

New Zealand Territories

Scattered like confetti across the Pacific Ocean south of the Equator are the islands that make up New Zealand's overseas territories.

The **Cook Islands,** a 15-island cluster, include lush, volcanic Rarotonga, long regarded as a Polynesian paradise. Islanders grow export crops of coconuts, citrus fruit, and pineapples or work in the tourist and clothing industries.

Niue (pronounced New-way), a limestone plateau, rises sheer from the sea west of the Cook Islands. Niue takes its name from *Niu*, a Polynesian word for coconut tree, and *e*, meaning behold. It is one of the world's largest coral islands. Many of its cliffs have been carved by pounding waves into a wonderworld of caves, pools, and grottoes. Self-governing since 1974, Niue earns income through exports of copra, coconut cream, passion fruit, honey, limes, and crafts.

North of Niue, close to the Equator, lies **Tokelau,** a trio of low-lying, typhoon-prone atolls. Tokelau has thin soil and few natural resources aside from fish and shellfish. Many of its people have resettled in New Zealand.

New Zealand's three Pacific territories support small Polynesian populations. Most of the people live on crops of coconuts, taro, and yams, and they raise pigs and poultry. The islanders depend on aid from New Zealand, as well as on money sent home by relatives who have moved away to better their lives.

French Territories

On the highest slopes of Raiatea Island in **French Polynesia** lives one of the world's unusual plants. It is a slender-leaved gardenia with five white petals that look like the outstretched fingers of a hand. The plant grows only on Raiatea. Islanders say that its flower is the hand of a princess who died of a broken heart when forbidden to marry a young man from another island.

A delightfully romantic tale, of course. But how fitting that such a story should come from these lush, tropical islands that long have inspired artists, writers, and adventurers to thoughts of earthly paradise. Even crusty Lt. William Bligh, master of the *Bounty* and its mutineering crew, thought one of the islands, Tahiti, "the finest island in the world."

Located halfway between South America and Australia, French Polynesia is made up of some 120 islands grouped into four archipelagoes. Altogether the islands cover an ocean area about

half the size of the United States. But the land part is tiny—about the size of Rhode Island. Some islands are volcanic, with cloud-wreathed peaks rising straight out of the sea. Others are coral atolls covered with coconut palms.

A French protectorate since the 1800s, French Polynesia became one of France's Pacific territories in 1957. The others are the **Wallis and Futuna Islands** and mineral-rich **New Caledonia,** one of the world's largest producers of high-quality nickel used to make steel alloys.

Tahiti, the largest and most heavily populated of the French Polynesian islands, earns much of its income from tourism. Its biggest city, Papeete, is a busy port for shipping coconut oil and serves as the capital for all of French Polynesia.

But even paradise has problems. Since 1966 France has tested atomic weapons on remote atolls, and in New Caledonia a drive for independence has brought violence and bloodshed.

Pitcairn Island

Fletcher Christian knew how to hide. When in 1789 he and his fellow mutineers took over H.M.S. *Bounty* and cast its skipper, Lt. William Bligh, adrift in an open boat, he sailed away to one of the world's most remote islands—Pitcairn. The flat-topped island, a British colony, lies 1,350 miles (2,170 km) from the nearest commercial port. Its cliffs rise like a fortress from the sea. Volcanic soil supports crops for a dwindling population of *Bounty* descendants.

Official name: *Pitcairn Islands (3 uninhabited)*
Area: *18 sq mi (47 sq km)*
Population: *60*
Capital: *Adamstown (pop. 60)*

Easter Island

Lips pursed, backs to the sea, great stone figures known as *moai* line the coastal cliffs of this remote volcanic island owned by Chile. Carved with stone picks and hoisted into place, the giant statues honor clan ancestors.

The Easter Islanders, mostly descendants of the Polynesians who settled here 1,600 years ago, fish, farm, or raise livestock for a living. Dutch explorers discovered the island on Easter Sunday, 1722, hence its name.

Official name: *Easter Island*
Area: *63 sq mi (164 sq km)*
Population: *1,928*
Capital: *Hanga Roa (pop. 1,928)*

1 *Tahiti, French Polynesia*

2 *Marutea, French Polynesia*

French Polynesia

1 *Legendary beauty of Tahitian women reflects a blend of several nationalities.*

2 *Rare black pearls, cultivated in a lagoon, take several years to grow and may be worth thousands of dollars.*

3 *The island of Moorea rises from a reef-fringed lagoon, an unspoiled retreat within sight of its sister island, Tahiti.*

Marshall Islands

4 *Americans shop for groceries at a supermarket on Kwajalein. Some 3,000 civilians and U. S. Army personnel work at this island's missile-testing facility.*

Western Samoa

5 *Paddling his outrigger canoe, a fisherman from Savai'i Island preserves seamanship skills prized by his Polynesian ancestors.*

Easter Island

6 *Stone faces of Easter Island, some weighing up to 85 tons (77 metric tons), seem to watch the arrival of Halley's Comet in this double exposure.*

3 *Moorea, French Polynesia*

4 *Kwajalein, Marshall Islands*

5 *Western Samoa*

6 *Easter Island*

1 *Upolu, Western Samoa*

2 *Papua New Guinea*

3 *Federated States of Micronesia*

4 *Palau*

Western Samoa

1 *Thatched houses called* fales *have open-wall air-conditioning in a village on the island of Upolu. Palm mats can be let down to keep out rain and sun.*

Papua New Guinea

2 *Daubed with clay body paint, Gimi story-tellers of the Eastern Highlands dramatize tribal myths and legends—in this case part of a boys' initiation ceremony.*

Federated States of Micronesia

3 *A farmer of Kosrae displays his produce. Easternmost of Micronesia's four federated states, Kosrae is known locally for its fine limes, oranges, tangerines, and bananas.*

Palau

4 *Diver in a bubble bath? No, these are the jellyfish that swarm in some of the 80 or so salt lakes that dot these South Pacific isles.*

South Orkney
Islands

SOUTH ATLANTIC OCEAN

Sanae
SOUTH AFRICA

Dakshin Gangotri
INDIA

Georg von Neumayer
GERMANY

Novolazarevskaya
SOVIET UNION

Georg Forster
GERMANY

INDIAN OCEAN

Asuka
JAPAN

Syowa
JAPAN

South
Shetland
Islands

Riiser-
Larsen
Ice
Shelf

Molodezhnaya
SOVIET UNION

Esperanza
ARGENTINA

NEW SCHWABENLAND

ENDERBY LAND

QUEEN   MAUD   LAND

General
Bernardo
O'Higgins
CHILE

Marambio
ARGENTINA

WEDDELL SEA

Halley
UNITED KINGDOM

Antarctic
Peninsula

Palmer
UNITED STATES

Faraday
UNITED KINGDOM

General Belgrano II
ARGENTINA

Mawson
AUSTRALIA

MAC. ROBERTSON
LAND

San Martin
ARGENTINA

Amery
Ice Shelf

PALMER LAND

Rothera
UNITED KINGDOM

Alexander
Island

Filchner
Ice
Shelf

Ronne
Ice
Shelf

Berkner
Island

Progress
SOVIET UNION

Davis
AUSTRALIA

Zonghshan
CHINA

BELLINGSHAUSEN
SEA

Vinson Massif
16,067 FEET
4,897 METERS
Highest point
in Antarctica

POLAR PLATEAU

AMERICAN
HIGHLAND

ELLSWORTH MOUNTAINS

ELLSWORTH LAND

WEST
ANTARCTICA

SOUTH POLE

ANTARCTICA

EAST
ANTARCTICA

Amundsen-Scott
UNITED STATES

Mirnyy
SOVIET UNION

SOUTH PACIFIC OCEAN

-8,327 FEET
-2,538 METERS
Lowest point
in the world

TRANSANTARCTIC

MARIE

Byrd Station
UNITED STATES

BYRD

LAND

QUEEN MAUD MOUNTAINS

Vostok
SOVIET UNION

Shackleton
Ice
Shelf

AMUNDSEN
SEA

WILKES LAND

Casey
AUSTRALIA

Ross Ice Shelf

Roosevelt
Island

Russkaya
SOVIET UNION

Scott Base
NEW ZEALAND

McMurdo
UNITED STATES

Mount Erebus
12,448 FEET
3,794 METERS

VICTORIA LAND MTS.

ROSS SEA

Dumont d'Urville
FRANCE

Leningradskaya
SOVIET UNION

EQUATOR   0°

AFRICA

ATLANTIC
OCEAN

30°S

SOUTH
AMERICA

30°W   0°

30°E

60°S

60°E

INDIAN
OCEAN

60°W

90°E

90°W

ANTARCTICA

SOUTH POLE

AUSTRALIA

120°W

ANTARCTIC CIRCLE

ANTARCTIC CIRCLE

■ Research Station

0   KILOMETERS   700

0   STATUTE MILES   400

For map legend see page 21.

The Poles

Antarctica

In the 1770s British explorer James Cook sailed completely around this great white continent without ever sighting land. But he got close enough to conclude that if any land did lie beyond the ice-choked seas, "the world would not be benefited by it." The seal hunters, whalers, and explorers who came later found that land did, in fact, lie farther south, nearer to the South Pole. But Cook's assessment seemed correct.

Earth's southernmost continent, one-tenth of the world's land, is covered by a sheet of ice averaging two miles (3.2 km) thick. Winds howl across it at speeds up to 200 miles (320 km) per hour, and temperatures can plunge to minus 121°F (-85°C). So harsh is the climate that only a few mosses, lichens, and insects live on land.

Antarctica's interior remained largely unexplored until the early 1900s, when rival teams led by Norway's Roald Amundsen and Great Britain's Robert F. Scott raced each other to the South Pole. With the aid of dogsleds and good weather, Amundsen planted his flag at the Pole on December 14, 1911. Hauling their own sledges, Scott's party arrived 35 days later. On the way back, a blizzard trapped the British explorers in their tent, and they died of starvation.

The United Kingdom, Norway, and several other countries—Chile, Argentina, Australia, New Zealand, and France—have made sometimes overlapping claims to portions of Antarctica. But in the Antarctic Treaty, which went into effect in 1961, they agreed not to press those claims. This treaty, signed by 38 countries, also decreed that Antarctica be used only for peaceful, scientific purposes.

Today more than 40 year-round research stations dot the Antarctic ice. Among other things, scientists are studying Antarctica's ice sheet to see how it is being affected by global warming. Scientists have warned that increases in Earth's temperature, due to the "greenhouse effect," could cause polar ice sheets to melt, raising ocean levels worldwide.

Scientists are also monitoring the "hole" that has been discovered in the ozone layer over Antarctica. Ozone shields Earth from the lethal effects of ultraviolet rays. Researchers are trying to discover whether excess radiation over Antarctica is slowing the growth of tiny marine organisms known as phytoplankton. Declines in phytoplankton could cause drops in other species, such as shrimplike krill, whales, penguins, and fish that abound in these coastal waters.

Antarctica isn't only of scientific interest. Petroleum may exist under the continental shelf in large quantities, and other minerals, including coal, are known to lie underground.

So far, the Antarctic Treaty and the huge costs of extraction have kept any minerals safely locked up in this frozen vault. But in 1988 the Antarctic Treaty nations hammered out a new agreement, the Wellington Convention, which set up conditions under which exploration or mining could go forward.

Environmentalists object to development in Antarctica. They say that oil spills or other industrial mishaps could seriously harm this fragile and still relatively unspoiled continent. In 1989, France and Australia joined conservationists in calling for Antarctica to be set aside as a wilderness reserve, off limits to development.

The continent that was once considered worthless is now the subject of a growing debate over how best to use its resources. As the 1990s unfold, the treaty nations must decide whether to open this frigid frontier to development, or to protect Antarctica for the contributions it can make to global scientific understanding.

Arctic Regions

Earth's two polar zones are opposite in more ways than location on the globe. While Antarctica is an ice-covered continent surrounded by sea, the Arctic is an ice-covered ocean ringed by continents: North America, Europe, and Asia.

Because the Arctic ice pack is sea ice full of meltwater and open channels, it reflects less of the sun's heat back into space, and the region within the Arctic Circle is warmer. Temperatures over the ocean hover around 32°F (0°C) in summer and minus 30°F (-34°C) in winter.

In summer the ice pack shrinks, and the ocean abounds with fish, whales, and seabirds. Seals raise pups on floating ice-top nurseries, occasionally becoming prey of polar bears or human hunters. Summer also melts the snow cover on the lands ringing the ocean. They spring alive with blossoming plants, shrubs, and grasses and support hares, foxes, caribou, and reindeer. Arctic lands are also home to several native peoples who have adapted to this frigid climate.

Adventurers from warmer lands have long been attracted to Arctic challenges. Sea captains nudged their boats along the Arctic's icy coasts, looking for northern trade routes. Later, explorers came seeking the North Pole. America's Robert E. Peary reached it first, in 1909.

More recently, developers have come north to tap the region's mineral wealth, which includes impressive stores of oil and natural gas, as well as coal and iron ore. Scientific studies have examined such problems as the transport of air pollutants from northern industrial areas and the extent of ozone loss.

In 1988, as concern grew over global climate and atmospheric changes, eight Arctic rim nations created a committee to coordinate Arctic research in hopes of improving international understanding of these problems. In 1989, after an American oil tanker wrecked in Alaskan waters, seriously harming fish and wildlife, calls increased for efforts to protect this region's fragile environment and to preserve its value as a natural laboratory.

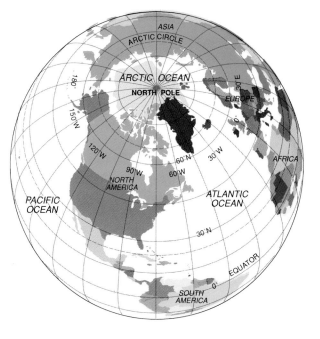

1 *Ellesmere Island, Canada*

2 *Baffin Island, Canada*

3 *Alaska, U. S.*

4 *Antarctica*

5 *Antarctica*

Arctic Regions

1 *An Inuit paddles his kayak past the village of Grise Fiord 950 miles (1,530 km) from the North Pole.*

2 *An Inuit grandmother at Pond Inlet baby-sits while stretching hides for use in clothing. The temperature around her is 40°F below zero (-40°C).*

3 *One of a migrating herd, an antlered caribou bull grazes the tundra. As summer draws to an end, caribou eat constantly to store up body fat for the long Arctic winter.*

Antarctica

4 *Emperor penguins stand with a two-week-old chick at their winter breeding ground on an ice shelf. Some penguin breeding colonies here number in the millions.*

5 *A scientist at the U. S. Amundsen-Scott Station at the South Pole checks solar radiation sensors to measure ozone-damaging air pollutants.*

Illustrations Credits

Abbreviations for terms appearing below: (t)-top; (b)-bottom; (l)-left; (r)-right; (c)-center; NGP-National Geographic Photographer; NGS-National Geographic Staff.

Cover, Michel Tcherevkoff. 2-3, Shusei Nagaoka. 6-7, Mapping Specialists, Ltd.

Mapping Our World
9, Michel Tcherevkoff. 10-20, paintings by Shusei Nagaoka.

North America
22, (t) Annie Griffiths Belt; (c) Paul Chesley; (b) Philip Schermeister. 23, Tibor G. Toth. 25, Stephanie Maze. 28, Sandy Felsenthal. 29, (tl) NASA; (tr) Bruce Davidson; (bl) Wilbur E. Garrett; (br) C. C. Lockwood. 30, (t) Phil Schofield; (b) Bruce Dale, NGP. 30-31, Art Wolfe, Allstock. 31, (t) Robert W. Madden, NGS; (b) Bill Hess. 34, George F. Mobley, NGP. 34-35, Ann E. Yow. 35, (t) Paul von Baich, First Light; (c) Yva Momatiuk and John Eastcott; (bl) George F. Mobley, NGP; (br) Ivars Silis. 38, (t) Mark Godfrey; (b) David Hiser, Photographers/Aspen. 38-39, David Hiser, Photographers/Aspen. 39, (t) and (cl) Danny Lehman; (cr) Chuck Place; (b) Sisse Brimberg. 43, Nicholas DeVore III, Photographers/Aspen. 44, (t) Danny Lehman; (bl) Alain Keler, Sygma; (br) James Nachtwey, Black Star. 45, (t) Joseph J. Scherschel; (bl) David Alan Harvey; (br) Loren McIntyre. 51, (t) Jodi Cobb, NGP; (bl) Tor Eigeland; (br) Cotton Coulson. 52, (t) Carole E. Devillers; (bl) and (br) Steve Raymer, NGS. 52-53, Bruce Dale, NGP. 53, (t) James L. Stanfield, NGP; (b) Tony Arruza.

South America
54, Loren McIntyre. 55, Tibor G. Toth. 57, William Albert Allard. 60, (t) O. Louis Mazzatenta, NGS; (bl) Fred Ward, Black Star; (bc) José Azel, Contact Press Images; (br) Georg Gerster. 61, (t) Uwe George, GEO Magazin; (b) Loren McIntyre. 64, (t) Cary Wolinsky; (b) Martin Rogers. 64-65, Ric Ergenbright. 65, (t) William E. Townsend Jr., Photo Researchers, Inc.; (b) Dieter and Mary Plage, Survival Anglia. 68, (t) Stephanie Maze; (b) Andrew L. Young. 68-69, Stephanie Maze. 69, Carole E. Devillers. 72, (t) O. Louis Mazzatenta, NGS; (b) Loren McIntyre. 72-73, O. Louis Mazzatenta, NGS. 73, Loren McIntyre. 76, (t) O. Louis Mazzatenta, NGS; (bl) James P. Blair, NGP; (br) Frans Lanting, Minden Pictures. 76-77, David Alan Harvey. 77, Loren McIntyre.

Europe
78, (t) Farrell Grehan; (b) Cotton Coulson. 79, Tibor G. Toth. 81, (l) Adam Woolfitt; (r) Horst Munzig. 84-85, Bob Krist. 86, (l) Sisse Brimberg; (r) Tor Eigeland. 87, (tl) Jodi Cobb, NGP; (tr) Bernhard Wagner; (b) Sven Hörnell. 90, (t) John Bulmer; (bl) Linda Bartlett; (br) Nathan Benn. 90-91, O. Louis Mazzatenta, NGS. 91, Cotton Coulson. 94, (t) Cotton Coulson; (b) James L. Stanfield, NGP. 95, (l) Jean-Paul Nacivet, After Image; (r) Nathan Benn. 98, Yva Momatiuk and John Eastcott. 98-99, James L. Stanfield, NGP. 99, (t) Yva Momatiuk and John Eastcott; (b) Yva Momatiuk and John Eastcott, The Image Works. 102, James P. Blair, NGP. 103, (tl) Stephanie

Maze; (tr) Tor Eigeland; (b) Bernard Wolf. 106, French National Railroad. 106-107, James L. Stanfield, NGP. 107, (tl) Charles O'Rear; (tr) Jodi Cobb, NGP; (b) Cotton Coulson. 110, O. Louis Mazzatenta, NGS. 111, (tl) Thomas Nebbia; (tr) and (br) James L. Stanfield, NGP; (bl) Cotton Coulson. 114, Adam Woolfitt. 115, (tl) Adam Woolfitt; (tr) Cary Wolinsky; (b) Jonathan Blair. 118, Higuchi, Miller Comstock, Inc. 119, (tl) James P. Blair, NGP; (tr) James L. Stanfield, NGP; (b) Hans Madej, Bilderberg.

Asia
120, (t) William Thompson; (b) Dean Conger. 121, Tibor G. Toth. 123, David Alan Harvey. 126, (t) Nicolai Rachmanov, Desertina Verlag; (b) Steve Raymer, NGS. 127, (t) Vladimir Vyatkin; (bl) Bruce Dale, NGP; (br) Jay Dickman. 131, James L. Stanfield, NGP. 132, (tl) Steve Raymer, NGS; (tr) James L. Stanfield, NGP; (b) Jodi Cobb, NGP. 133, Steve McCurry. 136, Steve Raymer, NGS. 137, Mohamed Amin, Camerapix. 138, (tl) Thomas J. Abercrombie, NGS; (b) Jodi Cobb, NGP. 138-139, Robert Azzi, Woodfin Camp, Inc. 139, (t) Steve Raymer, NGS; (b) Lynn Abercrombie. 142, (l) Steve Raymer, NGS; (r) Michael Coyne, The Image Bank. 143, (tl) and (tr) Steve McCurry; (b) James L. Stanfield, NGP. 147, Henry Wilson. 148, Steve McCurry. 148-149, Raghubir Singh. 149, (t) David Hiser, Photographers/Aspen; (bl) Steve McCurry; (br) Raghubir Singh. 152, (t) James L. Stanfield, NGP; (b) Cary Wolinsky. 153, (l) Bruce Dale, NGP; (tr) Thomas Nebbia; (br) H. Edward Kim. 154, Reinhold Messner. 154-155, Steve McCurry. 155, Dean Conger. 158, (l) Charles O'Rear; (r) Michael S. Yamashita. 158-159, George F. Mobley, NGP. 159, (t) David Alan Harvey; (bl) and (br) Nathan Benn. 162, James L. Stanfield, NGP. 163, (tl) Seny Norasingh; (tr) and (br) David Alan Harvey; (bl) Steve Raymer, NGS. 166-167, Steve McCurry. 168, Dean Conger. (tl) James P. Blair, NGP. 169, Charles O'Rear; (b) David Robert Austen.

Africa
170, (t) Richard Packwood, Oxford Scientific Films, Ltd; (b) George F. Mobley, NGP. 171, Tibor G. Toth. 173, Steve Jackson, Black Star. 176, David Alan Harvey. 177, (t) Carol Beckwith; (b) Steve McCurry. 178-179, Bruno Barbey, Magnum. 179, (t) and (bl) Steve McCurry; (br) Pierre Boulat, Woodfin Camp Cosmos. 182, Anne B. Keiser. 182-183, (t) Dick Durrance II, Woodfin Camp, Inc.; (b) Robert Caputo. 183, (t) James L. Stanfield, NGP; (bl) Steve McCurry; (br) Robert Caputo. 187, Olivier Martel, Gamma Presse Images. 188, Michael and Aubine Kirtley; (tl) Susan Pierres, Peter Arnold Inc. 189, (l) Arthur Tress, Magnum; (r) Eugene Gordon. 192, (t) Douglas Waugh, Peter Arnold Inc.; (b) William Campbell, Sygma. 193, (tl) Georg Gerster; (tr) John Sleezer; (b) Anthony Suau. 196-197, Anthony Suau. 198, (t) Robert C. Bailey; (b) James A. Sugar. 198-199, Georg Gerster. 203, (t) Mitsuaki Iwago; (b) George F. Mobley, NGP. 204, (t) Kevin Fleming. 204-205, Robert Caputo. 205, (t) Gerry Ellis, Ellis Wildlife Collection. 208, Frans Lanting. 209, Steve Raymer, NGS; (tl) Michael Friedel. 212, (t) Susan Meiselas, Magnum. 212-213, Eli Reed, Magnum. 213, (b) Susan Pierres, Peter Arnold Inc. 217, (l) Carol

and David Hughes; (r) Jim Brandenburg. 218, (l) Nicholas DeVore III, Photographers/Aspen; (r) Frans Lanting. 219, (tl) David Turnley, Black Star; (tr) Thomas Nebbia; (b) James L. Stanfield, NGP.

Oceania
220, (t) Gordon W. Gahan; (c) Georg Gerster; (b) David Doubilet. 221, Tibor G. Toth. 224, (t) Penny Tweedie; (b) David Robert Austen. 224-225, George Hall, Weldon Trannies. 225, (t) Jim Brandenburg; (bl) Anne B. Keiser; (br) Yva Momatiuk and John Eastcott. 232, (tl) Nicholas DeVore III, Photographers/Aspen; (tr) Fred Ward, Black Star. 232-233, David Hiser, Photographers/Aspen. 233, (tl) Melinda Berge, Photographers/Aspen; (tr) David Hiser, Photographers/Aspen; (b) James Balog. 234, David Hiser, Photographers/Aspen. 235, (tl) David Gillison; (tr) David Hiser, Photographers/Aspen; (b) David Doubilet.

The Poles
238, (t) Jim Brandenburg; (bl) Kevin Fleming; (br) Michio Hoshino. 239, (t) Doug Allan; (b) George F. Mobley, NGP.

Acknowledgments

We wish to thank the many individuals who helped in the preparation of the *National Geographic Picture Atlas of OUR WORLD:* Larry Armentrout; Bonnie Bracey; Lynda Bush; Kathryn Champion, Metropolitan Toronto Convention & Visitors Association; Ted Dachtera, NGS; Debra G. Daggs, Roger M. Downs, and Lynn S. Liben, Pennsylvania State University; Harm de Blij; Aubrey Diem, University of Waterloo; Charles Drake, Dartmouth College; Charles Dunne, U. S. Department of State; Carl Haub, Population Reference Bureau; Charles M. Love, Western Wyoming College; Cathy Riggs-Salter; Christopher L. Salter; Whitney Smith, Flag Research Center; John P. Snyder, U. S. Geological Survey.

We are grateful to the National Geographic Society Library, including its Map and News Collections; Administrative Services; Cartographic Division; Geography Education Program; Illustrations Library; Messenger Center; Photographic Services Division; Production Services, Pre-Press Division; Records Library.

We found the following general reference works most helpful: The American University Area Handbook Series of *Country Studies;* Central Intelligence Agency, *The World Factbook 1989;* U. S. Department of State, *Background Notes; Encyclopaedia Britannica 1989 Book of the Year; The Europa World Year Book 1989;* Facts on File, Inc., *Encyclopedia of the Third World;* National Geographic *Atlas of the World;* Reader's Digest, *Guide to Places of the World; The Statesman's Year-Book 1989-1990; The World Almanac 1990.*

Facts at Your Fingertips

Earth's Extremes

Rainiest Spot
Mount Waialeale, Hawaii, U. S.; annual average rainfall 661 inches (1,680 cm). Heaviest rainfall ever recorded: Barst, Guadeloupe, November 26, 1970; 1.5 inches (3.8 cm) in 1 minute

Driest Spot
Atacama Desert, Chile; rainfall barely measurable

Coldest Recorded Temperature
Vostok, Antarctica; -128.6°F (-89.2°C), on July 21, 1983

Hottest Recorded Temperature
Al Aziziyah, Libya, south of Tripoli; 136.4°F (58°C), in 1922

Highest Point
Mount Everest, Nepal-Tibet; 29,028 feet (8,848 m)

Lowest Point
In West Antarctica; 8,327 feet (2,538 m) below sea level

Longest River
Nile, Africa; 4,145 miles (6,671 km)

Highest Waterfall
Angel Falls, Venezuela; 3,212 feet (979 m)

Largest Gorge
Grand Canyon, Colorado River, Arizona, U. S.; 290 miles (466 km) long, 600 feet to 18 miles (183 m to 29 km) wide, 1 mile (1.6 km) deep

Deepest Gorge
Colca River Canyon, Peru; 2.25 miles (3.62 km)

Biggest Cave
Mammoth-Flint Ridge cave system, Kentucky, U. S.; more than 330 miles (531 km) of passageways

Largest Desert
Sahara, North Africa; 3,500,000 square miles (9,064,958 sq km)

Longest Reef
Great Barrier Reef, Australia; 1,250 miles (2,012 km)

Deepest Ocean Trench
Mariana Trench, Pacific Ocean; 35,810 feet (10,915 m)

Highest Tides
Bay of Fundy, Nova Scotia, Canada; 52.5 feet (16 m)

Largest Ocean
Pacific; 64,185,999 square miles (166,241,000 sq km), average depth 12,925 feet (3,940 m)

Largest Sea
South China; 1,148,499 square miles (2,974,600 sq km), average depth 4,803 feet (1,464 m)

Largest Lake
Caspian Sea, Europe-Asia; 143,244 square miles (371,000 sq km), 3,363 feet (1,025 m) deep

Deepest Lake
Lake Baykal, U.S.S.R.; greatest depth 5,315 feet (1,620 m)

Highest Lake
Unnamed glacial lake near Mount Everest, Nepal-Tibet; 19,300 feet (5,883 m) high

Lowest Lake
Dead Sea, Israel-Jordan; surface of water 1,312 feet (400 m) below sea level

Largest Island
Greenland; 840,004 square miles (2,175,600 sq km)

Highest Town
Wenquan, China; 16,732 feet (5,100 m) above sea level

Lowest Town
Ein Bokek, Israel, on the shore of the Dead Sea; almost 1,300 feet (396 m) below sea level

Northernmost Capital
Reykjavik, Iceland; latitude 64°09′N, longitude 21°57′W

Southernmost Capital
Wellington, New Zealand; latitude 41°18′S, longitude 174°47′E

Largest Continent by Area
Asia; 17,176,102 square miles (44,485,900 sq km)

Smallest Continent by Area
Australia; 2,966,153 square miles (7,682,300 sq km)

Largest Continent by Population
Asia; 3,132,638,000

Smallest Continent by Population
Australia; 16,820,000

Largest Country by Area
U.S.S.R.; 8,649,538 square miles (22,402,200 sq km)

Smallest Country by Area
Vatican City; 0.2 square miles (0.4 sq km)

Largest Country by Population
People's Republic of China; 1,103,923,000

Smallest Country by Population
Vatican City; 830

Most Crowded Country
Monaco; 46,667 people per square mile

Least Crowded Country
Mongolia; 3.5 people per square mile

Largest Metropolitan Area Population
Tokyo-Yokohama, Japan; 30,394,532

Engineering Wonders

Highest Bridge
Royal Gorge, Arkansas River, Colorado, U. S.; 1,053 feet (321 m) above water

Longest Bridge Span
Humber Estuary, Hull, England; 4,626 feet (1,410 m)

Longest Big Ship Canal
Suez Canal, Egypt, links the Red Sea and the Mediterranean; 100.6 miles (162 km)

Biggest Dam (Concrete)
Grand Coulee, Columbia River, Washington, U. S.; 10,585,000 cubic yards (8,093,000 cu m)

Biggest Dam (Earthfill)
Pati Pavana River, Argentina; 311,527,000 cubic yards (238,193,544 cu m)

Tallest Dam
Nurek, U.S.S.R.; 984 feet (300 m)

Great Pyramid of Cheops
Giza, Egypt; 450 feet (137 m) high; base covers 13.1 acres (5.3 ha)

Great Wall of China
3,930 miles (6,325 km) long; averages 25 feet (7.6 m) high; 15 feet (4.6 m) wide at top; 25 feet (7.6 m) wide at base

Largest Artificial Lake
Lake Volta, formed by the Akosombo Dam on the Volta River, Ghana; 3,500 square miles (9,065 sq km)

Tallest Office Building
Sears Tower, Chicago, Illinois, U. S.; 1,454 feet (443 m); 110 stories

Longest Railroad
Trans-Siberian Railroad, Moscow to Nakhodka, near Vladivostok, U.S.S.R.; 5,864 miles (9,437 km)

Tallest Tower (Freestanding)
Canadian National Railroad Tower, Toronto, Canada; 1,815.5 feet (553.3 m)

Longest Rail Tunnel
Seikan Undersea Tunnel, from Honshu to Hokkaido, Japan; 33.46 miles (53.85 km)

Longest Road Tunnel
St. Gotthard, from Göschenen to Airolo, Switzerland; 10.1 miles (16.3 km)

Longest Artificial Waterway
St. Lawrence Seaway, on the St. Lawrence River from Montreal, Canada, to Lake Ontario; 189 miles (304 km)

Deepest Water Well
Stensvad Well 11-W1, Rosebud County, Montana, U. S.; 7,320 feet (2,231 m)

Glossary

Fact box explanation
At the end of each country account, you will find a fact box listing the country's vital data, such as area, population, and so on. Most of the headings are self-explanatory. When the population of a capital city is preceded by the abbreviation *pop.* (meaning *population*), the figure includes only the people within the city limits. Sometimes the figure includes the whole metropolitan area, *met. pop.*

Under the heading **Ethnic groups,** you will find descriptions of the people who live in each country. Where the populations are long established, as in Europe, country names may be used. Where they originate from a mixture of nationalities, as in the United States, terms such as *white* and *black* are more suitable. In some cases, continental ethnic origin is listed; such references may be explained in the country story. Only major ethnic groups, religious groups, and languages are listed, and we put the country's official language first.

The **Economy** of each country is split into agriculture *(Agr.)* and industry *(Ind.).* Each is listed in roughly descending order of importance. *Agriculture* includes both food and export crops. In the countries where subsistence farming is of prime importance, food crops are listed first. *Industry* focuses on commercial activities that support a country's economy, including exports.

Abbreviations used in this book
Many of the figures and metric conversions have been rounded off.

°C—degrees Celsius or Centigrade	kg—kilograms
	km—kilometers
cm—centimeters	m—meters
cu m—cubic meters	mi—miles
°F—degrees Fahrenheit	sq km—square kilometers
ft—feet	sq m—square meters
ha—hectares	sq mi—square miles

adobe—brick made of sun-dried mud or clay.
alpaca—a domesticated mammal with long, woolly hair; related to the llama.
altiplano—a high plateau or valley between higher mountains.
apartheid—a government policy of racial segregation and discrimination in South Africa.
aquifer—an underground reservoir of water contained within a porous rock layer.
Arabic—referring to the language and culture of the Arabs.
archipelago—a group or chain of islands.
atoll—a ring of coral islands encircling a lagoon.
autonomy—the right of self-government or freedom from external control.

balkanize—to break up a large political region into smaller units or regions.
basin—a depression in the Earth's surface, often filled with water at its lowest point; also the entire area drained by a river system.
bauxite—aluminum ore; an earthy, reddish-colored material used in the manufacture of aluminum.
bay—a body of water partially surrounded by land; bays are usually smaller and less deeply indented than gulfs.
Bedouin—a nomadic Arab of the desert.
Benelux—the countries of Belgium, the Netherlands, and Luxembourg in an economic alliance for tax-free trade.
Berlin Wall—the wall built after World War II between East Berlin and West Berlin to prevent free movement from one part of the city to another.
Buddhism—a religion of Asia that grew from the teachings of Gautama Buddha in the 6th century B.C. He taught salvation through self-purification.
CFA franc—currency of the Communauté Financière Africaine (African Financial Community); worth half a French franc.
cacao—a tropical tree bearing seeds called cacao or cocoa beans, used to make cocoa and chocolate.
campesino—a resident of a Latin American rural area.
canyon—a deep, narrow valley with steep sides; it is wider and longer than a gorge.
cape—a piece of land that extends into a river, a lake, or an ocean.
capitalism—an economic system based on private ownership of businesses and a competitive market.
cash crop—a crop grown for sale, as opposed to food crops grown for family use.
cassava—a plant grown in the tropics for its edible, starchy root; sometimes called manioc.
caste—a hereditary social class in Hinduism.
chaco—lowland plain; specifically, the Gran Chaco of Argentina, Paraguay, and Bolivia.
channel—a waterway between two landmasses; also the part of a river that is deepest and carries the most water.
Christianity—a religion based on the teachings of Jesus Christ, who is believed to be the son of God.
city-state—an independent country made up of a city and sometimes the surrounding area.
civil war—armed conflict between opposing groups of citizens of the same country.
coca—a shrub whose leaves are made into a drug called cocaine.
collective farm—a collection of land holdings operated as a single unit, especially one owned and operated by a communist government; the workers receive a share of the returns.
colony—a foreign territory that enjoys some autonomy, but retains ties with its parent country.
the Commonwealth—a voluntary association of independent countries that maintains ties of friendship, cooperation, and assistance. The British monarch is the symbolic head.
communism—an economic system based on the idea that property is owned in common rather than privately, and goods are distributed as needed.
conquistador—a soldier in the Spanish conquest of the Americas.
contiguous U. S.—the 48 states that adjoin each other in the United States; noncontiguous states

are Alaska and Hawaii.
continent—one of the seven main land areas on the Earth's surface: North America, South America, Europe, Asia, Africa, Australia, and Antarctica.
continental shelf—the shallow, gently sloping seafloor that surrounds each continent.
contras—an organized group of rebels who fought the Sandinista government in Nicaragua.
copra—dried coconut meat that yields oil.
coral—hardened skeletons of tiny marine animals, called coral polyps, which form reefs and islands.
cottage industry—an industry whose labor force consists of family members working at home with their own equipment.
coup, coup d'état—a sudden, usually successful act to overthrow a government from within.
Creole—a mixture of several languages, which serves as an indigenous form of speech.
crown colony—a colony of the United Kingdom over which the crown retains some control, such as Gibraltar.
delta—the lowland composed of silt, sand, and gravel deposited by a river at its mouth.
democracy—a form of government in which power is held by the people and is exercised by them directly or through their elected representatives.
dependency—a geographically separate territory under the jurisdiction of a parent country.
dhow—an Arab boat with a triangular sail.
dialect—a regional variety of a language.
divide—the high boundary between areas drained by different river systems; water flows in a different direction on either side.
dormant volcano—a temporarily inactive volcano; a totally inactive one is called extinct.
drought—a long period without rain.
duchy—the territory ruled by a duke or duchess.
dynasty—a succession of rulers coming from the same line of descent.
economy—the system or structure of a country's production, distribution, and use of goods and services.
emigration—the act of leaving one's native country or region to settle in another one; usually means moving to a foreign country.
enclave—a small land area entirely surrounded by foreign territory.
escarpment—a cliff separating two nearly flat land surfaces that lie at different levels.
estuary—the widening mouth of a river where it meets the sea; tides ebb and flow within this area.
ethnic group—a group of people who share a common racial, linguistic, cultural, or regional background.
European Community—a Western European trade organization with headquarters in Brussels.
fallow—farmland left unplanted during the growing season.
federation—a group of independent countries united by a treaty or alliance for joint action.
fjord—a narrow, steep-sided ocean inlet that reaches far into a coastline.
geothermal power—energy provided by heat from inside the Earth.
glacier—a large, slowly moving mass of ice.
gorge—a narrow passage or valley with steep sides; it is narrower and shorter than a canyon.
griot—an oral historian, a singer-storyteller.

guanaco—a mammal with a soft, thick coat; probably the original ancestor of both the alpaca and the llama.

guerrilla—a person who carries on warfare behind enemy lines through ambushes, raids, and sabotage of transport and communications.

gulf—a portion of the ocean partly enclosed by land.

hacienda—a large estate or plantation in Latin America, or its main house.

harbor—a body of water sheltered by natural or artificial barriers and deep enough to moor ships.

heavy industry—manufacturing that processes large amounts of raw materials, such as coal and iron ore, and uses heavy machinery.

Hinduism—the major religion of India; it teaches righteous living to achieve a final union with Brahman, the supreme power of the universe.

homeland—an area set aside for a people of a particular national, racial, or cultural origin.

hydroelectric power—electricity produced by capturing the energy of moving water.

ice sheet—a broad, thick layer of glacial ice that covers a large area.

iceberg—a large floating chunk of ice broken away from a glacier or an ice shelf.

immigration—the legal or illegal movement of people into a country of which they are not native residents.

Inca—an empire in the Andes that ruled an area from Colombia to Chile before the Spanish conquest.

irrigation—artificial watering of farmland.

Islam—a religious belief that Allah is the only God and that Muhammad is his Prophet.

isthmus—a narrow strip of land that connects two larger landmasses and has water on two sides.

Judaism—a religion developed by the ancient Hebrews that teaches belief in one God.

kingdom—a form of government headed by a king or a queen.

ladino—a term used chiefly in Guatemala to describe a person who has adopted European ways of living.

lagoon—a shallow body of water that opens on the sea but is protected by a sandbar or coral reef.

landlocked country—a country surrounded by land, without access to the sea.

legumes—edible seeds such as peas, beans, lentils.

light industry—manufacturing that uses small amounts of raw materials and employs light or small machines; one example is food processing.

llama—a mammal used as a pack animal and a source of wool; related to the camel.

llano—an open, grassy plain.

loess—deposit of fine silt or dust that settles on the ground after being carried by the wind.

maharaja—a Hindu prince.

maritime—bordering the sea; concerning navigation or commerce on the sea.

Maya—an Indian civilization of Central America, which built cities and temple-pyramids and devised a calendar and a writing system.

medieval—referring to a period of European history known as the Middle Ages, roughly from A.D. 500 to 1500.

mesa—a broad, flat-topped landform with steep sides found in arid or semiarid regions.

mestizo—a Latin American of mixed European and American Indian ancestry.

metric—a system of measurement based on units of ten; the meter is its principal unit.

millet—a grass cultivated for its grain, used for food.

monarchy—a government having undivided rule by a single person, such as a king or a queen.

monsoon—a wind that produces dry and wet seasons in southern and eastern Asia.

moor—an open expanse of rolling land covered with grass or other low vegetation.

Moors—North Africans of mixed Arab-Berber descent; Moors ruled parts of the Iberian Peninsula between A.D. 711 and 1492.

moraine—an accumulation of debris carried and deposited by a glacier.

mosque—an Islamic house of worship.

mouth (of a river)—where a river ends by flowing into a large body of water, such as a sea or ocean.

mulatto—a person of mixed white and black ancestry.

Muslim—a follower of Islam.

nomads—usually herders, who travel from place to place seeking supplies of food and water.

oasis—a green area in a desert, with a spring or waterhole, often fed by an underground aquifer.

oil palm—a palm growing chiefly in western and central Africa, whose fruit and kernel yield oil.

outback—the remote backcountry of Australia.

outcrop—the part of a rock formation that appears at the surface of the ground.

pagoda—a tower with several successive roofs, used as a temple or memorial in the Far East.

pampa—an extensive grassland.

parliament—a group of representatives who meet to discuss national affairs and make laws.

patois—a regional dialect.

peer—a member of the British nobility, such as a duke, marquess, earl, viscount, or baron.

peninsula—a long piece of land almost surrounded by water, but connected to a larger landmass.

per capita—a way of averaging "by heads," meaning by individuals; income, production, or other data are often given per individual.

permafrost—permanently frozen subsoil and bedrock, up to 1,500 feet (450 m) deep, that can produce the effect of completely frozen ground.

phosphate—organic compound used in fertilizers.

pidgin—simplified speech consisting of words adapted from other languages; used between people who speak different languages.

pilgrimage—a journey to a place of great religious significance.

plantain—a starchy fruit, similar to a banana, that is a staple in the diet of people living in the tropics.

plantation—a large estate that grows a cash crop; usually worked by unskilled or semiskilled labor.

plateau—a large, flat area that rises higher than the land around it; larger than a mesa.

poach—to capture or kill wild animals illegally.

polder—a tract of land reclaimed from the sea and protected by dikes. About 40 percent of the Netherlands consists of polders.

polyglot—a mixture of languages.

populous—having a large population; densely populated refers to the number of people per area.

principality—a territory or jurisdiction of a prince.

Pygmies—groups of central African peoples who usually stand less than five feet tall.

pyrethrum—a chrysanthemum that is a source of insecticides.

rain forest—dense forest composed mainly of broad-leaved evergreens found in wet tropical regions.

reef—an offshore ridge of rocks, coral, or sand, that lies at or near the water's surface.

republic—a form of government whose chief of state is usually a president, not a monarch; also a country having such a government.

rift valley—a trough-shaped valley formed when the Earth's crust sinks between parallel faults.

root crop—a crop grown for its large, edible roots, such as potatoes, turnips, cassava, taro.

Russia—until 1917 an empire in Eastern Europe and northern and western Asia; today it is the dominant republic of the Soviet Union; often used incorrectly for the entire U.S.S.R.

Sahel—the semiarid grassland directly south of the Sahara in western and central Africa.

savanna—a tropical grassland with scattered trees.

scale—the ratio of map distance to distance on the Earth's surface, shown as a bar graph.

secession—formal withdrawal, such as from a country or federation.

socialism—an economic system based on the idea that a government should distribute the society's wealth equally.

sorghum—a tropical grass whose grain is used for food or whose stem may yield syrup.

sound—a long, broad ocean inlet usually parallel to the coast, or a long stretch of water separating an island from the mainland.

steppe—a grassland in the temperate zone where limited rainfall prevents tree growth and keeps most grasses from growing any taller than 20 inches (50 cm).

strait—a narrow passage of water that connects two larger bodies of water.

Sudan—the largest country in Africa, in the northeast; also the name given by Arabs to the region in north-central Africa between the Sahara and the equatorial forests. It includes the Sahel.

tableland—an extensive region of elevated land, usually with a level surface.

taiga—subarctic coniferous forest largely consisting of firs and spruces.

taro—a plant raised throughout the tropics for its edible, starchy root.

tartan—a plaid textile design usually associated with a distinctive Scottish clan.

territory—a geographical area belonging to or under the jurisdiction of an external government; also an administrative subdivision of a country.

traditional—refers to beliefs, customs, dress, and behavior handed down from one generation to another, often with no written record.

tributary—a stream that flows into a larger river.

tundra—a treeless plain found mostly in Arctic regions, that has permanently frozen subsoil and low-growing plants.

urban (metropolitan) area—the city and its surrounding built-up area and population, as far as the outer suburbs.

World War II—the name given to the global conflict of 1939-1945; battles were fought in Europe, Asia, Africa, and the Pacific islands.

yurt—a circular tent of felt or animal skins used by nomads in central Asia; also called a ger in Mongolia.

Index

Map references are in **boldface**
(74) type. Letters and
numbers following in lightface
(P5) locate the place-names.
Refer to page 21 for more
detail. Illustrations appear in
italic (220) type, and text
references in lightface (106).
Diacriticals in the index
reflect what is in the book:
They appear in the text, but
not on the maps.

249

Type composition by the Typographic section of National Geographic Production Services, Pre-Press Division. Color separations by Chanticleer Co., Inc., New York, N.Y.; The Lanman Companies, Washington, D. C.; Phototype Color Graphics, Pennsauken, N.J. Printed and bound by Ringier America, Inc., New Berlin, Wisconsin. Paper by Repap Sales Corp., New York, N.Y.

Library of Congress CIP Data

National Geographic Society (U.S.)
National Geographic picture atlas of our world.

Includes index and glossary.
1. Atlases. I. Title. II. Title: Picture atlas of our world.
G1021.N4 1990 912 90-675180
ISBN 0-87044-812-9 (alk. paper)
ISBN 0-87044-813-7 (Lib. ed.: alk. paper)